The Taste of America

Other books by John L. Hess:

The Case for De Gaulle: An American Viewpoint, 1968.
The Grand Acquisitors, 1974.
Vanishing France, 1975.

Other books by Karen Hess:

English Bread and Yeast Cookery by Elizabeth David,
Editor of American edition, 1980.
Martha Washington's Booke of Cookery, 1981.
The Virginia House-Wife by Mary Randolph (1824),
editor of facsimile edition, 1984.

The Taste of America

John L. Hess & Karen Hess

The University of South Carolina Press

The Taste of America, by John L. Hess and Karen Hess.
New York: Grossman/Viking, 1977; Penguin, 1977. This,
the third edition, is based on the Penguin edition, with a
new preface by the authors.

Library of Congress Cataloging-in-Publication Data
Hess, John L.
    The taste of America / John L. Hess and Karen Hess. — 3rd ed.
      p.   cm.
    Bibliography: p.
    Includes index.
    ISBN 0–87249–640–6.   —   ISBN 0–87249–641–4 (pbk.)
    1. Food.   2. Cookery.   3. Food industry and trade.   I. Hess,
Karen.   II. Title.
TX353.H47   1989
641'.01'3—dc19   89–4763
                                                                    CIP

Printed in the United States of America

Portions of this book originally appeared in The Atlantic
Monthly, Harper's Magazine, House & Garden, and Organic
Gardening Magazine.

ACKNOWLEDGMENTS:
The New England Journal of Medicine: "Impasse" by David
Kritchevsky, Vol. 262, page 619, 1960; reprinted by permission
    from The New England Journal of Medicine and David
Kritchevsky. The New York Times: Copyright © 1973 and
1974 by The New York Times Co.; reprinted by permission.
Quadrangle Books: "Mustard Soup Tisel" from The Hellfire
    Cookbook, by John Philips Cranwell, Copyright © 1975 by
John Philips Cranwell; reprinted by permission of Quadrangle/
    The New York Times Co. Random House, Inc.: From The
Americans, by Daniel J. Boorstin, Copyright © 1973 by Daniel
J. Boorstin. Time: Excerpts from "The Burger That Conquered
the Country," reprinted by permission from Time; Copyright
Time Inc. The Wall Street Journal: From "Most People Have
No Taste; It's Been Lost in the Process," by Mary Bralove,
excerpted from The Wall Street Journal, April 30, 1974, by
permission.

*To our children
and our children's children
Peter, Michael, Martha,
Emerick, Anna Magdalena,
and those who follow*

We wish to express our appreciation to Daniel Okrent, Elisabeth Sifton, and Barbara Burn, editors. And to Eleanor Lowenstein of the Corner Book Shop, Maud Cole of the Rare Book Collections at the New York Public Library, James Mooney, director of the Pennsylvania Historical Society, and Gregory Johnson of the Alderman Library, University of Virginia, all of whom extended special courtesies to us in our research. And to Lord O'Hagan, by whose gracious permission we quote from the Towneley Manuscript. And to Elizabeth David, who was so generous and helpful to us. And to other friends who have shared their knowledge and experience with us. We thank one and all.

They ate frozen meat, frozen fried potatoes and frozen peas. Blindfolded, one could not have identified the peas, and the only flavor the potatoes had was the flavor of soap. It was the monotonous fare of the besieged ... but ... where was the enemy?

John Cheever, in *The Wapshot Scandal* (1963)

Contents

17 / 283
Manicured Chickens

18 / 303
The Green Revolution

19 / 329
Hope

A CO-AUTHOR'S NOTE 337

Preface to
the Third Edition

THESE ARE dizzying times. In the fourteen years since we wrote this book, "Kool-Aid like Mother used to make" has become "Kool-Aid like Grandma used to make"—in other words, Americans are one more generation removed from the memory of real food. Not just Americans, of course. A journalist in Sydney told us our book might just as well have been titled "The Taste of Australia," and the invasion of the Champs-Élysées and the Boul' Mich' by le fast food suggests that the book may some day fully describe "The Taste of France," though not, we pray, in our lifetime. As for the tragicomedy of American foodways and foodwriting, nothing, alas, has happened to justify our changing a line.

It's not that nothing has happened. On the contrary, these have been years of turbulence, of obsession with food, and with change. But the more things changed, the more they were the same. The funny things got funnier, the bad things worse, and the hopeful signs . . . well, they remain hopeful.

For example, soon after our book appeared, the Hudson River was found to be poisoned with PCB's and the authorities advised consumers to eat its fish no more than once a week. Then Lake Erie was poisoned, leading to the same warning. We broadcast a suggestion that all we needed now was to find five more poisoned bodies of water and we could eat fish every day of the week. Well, that warning has since become official for many of the commercial freshwater fisheries of the nation. In the Northeast, coastal waters have become so polluted that the noble striped bass has been banned from our tables, and maitres d'hôtel assure clients that their seafood comes from distant waters. Although possibly safe, it cannot possibly be fresh, but hardly anybody thinks about freshness anymore.

The establishment has stopped making fun of environmentalists and their fears of acid rain, pesticide runoff, the greenhouse effect, and other by-products of technological progress, but that progress continued unabated—indeed, environmental protection was all but suspended during the Reagan administration. While another third of a million farmers were squeezed off the land, agribusiness pursued its agenda, nicely expressed in an advertisement of the National Starch and Chemical Corporation headed, "Eat your heart out Mother Nature."

This was in the printed program of the 1980 convention of the Institute of Food Technologists in New Orleans, which featured the latest research on the effect of PHMB on the shelf life of shrimp, why cottonseed flour turns brown in biscuits, the flowability of mozzarella cheese, and the characteristics of comminuted fish and meat. En route to the affair, we shared a cab with a researcher for General Foods (now a subsidiary of something else). "In five years," she said, "we'll have wonderful things. Everything will be balanced nutritionally, like pet food. All we need is to educate the public." After she debarked at her hotel, the driver said, "I don't want no Alpo diet."

His was the minority view inside the Superdome, which eight years later would serve up to the nation George Bush and J. Danforth Quayle III. On that day in 1980, the 9,700 registrants could sample what lay ahead for the electorate: a new artificial sweetener, real (that is, 10 percent, later cut to 5 percent) fruit juices, synthetic cheeses, soy-based ice cream, ham made of viscoelastic gluten, imitation bacon, extended crab paste, and veal-flavored rabbitburgers. It was the flavor, not the rabbit that was on sale. A chemist who had helped fabricate it said it tasted like beef. Asked why not sell rabbit that tasted like rabbit, one representative said rabbit was too gamy and the chemist said it was too bland, which he explained was what the public understood as gamy.

That is, of course, the point we began with, that few Americans knew any more what real food tastes like; few had ever tasted good bread, good Jersey cream or cheese, ripe-picked tomatoes, barnyard fowl, fresh fish, newly roasted coffee, proper beer. Indeed, a phrase in the language meant to express admiration for ingenuity is "the greatest thing since sliced bread"—a gastronomic disaster hailed by its victims. As for veal, gourmet writers at the time were clucking over turkey breast that tasted the same to them.

At New Orleans, a vision of the future was a line of batters and breadings to coat prepared "convenience" products, the crisp coatings designed to conceal an absence of flavor. The line was called Newlywed Foods. . . . A chemist from Minneapolis told us that industry was in a race that would make a fortune for the winners, to find "a way to put a crust on something in a microwave."

This has since been achieved, more or less. Our book makes fun of the microwave oven, whose chief useful function is to thaw TV dinners. But in a triumph of marketing over common sense, the gadget has been sold to a majority of American households. Applying Thorsten Veblen's brilliant dictum that invention is the mother of necessity, the industry has engaged food writers and editors to demonstrate how a microwave oven may be conscripted to do almost anything a stove can do, nearly as well and with only a little more trouble and risk. Our favorite in this campaign, by the leading microwave hustler, calls for making a lemon meringue pie in no more than 20 incredibly adept steps, timed to the microsecond if you can manage it. (As for those crisp surfaces and film covers, trouble is brewing over the side effects of ingesting microwaved plastic, but that is not our department.)

As these lines were being written, a food-page column called Micro Ways offers a recipe for Saltimbocca alla Romana that calls for browning the veal on the stove, then microwaving it on HIGH 6 to 7 minutes and on MEDIUM 6 to 7 minutes more. (The classic recipe calls for a maximum cooking time of 5 minutes, on a stove, of course.) The column also tells how to microwave scallops for 23 minutes or so in eight steps, followed by a final minute on the old stove. Truly weird.

When this book first appeared, the phenomenon called *nouvelle cuisine* was still new; we had in fact attended its birth in Burgundy and Paris and knew its creators well. As we noted, it had its good and its bad sides. On the one hand, it was a brilliant effort by young chefs to lighten the classic cuisine, featuring a fanatic pursuit of the dwindling sources of fine *artisanal* produce. On the other hand, it had been taken up by the fashion world, obsessed with the shock of novelty for its own sake. A line about this disappeared unaccountably from our final "De Gustibus" column in *The New York Times*. It said, "As long as fashion editors tell us what to eat, we shall eat badly."

The takeover of high cookery by fashion soon became total. Like clothing and decor, food had to be new, it had to be now, it had to be different. It became not good but glamorous. Thousands of bright young people spurned other arts and professions to slave over the hot stove, which French cooks ironically call the piano. In these go-go years, vast amounts of venture capital financed a proliferation of tax-sheltered eating places for the expense-account throng, and won breathless coverage in a proliferation of food pages. The kiwi speckled the national table, vegetables shrank like Alice in Wonderland, the jalapeño pepper burned every yuppie palate, and blackened fish, the invention of a cagey Cajun, darkened menus across the land. All this experimentation had to bring forth some good as well as much evil but, as we forever quote, nothing goes out of fashion like fashion, so that good fads tend to die like bad ones. (A few years ago, for example, a score of shops selling old-fashioned ice cream blossomed in our part of town, attracting queues of eager conformists. Not one of the shops has survived.)

Food was fashionable, but who was to teach the new cooks and the new clientele? The teachers and writers are now themselves, like their pupils, one more generation removed from the memory of good food. We described (in Chapter 12) the off-duty snack preferences of our food mavens as reported in 1974; *The Times* in 1986 found the current culinary stars staving off hunger with Doritos-and-guacamole, frozen Snickers, pretzels, M&M's, Oreos, fortune cookies, franks-and-beans and, in the case of the impresario Joe Baum, "anything from any street corner that has fried onions." Baum, incidentally, is credited with the invention of the theme restaurant (actually a reinvention) and of that obnoxious refrain, "Hello, I'm Bruce and I'll be your waiter this evening," followed by all the mad unpriced dishes that are not on the printed menu. Another veteran entrepreneur, George Lang, recently denounced this plague and the nouvelle follies in general, at a recent conference of foodies, as they now revoltingly call themselves. Lang satirized "Bruce" as recommending "the breast of guinea hen marinated in lavender vinegar, wrapped in cherrywood-smoked salmon, stuffed with goat cheese, and topped with a dandelion beurre blanc." Lang was dismayed when several of the foodies asked for the recipe for their restaurants.

A generation of new food writers has been winging it by emulating *The Times*. It is in that paper, we believe, that the Oxymoronic Critic was born: One high-tone restaurant was "glowing and plush if undistinguished," another "undistinguished" yet "bright and felicitous," a third "colorful and refreshing but head-splittingly noisy," and a fourth "pleasant, comfortable, and unprepossessing." In a fifth, the beef was "fine if served rare but dull if overcooked" and in a sixth it was the pasta that was fine, "provided it is not undercooked or overcooked."

That last restaurant received a good deal more praise and abuse, and a rating of three stars ("Excellent"). In other words, the reader is invited to spend a lot of money there, and can't say he wasn't warned if the experience proves awful or wonderful, as the case may be. It was there, also, that "Drinks are large, so wine is superfluous, which is just as well because the selection is mundane." We have never dared ask what mundane selection is like, for fear of revealing our gaucherie.

The Times sets the tone. In other journals we have come to read that service was "polite but could be more attentive," scallops were "good but overcooked," and puff pastry was "good, but too doughy." We have also seen them sampling, or pretending to sample, every dish on the menu, some of them several times, just like the iron-stomached *Times*.

Something of a climax came in the late spring of 1988, when a young star from Seattle arrived with éclat at Maxwell's Plum, that pioneer New York cafe for swinging singles. Required against her will to serve hamburgers, she insisted that they be designer burgers, triangular in shape with we know not what garnishes. She lasted three weeks. Her successor, a darkly handsome male, was called a "hot new hero" by *New York* magazine's Gael Greene, whose rave appeared, unfortunately, a day after Maxwell's Plum had shut down. The restaurant and Ms Greene were victims of a trend she herself had done much to promote, the chase after the shockingly new. All over town and across the land, new restaurants that had been smash hits for three months or so were closing their doors.

You could not easily detect the slump from the food pages. They had come to describe $50 meals as moderately priced, but the number of readers who can afford them is limited. The rest of the population has turned perforce to pizza, fast food, junk food, takeout, and frozen precooked meals. With most adults now employed outside the home, there was little time to cook and hardly anybody to teach what real American food used to be like. The term has so lost its meaning that a recent review in *The Times* raved about a "patrician" restaurant that had dropped its French menu in favor of American cuisine, which, it told us, was now back in fashion. The American menu: raw tuna seared black, smoked quail vinaigrette, vegetable terrine, crab ravioli, foie gras on fava beans, baby corn and shredded confit. . . . There is more, and some of it is funny, but one gets the idea. American indeed.

Now for the good news. The palate lives, not yet adapted by genetic engineering to the progress of food technology. All the attention dedicated to eating has had to encourage rediscovery of quality, along with the folderol and follies of fashion. Some publishers have heeded our appeal for reprints of good old American cookbooks and there has been a heartening growth of a relatively new discipline, that of food history. (Alas, progress is slow and uneven. *The Times* still solemnly informs us every August that tomatoes were not used in America until around the 1880s [the 1780s is more like it], and just recently reminded us that Marco Polo brought pasta from China to Italy in the fifteenth century, no less [the Italians had been eating pasta in all manner of shapes for centuries and, of course, Polo made his famed voyage in the thirteenth century]. And on the scholarly scene, a work published by Oxford University Press told us that, "Asparagus, for example, was practically unknown in the United States until the 1920s. . . ." ["*Sparagus* thrives exceedingly" in New England, according to John Josselyn in 1672, and no American gardening manual or cookbook of the eighteenth and nineteenth centuries is without copious reference to this popular vegetable.])

Heartening is the news that farmers markets are thriving and that here and there some farmers are introducing oldtime strains of vegetables and fruits, especially apples. Consumers are enthusiastic and public officials have learned that the markets are economic assets. Our complaint about New York having driven them out led the urbanist Barry Benepe to organize Greenmarkets, which have become a cherished institution in that city, supporting scores of farmers who otherwise would have left the land.

Our list of good happenings is a short one. We are obliged to note that pollution of land, water, and air has generally worsened, to the point of blighting the last summer season for beach resorts, ruining whole fleets of fishing boats and forcing national, state, and local governments to consider enormously costly attacks on the problem. Things had to get this bad to arouse public action. We dare say things must get even worse before they can get much better. But nature has great powers of resilience. This book is one effort to raise understanding about one basic element of the quality of life. We hope that it will continue to serve.

New York, New York   John L. Hess and Karen Hess
January, 1989

The Taste of America

1
The Rape
of the Palate

Most People Have
No Taste; It's Been
Lost in the Process

Headline in The Wall Street Journal, *April 30, 1974*

WE WRITE with trepidation. How shall we tell our fellow Americans that our palates have been ravaged, that our food is awful, and that our most respected authorities on cookery are poseurs? Can most Americans be wrong? Considering our recent political and social history, the answer is evidently yes. But that is the wisdom of hindsight, imposed upon us by Vietnam and Watergate. In challenging our very taste, we must confront the housewife interviewed on a television program not long ago. She claimed that she prepared a wholesome balanced diet, but her children preferred junk food "because it tastes good."

"Food is for health," she wailed. "Why does it have to taste good?"

How shall we tell her that she is a terrible cook, and that junk food does not taste good? When she says "taste good," she simply means "taste sweet." If she is a typical American, and she sounds like one, her very first mouth-

ful of nourishment was a synthetic, sweetened bottle formula; she was weaned on starchy baby foods loaded with
sugar and monosodium glutamate, and she grew up
on soda pop, candy, corn flakes, ketchup-doused hamburgers, and instant coffee. Her grandmothers may have
known how to cook, but her mother probably did not.
Her cooking teacher in public school knew no more, and
the authors of the recipes she now relies upon are very
nearly as ignorant as she is.

The truth is that good food in America is little more
than a memory, and a hope. We were one of the best-fed
countries in the world; we have become one of the poorest. Poorest in sensual pleasure, we mean, although our
"nutrition" has been worsening for decades. The decline
in the taste of our food began more than a century ago,
and has turned into a catastrophic depression in recent
years. The rest of the world has been following us down
this slope, but more slowly, so that the American traveler
now can find tastier victuals in such countries as Turkey
or Morocco than he can find at home.

Since everybody is born with a palate, this ought to be
self-evident. But Americans have been mouth-washed by
generations of bad food and brain-washed by generations
of bad advice about food, culminating in the gourmet
plague. So if we are to recapture the joy of good eating,
we must free our palates from their daily glop, and our
minds from entrenched myths.

It is, for example, a myth that our standard of living is
the highest in the world and is forever rising. This was
true in nearly every sense two centuries ago, when Tom
Paine told his fellow Englishmen that American freemen
lived better than *they* did. To repeat that today, however, poses a problem of definition: what is the standard
of living, and what Americans are we talking about?

The computer analysts who have taken over economics
in recent years, with such disastrous results, have given us
a measure called per capita Gross National Product—in
other words, dollars spent. By this measure, a man behind

the wheel of a new Cadillac in a traffic jam is living five times better than the man in the Volkswagen alongside, and both are living infinitely better than the eccentric who is picking dandelion greens in the meadow beside the turnpike. One who eats a poor meal at a cost of $30 is six times better off than one who manages a decent meal at $5. A vandal who throws a rock through a store window enriches us all by the cost of its replacement, and the ultimate vandal, war, produces the ultimate standard of living.

Even by this crass measurement in dollars, our standard of living has been declining since 1973. But if it is measured by the satisfactions that life should afford, by the air we breathe, the food we eat, our relations with our neighbors and with nature, then the decline began much earlier. As Scott Sullivan of *Newsweek* reported from Paris in mid-1973, "The truth is that when it comes to that difficult-to-define experience known as the quality of life, millions of Europeans live better than we do." More blunt was the comment of a New Jersey woman in a letter to *The New York Times*:

> To the Editor:
> What a rotten world we are handing down to our grandchildren.
> Violence and football on TV, Benjamin Britten on Saturday matinee at the Metropolitan, screaming records on radio and adulterated foods to eat.
> I am 89 and have known better days.
> Louise Wilde Perry

But most professional writers have always followed the motto of Voltaire's Dr. Pangloss: "All is for the best in this best of all possible worlds." Thus, in this bicentennial period, such quasi-official historians as Daniel J. Boorstin and James Beard assure us that we have never had it so good—that colonial Americans were primitives and ignoramuses in matters gastronomic, while the table of the ordinary American today is graced by delights formerly known only by the very rich.

The truth is almost precisely the contrary. The Founding Fathers were as far superior to our present political leaders in the quality of their food as they were in the quality of their prose and of their intelligence.* And if we leave aside for the moment the most depressed urban and rural slums of nineteenth-century America, no class of Americans—rich, middle-class, or even poor—eats as well today as its counterpart did a century ago. A millionaire today cannot at any price buy, in commercial channels, many of the pleasures of the middle-class table of the eighteenth and nineteenth centuries, nor the skilled and loving cookery that enhanced them. For today's middle class and poor (aside from those who garden or hunt or fish), to find even an occasional item of real taste is a stroke of luck, like finding an arrowhead in the woods. Good food, in short, is outside the mainstream of our economy.

This historic disaster has been obscured by great gains in productivity and wages, which have elevated a large section of our people into middle-class affluence. Many millions whose forebears were often *hungry* now have the wherewithal to stuff themselves with what looks like an enormous variety of what passes for food. But unlike us, when our forebears did have the modest price, they could obtain a considerable variety of really delicious food, and they knew how to prepare it. This whether they lived in Europe, Africa, Asia, Latin America, or the United States.

The disaster has been obscured also by a multibillion-dollar smokescreen of food advertising and by the propaganda of collaborationist food writers. But the most ominous development is what has happened to the American palate.

There is some evidence suggesting physical damage. The switch from breast feeding to sugared formulas is known to have affected babies' teeth and to have promoted obesity; it is at least possible that it has harmed the palate.

---

*For the food tastes of our recent Presidents, see Chapter 2. For the food tastes of Congressmen, see Appendix.

Zinc deficiency in the soil, in crops, and in diet has been turning up in many areas; among its less horrifying symptoms is a loss of ability to taste. Conceivably, some others among the thousands of additives and (to coin a word) subtractatives of modern food technology may have spoiled our palates. There is no question, however, about their having been badly conditioned.

The food industry knows this well. Publicly, it advertises this year's improved glop as even more delicious than last year's; privately, its analysts say the public *prefers* bad food to good. That's what they told *The Wall Street Journal*, as reported in an article headlined, "Most People Have No Taste; It's Been Lost in the Process." One informant told of a company that had developed a ketchup with natural tomato flavor. It flopped, until the product was slightly scorched and a metallic component added to give it the taste of "real" ketchup.

"Despite the clamor in recent years for a return to 'natural' foods," wrote Mary Bralove of the *WSJ*, "most Americans have grown so accustomed to mass-produced, artificially flavored foods that anything else tastes peculiar."

Tests have shown that fresh fruit juices taste odd and hence unpleasant to people raised on processed and imitation juices. William Downey, a food chemist, said, "We've moved away from the utilization of fresh flavor. It isn't familiar any more."

"Indeed," wrote Bralove, "food manufacturers are beginning to insist that flavorists forsake their search for natural flavors in favor of imitations of imitations. 'More than ever before, manufacturers request the taste of a product as it is usually found in the marketplace—processed, concentrated, freeze-dried, powdered or canned,' says Charles Grimm, director of flavor creation for International Flavors & Fragrances, Inc. Using this rule of thumb, Mr. Grimm says that if he were developing a bread flavor today, he would aim for the taste of Wonder Bread rather than homemade bread."

Kurt Konigsbacher, vice president for food activities of Booz, Allen & Hamilton, the management consultants, told Bralove he had once tasted flavors duplicating raw beets and raw asparagus, and they were awful. "If you give somebody strawberry ice cream made with fresh strawberries, you'd have a totally unacceptable product," he asserted. "People would say, 'I wouldn't eat that artificial stuff.'"

One may wonder how familiar Grimm was with the taste of homemade bread, or Konigsbacher with real strawberry ice cream. The recent boom in home baking and gardening suggests that many Americans would disagree. But they are a minority, and the food industry, like the television industry, goes by the ratings.

On the networks, family situation comedies perpetuate the myth that Americans come to table for three square meals a day in togetherness. The commercials for junk foods and soda pop are closer to the awful truth. The most devastating report we have seen on how Americans really eat was made by Dr. Paul A. Fine, a psychological consultant to major food companies. He presented his findings to a symposium of the American Medical Association and later discussed them in an interview.

It was appropriate that the study should be done by a psychologist because the dietary behavior of Americans abounds in symptoms of neurosis: divorce from reality, guilt feelings, a profound sense of inferiority and insecurity. Thus, when Dr. Fine's canvassers asked housewives to describe their families' eating patterns, they came up with the traditional three squares. But when they were persuaded to keep diaries of actual food consumption, they were, he said, "almost always surprised."

Three out of four American families do not eat breakfast together, he reported, and many don't eat breakfast at all. As for the hallowed evening meal, it can take place "as seldom as three days a week or less"—and then often lasts no more than twenty minutes.

The real American pattern of feeding is the snack. It

lasts from early morning to bedtime. "Even then it doesn't end," Dr. Fine said. "People can't sleep—they are restless —they are hungry. They get up and raid the leftovers they would not eat at dinner." This makes for an average of twenty "food contacts" a day, instead of three squares. And what is in these food contacts? Dr. Fine replies that the diet of the "American mainstream" is—

Oreos, peanut butter, Crisco, TV dinners, cake mix, macaroni and cheese, Pepsi and Coke, pizzas, Jell-O, hamburgers, Rice-a-Roni, Spaghetti-O's, pork and beans, Heinz ketchup and instant coffee.

Nevertheless, Dr. Fine said he did not regard the typical housewife as irrational, indifferent, or even unaware of how her family should eat, but rather as being "hooked into a dilemma she cannot solve." He explained:

The whole structure of modern life is such that she cannot usually do in reality what she thinks she is doing to compromise various pressures to "make things come out right." So deep is the strength of the ideal "shoulds" with regard to food and eating that the topic engenders much social lying—sheer refusal to talk in a group, to let others know the truth about what really goes on in one's family with regard to eating.
     There is also much self-deception. Women often think of the regular eating patterns of their families as exceptional cases, or "a stage someone is going through." Or they simply do not perceive their own reality fully.... It may be easier to get people to talk with complete frankness about their sex life than about the eating patterns of the family they are supposed to be in control of and toward which they feel an enormous sense of responsibility.

The woman who still believes that her sole and sacred role is to be a homemaker is in a particularly painful situation. "To spend a couple of hours or more preparing a meal that is over in twenty minutes or so seems senseless, and women say so," Dr. Fine reported. "The same women in places like Georgia or South Chicago who say with heat and anger, 'We don't want to be liberated,' also say, 'I will not be a slave in the kitchen like my mother was.'" His study described the actual life of these women, however, as a daylong drag: no breakfast to speak of, coffee-and in midmorning, abstinence from lunch in order to "diet," and perpetual replenishing of the family snack larder.

The foregoing is Dr. Fine's description of what he calls "the American mainstream," which is constantly being swelled by immigration from abroad and from the rural hinterland. These "ethnics," and especially their children, respond to pressures to conform, to "be American," by abandoning their cultural traditions, including their foods. On the other hand, a segment of the middle class is struggling to get out of the mainstream and into new "life styles." But these are people who were *born* in the mainstream. They have been out of touch with real food and real cookery for one, two, even three generations. Weaned on junk foods and soda pop, their palates have been numbed. Subject to the same neurotic pressures as their conformist neighbors, yet desperate to be chic and with-it, they are pathetically easy marks for the "gourmet" quacks.

Yet there is hope. The consumerists, the environmentalists, the gardeners, the home bakers, and the experimenters with foreign foods all have engaged in a resistance that sometimes wins victories. Mainly concerned with pollution and prices, or with novelty and status, they are weak in defending the sensual pleasures of good eating. Let us examine how we lost those pleasures, and how we may regain them.

2

Onward
and Downward

... the settlers who came to the New World were too busy with basic needs to bother about the niceties. In America, food initially was a matter of survival; later it was little more than a function. It wasn't until the end of World War II, says James Beard, the doyen of America's burgeoning food fraternity, "that Americans began to think of eating as a pleasurable thing, a sensual delight."

Horace Sutton, in The Saturday Review

Day in and day out, Mr. Ford eats exactly the same lunch—a ball of cottage cheese, over which he pours a small pitcherful of A.1. Sauce, a sliced onion or a quartered tomato, and a small helping of butter-pecan ice cream. "Eating and sleeping," he says to me, "are a waste of time."

John Hersey, in The New York Times

THE ESTABLISHMENT version of our food history has been packaged by Daniel J. Boorstin in *The Americans: The Democratic Experience*. His credentials are the best: President Cottage-Cheese-and-Ketchup named him director of the Smithsonian's National Museum of History and Technology, and President Cottage-Cheese-and-A.1.-Sauce promoted him to Librarian of Congress.

Jack Anderson complained that Boorstin had used $65,000 worth of the Smithsonian's hired help and facilities to assemble this clumping textbook, which won a Pulitzer Prize. The Senate Rules Committee nonetheless approved his elevation, while asking him not to use the Library of Congress as a writing stable. But this sort of subsidized peonage is not unusual in academe. What Anderson should have exposed was the extent to which Boorstin's assistants seem to have relied upon the company histories of such pioneers as Borden, Armour, and Swift.

A historian who did his own research and went to original sources would hardly declare, as Boorstin does, that the nineteenth-century restaurateur Delmonico helped Americans "discover salads" and showed them "how salads could be made from common New World plants." (Like iceberg lettuce and cottage cheese?) James Beard in his *American Cookery* (1972) puts the discovery even later: "The dish we normally associate with salad—greens, with or without other ingredients, mixed with a dressing— did not come into use until the late nineteenth century, and not until the twentieth century, about 1912, did the balance in flavor of sour to bland begin to achieve sophistication."

Neither historian offers any documentation for these absurdities. Reason alone should have made them reflect that the American Indians just might have known a thing or two about common New World plants, and that the settlers, being Europeans, would have been fond of salads, as their ancestors had been since antiquity. At the risk of being considered by his sponsor, Spiro Agnew, as an effete

Eastern intellectual, Boorstin might have noted that the Roman poet Martial discussed whether salads go best at the beginning or the end of a meal. In *The Forme of Cury*, a manuscript collection compiled by the cooks of Richard II about 1390, we find this charming recipe for a *Salat*: Take parsley, sage, garlic, chives, onions, leeks, borage, mint, maiden's leek, cress, fennel, rue, rosemary, purslaine, wash them clean, pluck them small with thine hand and mix them well with raw oil [olive]. Lay on vinegar and salt, and serve it forth.* And Beard, who calls iceberg lettuce "the most generally maligned and mis-treated" of all salad greens and maintains that their hearts "have good flavor and interesting texture," might learn something about sophistication from the English poet Milton. In *Paradise Lost*, which was surely familiar to our cultivated forebears, we find Eve assembling a salad for "her Angelical Guest," pondering:

> What choice to choose, for delicacy best;
> What Order so contrived, as not to mix
> Tastes not well join'd, inelegant, but bring
> Taste after Taste, upheld by kindliest change.

The lines are quoted by the English diarist John Evelyn in *Acetaria: A Discourse of Sallets*, a work published in 1699 and read in the colonies that puts our present "salad" abominations to shame. Evelyn lovingly considers the most desirable proportions for blending greens, listing scores that were available. The dressing, he says, should be a "discreet choice and mixture, neither the *Prodigal*, *Niggard*, nor *Insipid*," of olive oil from the Lucca region of Italy, the "best Wine Vinegar ... impregnated with the infusion of Clove-gilly-flowers, Elder, Roses, Rosemary, Nasturtiums, &c." or verjuice from green grapes,† and

* Transcribed into modern English by author. —K.H.
† Verjuice is, as Evelyn says, the juice of unripe grapes. Some authorities maintain that in England only crab apple juice was used, but many references make it clear that the grape was preferred. In a number of fifteenth-century English manu-

"the brightest Bay grey-Salt." Compare this with a sophisticated concoction that Beard recommends: "1½ cups sugar, 2 teaspoons dry mustard, 2 teaspoons salt, ⅔ cup vinegar, 3 tablespoons onion juice, 2 cups vegetable oil—not olive oil, 3 tablespoons poppy seeds."*

Now, why would anyone think that the English colonists abandoned salads? They didn't. Colonial gardens and markets offered a rich variety of greens. William Byrd, a contemporary of Evelyn's, lists dozens in his *Natural History of Virginia* (1737). Thomas Jefferson in a garden book mentions as regularly available in the market of Washington during his years in the White House (1801–1809) not only lettuce, tomatoes, parsley, radishes, cucumbers, celery, and cabbage but also corn salad, sorrel, endive, and cress, which would be more difficult for the modern housewife to find. Mrs. Randolph (*Virginia Housewife*, 1824) tells us in her recipe, "To dress salad: To have this delicate dish in perfection, the lettuce, pepper grass, chervil, cress, &c. should be gathered early in the morning, nicely picked, washed, and laid in cold water, which will be improved by ice: just before dinner is ready to be served, drain the water from your salad, cut it into a bowl, giving the proper proportions of each plant." She then gives a typical English dressing of the time based on hard-boiled egg yolks. The English had forsaken the classic oil and vinegar of Chaucer's time, and Evelyn's, and when it was reintroduced to England and America toward the end of the nineteenth century it was called French dressing. By now, commercial French dressings have been so debased (with recipe books following suit) that most serious cooks prefer the French *vinaigrette*; even here, one now finds recipes that depart from the classic olive oil, wine vinegar or lemon juice, salt, and pepper.

The earliest known cookbook written by an American,

---

scripts (Harleian Ms. 4016, about 1450) recipes occasionally called for *vinegre* or *vergeous*.
* In *American Cookery*.

Amelia Simmons's estimable *American Cookery* (1796), mentions several varieties of lettuce, and recommends purple cabbage for slaw. It is only in our own time that iceberg lettuce and cotton tomatoes have driven tasty greens and real tomatoes from the market, while horrid "chef" concoctions topped with synthetic dressings have flouted the artful balance sought by Eve for her Heavenly visitor—Paradise lost, indeed.

As if to indicate the nature of American eating habits before Borden, Armour, and Swift came along, Boorstin opens his food history with the story of the 1846 Donner party, who ate one another. This, he says, inspired Gail Borden to invent a meat biscuit. It tasted so awful that Frederick Law Olmsted, on a journey in Texas, "finally fed his to the birds, declaring that he would 'decidedly undergo a very near approach to the traveler's last bourne, before having recourse to it.'" Taste has ever been an obstacle to progress.

But Borden had a vision about compacting space and time. He told his pastor: "Condense your sermons.... The world is changing....Even lovers write no poetry, nor any other stuff and nonsense, now. They condense all they have to say, I suppose, into a kiss." Napoleon never took more than twenty minutes to eat, Borden observed, and "*I* am through in fifteen." Here Boorstin missed a chance to pay a similar compliment to Gerald Ford, for whom eating is "a waste of time." *The New York Times* reported (June 19, 1974):

> Vice President Ford told the Grocery Manufacturers of America at their convention in White Sulphur Springs, Va., that he felt a particular affinity for the makers of instant coffee, instant tea and instant oatmeal.
>
> "I happen to be the nation's first instant Vice President," he said. "I only hope that I prove to be as pure, digestible, and as appetizing to consumers who did not have a chance to shop around for other brands of Vice President when I was put on the market."

Although Borden used what looked suspiciously like bribery to promote his meat biscuit, the Army could not stomach it. But he kept trying to dehydrate "useful dietary matters," declaring, "I mean to put a potato into a pillbox, a pumpkin into a tablespoon, the biggest sort of a watermelon into a saucer." He was ahead of his time on these, but he hit the jackpot with condensed milk.

Boorstin wistfully mentions the tale that Borden invented his process because he had heard babies crying for milk during a transatlantic crossing. To be fair, he doesn't vouch for it, but he could hardly pass it up. Pop historians like Boorstin and James Beard are patsies for the neat anecdote: the apple fell on Newton, so he discovered gravity; the Donner party resorted to cannibalism, so Borden made a meat biscuit; Birdseye saw a frozen fish thaw out, so he invented quick-freezing.

Typical of this genre of historical fiction is the story of *pommes soufflées*: The inaugural train from Paris to St. Germain-en-Laye (1837) was delayed, so Chef Collinet snatched his French fries out of the pan half cooked. When he heard the train whistle, he put them back in and presto! they exploded into golden shells of hot air. Hundreds of writers have repeated this children's tale of the choo-choo train that finally made the grade, among them James Beard in *American Cookery* (although what *pommes soufflées* have to do with American cookery is not clear). *Larousse Gastronomique* also tells the story, but our yarn spinners failed to notice that it is told in the subjunctive, indicating some doubt, and with a further disclaimer, *on pretend* (it is claimed).

Just so, the invention of *béchamel* sauce is always attributed to Bechameil, Marquis de Nointel, although one can easily find recipes for the sauce printed long before his time. (It should be noted that those seventeenth-century recipes were all based on a reduction of veal or chicken broth and heavy cream; they had not the least resemblance to the *béchamel* of today.)

In virtually all such cases, the truth is more interesting

though less tidy than the anecdote, but to find it requires tedious and meticulous research. And of course, the anecdote grows more pat with each telling. Beard asserts without qualification: "When Lord Sandwich sent out for some meat to be placed between two pieces of bread so he could continue with his game of cards, he had no idea what a revolution in food he was causing. He influenced the food habits of the Danes, the English and the French. But for Americans, he started a way of life." With a moment's thought, Beard might have reflected that people had been folding meat or fish or beans into bread as far back as antiquity. All responsible sources simply suggest that *a* sandwich was named in honor of the fourth Earl of Sandwich, and the name stuck, in English. That is plausible; to say the Earl invented the sandwich and conferred it upon the Danes is a little much.

Boorstin, too, likes to stretch the exploits of his heroes. He tells us that Borden not only eliminated the need for fresh milk but also "turned the dairy farmer into a milk wholesaler who no longer had to peddle his milk, or churn butter or mold a cheese." And where Borden failed, in taking the juice out of meat, Swift and Armour eventually succeeded. Both were meat packers who, like Borden, made fortunes in the Civil War. All were patriots. "Armour foresaw that a Union victory would soon bring pork prices down," Boorstin says. "He went to New York to sell pork futures and found many takers. When Union victories sent pork prices plummeting, Armour was able to buy for $18 a barrel pork which he had already sold for more than $30. So he was well rewarded for his patriotic confidence in the Union. . . .

"His reputation, like Swift's, was not improved by the scandal of 'embalmed beef,' a supply of bad beef sent to the troops in the Spanish-American War. But Armour and Swift both became generous philanthropists."

They also endowed the world with a new way to conserve meat, says Boorstin. "Now the most popular mode of preservation was no longer salting, spicing or smoking, all of which had been known from ancient time, but was canning." Actually, as he mentions in passing, modern industrial canning had been developed by the French and, as in this country, got a great lift from war contracts. But it took merchants to turn field rations into staples of civilian diet. César Ritz and his chef, Escoffier, got a piece of the business. M. F. K. Fisher gives us, deadpan, this boast by Ritz: "Only the other day, an Englishman who had lived many years in India told me, 'Thanks to Escoffier's tinned and bottled foods, I was able for many years to enjoy good French cooking in the wilds.'" The sun never set on Fortnum & Mason. In the middle of India, with its marvelous array of aromatic foods, this Englishman dined, properly dressed no doubt, on canned goods. God save the Queen.

With equal lyricism, Boorstin says of canning that this "new source of everyday miracles would make prose out of many an old poetic metaphor." He proves it by quoting an industry puff published in 1924:

> Canning gives the American family—especially in cities and factory towns—a kitchen garden where all good things grow, and it is always harvest time.... A regular Arabian Nights garden, where raspberries, apricots, olives, and pineapples, always ripe, grow side by side with peas, pumpkins, spinach, a garden with baked beans vines and spaghetti bushes, and sauerkraut beds, and great cauldrons of hot soup, and through it running a branch of the ocean in which one can catch salmon, lobsters, crabs and shrimp, and dig oysters and clams.

This prose miracle of canning, Boorstin writes, canceled out the poetry of Ecclesiastes: "To every thing there is a season." In the new garden of Eden, where "the diet of the common American citizen was more varied than that of many a European man of wealth," not only canned but also fresh tomatoes are available year-round. A century ago, "carrying quality, not to mention such fine points as appearance and texture, did not enter much into the farmer's calculation." A revolution in transportation, refrigeration, and agriculture changed all that; "another step was being taken toward democratizing the national diet and increasing the variety of foods of the ordinary season."

Regions and seasons homogenized, the diet democratized by patriotic entrepreneurs who are rewarded by listing on the New York Stock Exchange and are ultimately conglomerated like their products—it is indeed a tale to thrill the house historian of a cottage-cheese-and-glop Administration. It is marred, however, by one whopping injustice and one whopping omission. The injustice is Boorstin's suggestion that pure food laws and other improvements in living standards were the gift of his business heroes, rather than of reformers and muckrakers who, down to our time, have always had to fight the industry every inch of the way. The omission is the fact that the history of American food is the history of the destruction of its taste.

"*De gustibus non disputandum est*" (there's no arguing about taste) is a notion that we shall dispute to our dying breath. It implies that we cannot maintain that Bach is better than the latest noise on the Hit Parade, that Tolstoy is better than Herman Wouk, that homemade bread with Jersey butter is better than Wonder Bread with margarine. Nature has endowed every living species with a set of taste preferences that are part of the overall structure of survival; it is no accident that growing fruits are rather suddenly transformed from green, tough, and unsavory things to ripe, juicy, aromatic, and delicious—even more nourishing—things at the very time that their seeds are mature, and ready to be broadcast by the creatures that eat them.

Taste is a product not only of a species but also, and above all, of soil and water. Just as oysters from any arm of the sea taste different from those anywhere else, so every form of edible life tastes of its environment and its food. In plants, the flavor and aroma are an amalgam of microclimate, water, and the structure of the soil, with its trace elements and its living and decaying matter. A single variety of grape will produce a great red wine in Burgundy, a great white in Champagne, a mediocre table wine elsewhere; for that matter, any taster fortunate enough to make the comparison can detect a difference between wines from adjoining fields. Cigar smokers are familiar with the same phenomenon; tradition has it that the seed of Havana tobacco was smuggled out of Cuba in a pilgrim's staff, but the Vuelta Abajo of Cuba has not lost its aromatic supremacy. The quality of coffee, of course, varies dramatically among regions, and at different altitudes. And these distinctions are not limited to "noble" products like wine, tobacco, and coffee. "Idaho" potatoes grown in other parts of the country are not as good, and New England connoisseurs swear that the best turnips come from near Wellfleet. In Paris markets, good house-wives insist on potatoes from the Ile de Ré and turnips from Nantes or Croissy, in season, and butter from Deux-Sèvres or Isigny, poultry from Bresse, Le Mans, or the Périgord, beef from the Limousin or Charolais. Those beef cattle are, of course, raised in fat meadows, and those chickens are, of course, raised in the barnyard, feeding only on grain and what they pick from the ground.

French peasants believe that a hectare of ground has only so much taste to impart to a crop, so that, all other things being equal, the bigger the crop, the smaller the flavor in a bushel—*c'est mathématique*, they say. This principle is so well established that any region allowed to market its wine under an *appellation controlée* or local label must limit the production per hectare in order to maintain quality; the volume is from one-sixth to one-third of what may be obtained by growers of *vin ordinaire*. (There is naturally considerable cheating, but the palate can tell.) Unfortunately, such taste control applies only to wine and to a few other products of prestigious local origin. An old grain merchant in Paris told us that one reason why bread was not as good as before the war was that wheat production per hectare had more than doubled, as a result of the use of new plant species, chemical fertilizers, insecticides, and fungicides.

The trace elements that help give each crop its savor are not inexhaustible, as was demonstrated by the appearance of zinc deficiency in intensively cultivated soils of the American West during the 1930s. This stunts vegetables, and children, too. The deficiency can be treated by the addition of zinc to the diet, and to the soil, but what of all the other trace elements? Most of them have not yet been studied, because crop damage has not been so dramatic as with zinc. Only our taste buds tell us that something is missing.

Writing in the middle of the eighteenth century, Samuel Pegge reported that the perfume of American fruits was so strong as to upset refined European palates, while European fruits seemed insipid to Americans. (Just so, the traveler familiar with the heady aroma and flavor of native species of bananas can never make do with the bland, green-picked variety developed by American companies.) The estimable Amelia Simmons advised a little later that "all Cabbages have a higher relish that grow on *unmatured* grounds." And if memory serves, that cultivated traveler Olmsted, who spat out Borden's meat biscuit, once made the precious observation that as he approached the virgin lands of the frontier, the bread tasted better.

In the beginning, then, Boorstin and Beard notwithstanding, the food of the New World was more flavorsome than that of the Old. Now that, among other things, the soil of the New World has become prematurely aged by chemical exploitation, it's the other way around. The rule of tongue is that the older—that is, the more primitive —the society, the tastier its food. Small, varied production of species locally developed, rotation of crops, the return of wastes to the soil, the thriving population of insects and worms, all these appear to preserve a balanced, living ecology that gives savor to food. The best bread we have tasted in decades we ate in a Greek mountain village where the wheat was grown in small patches, cut with sickles, ground by donkey-powered millstones, and baked in the village oven. The tastiest chickens were scrawny birds pecking around mud huts in Morocco.

The objection will be raised that we produce more food per capita and live better in nearly every other way than the poor of these countries. We will argue later that it is not necessary for a country to be poor to eat well; the subject now is taste. But be it noted that the foods of affluent Western Europe, wherever traditional methods of farming and marketing have survived, now are incomparably more flavorsome than ours.

This is, of course, a reversal of established dogma. In fact, our food history has generally been told backward, and upside down. Before we further analyze that revolution which, according to Boorstin, made this country an Arabian Nights garden where canned spaghetti grows on bushes, we must try to sketch the true story of our food, from the beginning. It is, as far as we know, a story never properly told.

3

Colonial Eden

Most of the *American* fruits are exceedingly odoriferous, and therefore are very disgusting at first to us *Europeans*: on the contrary, our fruits appear insipid to them, for want of odour.

Samuel Pegge, The Forme of Cury (1780)

WILLIAM BYRD called Virginia the Garden of Eden. A fellow of the Royal Society then headed by Sir Isaac Newton, Byrd was the founder of Richmond and, to be sure, a booster. In his *Natural History of Virginia* (1737), he reported that the colony had long been growing every kind of European fruit and vegetable, such as artichokes, "beautiful cauliflower...very large and long asparagus of splendid flavor, white as well as red...watermelons and fragrant melons" and all manner of pumpkins, squashes, and cucumbers. He was ecstatic about the fruits, especially the peach, and listed twenty-four kinds of apples, explaining that he "wanted only to describe the best species of them." He mentioned apricot, pear, plum, quince, fig, cherry, mulberry, and many nut trees as reasonably common, and added that even almond, pomegranate, coffee, and tea grew in the gardens of "fanciers of beautiful fruits."

In a section headed "What One Generally Eats and Drinks in Virginia," Byrd said that the beef, veal, mutton, and pork were "always as good as the best European [equivalents] can be, since the pastures in this country are very fine." A pound of the best meat "is commonly sold for a Virginia penny," a large fat capon for 8 to 10 pence and "a large fat turkey-hen which weighs from thirty to forty and even more pounds" for 24 to 30 pence. The ordinary bread was made of wheat, but Byrd said that old settlers often preferred corn mixed with rice.

A contemporary of Byrd's, Robert Beverley, put it that the bread in "Gentlemen's Houses" was usually of wheat, "but some rather choose the Pone, which is the bread made of Indian Meal." He noted that the word came from the Indian name *Oppone*; Captain Smith mentioned it as early as 1612.

Modern writers who describe the colonists as ignorant of "the niceties" of gastronomy utterly ignore the contribution of the Indians both to the variety of our diet and to the intelligence of its preparation. Robert Beverley devoted a chapter to Indian cooking in his *History and Present State of Virginia* (1705). Two staples of Southern cookery are there. "Homony: This is *Indian* Corn soaked, broken in a Mortar, husked, and then boil'd in Water over a gentle Fire." When meat is broiled "by laying it upon Sticks rais'd upon Forks at some distance above the live Coals . . . this they, and we also, from them, call Barbacue-ing."

The Indians baked their bread, Byrd said, "either in Cakes before the Fire, or in Loaves on a warm Hearth, covering the Loaf first with Leaves, then with warm Ashes, and afterwards with Coals over all." This would later become the Southerners' hoecake. The Indians made it of corn, wild oats, or sunflower seeds, Byrd wrote. "They delight much to feed on Roasting-ears; that is, the Indian corn, gathered green and milky, before it is grown to its full bigness, and roasted before the fire, in the Ear." Let our agricultural scientists note that the Indians had a great number of varieties of corn, so that they could have a long season, beginning in the middle of May, according to Byrd, who added, "And this indeed is a very sweet and pleasing Food."

These primitives also cultivated an extraordinary number of fruits and vegetables, among them peaches, strawberries, melons, "Pompions" (pumpkins), and many varieties of beans, and they gathered chestnuts, hickory nuts, and black walnuts. In the uplands, Beverley reported, the Indians milked the sweet pods of the "Honey Tree" (apparently honey locust) and the sap of the "Sugar Tree." "This Juice is drawn out, by wounding the Trunk of the Tree, and placing a Receiver under the Wound. The *Indians* make One Pound of Sugar out of Eight Pounds of the Liquor. Some of this Sugar I examined very carefully. It was bright and moist, with a large full Grain; the Sweetness of it being like that of good Muscovada. Though this Discovery has not been made by the *English* above Twelve or Fourteen Years; yet it has been known among the *Indians*, longer than any one now living can remember." All in all, it would seem that the settlers learned as much from the Indians about dealing with this strange land and its strange produce as the Indians learned from them.

"As for Fish, both of Fresh and Salt-Water, of Shell-Fish, and others, no Country can boast of more Variety, greater Plenty, or of better in their several Kinds," Beverley declared. He mentioned herring, shad, lamprey, flounder, whiting, bass, crabs, oysters, mussels, cockles, shrimp, eels, conger, perch, and catfish, among others, and said that before the English came, fish were so plentiful that Indian children would take them with pointed sticks. There were swans, geese, several kinds of ducks, and "many other Kinds of Water-Fowl, that the Plenty of them is incredible." There were also snipe, woodcock, larks, pheasant, partridge, "Wild Turkeys of an incridible [*sic*] Bigness," and deer, hare, squirrel, and wild hogs.

These last were the contribution of the earliest settlers,

and less than a century after their arrival, Beverley could report that "Hogs swarm like Vermine upon the Earth, and are often accounted such," being eliminated from estate inventories. "The Hogs run where they list, and find their own Support in the Woods, without any Care of the Owner." When a planter took the trouble to mark any part of a litter, it was accepted that the whole "Gang of Hogs" would belong to him; "as they are bred in Company, so they continue to the end." This, then, was the beginning of the justly celebrated Virginia ham. Those lean pigs, fed on acorns and other fallen fruits and nuts, must have been delicious, as are those of Corsica which range in chestnut forests. The custom of running hogs free persisted into our time in some parts of the South.

Beverley records the little-known fact that as early as 1622—we repeat, 1622—"some *French* Vignerons were sent thither [to Virginia] to make an experiment of their Vines." They reported to their employers that the wine "far excell'd their own Country of *Languedoc*." The wines of Languedoc are not among France's greatest, and one may assume that these vintners did not understate the quality of their Virginia product. We hear no more of them, but Sir William Berkeley, the Royal Governor of Virginia, fostered a number of experiments in the middle of the century. These, too, were failures; Beverley correctly observed that wine grapes prefer gravelly slopes and do not do well in company with the pine tree. Later, the Huguenot refugees "began an Essay of Wine" and, Beverley said, made a "Noble strong-bodied Claret, of a curious flavour." The Huguenots apparently forsook their vines, but they did leave important traces in the cuisine of Virginia, which we will examine later.

It should be noted that the English who settled in Virginia were, in the main, either the younger sons of gentry or, not to put too fine a point on it, ex-convicts and other dispossessed people who had little to gain by staying in England. There were few real farmers among them; indeed, industry was not one of their prime virtues. In his final chapter, Beverley reproached them for indolence and failure to make full use of the unparalleled richness of the tidelands: "No Seed is sowed there, but it thrives, and most Plants are improved, by being Transplanted thither. And yet there's very little Improvement made among them, nor any thing us'd in Traffique, but Tobacco." With brilliant foresight, he warned of the dangers of a one-crop economy, dependent upon England for products that could readily be made in Virginia. He closed with these words:

> Thus they depend altogether upon the Liberality of Nature, without endeavouring to improve its gifts, by Art or Industry. They spunge upon the Blessings of a warm Sun, and a fruitful Soil, and almost Grutch the Pains of gathering in the Bounties of the Earth. I should be asham'd to publish this slothful Indolence of my Countrymen, but that I hope it will rouse them out of their Lethargy, and excite them to make the most of all those happy Advantages which Nature has given them; and if it does this, I am sure they will have the Goodness to forgive me.

(Beverley did not, unfortunately, mention the contribution of slavery to the indolence of his countrymen, nor did he question the morality of the peculiar institution. It is interesting to note, however, that as early as June 1680 the colony outlawed meetings of blacks "under pretence of feasts and burialls" and forbade a slave "to lift up his hand in opposition against any christian.")

Unlike the lush tidelands of Virginia, the stony soil of New England could hardly be called a Garden of Eden. But its forests did not lack for game, and its cold coastal waters teemed with seafood even more delicious than that of warmer shores. The winters were long and harsh, and each spring the rocks boiled up through the soil and had to be cleared away again, but the Pilgrims made up by industry and husbandry what nature did not offer freely. By 1629, they were already harvesting apples; earlier, the Indians had taught them to grow corn and gather blueberries, cranberries, and other wild fruits and lay them by for the winter. While their cookery never reached the elegance of Virginia's, New England housewives made the best of what they had; their chowders and their bean dishes, for example, would honor our American cuisine in any international competition.

We will explore the history of our cooking (as distinct from the produce itself) later on, but let us in passing bury the myth that our Puritan heritage is responsible for the lamentable state of American food today. It would seem, on the contrary, that the various more or less Calvinist strains of our society adopted the sensual pleasures of the table as a subliminal replacement for the other joys that they abjured. It was better to eat than to burn.

It is difficult to understand how anybody reared on the tradition of the Thanksgiving feast, or even slightly familiar with our recent past, could think otherwise. In New England, the rich Bostonians and other Yankee industrialists may have shunned ostentation, but they early provided a market for the most elegant foods and for French wines. Devout Protestants everywhere were great trenchermen. There is a remarkable manuscript cookbook at the Pennsylvania Historical Society that belonged to the Quaker family of William Penn—a cookbook lavish not only in ingredients but also in techniques. The Amish and Mennonites, also, did not deprive themselves of good eating, nor did the Methodists and Baptists.

New Orleans and Richmond were never afflicted with Puritan traditions, yet their fare has suffered the same decline. Italians cannot be accused of Calvinism; theirs is a joyous cuisine. How, then, can we explain the limp factory pasta drowned in watery ketchup that is served in most Italian-American restaurants today? Further, the Puritan tradition has certainly faded in our attitudes toward sex; why has our new hedonism not kept our food from going to slop?

Until a few years ago, church suppers and cake sales were a precious resort of serious eaters. One of the authors of this book is the daughter of a Midwestern Danish Lutheran pastor—of the Beckian or Calvinist persuasion, be it noted, not the Gruntvigian, or "Merry Lutherans"—and her girlhood was one long round of competition among women of the congregation to impress the pastor with their culinary artistry. They were all fine cooks and bakers, most kept cows, chickens, and gardens, and each tried her best to outdo her Christian sisters in the most un-Christian fashion. The pastor was well fed.

Alas, this has changed, but it was not Puritanism that did it in. Even in those days, before the war, the worm was in the apple. The sons of one champion baker were embarrassed to take homemade bread to school and whined, "Gee, *Mor*, why can't we have store bread like everybody else?" She never baked bread again. Another woman made the best lemon meringue pie we ever ate—until she discovered Realemon. Recently, we sat down with her son at a church-connected dinner. It was catered by Kentucky Fried Chicken, whose product has been described by no less an authority than Colonel Sanders himself as "nothing but a fried doughball wrapped around some chicken" served with gravy that was like "wallpaper paste." It was July in Nebraska, and there was not even an ear of corn on the table, not to mention real chicken and dumplings, farm pickles, or homebaked pies such as would have graced the table a generation ago. But the son insisted, "America is the best-eating country in the world."

A New England church we know abandoned its cake sales when it found that all the cakes were now either store-bought or made from mixes; it asked the women to donate cash instead. We used to haunt church suppers in the Berkshires, where the food ranged from good to marvelous. When we returned not long ago, we found that the members, having abandoned gardening, dairying,

and old-fashioned cookery, were now begging chickens
and canned peas from supermarkets and serving steam-
table glop and gelatine salads.

The modern gourmets were not the first to look down
their noses at colonial food. English snobs of the period
refused to believe that it could be civilized, not to say
better than theirs. We have quoted Samuel Pegge's observation that American fruits were too "odoriferous"
for refined European nostrils. A similar prejudice had
inspired an anonymous letter in the *Gazetteer* of London
in 1765, deriding the threat of the colonists to boycott
tea in protest at the Stamp Act. It said, "the Americans,
should they resolve to drink no more tea, can by no means
keep that Resolution, their Indian corn not affording an
agreeable or easy digestible breakfast." Benjamin Franklin,
then in London as a colonial delegate, fired back:

> Pray, let me, an American, inform the gentleman,
> who seems ignorant of the matter, that Indian corn,
> take it for all in all, is one of the most agreeable and
> wholesome grains in the world; that its green leaves
> [read: ears] roasted are a delicacy beyond expression;
> that samp, hominy, succatash, and nokehock, made
> of it, are so many pleasing varieties; and that johny
> or hoecake, hot from the fire, is better than a York-
> shire muffin — But if Indian corn were so disagreeable
> as the Stamp Act, does he imagine we can get noth-
> ing else for breakfast? —Did he never hear that we
> have oatmeal in plenty, for water gruel or burgoo;
> as good wheat, rye and barley as the world affords, to
> make frumenty; or toast and ale; that there is every
> where plenty of milk, butter and cheese; that rice is
> one of our staple commodities; that for tea, we have
> sage and bawm in our gardens, the young leaves of
> the sweet hickery or walnut, and above all, the buds
> of our pine, infinitely preferable to any tea from the
> Indies; while the islands yield us plenty of coffee and
> chocolate? —Let the gentleman do us the honour of a
> visit in America, and I will engage to breakfast him

every day in the month with a fresh variety, without offering him either tea or Indian corn.*

Thomas Jefferson's passion for fine food and wine is sufficiently well known to pose a problem for those who sneer at the colonial table. Boorstin meets it by quoting Patrick Henry as calling Jefferson the gastronomic equivalent of an effete Eastern intellectual. But Franklin was a self-taught man of the people, who described himself as having been raised in a home indifferent to food, yet his letters to his wife, Deborah, are marked with grateful acknowledgment of the fruits and pies she had shipped to him, and with complaints about the austerity of his diet in London. Unlike Jefferson, he was not enchanted by French *haute cuisine*, but he evidently cared about food; apparently homesick for American cookery, he translated a number of recipes into French during his sojourn in Paris.

Jefferson is precious to us here because he kept a garden book from 1766 to 1824 and especially because he set down an extraordinary record of some of the produce available in the market at Washington, D.C., during his terms as President. The garden at Monticello may be ruled out as the hobby of a wealthy enthusiast, who cadged seeds and cuttings from friends in many countries. We may similarly pass over, as historians have done, the astonishing proportion of his correspondence that concerned his purchases of French wine. But the market list cannot be so dismissed. Where Boorstin holds that early Americans suffered from a lack of variety in the diet, we find here vegetables, regularly appearing, that one is hard put to find in most American supermarkets today. How often do you see corn salad or sorrel, for instance? Sorrel has a long growing season, and lettuce, spinach, and parsley were available all year round. Nor does the absence of an item from the list imply that it was absent

* Quoted in *Benjamin Franklin on the Art of Eating* (American Philosophical Society, 1958).

A Statement of the Vegetable market of Washington, during a period of 8. years, wherein the earliest & latest appearance of each article within the whole 8. years is noted.

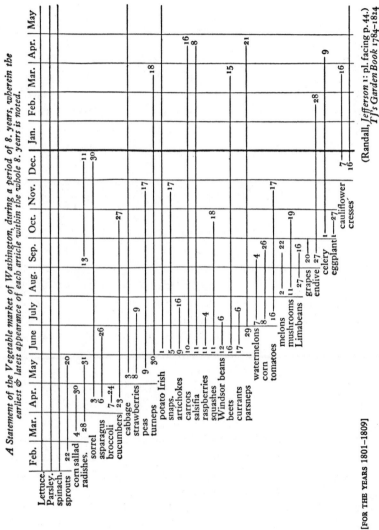

[FOR THE YEARS 1801–1809]

(Randall, *Jefferson* i: pl. facing p. 44.)
TJ's Garden Book 1784–1834

from the market. Apparently, Jefferson listed only a selection, for he did not mention such staples as sweet potatoes (often called Spanish potatoes), chestnuts, and tree fruits such as apples, peaches, cherries, plums, and pears. Note the presence, however, of tomatoes and eggplants, which gourmet historians tell us were introduced much later.

Perhaps the most remarkable thing about the list is the way it charts the seasons, whose suppression Boorstin regards as a triumph of modern industry. We are now so conditioned to cottony strawberries and tomatoes in January that we have forgotten the pleasures of anticipation, and the excitement when they finally came in, ripe, tart, and delicious. (The food chemists who say people don't like the taste of the real thing probably never had eaten it themselves. A grandson of ours, born in France, spat out the first strawberry he encountered in California, announcing, "It tastes like Lysol.") Even in the most difficult months, January and February, Washingtonians in Jefferson's time could buy at least fourteen kinds of fresh fruits and vegetables. And this, of course, was in addition to the stores of food that all self-respecting housewives had put by—dried, salted, pickled, or preserved in sugar.

If provisions were precarious and cooking rough-and-ready on the frontier, it can be seen that in the settled areas, Americans of the seventeenth and eighteenth centuries ate extremely well. No less an authority than Brillat-Savarin praised the quality of our provender. In his *La Physiologie du Goût*, he recalls a visit to a farm "five killing leagues" from Hartford, Connecticut, in October 1794. Dinner was "a superb piece of corned beef, stewed goose, a magnificent leg of mutton, then, all manner of root vegetables, and at both ends of the table two enormous pots of excellent cider of which I couldn't get enough." The occasion was a turkey hunt and, if we are to believe him, it was Brillat-Savarin who brought in the only turkey.

Everything at the farm fascinated the young Frenchman: the luxury of a fire in mild weather, the absence of
locks on the doors, the open way of the American parents
with their four daughters. He himself took charge of
cooking the hunt dinner: partridge wings *en papillotte*,
gray squirrel simmered in Madeira, and the roasted turkey.
He modestly admits that it looked charming, smelled good,
and tasted delicious, and he breaks into English to quote
one diner as exclaiming, "Oh! dear sir, what a glorious
bit!"

The raising of turkeys was by then a large commercial
affair in France; the bird was considered an elegant offering at festive dinners, stuffed with sausages, chestnuts, or
truffles. Brillat-Savarin told his French readers that the
flesh of the wild bird was "higher colored and more
aromatic than the domesticated turkey," and he therefore
approved the advice of one Monsieur Bosc to turkey
growers, "give them all possible liberty, take them to the
fields, and even the woods, to heighten their taste and make
them approach as much as possible the original species."
The advice would be even better directed, alas, to the
present-day American producers of caged, hormoned,
injected, frozen, and tasteless turkeys.

The golden age of American foodstuffs carried into the
first half of the nineteenth century. Washington Irving
sketches it in his "Legend of Sleepy Hollow." Compare
the Hudson Valley farm of Baltus Van Tassel with
Boorstin's 1924 Eden of canned-spinach bushes and canned-
sauerkraut beds. The time is a century earlier. Ichabod
Crane surveys the rows of pigeons, the troops of porkers,
the squadron of geese, the whole fleets of ducks and
regiments of turkeys, "and guinea-fowls fretting about"...

In his devouring mind's eye he pictured to himself
every roasting-pig running about with a pudding in
his belly, and an apple in his mouth; the pigeons were
snugly put to bed in a comfortable pie, and tucked
in with a coverlet of crust; the geese were swimming
in their own gravy; and the ducks pairing cosily in

dishes, like snug married couples, with a decent com-
petency of onion sauce. In the porkers he saw carved
out the future sleek side of bacon and juicy relishing
ham; not a turkey but he beheld daintily trussed-up,
with its gizzard under its wing, and peradventure, a
necklace of savory sausages; and even bright chanti-
cleer himself lay sprawling on his back in a side dish,
with uplifted claws, as if craving that quarter which
his chivalrous spirit disdained to ask while living.

As the enraptured Ichabod fancied all this, and as he
rolled his great green eyes over the fat meadow-lands,
the rich fields of wheat, of rye, of buckwheat, and
Indian corn, and the orchards burthened with ruddy
fruit, which surrounded the warm tenement of Van
Tassel, his heart yearned after the damsel who was to
inherit these domains. . . .

Fain would I pause to dwell upon the world of
charms that burst upon the enraptured gaze of my
hero, as he entered the state parlour of Van Tassel's
mansion. Not those of the bevy of buxom lasses, with
their luxurious display of red and white; but the
ample charms of a genuine Dutch country tea-table in
the sumptuous time of autumn. Such heaped-up
platters of cakes of various and almost indescribable
kinds, known only to experienced Dutch housewives!
There was the doughty dough-nut, the tenderer oly
loek, and the crisp and crumbling cruller; sweet-
cakes and short-cakes, ginger-cakes and honey-cakes,
and the whole family of cakes. And then there were
apple-pies and peach-pies and pumpkin-pies; besides
slices of ham and smoked beef; and, moreover, delectable dishes of preserved plums, and peaches, and
pears, and quinces; not to mention broiled shad and
roasted chickens; together with bowls of milk and
cream, all mingled higgledy-piggledy, pretty much
as I have enumerated them, with the motherly tea-pot
sending up its clouds of vapour from the midst.

And then Boorstin's heroes came along.

4

"Better Than Fresh"

You can't get good ice cream anymore. . . .
It tastes like gum and chalk. . . . The world
is winding down. You can't get good bread
anymore even in good restaurants (you get
commercial rolls), and there are fewer good
restaurants. Melons don't ripen, grapes are
sour. . . . Butter tastes like the printed paper
it's wrapped in. Whipped cream comes in
aerosol bombs and isn't whipped and isn't
cream. People serve it, people eat it. Two
hundred and fifty million educated Americans will go to their graves and never know
the difference. . . . That's what Paradise is—
never knowing the difference.

Joseph Heller, in Something Happened

Humiliating to an American is a visit to any good fish
market in Madrid, Ankara, or Marrakech. His eyes and
his nose tell him that the saltwater fish in these *inland*
cities of poor countries is fresher than he can find in most
markets of *coastal* cities in the United States. Our only
explanation is that refrigeration has come to these back-

ward lands only recently; the catch is rushed over the mountains by dawn and must be consumed that day.

We used to handle fish the same way. Old merchants in New York remember when the day's catch would be landed at Fulton Fish Market—some of it kept alive in floating tanks—and sold before dawn, often still curved in rigor mortis. Progress has changed all that. The boats now go out for weeks at a time. Most of the fish is filleted and frozen in blocks, some of it aboard ship, some ashore; two-thirds of the carcass is ground into feed and fertilizer, the rest processed for human use. The 5 or 10 percent of the catch that is delivered as fresh may have been treated with antibiotics to postpone decay, although that has been illegal in the United States for some years now. (There is no sanitary inspection of fish.) More likely, the catch will have been soaked in some brine and chemical solution that has not yet been outlawed.

Fishermen, like farmers, tend to overuse chemicals that promise to increase yields. A state bulletin to Florida shrimpers warns them that they have been using too much sodium bisulfite, a cosmetic measure to prevent the harmless black spot that normally appears on shrimp some days or weeks after they have been taken. The overdose, according to the bulletin, "causes discoloration and a sharp flavor" that bring consumer complaints. This is a little mystifying, since fresh—that is, unfrozen—shrimp have virtually disappeared from our markets.

Boorstin reports with condescension the belief of Gail Borden that milk is a "living fluid" which "as soon as drawn from the cow begins to die, change and decompose." The historian suggests that modern chemists would smile, but he doesn't seem to have asked one. Borden was, of course, right. What he said of milk applies to most foods. Modern urbanites have so lost touch with this truism that they put up with television commercials assuring them that synthetic orange juice is better than fresh—indeed, polls have shown that many consumers now agree. Most gardeners are aware of the difference between fresh and stale, but even some of them have been conditioned to find the real thing upsetting. Seed companies have found a good market for bland varieties; tomatoes, for example, have traditionally been safe for home canning because their acid is inhospitable to bacteria, but a recent outbreak of botulism was traced to a variety whose acidity is so weak that the botulin is said to thrive in it.

A preference for fresh taste lingers in our folk wisdom. Mark Twain wrote that the only way to fix corn was to boil a pot of water in the field and shuck the ears into it. As for fish, the Provençals say it should swim in water and die in oil (olive oil, of course), meaning that it should be almost alive when it hits the pan. But the number of Americans who have any acquaintance with fresh food is dwindling. In a village store in the Berkshires one recent summer evening, a clerk pointed to a mound of sweet corn that had been delivered by a farmer that morning. The tag said 59 cents a dozen. "We sold two dozen," he said. "Now we'll husk them and put them in cartons with Saran wrap, and we'll sell them out, at five ears for sixty-nine cents."

We once lived in a town on the Atlantic Coast that had a small fishing fleet. The manager of the supermarket was not authorized to buy locally; his fish came hundreds of miles by train and truck from Boston. The local catch went to a few good fish restaurants in New York and a peddler or two, all since gone. Restaurateurs today no longer shop for fresh fish; like the surviving fish retailers, they sleep late mornings and get their deliveries from commercial wholesalers. Even shore restaurants generally do the same, ignoring local fishermen and farmers.

"Few stores have fresh-fish counters any more," said Roland Finch of the National Fisheries Institute in Washington. "People have little experience, interest, or even knowledge about it."

It will get worse. The city fathers of New York began

to build a new plant in a garbage-fill wasteland of the Bronx, to replace the old Fulton Fish Market on the downtown waterfront. The new market would use lift trucks instead of hand trucks, and have lots of modern refrigerator space, but no dock for fishing boats. The colorful old market was to be razed to make way for a highrise eyesore, but in pure sentiment the authorities preserved a tiny sector of the waterfront as a museum—complete with an idle fishing schooner—to show nostalgics what it used to be like. "Delivering by boat is an inefficient way," a fish broker explained. "The efficient way is by airplane." Fish has in fact become so expensive that it adds only a little more to the price to freight it by air. But to save weight, air shippers use dry coolant instead of crushed ice, further damaging the quality of the fish.

In London and Paris, in New York, Baltimore, New Orleans, and hundreds of other cities being strangled by the automobile, the old wholesale markets have been exiled to modern, bleak complexes in the suburbs. To justify the eviction of farmers and dealers from the old French Market in New Orleans, the civic promoters explained to *The New Orleans Statesman* that "the market's old function as a daily fresh meat and produce area was no longer viable in an age of automobiles, supermarkets and home freezers."

The promoters always promise that the new markets will be more efficient and will save lots of money for consumers through the economy of scale. Always, these promises have failed. Consider the old Washington Market in downtown Manhattan, across the island from the Fulton Fish Market. When the city decided in 1967 to raze them both, *The New York Times* commented:

> The old markets are among the most expensive working antiques the city has. Every year it costs more and takes longer to bring in and get out fewer things for which there is increasingly less space in the fine, ruinous buildings and narrow streets. Even in their

decline, though, they are Breughelian in aspect, peacefully brawling, good to look at, to savor and listen to....

Wherever they are going, the markets will operate more efficiently, no question, and whatever takes their place will be quite modern and shining. But when they are gone, two more of the very few connections between the city's past and its present will be gone too.

Officials promised that the new complex at Hunts Point in the Bronx would be "a grocer's dream" and "a housewife's dream of convenience," saving 28 cents on the dollar of handling costs and providing consumers with fresher produce. The "fine, ruinous buildings" of Washington Market were replaced by the ugly dominos of a housing development and the World Trade Center, a Rockefeller project that has cost taxpayers a billion dollars, remains partly vacant, and has ruined real-estate values in Manhattan. As for Hunts Point, a bleak fenced-in stretch of sheds that has cost the city some two hundred million dollars, no housewife does her shopping there, and fewer and fewer grocers bother to drive there and pay the tolls. Most of the small merchants of Washington Street went out of business when that market died, or went broke trying to pay the rent at Hunts Point, which ran some five times higher. One survivor snapped: "Cheaper? It's more dear. Downtown, you had a customer for everything. You could get rid of it all there. Here, you got to keep it till next morning. *We* should have what they waste here in a year."

The same complaint has been made by survivors of Les Halles, that redolent and colorful, utterly enchanting market in the center of Paris. In early morning, after the trade buyers and the night revelers had left, gongs would sound and crowds of thrifty shoppers would be let through the gates of the grand iron pavilions to buy up whatever fish and produce were left. There was not much refrigeration—it was hardly needed. Les Halles kept up a tradition that goes back many centuries, when inspectors would tour markets at the close to ensure that all perishables were gone. But motorists complained about the traffic bottleneck, and the authorities decided to destroy this vibrant monument, an act comparable to razing Notre Dame. They promised that the new market, near Orly, would be more efficient, and cheaper. That was in 1969. Les Halles now is a gaping hole, which the authorities hardly know how to fill. Most of the little merchants are gone. No tourists or housewives go to the new market, and most shopkeepers and restaurateurs order by phone. The produce and fish are delivered to Paris hours later than before, and the market's leftovers go back into the spacious refrigerators. Parisians' food costs more, and is less fresh, because they allowed Les Halles to be destroyed.

From the beginning of civilization, towns have been fed by the surrounding countryside—what urban planners now wistfully call the greenbelt. The produce followed the seasons, which did not rule out an extraordinary variety, as Thomas Jefferson's market list shows. What farmers picked in the cool morning or evening hours was on the citizens' tables within half a day. As Boorstin says, progress has liberated us from all that. Strawberries in January...

Hardly any farmers come to Hunts Point. Suburban sprawl has erased many of them, and the greenbelt with them. Those surviving are not welcome at Hunts Point. Its produce comes, as Boorstin sings, from Florida and California and Mexico and the Dominican Republic, from Tenneco and Gulf & Western and Dow Chemical and other agribusinesses. Yes, there are strawberries in January, and tomatoes, too—but what strawberries! what tomatoes!

The taste of the seasons is gone; it has been replaced by "carrying quality." (It is noteworthy that Boorstin puts this feature, and appearance, ahead of taste.) More and more of the produce grown in those far-off factories of the soil is harvested by machine. It is bred for rough handling, which it gets. A chemical is sprayed on trees to force all the fruit to "ripen"—that is, change color—at once, in time for a monster harvester to strike the tree and catch the fruit in its canvas maw. Tomatoes are picked hard green and gassed with ethylene in trucks or in chambers at the market, whereupon they turn a sort of neon red. Of course, they taste like nothing at all, but the taste of real tomatoes has so far faded from memory that, even for local markets, farmers now pick tomatoes that are just turning pink. This avoids the spoilage that occurred when they used to pick tomatoes red-ripe.

In the old Washington Market, in tomato time, one could find ripe fruit, tart, sweet, and bursting with juice. Reactionaries, dedicated to the taste of the real thing, would eat tomatoes only in season. Now, there is not a ripe-picked tomato to be found *even in tomato time*. (Several Hunts Point merchants denied that vigorously one August morning. Challenged to find a ripe tomato, they showed cartons of green-pink fruit. The very word "ripe" has been subverted.) So we can have tomatoes year-round, but now we cannot buy tomatoes worth eating at any time of year. Nor strawberries. In fact, we can no longer tell the difference between tomatoes and strawberries.

(Whenever the authors write about the dismal situation of American food, we get a response such as Dr. Johnson drew when he asserted that there was not a tree in the Highlands. An indignant Scot wrote that there was, too, a tree, not ten miles from where he lived. So kind readers tell us about a fishing dock here, a roadside market there, a Wisdom apple tree—literally, one apple tree—somewhere else. Let us concede that if you are Nero Wolfe, the detective, and if you have Archie Goodwin to chase down food supplies, you can eat well in America, year-round.)

The merchants point out that the fruit *looks* beautiful, and they insist that that's all that consumers want. There is a germ of truth in this, but it does not explain why the consumption of fresh fruit and vegetables has been declining for decades as they have been getting more and more beautiful. One government study found that children tended to *like* vegetables if their parents had kitchen gardens, or lived in the country. (*Produce News*, reporting this, commented, "it's a wise child that knows its fodder.") The mother quoted in the first chapter, who thought her children ate junk food because it tasted better, was evidently not one of these. Our own children, now grown, have always been mad about greens, lightly cooked in their own moisture. Readers who grew up abroad or in old-fashioned families have written us that this is so in their homes as well.

In the spring of 1974, the Department of Agriculture polled consumers at the request of food manufacturers and supermarket chains, and reported: "Two-thirds of the survey's 1,183 respondents said they were always or almost always satisfied with food products they buy for their households. Thirty per cent were sometimes satisfied, but only 4 per cent said they were rarely or never satisfied." Considering the drumbeat of advertising and the normal inclination of respondents to tell polltakers what they presumably want to hear, this may have shown a creditable proportion of dissent. Further, when questions were asked about individual products, complaints ran somewhat higher, with tomatoes and precooked frozen foods heading the gripe list. Exploring this further, *The New York Times* quoted a shopper in Long Island as saying, "I buy very few tomatoes, just a few to make my daughter's sandwiches a little wet. They're rotten, they're not ripe and they have no flavor. I think that with the advent of frozen foods, those companies have taken the pick of the crop." It is not clear why her daughter's sandwiches should be wet, but it is clear that consumers get no pleasure from tomatoes, and buy them only from habit and conditioning, if at all.

The freezing industry is out of the picture here because tomatoes do not support freezing. More to the point was a comment by a Florida grower: "They've bred the taste out of them. Twenty years ago, we had tomatoes that had thick enough skins to be shipped and they had good flavor, but the yield was only two hundred bushels per acre. Now we get four hundred bushels per acre. They gave up taste for yield." They also gave up taste for "carrying quality" and capability of being harvested by machine. A longtime favorite of ours was the tart, juicy Rutgers tomato, whose name honors the university where it was bred. Rutgers's new pride is called the Red Rock. . . . Other government-subsidized agricultural stations have in this manner solved many of the problems of machine picking, of lettuce at Salinas, of cantaloupe at Kansas State, of asparagus at Davis, California, of "extremely firm" strawberries at the University of Arkansas, and so on. For many years, the authorities have been urging farmers to buy hugely expensive harvesting machines, in order to get rid of harvest workers. When Florida citrus growers resisted, because they found hand labor cheaper than machines, the state in 1974 paid them a bonus of twenty cents a box for machine harvesting. The state also, according to *Consumer Reports*, set size standards for vine-ripened tomatoes more stringent than for machine-picked ones. The seasonal labor thus eliminated presumably moved North to join the city welfare rolls.

Consumers *have* been conditioned for generations to accept appearance as a substitute for taste. A "filler" item sent by the government to newspapers for food pages advises: "Why pay more for freestone peaches? They're more flavorful to use in pies and cobblers—but, they don't hold their shape as well." Damn the flavor . . . Consider the avocado (or the canned truffle or mushroom or *foie gras* or any other "gourmet" ingredient). Before World War II, only a relatively few Californians and Floridians, and Latin communities in the Northeast, ate avocados. The thin-skinned, ripe fruit arrived bruised but heady with perfume and flavor. After the war, gourmet writers helped make it snob fare, hence popular, and agribusiness made it a staple. A leather-skinned variety was developed that is picked stone-hard and can be shipped almost like coal. It never bruises. It has hardly any taste, but the gourmets haven't noticed.

A Parisian named Nestor Roqueplan, back in 1869, wrote: "Once, more than two hundred kinds of pears were known, honored, cultivated; our gardeners thought that because the Bastille had been destroyed, privileges and provincial customs abolished, laws codified, the postage unified and the whole Army decked in red trousers, then they must destroy the ancient pears, codify them, red-trouser them and reduce them to one type, the Duchess pear." Roqueplan was exaggerating; there must still be a dozen varieties of pears adding their fragrance to the Rue Mouffetard as the seasons change. But this standardiza-tion—Jacobinism, Roqueplan would call it; homogeniza-tion, Boorstin would say—is a real plague of our time.

At the end of the nineteenth century, eight thousand growing varieties of apples were still listed by our De-partment of Agriculture. As recently as our own child-hood, scores could be found in good markets. There were summer, fall, and winter (long-keeping) apples, there were apples for hand-eating and apples for pie, for sauce, for apple butter, for jelly, for cider. Most of these are gone from the markets: the Baldwin, the Russet, the Northern Spy, the Red Astrakhan, the Gravenstein, the Spitzenberg, the Pippin, the Red Spartan, the Opalescent, the Idaho Red, the York Imperial, the Sheep's Nose, the Winter Banana, the Maiden Blush. In some seasons and in some areas, one still finds the Jonathan, the McIntosh, the Winesap, the MacCoun, or the Rome Beauty—which Webster's Unabridged called "a rather mediocre but long-keeping American variety" (evidently, the lexicographers had never eaten a properly baked Rome Beauty). The Rhode Island Greening is still grown commercially, but the canning industry takes most of the crop; the consumer who loves that tart bite may, in season, find costly Granny Smiths—from Australia. But the only apple most Ameri-cans eat today is the Delicious, which looks like an apple in a child's coloring book, has superb carrying quality, and has hardly any taste at all. Except for the color, there is no real difference between the Red and the Golden Delicious. The Golden is actually recommended for cooking; Julia Child prefers it above all others. One might as well follow the directions on a carton of Ritz Crackers and make a "Mock Apple Pie: no apples needed!" It is indeed only a short step from Delicious to no apple at all. To discourage the public from abandoning apples altogether, industrial growers have not thought of returning to tasty varieties; instead, they have joined with Kraft in an advertising campaign to promote the Waldorf Salad: Delicious apples, Miracle Whip dressing . . .

Kraft brings us back to Gail Borden, who liberated the American farmer from cheesemaking. This is the first example given by Boorstin of the food revolution that he says introduced variety into the American diet. Before that, dairy regions that could not sell all their milk directly to nearby cities had little cheese factories spaced every few miles. There were never so many varieties as in France, where an engineer once told us sadly, "Every time we build a dam and flood a valley, a cheese dies," and where a girl in a country inn, asked for the name of the cheese she was serving, replied, "*Mais, c'est le fromage de Papa.*" But America once did have dozens of distinct and delicious kinds, and within each kind scores of subvariations, reflecting the quality of the milk, the season, and the skill and preference of the cheesemaker. And it was cheap, workingman's food. There was real buttermilk, faintly acid and delicious, also cheap. And there was real, rich milk. The cream was often "so thick you could skate on it"; you could skim it off and whip it, easily. And there was butter, golden when the cows were in pasture, pale yellow when they were on hay . . .

The little cows that gave us this miracle were Jerseys and Guernseys, now virtually extinct. They have been replaced by the Holstein, a giant machine that gives twice as much milk, with much less cream. Homogenization concealed the switch from the public. A side effect of

Holsteinization is that the number of dairy cows has dropped by half since World War II, and with it the number of veal calves. This in turn had a curious result: Before the war, unscrupulous purveyors would use cheap veal in place of expensive chicken in Chicken à la King. Today, veal is so dear, and chicken so relatively cheap, that we have met chicken labeled as veal. No matter— they're both fed the same and look the same, and would taste the same if they had any taste at all.

Boosters like Boorstin love to recall the nineteenth-century scandals of blue milk, from cows fed on distillery swill. But the scandals would seem to reflect more on the morals of Boorstin's entrepreneurs than on the state of technology of that period. Reformers forced the introduction of hygiene, but the entrepreneurs do not seem to have changed their ways, judging from recent scandals involving milk, wheat, hamburgers, and all manner of processed foods. A major New York dairy supplier was indicted for reconstituting dried and rancid milk and selling it as fresh; this had gone on for years, and consumers never noticed. Our predated, homogenized milk has so suffered in quality as it has gained in shelf life that the public couldn't tell the difference.

To get decent butter, the authors have been reduced to churning the best cream we can find. To most consumers, the only difference between butter and margarine is that the latter is thought to be free from saturated fats (often erroneously, by the way, and even polyunsaturated fats turn saturated in processing and cooking). Borden's condensed milk began to turn Americans away from real cream; now they "whiten" their instant coffee with a synthetic powder or a superpasteurized fluid that needs no refrigeration, and they apply an aerosol chemical to their desserts in place of whipped cream.

As for cheeses, there is really only one, though it comes in as many flavors as Jell-O. It is a compound of milk solids and lots of water and chemicals, synthetically flavored, and it is sold, often presliced, in airless packages that might have shocked Gail Borden himself. And it is expensive. The well-to-do in major cities can buy imported cheeses, but the dairy lobby has imposed a requirement that the fresh ones be pasteurized, so that although they look beautiful, they are almost as bland and characterless as American cheese.

Real sour cream, after a long and disastrous slump in quality, is now being replaced by a gleaming white synthetic that looks and tastes like toothpaste flavored with hair oil. The chef at a popular New England shore restaurant, where we first met it, told us he'd made the switch two years before. "If people complained," he said, "I guess we'd go back to the dairy. They eat these TV dinners and all, and maybe they can't tell the difference." One fast-feeding chain serves this synthetic sour cream in little paper cups topped with a tiny American flag. It is a desecration more obscene than our youthful rebels of the sixties ever dreamed of.

Boorstin expresses a dim awareness that people from ancient times had developed many ways to preserve foods before Borden, Armour, and Swift came along. He nowhere suggests how delicious these ways were: drying, salting, pickling, fermenting, spicing, smoking—even home canning. In winter, early Americans ate hams, sausages, dried codfish, peas and beans, corned beef, all manner of pickled foods, dried fruits, and conserves. The intensity of flavor was such that foods preserved in these traditional ways are still popular with us—in fact, those who care about taste find them almost the last way of enjoying it.

What Boorstin means by variety is suggested by the annual National Sandwich Idea Contest, sponsored by the Department of Agriculture and the grain, meat, and dairy industries. One winner, submitted by a food specialist of the Greyhound Corporation, was made of peanut butter, crushed pineapple, and cranberry-orange relish, spread on buttered factory bread and grilled. Another was the U-Betcha: factory cheese, bologna, and pineapple, coated with relish, barbecue sauce, and horseradish, grilled. What we have is not variety, but the substitution of multi-colored, multiseasoned blandness for real taste. The poet Howard Nemerov, in his "Eggs Maledict," put it this way:

> Instead of English muffins, Wonder Bread,
> Instead of ham, Spam,
> Instead of hollandaise, Kraft mayonnaise,
> Eggs fried instead of coddled.

In the bad old days, a poor workman could lunch on a chunk of good bread, smelling of the earth and golden grain, with a sweet onion, or cheese, or a chewy slice of sausage or lean country ham, and a draft of real beer or cider or homemade wine. Talk of variety—how many hundreds of delicious varieties there were! Talk of convenience—what could be more simple to prepare than such a meal? And yet that workman was eating better than a Wall Street broker can today at Delmonico's, with its stock ticker in the bar clattering the prices of the conglomerates that feed us now.

The real flavors have been bred and processed out of our fruit and vegetables, our fish, our dairy products, our chicken, of which Vance Bourjaily has written that "the only flavor they have is what will be absorbed by the cardboard and plastic wrappings they're presented in."* Our broiler factories feed their millions of chicks a concentrate spiked with antibiotics and hormones that force them to eat the stuff like mad, with the lights on at night so they won't sleep. The poor insomniacs bloat to market size in eight weeks, instead of the normal thirteen; the flabby white flesh is then colored yellow to look real. The old hen, now an egg-laying robot, goes from her cage on the assembly line to a soup factory, and the old red rooster not only don't crow like he useter, he don't go into fricassee and dumplings any more. Our veal calves and our pigs are raised much the same way. Because, like us, they are mammals, the horrors of their incubation seem all the

* *Harper's*, March 1972.

more unspeakable. And it is a pointless cruelty, designed to produce a flabby, pale, and tasteless flesh. Pork is cured on the line with injections of water and synthetic smoke; this originally had the commercial advantage of appealing to people who didn't like the tang of real country-smoked pork, while those who did simply had to put up with the bland travesty. (Ironically, the new hams must be refrigerated, which means that the very point of curing pork has been lost with the flavor.)

The suppression of flavor is sometimes incidental, sometimes deliberate. When the University of Wisconsin developed a process for making mozzarella in five and a half minutes instead of four hours, it commented that the product was "mild, but satisfactory for normal uses," whatever that means.* A braumeister in the Middle West grumbled: "We don't make beer, we make flavored water for people who don't like beer." Many years ago, the Department of Agriculture set out on purpose to breed a lamb that would not taste like lamb. The problem has now been solved, for consumers who don't care for lamb. Those who do care must make do.

Beef is the last of our major foods to be losing its soul. Americans have long taken it as an item of faith that ours is the best in the world. This was always contestable; the Aberdeen Angus, the Limousin and some Charolais and Norman steers, grass-fattened for at least three years in rich meadows, can easily challenge that claim. But the best of our marbled, cornfed beef is fine indeed; along with Idaho potatoes, it is one of the few store products we are not ashamed to serve to foreign guests. It is getting harder to find, however, as the old butchers who care about beef close down, one by one. Just as the Colt .45 made all men equal, so tenderizers, MSG, and pink fluorescent lighting in supermarkets make all beef equal. New airtight plastic packaging, some of it with citric acid crystals inside, also helps. And, time being money, our steers

* *Hard Tomatoes, Hard Times*, by Jim Hightower (Agribusiness Accountability Project, 1972).

are shot up with the hormone diethylsilbesterol (DES) to make them eat faster. DES is banned in many countries as a cancer threat, but our Department of Agriculture up to this writing has refused to ban it—except on beef exports to Canada, which refuses to take a chance.

DES, incidentally, was developed by Iowa State University, one of those federally supported agricultural schools that have been dedicated to the promotion of farm technology and the elimination of taste. The school assigned the enormously valuable patent, without bidding, to Eli Lilly & Co., in return for a 5-percent royalty. At that, it was smarter than the New York Botanical Garden, where puffed cereal was invented in 1901. The society never got a penny of royalty from the multibillion-dollar industry that arose from the invention. Serves it right.

Speaking of drugged cattle, what is left of the beef critter is ground up and "extended" with water (10 percent), fat, soybean flour, sugar, nitrates, and other additives to be served on a sweet bun. The hamburger and the hot dog are the modern American's substitute for our ancestors' bread-and-cheese. Since 1945, according to William Robbins of *The New York Times*, the fat in frankfurters has risen from 14 to 33 percent, while the protein has declined from 15 to 11 percent. The protein in an "all-beef" hot dog cost the consumer $7.18 a pound in early 1972....

All of these improvements have been triumphs of salesmanship. The long-used preservative nitrate, now suspected with its associate nitrite of causing cancer, turns cured meat red; consumers were persuaded that red is the normal and desirable color of a sausage.

Folk wisdom holds that the exception proves (that is, tests) the rule. An apparent exception to the rule that every advance in food processing has been at the expense of taste is quick-freezing. It *was* an improvement, at first. One of the authors of this book worked briefly in the thirties on a farm that grew peas and lima beans for Birdseye; he can testify that the crop, harvested young and frozen within an hour or two, was superior to the usually overmature and not very fresh legumes then available in city markets, although it could never be as good as peas and beans picked in the garden just before supper.

In those pioneer days, Clarence Birdseye didn't freeze just anything, and he was ferocious about maintaining quality—he would remove his product from a store that did not keep it well frozen. This did not last. The abuse of frozen foods—its repeated thawing en route to stores, in stores, and at home—is so prevalent that the industry recently conducted a rather pathetic "Mark of Zero" campaign, to persuade handlers to keep the product at no more than 0°F, whereas the recommended maximum temperature is 10 degrees below that. Housewives are of course aware that the product in the display cabinets at the supermarket is often mushy, and that it is not helped by the trip home or the sojourn in the refrigerator. They are concerned not so much about the taste, it would seem, as about the danger of bacterial contamination. Friends of the industry are now trying to reassure them, as in an article in *The New York Times* headlined, "Some Food Can Be Refrozen, Even if Package Says Not To." Dr. Walter A. Maclinn of Rutgers said Birdseye put those warnings on his packages because he didn't want people to "decide that Birdseye products weren't any good." The article continued:

> According to Dr. Maclinn, this hasn't been stressed for a good many years. "You don't see many such signs these days," he said. But not many people seem to have noticed their absence: The same thinking about refreezing has continued.
>
> Now, however, Dr. Maclinn is coming right out and saying that if foods are still partly frozen, "just refreeze them; they may lose some quality, but they're safe to eat."

Dr. Maclinn goes on to endorse the refreezing of fully thawed food, provided it doesn't actually stink, and Dr.

D. G. Guadagni of the USDA at Berkeley is quoted as saying, "If the package gets soft once or twice, it shouldn't matter. Actually, it could get soft several times but it might not taste as well." A few other scientists are quoted as having some fears about those bacteria, but the Department of Agriculture closes the discussion on safety with, "In general, if a food is safe to eat, it is safe to refreeze." Again, the department confirms rather offhandedly that the "eating quality" will suffer, but this has never been a serious consideration with nutritionists.

Even the best prevailing industrial technique, flash freezing and drying at 52° below zero, damages texture and flavor. Cryogenic freezing, at more than 320° below, is better but requires costly equipment, and its advocates claim only that the product is "almost as good" as fresh. (All claims assume that the food is subsequently kept at minus 10° and is then thawed properly, which is far from common practice.) Now, each food, and in fact each component of a food, responds differently to freezing and thawing. Few do as well as peas and beans; most frozen greens are poor, tomatoes and carrots impossible. In the present state of marketing, frozen berries and peaches tend to be better than the fresh, but that is not saying much, and in any case the frozen product is after all a very different thing from fresh berries. Good homemade bread freezes well, but must be eaten immediately after it is reheated. Dough, a living culture of yeast, suffers on freezing, despite the popularity of the practice, which requires a heavy added dose of sugar for the yeast to survive at all. (Incidentally, home freezing works *better* than industrial freezing, despite the inferiority of the equipment, precisely because of the abuse that food receives in commerce. A householder who has an oversupply of garden produce, a good day's catch of fish or game, or a bargain special from the store may well find the freezer the best place to keep it—provided it does not stay there too long. We had an inquiry once from a reader who wanted to know what to do with a turkey she had stashed away two years before; we told her to throw it out. Freezing only slows decay, it does not halt it. The shorter the stay in the freezer, the better.)

As for meat, try this experiment. Get a fine piece of nonfrozen beef and put half in the cooler and half in the freezer. A day or two later, thaw the frozen half and cook both halves in the same manner. The frozen piece should be edible, but if you cannot tell the difference between it and the unfrozen one, your palate and your sense of texture are in trouble.

If you need scientific evidence, the government has found it: in fresh beef, the ratio of Enzyme A to Enzyme B is 9 to 1, while the ratio in frozen beef is 1 to 1. We don't know what that signifies in terms of nutrition, but something has certainly happened in the freezer.

Louis Roncivalli, director of the Atlantic Fishery Products Technology Center at Gloucester, Massachusetts, told us, "The freezing act itself takes away maybe ten to twelve percent of the quality." Yet, as we have noted, 90 to 95 percent of the catch is filleted either at sea or, more often, ashore, then frozen into blocks, then thawed and either repackaged in retail sizes or cooked and refrozen, then hauled to distribution plants, stored, redistributed, restored, and, finally, reheated and served. The danger to health grows at every step. The destruction of texture and taste is total. One widely published recipe calls for poaching a foil-wrapped frozen fish in the dishwasher.

Precooked frozen food is a disaster. To take the simplest item, frozen French fries may be reheated to a crisp, but the interior will inevitably be mushy and tasteless. The more complex the dish, the more it suffers. Worst of all are "gourmet" dishes. Aside from the fact that some of their many ingredients don't take to freezing—eggs, carrots, dairy products, oils—each calls for a different rate of thawing and reheating, which is practically impossible to achieve.

Ah, but how convenient. In this mechanized society of ours, everything is done to eliminate work and enhance leisure, yet we never seem to have any time. To cut bread took too much time; it comes sliced now. To brew a pot of tea took too much time; we switched to teabags and then, God save us, to instant tea, which is only one step short of intravenous feeding. Shopping takes too much time, so we've got big refrigerators and shop only once a week, driving to a huge supermarket with miles of shelves loaded with thousands of gaudy packages of nothing. An executive of a high-priced restaurant chain, complaining about the high cost of labor, observed enviously one day that the supermarket had a great advantage: it put the customer to work. How many Americans remember when the middle-class housewife would telephone her order to the grocer, and a boy would deliver it on a bicycle? There was less "variety" but more taste; the produce was seasonal but the quality was generally far superior to what one can find in your friendly neighborhood shopping center today.

It was cheaper, too. Despite the claims of the Department of Agriculture and other flacks for the industry, consumerists have demonstrated the obvious fact that convenience foods are, more often than not, much more expensive than the sum of their parts. (After the foregoing lines were written, we came across the following advertisement in a butchers' trade paper: "As profitable as Perdue whole birds are, the profits aren't as great as the sum you can make on the parts. Perdue chicken parts are probably the single most profitable item in the chicken business. Your customers pay about 35¢ a pound premium for Perdue chicken breasts over the price of the whole bird. Up to 20¢ a pound premium for legs. And there's absolutely no work in it for you.") Health officers are worried, too, and doubtless with reason, about the additives and subtractives. But no organized group, to our knowledge, has yet sounded the alarm about the taste of our food. Or rather, the absence of taste.

A young French chef we know who immigrated to New York observed with sorrow one day that five out of six of his clients salted and peppered his sauces—before they had tasted them. Another transplant, Jacques Pépin, said that on a visit home, his mother asked why he was seasoning the food so heavily. Pépin had insensibly fallen into the habit of hyping up our bland produce to a degree that would overwhelm the natural taste of *French* produce.

Americans are starved for flavor. That is the reason for the ketchup on the Presidential cottage cheese—the ketchup whose flavor is such that, so *The Wall Street Journal* reported, a metallic and slightly burnt taste had to be added to make the product acceptable. That is a reason for our addiction to sugar, or to dangerous substitutes for sugar among the millions who are perpetually dieting to combat our national affliction of obesity. That is a reason, no doubt, for the recent popularity of "hot" foods—incendiary chilies, curries, and "Szechuan" or "Hunan" dishes guaranteed to create a sensation on the palate. An addict we know says the Szechuan fad was touched off when Jacqueline Onassis was seen in a restaurant of that persuasion, but snobbery alone cannot explain the duration of the fashion. When the actors have to set fire to the house in order to get a reaction from the audience, then the theater is in trouble.

Now, how did we get into this state? A clue may be found in the recent introduction of cottonseed flour to "enrich" (that is, impoverish) hamburgers, frozen desserts, and a variety of baked goods. It's an improvement on soybean flour, its promoters say, because it's bland and so "can be added to a large number of other foods to enrich them without affecting their taste."* Cottonseed contains a substance charmingly called gossypol, which is not so charmingly poisonous to humans, but our Agriculture Department found a way to get the gossypol out. As is our custom, we first tried the product out on the Third World. We built a pilot plant in India, but the Indians spurned the stuff in great numbers. Our developers were not discouraged. *The New York Times* reported Mrs. Wilda H. Martinez, chief of the project, as saying (in

* *New York Times*, July 10, 1975.

paraphrase): "That should not be a problem in the United States, because American eating habits are more sophisticated and most of the cottonseed flour will be used as an ingredient in other foods."

The key word here is "sophisticated." Basically, it seems to mean "easily conditioned," like Pavlov's dog, but there are flattering overtones of snobbery and superiority. It is in fact an insult to Americans. We did not surrender easily; there was resistance to every assault by commerce on our taste, and there is such resistance today. But we were disarmed—we are disarmed—by the very professionals whom we pay to defend us: the scientists, the advertisers, the food editors and publishers, the home economists, and, most ignoble of all, the gourmet frauds who have persuaded Americans that fancy means good and that expensive means sophisticated.

The deterioration of our food is not new, and the infatuation with phony elegance is not new. Our latter-day gourmets, who claim to have introduced us to Escoffier, have only traduced him; they have contributed nothing. It may be said for their predecessors, beginning with Fannie Farmer, that the decline of food quality in their time was so gradual that their collaboration may have been innocent. But since World War II, the slide has accelerated at such a rate that it is now visible from week to week, in supermarkets, restaurants, and television commercials. It is a national disaster. Like Dr. Pangloss, the hacks tell us that all is for the best in this best of all possible worlds; like Coué, they tell us that every day in every way things are getting better and better. It is as if our art critics were to say, of Venice sinking beneath the polluted sea, that it is even more beautiful under water. These gourmets are the maraschino cherry on the aerosol whip on the packaged mousse of our gastronomic humiliation.

5

Let Them
Eat Cake

With good bread the coarsest fare is tolerable; without it, the most luxurious table is not comfortable.

Mary Cornelius, in The Young Housekeeper's
Friend (*1845*)

"GOOD FLOUR," Mrs. Cornelius wrote, "adheres slightly to the hand, and if pressed in the hand retains its shape, and shows the impress of the lines of the skin.... Newly ground flour which has never been packed, is very superior to barrel flour, so that the people in Western New York, that land of finest wheat, say that the New England people do not know what good flour is."

Oddly, Boorstin's food history ignores the staff of life, so it omits one of the most fateful events in that history. As Mrs. Cornelius was writing, in the 1840s, flour milling was undergoing a revolution. The new mills ground fast and exceeding fine, but tended to overheat and get gummed up by the crushed wheat germ. So the germ was extracted in advance, along with most of the nutrients, and the flour, often doctored with nasty adulterants even in those days, went on the market. Mrs. Cornelius had observed that, as everybody knew, good flour was yellowish. The new flour was chalk white. Even the yeast bugs didn't care for it, so bakers added a little sugar to help the fermentation, much as vintners may cheat by adding sugar to the grape juice in a poor year.

The big millers managed nevertheless, with the help of complaisant food writers, to persuade much of the public that the starchy, lifeless flour was an elegant improvement, and by the 1880s, Washburn and Pillsbury had "swamped the country" with it.* The rich and the poor, but especially the poor because they were so dependent on bread, became victims of low-grade malnutrition. The bread got puffier and puffier because sugar feeds the yeasts and, with the starchy flour, absorbs more water. Small wonder that people turned to sugar, to stave the pangs of hunger.

The latter half of the nineteenth century was also the era of the American layer cake, a puffy debasement of older cakes that were made with natural leaveners such as yeast and eggs. The new cakes used chemical leavens, now called baking powders. Saleratus (usually bicarbonate of soda) and pearl-ash (potassium carbonate) had been used in "economy" cakes for some time; they saved on eggs and butter, and were speedier than yeast. Now, however, they became the norm. Inevitably, they were industrialized. In 1899 a war broke out between the American Baking Powder Association and the Royal Baking Powder Company, each accusing the other of poisoning the public with aluminic sulphate. According to H. E. Jacob, the resulting scandals and litigation, involving charges of bribery reaching into the Congress, raised a stench for years. The quarrel centered on the possible "deleterious effect on health," which is assuredly the most important issue, but nobody, including Mr. Jacob, seems to have commented on the damage these chemicals may have done to our palates.

Typical of the turn from yeast to baking powders is a

* H. E. Jacob, in *Six Thousand Years of Bread* (1944, first American edition).

manuscript recipe for Unfermented Bread from the Martha Randolph collection.* It is dated either 1862 or 1869 (the last digit is not clear), and calls for "3 lbs. of flour, a pint & ½ cold water, ½ oz sesquicarbonate of soda, 5 drachms of Muriatic acid." That's hydrochloric acid, and while it must be supposed that no one died from it, it can hardly have been delicious.

There is no sugar yet in that family recipe, nor had there been in most breads since antiquity. Consider this loving recipe brought to Virginia in the seventeenth century, in the so-called Martha Washington manuscript cookbook:

To make white bread

Take 3 quarters of a peck of fine flower & strow salt in as much as will season it, y^n heat as much milke as will season it Luke warme, & hould it high when you poure it on to make it Light & mingle wth y^r milke 4 or 5 spoonfulls of good yeast, worke y^r paste well, & Let it Ly a rising by the fire, y^r oven will be heated in an houre & halfe y^n shut it up a quarter of an houre, in wch space make up y^r Loaves & y^n set them in ye oven an houre & halfe will bake them.

The first all-American cookbook, Mary Randolph's *Virginia Housewife* (1824), has no sugar in any of the bread recipes. The standard loaf includes only the classic ingredients: flour, water, yeast, and salt. ("Sugar in bread is heresy to a Virginian," says *Virginia Cookery—Past and Present*, published in 1957 by the Woman's Auxiliary of Olivet Episcopal Church in Franconia.)

Mrs. Cornelius, in 1845, gave this fine recipe for:

* At the Alderman Library, University of Virginia. The earliest recipes in this collection date from the Thomas Jefferson household. One can trace the deterioration of American cookery by starting at the beginning and reading on.

Third Bread

Take equal parts of white flour, rye flour, and Indian [corn] meal. It is good made with water, but made with milk is much better. Add salt and a gill of yeast to a quart of water or milk. It should not be made so stiff as to mould, but as thick as you can stir it with your hand, or a large spoon. Like all other bread, it should be thoroughly worked together. Bake in deep pans.

By the time of the first *Boston Cook Book*, in 1883, the new flour was in such demand that its author, Mary Lincoln, was adding a tablespoonful of sugar in her standard batch. But she was defensive about it: "Many object to the use of sugar in bread. Flour in its natural state contains sugar; this sugar is changed in fermentation. Just enough sugar to restore the natural sweetness, but not enough to give a really sweet taste, is necessary in fermented bread."

James Beard, who has helped promote Pillsbury products, repeats this notion in his *Beard on Bread* (1974): "For yeast to become activated... it must have something to feed on. Give it a little sugar and the yeast cells are encouraged to go to work; thus when a sweetener is called for in a bread recipe, it is not simply serving as a flavor." Even his French bread has sugar in it. He dedicates the book to Elizabeth David, "who loves bread," but does not heed her when she says: "I find the sugar and milk business unnecessary and undesirable... because even... small quantities... will give a sweet or soft taste to the bread, and that is not my idea of good bread." (*The Baking of an English Loaf*, 1969)

Even with modern flour, an acceptable bread can be made with any of the old standard recipes, using no sugar; it just takes longer to rise. Mrs. Lincoln was sounder in opposing the increasing use of baking powders, which she thought were dangerous to health, and wrote that "for bread that will leave a sweet, clean taste in the mouth...

there is nothing equal to perfect, home-made yeast bread."
She added that dry yeast cakes were "generally liked more
for economy of time and trouble than for the quality of
their bread."

It is unfortunate that Mrs. Lincoln did not apply the
same reasoning to sugar. Her bread recipe called for 1
tablespoon of sugar to 8 cups of flour. When Fannie
Farmer wrote the *Boston Cooking-School Cook Book* in
1896, she used 1 tablespoon of sugar to 6 cups of flour,
and gave a recipe for Entire Wheat Bread that calls for 4
tablespoons of sugar to 4⅓ cups of flour. By the 1914
edition, she had upped the amount in regular bread to 2
tablespoons, and her Steamed Graham Bread called for
1 cup molasses (scant) to only 4 cups of flour...

"Miss Leslie," in her *Directions for Cookery* (1837),
gives a fine recipe for that buttery scone called Sally Lunn
(see page 100). No sugar. The same recipe appears in *Miss
Leslie's New Cookery Book* (1857), with this admonition:
"In mixing this cake, add neither sugar nor spice. They
do not improve, but spoil it, as would be found on trial.
It is the best of plain tea cakes, if properly made and
baked." Evidently, the sugar sickness was already taking
hold. Modern cookbooks all use sugar; Beard prescribes
⅓ cup. Poor Sally Lunn.

It has gotten to where, today, many restaurants around
the country serve sweet cinnamon buns and sweet rolls
with seafood and steak, and several pretentious ones in
New York serve a sweetened French breakfast croissant.
Even those surviving bakeries that make "ethnic" breads
have surrendered, one by one, so that their breads have
become soft, puffy, and sweet. What passes for pumper-
nickel is often not much more than a brioche dyed with
burnt sugar.

Ellen Semrow, who was president of the American Institute of Baking in Chicago, explained to us some time
ago that real, sugarless bread such as foreigners make
doesn't go through the slicing machine, and it stales rapidly. "I happen to love it," she said, "and it's getting very

popular. But if you're talking about making eleven hundred loaves of bread per man-hour, you have to change your formulas."

Read the label on that ghastly cloud of chemicals that passes for the staff of life in America today, keeping in mind that the list of ingredients is not complete because that is not required by law. At the instigation of the industry itself, some vitamins and minerals have been added, replacing some of the natural ones that have been processed away, so that baking companies may promote as "enriched" a product whose taste they have impoverished. (Admirers of sharp merchandising may enjoy the revelation that the added iron often comes in an indigestible form.)

We visited the laboratory of Quality Bakers of America in, of all places, Times Square. It has a miniature bread mill, where all those fearsome ingredients are mixed in vats and, after only two and a half hours, extruded into loaves that enter a heated tunnel on a moving belt and emerge to be sliced and packaged. Much sugar is used; it speeds the fermentation, absorbs added water, and, along with fungicides and other chemicals, assures softness and shelf life. "No kneading—that's the important part," said Dr. Simon S. Jackel, the director. When it was suggested to him that bread might have been better in the old days, Dr. Jackel replied: "Nobody was rushing. It was a more leisurely era. Our goal is rapidity and uniformity, the goal of an industrial society."

An industrial success story overlooked by Boorstin is the tale of Pepperidge Farm. Back before World War II, we are told, a well-to-do Connecticut housewife named Margaret Rudkin was advised by her physician that factory bread was bad for her son. (The physician, who surely deserves some of the glory, is not named.) Mrs. Rudkin obtained a standard recipe of the period for homemade bread (sweetened, but good for jams and toast), and lo! a business was born. A public famished for taste and texture snapped up the bread; Mrs. Rudkin and her broker husband, who became chairman of the corporation, were progressively impelled to eliminate kneading so as to speed production, and to improve shelf life so as to reduce the frequency of deliveries. The quality of course suffered, but by the late 1950s, a gush of gourmet food writers was at hand to drool over anything that sold at a premium price.

Craig Claiborne, who had just joined *The New York Times*, went wild over Pepperidge products, including a line of frozen puff pastries and "a truly remarkable bun" that he identified as "the famed French specialty, the brioche." To be sure, he had kind words for Pepperidge's competitors, too. Claiborne's first job in the food biz had been to promote Fluffo margarine, and he remained kindly disposed to brand products. In this he has never changed. In 1975, he would write in the ordinarily austere columns of *The Times*, "Medaglia d'Oro, we love you," and would publish a recipe calling for "¼ cup of brown sauce or canned beef gravy (we use Howard Johnson's)." The "we" represents Claiborne and his partner, Pierre Franey, whom *The Times* does not identify as the executive chef of Howard Johnson's.

The 1950s saw the introduction of precooked frozen gourmet glop. Claiborne greeted the aurora with typical poesy:

> In the field of food the clearest view of things to come is afforded, frequently, by a glance at the recent past. If such is the case, then 1958 is loaded with promise—especially for cooks on the run. The past twelve months initiated a trend that is sure to be developed more fully—the packaging of dishes with a so-called Continental touch that can be heated and brought to table within minutes—to the awe and delight of guests with educated palates.
>
> Approximately fifty-five items were introduced last year in the General Foods line of Gourmet Foods. Most of the foods offered in the line are packed in tins abroad and include such delicacies as Copenhagen

ham, Rock Cornish game hens and cocktail kick-shaws. . . .

The gourmet plague could not be better summarized. That flabby midget called Cornish game hen was, next to chocolate-covered ants, the gourmet racket's funniest joke on a gullible public. It has no more taste of game than a wad of cotton. That "so-called Continental touch" is the nameless cuisine taught in Swiss hotel schools such as Claiborne had attended, an amalgam of bad German, bad Hungarian, and pseudo-French cooking. The "awe and delight of guests with educated palates" is the aim of the game. Nothing has changed. Nearly twenty years later he would write: "An untrimmed sandwich is in my eyes vulgar, crude and uncouth."

A reader once asked us why an item in her supermarket cost 79 cents in the regular department, and $1.09 in the gourmet section. We replied that that was as good a definition of gourmet as we had seen. If it was more expensive, Claiborne was for it. In his salutes to Pepperidge and other "exciting products" of 1958, he found space to report that Seabrook was introducing "an inspired beef à la bourguignonne," Betty Crocker was adding a new instant meringue to "the line-up of glamorous foods," Borden was giving us Instant Starlac and Instant Whipped Potatoes, Carnation "excellent and quickly made" Golden Fudge, and Campbell Soup frozen fruit pies. The last competed with Pepperidge, but not for long. In 1960 the Rudkins merged with Campbell, for $28 million. By this time, their bread was not much better than the standard factory loaf.

Waiting in the wings are a host of eager Mrs. Rudkins. There has been a heartening resurgence of interest in home baking, and here and there "home-made" breads are appearing in offbeat stores and restaurants. But under the guidance of gourmets and faddists, the neophytes spurn the old basic bread. The soft loaves they sell have been doctored with soy flour, zucchini, curry, whole oranges, cheese, carrots—anything. Above all, they use lots of brown sugar, honey, or molasses, or all three. Thus the book *Bread*, by Joan Wiener and Diana Collier, correctly denounces factory bread as "a spongy, squooshy, ghastly white, dehumanized, denutritized, flavorized, proprionated, artificialized, shot-up, brought-down item more closely related to a Styrofoam cup than the staff of life." Then it gives 110 recipes for breads that would go well with coffee or tea, but hardly with real food. They are more cake than staff of life. The authors boldly describe their sugared "French" and "Italian" breads as better than what can be found in France or Italy. (In France, at least, sugar is banned from standard bread as an adulterant; in either country, it is a heresy.) Wiener and Collier explain: "Bad-mouthing on the part of health food mavens [maven is New York slang from the Yiddish and means expert] is creating a generation of 'sugophobics'—those who avoid sugar like bubonic plague. Undaunted, we're thoroughly hooked and continue to use it."

Hooked is the word. But they are wrong when they think they are exceptional. In a large office that we know well, the refreshment cart comes around twice a day. Five minutes before it's due, employes begin to gather in the aisle. If it's late, they ask one another nervously, "Has the cart *been* by?" What they're waiting for, of course, is their sugar fix. It comes in cakes, cookies, candy, coffee, and, above all, soda pop. Curiously, many of these addicts order "diet" drinks, which is what Wiener and Collier presumably mean when they talk of "sugophobics." Like heroin users who switch to methadone, they are getting their sweetening from substances that may be even more dangerous than the sugar they were hooked on.

Most other societies take their sweetening on occasion, usually in a dessert or between meals. The French and Italians have traditionally separated ice cream and cake from real eating, and regard a bit of fruit or cheese as a proper dessert for a proper meal (a tradition that is fading, to be sure). Some Orientals use sugar in main courses, but serve no dessert with meals. In short, mankind has used sugar with restraint, until our time.

We, on the other hand, have become a nation of sugar addicts. As noted, we give our babies a formula that provides something like two teaspoons of sugar per feeding, wean them on heavily sweetened baby foods, and raise them on double-sweetened frankfurter and hamburger buns, sweet ketchup, candy, and drinks. We consume more of this poor nutrient than any other society ever has—about one-third of a pound a day for every man, woman, and child—and we look for it in everything we eat—bread, meat, even soups, vegetables, and salads. No wonder we are afflicted with obesity, and no wonder we are phobic about it.*

We do not mean to suggest that it was only the steel-ground flour that turned the country on to sugar. The taste was fading in all of our principal foods, leading us to douse them up as much as possible and to overeat as well.

In his role as American food historian, James Beard tells us that it was not until after World War II that returning GI's and tourists brought home a taste for "the real thing." This sounds plausible, which is all a pop historian needs, but it fails to explain why the doughboys returning from France after World War I did not bring home a taste for French cuisine, nor why earlier expeditionary forces did not bring home a taste for the estimable Cuban or Filipino cuisines. Our own observations abroad, during both wartime austerity and postwar affluence, suggest that our troops were not so different from César Ritz's English gentleman, who dined out of cans in India. In the gourmet years of the sixties, a pamphlet issued to military wives at

---

* How phobic we are appeared when the FDA belatedly moved to ban saccharin in 1977. The soft-drink industry had no difficulty in whipping up a hysterical counterattack. Hardly anybody except the authors argued that diet drinks were not only dangerous but also tasted lousy and did nothing for fat people or diabetics. Given a choice between cancer and overweight, many chose cancer. It was a false choice.

European bases advised them to soak any local produce in a Clorox solution for forty-five minutes. The advice was hardly needed. Most of them shopped exclusively at the PX, where good old iceberg lettuce (a maligned vegetable, Beard says) was flown in from California, and we can testify from interviews with Army wives that many went home after a hitch in France without ever having eaten French food.

Travelers fare little better on guided tours or following *Europe on $5 a Day*. One morning, we observed a tour group in an Athens hotel refusing to follow their guide until the management came forth with their fix of instant coffee. (The supply had been locked up and the man with the key had to be fetched from home.) Snobs may shrug off those GI wives and bargain trippers as of the lower orders. But a leading gourmet food store in New York features one of those kits for travelers to heat water in a toothbrush glass to make instant coffee; the manager says she would not dream of going to Europe without it. And *New York* magazine, than which there is no publication more with-it, published a connoisseurs' guide to coffee supplies in the city, by two women who confessed that they were instant addicts, and who asserted that dark-roast coffee, such as is served in Latin America and in the Mediterranean countries, is so burnt that the quality of the bean doesn't matter!

Instant coffee is the end of a sad story, or, as Boorstin and Beard might put it, the culmination of a march toward the ultimate in convenience. Those early Americans who, according to Boorstin and Beard, had not yet learned the sensual delights of food, roasted their own coffee at home. As evidenced by eighteenth- and nineteenth-century recipe collections, families of culinary pretension also blended their own, and such varieties as Mocha, Java, Laguayra, and Rio were widely available. Americans also understood coffee. Says Eliza Leslie in *Directions for Cookery in Its Various Branches* (1837):

To have it very good, it should be roasted immediately before it is made, doing no more than the quantity you want at that time. It loses much of its strength by keeping, even in twenty-four hours after roasting. It should on no consideration be ground till directly before it is made. Every family should be provided with a coffee roaster, which is an iron cylinder to stand before the fire, and is either turned by a handle, or wound up like a jack to go of itself. If roasted in an open pot or pan, much of the flavour evaporates in the process.

In those unsensual days, the aroma of roasting coffee must have been a heavenly way to wake up, but it was, to be sure, a burden on the woman tending the roaster at the fire. So it was a real step forward for women when coffee-roasting shops appeared in every sizable town and every city neighborhood. (It is difficult to understand why the appliance industry, which has developed so many useful and useless kitchen gadgets, has not yet given us a coffee-roasting attachment for our stoves.)

Now it must be understood that the flavor and aroma of coffee are locked into the berry, to be released only when it is roasted. Many connoisseurs prefer the green beans aged several years; but once beans are roasted, they begin immediately to loose their fragrance into the air, which is why coffee shops smell so good. When coffee is ground, the evaporation of those aromatic oils is speeded enormously.

As long as housewives were picking up a few days' supply of fresh-roasted beans at the store and grinding it as needed in a hand mill on the kitchen wall, the loss in flavor was limited. But in the late nineteenth century, Borden's condensed milk was taking the place of cream, and the newfangled percolator was sweeping the country. There are many ways of making good coffee, but percolating is not one of them; except for expresso, all the good ways use water that is just below boiling point, and none reheats the coffee once it is made. Only the percolator keeps the coffee boiling and repasses it through the used grounds, picking up undesirable oils and breaking down the delicious ones. So by the end of the nineteenth century, many housewives were ready for the introduction of store-ground coffee, and the even more disastrous invention of "vacuum-packed" ground coffee.

There is of course some air in a can of vacuum coffee, and it is deadly to the flavor and aroma. At first, the packers urged shopkeepers to keep the cans in a cool place; they also took back and destroyed any that had not been sold within two or three weeks. In principle, at any rate. By the 1950s, these scruples had been so long forgotten that when Martinson's, a premium brand, changed the color of its can, we found the old cans on the shelves of our supermarket a year later. We tried one. It did not hiss when opened, the "vacuum" having long since been filled, and the coffee was quite dead. The manager said with a shrug that nobody else had noticed.

By then, many consumers already were using instant coffee when they were in a hurry, although only a few were yet serving it to company. But the quality of the bean mattered less and less. Today, according to the Pan-American Coffee Bureau, more than one-third of our coffee comes from West Africa, fit only to be made into instant, and most of the rest consists of the cheaper grades of Brazilian coffee. The finer grades are sold to affluent Europeans and, now, Japanese.

Few young Americans have ever drunk a good cup of coffee, and most of the older ones have forgotten what it tastes like, or what it takes to make it—to such a point that those instant experts at *New York* magazine thought that the quality of the bean could not affect the dark roast. When the scientists of *Consumer Reports* were testing rival brands of coffeemaking machines, they just measured "the percentage of extraction from the grounds." On this basis, the percolator scores high. In a blindfold test, an expert engaged by the magazine could easily distinguish between perk and drip, and of course preferred the drip.

But *Consumer Reports'* staff couldn't tell the difference, and concluded that it was "a matter of subjective taste evaluation." Similarly, *Craig Claiborne's Kitchen Primer*, in its instructions on making coffee, does not mention the quality of the bean or even the possibility of grinding it at home. It does say: "The grinds [*sic*], incidentally, may in almost all circumstances be put down the drain of the kitchen sink. They will not clog it." Claiborne seems to be more interested in where the grounds are going than in where they came from.

Yet, if Americans are not conscious of what has happened to our coffee, our subconscious appears to have told us something. According to the Pan-American Coffee Bureau, the average American drank 3.2 cups of coffee a day in 1952, and only 2.3 cups a day in 1972. Financially perturbed, the industry made the typical response: it raised its advertising budget. The goal of business is not to improve the product, but to persuade the client that it is good. Like hammering home the message that synthetic juice is "better than fresh."

6

The Art of
the Hearth

[Virginians] have a great Plenty and Variety of Provisions for their Table; and as for Spicery, and other things that the Country don't produce, they have constant supplies of 'em from *England*. The Gentry pretend to have their Victuals drest, and serv'd up as Nicely, as at the best Tables in London.

Robert Beverley, in 1705

THE HISTORY of the art of American cooking parallels the history of the quality of American foodstuffs. The Boorstins do not challenge this, they simply turn it upside down. They say colonial cooking was as crude as the colonial food supply. On the contrary, it was as fine as the food supply. Colonial housewives in the North and slave cooks in the South, working at open fires in the hearth, achieved a sophistication and a sensual balance that our modern gourmets would be at a loss to duplicate in their microwaved, temperature-controlled kitchen laboratories.

American cooking, properly so called, was a blend of many ingredients. We have mentioned the contribution of

Indians. That of blacks is harder to come by; there has been little serious study of the question, and most of the recent books on soul food are just gimmick cookbooks. The slave women who cooked in the planters' kitchens had to learn European techniques—mostly English and French—but they must have brought certain culinary tricks with them from Africa. Even two chefs of the same culture, following the same classic recipe, will produce subtly different dishes; the Chinese speak of "wok signature" or "wok presence" in describing such differences. In this country, different worlds were meeting.

The cuisine of New Orleans seems to have absorbed more black influence than that of Virginia. One reason may have been that the basic cuisine in New Orleans was not English but Spanish and French, in part via Haiti. This is important not only because the latter cuisines are more aromatic but also because the role of the mistress of the house was very different. Mulatto mistresses (in both senses of the word) were famous in New Orleans for their cooking as well as their beauty. In Virginia, if the white mistress of the plantation did not know how to cook, she could read to her cook from Hannah Glasse, for instance, or from one of those manuscript cookbooks that many families kept. Jane Carson, in her invaluable *Colonial Virginia Cookery* (Williamsburg Research Series), cites the recollection of a slave at Monticello, who said that Mrs. Jefferson used to "come out there with a cookery book in her hand" and read pastry recipes to the cook. Cookbooks directed to housewives were peculiarly English; they were exceedingly rare in France and Spain.

Among themselves, the blacks ate very differently. While they had little to work with, they handled it with great skill. They gathered wild greens and scavenged beet tops, and cooked them with the chitterlings, the jowls, the maw, the tail, and other lowly portions of the pig that were granted them. The dish was cooked a long time and was almost a soup; they called it a "mess o'greens" or "pot likker" and it remains one of the favorite foods in soul cooking. While they came from many cultures, most of them were from West Africa. Distinct regional cuisines were lost, what with strange produce and the intermingling of the tribes, but the segregation of the field slaves tended to perpetuate certain uniquely African characteristics. Black tradition says that they brought many seeds with them to America, among them *benne*, the Southern name for sesame seed. Very likely. Sesame is actually from the East (benne is a Malay word), but the Arabs, who called it *simsim*, had controlled the spice and slave trades for centuries and had long since penetrated Africa. Helen Mendes, in *The African Heritage Cookbook* (1971), says that they brought with them okra. Of this there is little question; the word itself, Webster says, is a corruption of *nkruman*, a Tshi word from the Gold Coast. However, if they were cooking with tomatoes in Africa, as she claims, it would have been due to the Portuguese, who had been in West Africa since the fifteenth century and who early and enthusiastically took to the tomato. The tomato, of course, is native to tropical America and the very word derives from *tomatl*, its Nahuatl name (Webster). It is amusing to think that the black slaves may have brought tomatoes to the South; it is there that we first hear of their use in the United States, and Jefferson reported in 1782 that they were common in Virginia gardens. However, at about the same time, recipes using tomatoes were beginning to appear in English cookbooks, so we cannot be certain.

The foundation of American cooking in most of the colonies was English cooking of the seventeenth and eighteenth centuries. Readers familiar with the sad state of English food today may not regard that as much of a heritage, but in fact, the level of cooking in those centuries was high indeed, as evidenced by the cookbooks and manuscripts that the settlers brought with them.

Consider this admonition, from Hannah Glasse's *The Art of Cookery Made Plain and Easy*, an English work popular in America all through the second half of the eighteenth century:

> Most people spoil garden things by over-boiling them. All things that are green should have a little crispness, for if they are over-boiled, they neither have any sweetness or beauty.

Alas . . .

Proper English housewives of the sixteenth and seventeenth centuries kept manuscript books of recipes, which were handed down from mother to daughter; one of the duties of girlhood, along with sewing fine seams for a trousseau, appears to have been copying these recipes and learning how to make them. While daughters may have made certain deletions, they tended to make fair copies, adding recipes as they themselves set up housekeeping. In the great houses, the manuscript belonged to the family, with each new mistress bringing her own additions. Others were simple compilations of recipes collected from friends and relatives. These women were not trying to dazzle a public; they were writing for themselves and for their daughters. Their manuscripts, largely ignored by historians, are pages from a living past.

Printed cookbooks addressed to housewives did not appear until the end of the sixteenth century, when publishers discovered this gold mine. All cookbooks of the seventeenth and eighteenth centuries are based on family manuscripts, and even those households affluent enough to buy such books still treasured their own, and brought them to the New World. Two of these, which may be presumed to have helped shape our cooking, survive in the keeping of the Pennsylvania Historical Society. One is the so-called Martha Washington cookbook, which has long been attributed to Frances Custis, the First Lady's first mother-in-law. The other is that of the William Penn family. Both are said to have been written down at the beginning of the eighteenth century, but the recipes are clearly at least half a century older.

In a general way, the two collections resemble each other, as well they might, both having come from upper-class English families of roughly the same period. Recipes for beautiful fricassees (unmarred by flour), splendid dishes of carp, puddings by the score, great cakes, fruit pastes, marzipans, ginger breads, and preserves of all kinds show that English women brought to the colonies a rich and varied cuisine that would become the warp, the unifying factor, of American cookery. There is, incidentally, virtually no herb or spice in use in our "gourmet" cookery of today that did not appear in these seventeenth-century manuscripts.

As for printed cookbooks, Jane Carson notes that Robert Beverley sold his copy of Robert May's *The Accomplisht Cook* (1660) and that John Evelyn's *Acetaria: A Discourse of Sallets* (1699) was in another eighteenth-century inventory. From her studies of inventories and sales records, she lists the most popular cookbooks in colonial Virginia; the same list would have been valid in England. Curiously, no cookbooks seem to have been printed in America until 1742, when William Parks of Williamsburg brought out a shortened version (very likely pirated) of *The Compleat Housewife* by E. Smith (first published in England in 1727). It is interesting not only because it is a first, and an excellent cookbook, but also because the printer specified that he had chosen recipes with regard to their suitability to American produce. Here are some samples:

An Amulet of Eggs, the Savoury Way

Take a Dozen of Eggs, beat them very well, and season them with Salt, and a little Pepper; then have your Frying pan ready, with a good deal of fresh Butter in it, and let it be thoroughly hot; then put in your Eggs with four Spoonfuls of strong Gravy; and have ready Parsley, and a few Chieves cut, and throw them over it, and when 'tis enough turn it; and when done, dish it, and squeeze Orange or Lemon over it.

A typical omelet of the time. The gravy is pure meat juice, not the floury glop of today. (Mutton was usually used in England, but the colonials often substituted venison.) The orange would be the bitter Seville variety, a common seasoning for all kinds of dishes but already becoming a little old-fashioned at the time.

To Make Plumb Porridge

Take a Leg and Shin of Beef to ten Gallons of Water, boil it very tender, and when the Broth is strong, strain it out, wipe the Pot, and put in the Broth again; slice six Penny-loaves thin, cutting off the Top and Bottom; put some of the Liquor to it, cover it up, and let it stand a Quarter of an Hour, and then put in five Pounds of Raisins, and two Pounds of Prunes, and let them boil 'til they swell; then put in three Quarters of an Ounce of Mace, Half an Ounce of Cloves, two Nutmegs, all of them beat fine, and mix it with a little Liquor cold, and put in three Pounds of Sugar, a little Salt, a Quart of Sack, and a Quart of Claret, the Juice of two or three Lemons; you may thicken with Sagoe instead of Bread, if you please; pour them into Earthen Pans, and keep them for Use.

A typical version of the English plum pudding as it was made in the seventeenth and eighteenth centuries. (Six penny-loaves probably amounted to around five pounds of bread at the time; the size varied with the price of wheat. Sack is dry sherry.) Wiping the pot free from scum before putting the strained broth back is a nice touch. It is an excellent recipe.

Oyster Loaf is usually associated with New Orleans cooking but here it is, only slightly different, in this English cookbook. (Gravy is natural meat juice.)

To stew Oysters in French Rolls

Take a Quart of large Oysters, wash in their own
Liquor, and strain it, and put them in it with a little
Salt, some Pepper, Mace, and sliced Nutmeg; let the
Oysters stew a little with all these Things and thicken
them up with a great deal of Butter; then take six
French Rolls, cut a Piece off the Top, and take out
the Crumb and take your Oysters boiling hot, and
fill the Rolls full, and set them near the Fire on a
Chafing-Dish of Coals, and let them be hot through,
and as the Liquor soaks in, fill them up with more,
if you have 'em, or some hot Gravy: So serve them
up instead of a Pudding.

Now here is an elegant stuffing for a fowl to be roasted
before the fire:

Chickens forc'd with Oysters

Lard and truss them; make a Forcing with Oysters,
Sweet breads, Parsley, Truffles, Mushrooms, and On-
ions; chop them together and season it; mix it with a
Piece of Butter and the Yolk of an Egg; then tie them
at both Ends, and roast them; then make for them a
Ragoo, and garnish them with sliced Lemon.

This was likely served with a

Ragoo of Oysters

Put into your Stew pan a Quarter of a Pound of
Butter, let it boil; then take a Quart of Oysters, strain
them from their Liquor, and put them to the Butter;
let them stew with a Bit of Eschalot shred very fine,
and some grated Nutmeg, and a Little Salt; then beat
the Yolks of three or four Eggs with the Oyster-
liquor and half a Pound of Butter, and shake all very
well together till 'tis thick, and serve it up with
Sippets; and garnish with sliced Lemon.

And finally:

A Soop or Pottage

Take several Knuckles of Mutton, a Knuckle of Veal, a Shin of Beef, and put to these twelve Quarts of Water, cover the Pot close, and set it on the Fire; let it not boil too fast; scum it well, and let it stand on the Fire twenty four Hours; then strain it through a Colander, and when it is cold take off the Fat, and set it on the Fire again, and season it with Salt, a few Cloves, Pepper, a Blade of Mace, a Nutmeg quarter'd, a Bunch of sweet Herbs, and a Pint of Gravy; let all these boil up for Half an Hour, and then strain it; put Spinnage, Sorrel, green Peas, Asparagus, or Artichoke bottoms, according to the Time of Year; then thicken it with the Yolks of three or four Eggs; have in Readiness some Sheeps Tongues, Cox combs, and Sweetbreads, sliced thin, and fried, and put them in, and some Mushrooms, and French Bread dried and cut in little Bits, some forc'd-meat Balls, and some very thin Slices of Bacon; make all these very hot, and garnish the Dish with Colworts and Spinnage scalded green.

This is a rich, well constructed soup. The language is early eighteenth century, but the recipe could have appeared in any early-seventeenth-century cookbook. The directions are very clear—this is a cook speaking to cooks. The skimming and degreasing are excellently arranged, and we see that the quartered nutmeg, so popular in the seventeenth century, was still in use. To give it body, Mrs. Smith uses egg yolks, an elegant touch typical of earlier fine English cooking. The variety and amount of greens in the soup were also typical; one wonders sadly where this kind of cooking disappeared to. (Colworts, by the way, referred to kale or other non-heading members of the cabbage family.)

Mrs. Smith gives a remarkable recipe for Scotch-Collops which illustrates nicely that Scotch in old English cookbooks has nothing to do with Scotland but refers to "scotching" or scoring the meat: "Cut thin Slices out of a Leg of Veal, as many as you think will serve for a Dish, and hack them...." Then you fry them in butter and serve with a sauce of oysters and their liquor, strong broth, shallots, white wine, seasoned with anchovy and nutmeg, and thickened with eggs and butter. No flour.

(The impression is around that the modern gourmets introduced the shallot to America. In Mrs. Smith's book there is scarcely a recipe, aside from the desserts, that does not call for "an Eschalot or two" and a glass of white wine or claret. This is typical of seventeenth-century English cooking, and of early American cooking as well.)

A magnificent recipe for stewed carp in the Smith book involves simmering the fish in a quart of claret, the blood of the creature, shallots, herbs, spices, anchovy, verjuice (classically, green grape juice, but vinegar was often used), and the whole beautiful sauce then thickened with half a pound of fresh butter and five or six egg yolks.

It cannot be overemphasized that these were not considered hifaluting, "Frenchified" recipes; they were normal dishes from everyday cookbooks. They were, to be sure, intended for comfortably situated families, but upper-class families "had" their recipes and their cooks, much as Boston ladies were said to "have" their hats. Yet this book was reprinted in America precisely because the English editions had been selling well here.

It had the customary long chapter on "All Sorts of Puddings," of a somewhat higher quality than usual, perhaps. There are the expected artichoke pies, sweet spinach pies, tansies,* quaking puddings, an interesting "English Katchup" (essentially "best white-wine vinegar" boiled with shallots, anchovies, spices, and mushroom liquor), and an exceptionally fine recipe for pancakes that starts out with a pint of cream, eight eggs, and a pound of butter. There are all sorts of typical English cakes, pastries, and cookies. There is an interesting recipe for "A Sweet

---

* Tansy: a sort of flat omelet, originally flavored with tansy. It was a Lenten dish and may be a vestige of the bitter herbs of Passover. By the eighteenth century, spinach often replaced tansy, and soon the dish was to disappear as well.

Chicken Pye" which calls for "*Spanish* potatoes" (sweet potatoes), chestnuts, bone marrow, barberries (not unlike cranberries), butter, and spices, all baked together with a cut-up chicken in a *coffin* (closed pastry crust). When done, one pours over it a *caudle*, a light, hot custard made of white wine, egg yolks, butter, sugar, and spices. "Have a care it does not curdle," Mrs. Smith warns. The recipe is a direct descendant of the great medieval pies.

The first recipe for ice cream known to have been published in America appears in Richard Briggs' *The New Art of Cookery* (1792). But Americans were making it long before that. Jane Carson reports that the French wife of Governor Thomas Bladen of Maryland served "some fine Ice Cream" among the "Rarities" at a splendid dinner in 1744. Marie Kimball, in *Thomas Jefferson's Cook Book*, mentions that George Washington bought a "cream machine for Ice" in 1784. Mrs. Kimball, who unfortunately never lists her sources, also gives a recipe that she says Jefferson copied down in France at about the same time. It calls for 2 bottles of good cream, 6 yolks of egg, ½ pound of sugar, and a stick of vanilla, cooked as a light custard and then frozen in a *sorbetière* using ice and salt.

In any case, good recipes for ice cream had been appearing in a number of English cookbooks widely circulated in this country. In *Syllabubs and Fruit Fools* (1969), Elizabeth David says that the earliest recipe she has found in English sources was in the 1756 edition of *The Art of Cookery* by Hannah Glasse. It was for "a simple raspberry puree and cream mixture which today we would call a raspberry fool," she says.* (The English may have got ice cream from the French; several recipes appeared in Liger's *Dictionaire Pratique du Bon Ménager* in 1715. The French got it from the Italians, of course, and for that matter, the English may have as well; the Italians are thought to have got it from the East.) None of these many recipes contained a grain of flour or any of the other nasty

* Mrs. David now tells us that she has found this same recipe in the appendix of the 1751 edition of Hannah Glasse.

thickeners that home economists and modern industry
have added. Briggs's recipe calls for a dozen ripe apricots
beaten fine, six ounces of sugar, and a pint of cream stirred
while freezing in a tin pail surrounded by ice and salt.
His recipe is virtually identical to one appearing at least
three years earlier in *The Experienced English Housekeeper* by Elizabeth Raffald.

A far more historic recipe appears in the 1792 book by
Briggs. It is worth giving here in full:

To dress Haddock the Spanish Way

Take two fine haddocks, scale, gut, and wash them
well, wipe them with a cloth, and broil them; put
a pint of sweet oil [olive oil] in a stew-pan, season it
with pepper and salt, a little cloves, mace, and nutmeg, beaten, two cloves of garlick chopped, pare
half a dozen love apples and quarter them, when in
season, put them in, and a spoonful of vinegar, put
in the fish, and stew them very gently for half an
hour over a slow fire; put them in a hot dish, and
garnish with lemon.

Tomatoes were called love apples (in Italian and French
as well) because of their supposed aphrodisiac qualities.
Although it is the earliest example we have seen of a
recipe that included tomatoes published in this country,
it is by no means the first one to circulate here. At least
as early as 1756, there appeared in Hannah Glasse's popular *Art of Cookery* a virtually identical recipe to the
above.* The olive oil and garlic, as well as the tomatoes,

* We had traced the recipe back to the 1767 edition; Elizabeth
David found it in the 1756 edition. Briggs evidently copied
it nearly word for word. Interestingly, a printer's error
changed *broil* to *boil* sometime after 1756; later editions, including the American ones, retained the error. Mrs. David
notes this, saying that she does not think that "Mrs. Glasse
would have done anything *quite* so preposterous as boiling a
haddock and then stewing it for half an hour." She comments
that all writers of the day "pillaged" earlier writers. "They

would suggest that it was actually a Spanish recipe; Gerard reports that the people of Spain ate tomatoes in salads and cooked in sauce. (*The Herball*, 1597). He felt that the English had best leave them alone, which they did for nearly two hundred years.

A charming tomato recipe, for which we are indebted to Elizabeth David, is for a sauce, the earliest such recipe we have seen. It is in a manuscript from Towneley Hall, Lancashire, dated 1759. (The recipe itself, she thinks, may possibly have been entered around 1780.)

Tomatoes, commonly called Love Apples

When they are quite red, roast them so as to be able to peel them, the peal is not made use of, Put the remaining part into a mortar bruise it well, add some gravy of the kind you are going to use, so as to make it of the consistency of pudding, when this operation is done put it in to a pot for to warme, it must not boil, then put it to anything to send to table.

Note the niceties of detail; roasting the tomatoes rather than simmering them gives a richer flavor, and the warning against allowing them to boil is perceptive. The gravy, as always, is meat juice. The most interesting aspect of the recipe, however, is that it illustrates how cookbooks lagged behind usage; although love apples were apparently well known at the time, the Hannah Glasse recipe noted above is the only one calling for them that we have been able to find in print for decades.

Considering how the tomato was to dominate American cooking, it took an uncommonly long time to get here. Still, judging by Jefferson's marketing notes, they were in popular use by the end of the eighteenth century (on

---

had absolutely no scruples," she says. "One does have the impression that Mrs. Glasse, Mrs. Raffald, Mrs. Rundell and some of the other women writers of the 18th century were more original than the men. E. Smith was good."

sale as early as July 16 and as late as November 17). So
it is surprising to read the authoritative James Beard
saying, in *American Cookery* (1972), "The first recorded
American recipes [including tomatoes] I found were in
Miss Leslie's books, dating from the 1850's and '60's." If
Beard had looked in Eliza Leslie's 1837 book, *Directions
for Cookery*, he would have found six recipes with
tomatoes. He would have found more in Mrs. Child's
American Frugal Housewife (1832) and in Mary Randolph's *The Virginia Housewife* (1824). They were
already called tomatoes and were so listed in the indexes.
Under love apples, he could have found them in the first
American edition (1805) of Hannah Glasse's *Art of
Cookery*. In fact, Beard could have looked in his own
book—he reprints one of Mary Randolph's tomato recipes!

Up to this point, we have been quoting cookbooks of
English origin, for the simple reason that they were the
only ones circulating in the colonies. But through the
seventeeth and eighteenth centuries, American housewives
from Maine to South Carolina were fashioning, without
benefit of cookbooks, a new and inspired array of cuisines.
It was only at the end of the eighteenth century that this
broke into print.

The first cookbook known to have been written by a
native is *American Cookery* by Amelia Simmons, "an
American Orphan," published in 1796 in Hartford, Connecticut. Many of her recipes are competent but routine
presentations of English cookery of the period, but Miss
Simmons knew her onions: "The Medeira white is best
in market, esteemed softer flavored, and not so fiery, but
the high red, round hard onions are the best; if you
consult cheapness, the largest are the best; if you consult
taste and softness, the very smallest are the most delicate,
and used at the first tables. Onions grow in the richest,
highest cultivated ground, and better and better year after
year, on the same ground."

Little is known about Miss Simmons, except that she

described herself as "not having an education sufficient to prepare the work for publication." So she entrusted her little book to someone who, she said, had made errors and substitutions "which were highly injurious...without her consent." (Already, serpents dwelt in the publishing world.) But she evidently was a real cook:

We proceed to ROOTS and VEGETABLES—*and the best cook cannot alter the first quality, they must be good, or the cook will be disappointed.* [Miss Simmons' emphasis.]

These words should be embroidered on samplers and hung in every kitchen, a reproach to all those modern gourmets and home economists who try to disguise the awfulness of our food with the awfulness of their cookery. We sadly note the fact that Miss Simmons' entire syllabub section— "To make a fine Syllabub from the Cow, Whipt Syllabub, Lemon Cream, Raspberry Cream, Whipt Cream, and a Trifle"—appears, virtually word for word, in Susannah Carter's *The Frugal Housewife* (first American edition 1772). They are all very fine recipes.

Miss Simmons mentions nine varieties of beans, seven of green peas, and most of the other vegetables and fruits that are popular today, with the interesting exception of the tomato. It was common in the South at that time; perhaps it was less so in New England. Or perhaps she was simply old-fashioned. She roasts turkey on the spit and says to "serve it up with boiled onions and cramberry sauce, mangoes, pickles or celery." (Elsewhere, she gives a recipe, "To Pickle or make Mangoes of Melons"; later writers specify green "muskmelons" to be gathered "a size larger than a goose egg.") She also gives an excellent recipe for a tart with "cramberries." Miss Simmons gives two recipes for that great American dessert, pumpkin pie; they seem to be the earliest of their kind in print. (As early as 1682, Hannah Woolley published a recipe for a "Pumpion-Pye" but it had no resemblance to ours.) Curiously, she gives them in the pudding section:

Pompkin

No. 1. One quart stewed and strained, 3 pints cream, 9 beaten eggs, sugar, mace, nutmeg and ginger, laid into paste No. 7 or 3, and with a dough spur, cross and chequer it, and baked in dishes three quarters of an hour.

No. 2. One quart milk, 1 pint pompkin, 4 eggs, molasses, allspice and ginger in a crust, bake 1 hour.

Her little book was so successful that a second edition appeared the same year "to accommodate a large and extensive circle of reputable characters." This Albany edition is a far more interesting cookbook: she tells us firmly, for example, in roasting beef that "rare done is the healthiest, and the taste of this age." She gives a remarkable fish recipe: "To dress a Bass." The stuffing is aromatic with herbs and wine and enriched with four ounces of butter; the fish is baked with thin slices of salt pork laid over, sauced with melted butter, and served up "with stewed oysters, cramberries, boiled onions or potatoes."

Her three recipes for "A Nice Indian Pudding" may be the first ever printed:

No. 1. 3 pints scalded milk, 7 spoons fine Indian meal, stir well together while hot, let stand till cooled; add 7 eggs, half pound raisins, 4 ounces butter, spice and sugar, bake one and half hour.

No. 2. 3 pints scalded milk to one pint meal salted; cool, add 2 eggs, 4 ounces butter, sugar or molasses and spice q.s. [to taste] it will require two and half hours baking.

No. 3. Salt a pint meal, wet with one quart milk, sweeten and put into a strong cloth, brass or bell metal vessel, stone or earthern pot, secure from wet and boil 12 hours.

The 12 hours in the last recipe was one of the editor's errata; Miss Simmons corrected it to 6. Now, anyone who has read English cookbooks of the seventeenth century would recognize that these are not *Indian* puddings but

English boiled and baked puddings using Indian—i.e., corn—meal. Craig Claiborne of *The New York Times* once upset informed readers when he called the dish "as American as the tomahawk" and offered some "old" recipes that were clearly twentieth-century, with such additives as baking soda.

Indian pudding is American in that it applied English cookery to an American product; the reason there are so many "authentic" ones is that English women brought their pudding recipes here and adapted them. An interesting one, because it calls for ginger and mentions whey (insisted upon by some purists), appears in Mrs. Lydia Maria Child's *The American Frugal Housewife* (1832):

> Indian pudding is good baked. Scald a quart of milk (skimmed milk will do) and stir in seven table spoonfuls of sifted Indian meal, a tea-spoonful of salt, a tea-cupful of molasses, and a great spoonful of ginger, or sifted cinnamon. Baked three or four hours. If you want whey, you must be sure and pour in a little cold milk, after it is all mixed.

Two recipes for Indian pudding appear in the first American edition (1805) of *The Art of Cookery* by Hannah Glasse. The book, first published in London in 1747, had apparently been the most popular cookbook of its time in the colonies; Gilbert Chinard, in the interesting monograph *Benjamin Franklin on the Art of Eating*,* suggests that Franklin had some Hannah Glasse recipes translated into French for the use of his cook when he was in Paris. The most interesting thing about the 1805 edition is a chapter called "Several New Receipts adapted to the American Mode of Cooking." It includes recipes for Buck-Wheat Cakes, Pumpkin Pie, Dough Nuts, Cranberry Tarts, Whafles, Maple Beer, and "A receipt to make Maple Sugar," as well as the Indian puddings. The recipes are authentically American. Mrs. Glasse had long since been laid to rest and no hint of authorship is given. They are *not* lifted from Amelia Simmons.

* American Philosophical Society, 1958.

The quality and richness of the recipes should surprise those who believe that Americans of those days ate only Spartan frontier food. "Whafles" start out with a pound of flour, a pound of sugar, a pound of butter, a glass of rose water.... No wretched package mix there. Nor in the pumpkin pie, which calls for a pint of pumpkin, a pint of milk, a glass of Malaga wine, a glass of rose water, seven eggs, half a pound of fresh butter, "and sugar and salt to taste."

The Art of Cookery gives The Order of a Modern Bill of Fare for each month. We must point out that this oldtime, sumptuous arrangement of dishes, *à la Française*, has more in common with a series of buffets or smorgasbords than with modern meals. Guests did not eat all those dishes; they simply reached for what they wanted. In our view, it was conspicuous waste, but not so wasteful and downright gross as the interminable menus stuffed down by the European and American upper classes in the Victorian era—and the cooking was demonstrably better in the eighteenth century. Hannah Glasse's bills of fare are interesting as a catalogue of available dishes. Here is the one for March:

FIRST COURSE
Soup.

Sheeps Rumps.	Almond Pudding.	Fillet of Pork.
Chine of Mutton and Stewed Celery.	Stewed Carp or Tench.	Lamb's Head.
Veal Collops.	Beef Steak Pie. Onion Soup.	Calves Ears.

SECOND COURSE
A Poulard larded and roasted.

Asparagus.	Blanc Mange.	Prawns.
Ragooed Sweetbreads.	A Trifle.	Fricasee of Rabbits.
Crawfish.	Cheesecakes.	Fricasee of Mushrooms.

Tame Pigeons roasted.

THIRD COURSE
Ox Palates shivered.

Tartlets.	Potted Larks.	Stewed Pigeons.
Cardoons.	Jellies.	Spanish Peas.
Black Caps.	Potted Partridge.	Almond Cheese-Cakes.
	Cock's Combs.	

It may be objected that this fare was not for every day, nor for everybody. Perhaps not; such lavish display was undoubtedly reserved for guests in wealthy homes, but the individual dishes were part of the homemaker's repertory of daily fare, and here lies the essential difference between eighteenth-century cookbooks and gourmet cookbooks of today. Rex Stout, in *The Nero Wolfe Cook Book*, appeals to the snobbery of the reader: "I beg you not to entrust these dishes to your cook unless he is an artist. Cook them yourself, and only for an occasion that is worthy of them." Ironically but typically, the gourmet dishes in Stout's book are not worthy of any occasion; its merit lies in the homelier American fare, and in Nero Wolfe's obsession with the quality of the ingredients, which sets him apart from the typical gourmet. This attitude, nearly lost today, impregnates cooking literature up to the late nineteenth century.

The first formally regional cookbook printed in America seems to be *The New-England Cookery*, by Lucy Emerson, published in Montpelier, Vermont, in 1808. It is sad to report that whole sections were lifted verbatim from Amelia Simmons—including the errors that Miss Simmons had noted in her 1796 edition. But Miss Emerson did insert a few recipes of her own, the most interesting of which is one for Oyster Soup:

Have ready a good fish stock, then take two quarts of oysters without the beards; bray the hard part in a mortar, with the yolks of ten hard eggs. Set what quantity of fish stock you shall want over the fire with your oysters; season it with pepper, salt and grated nutmeg. When it boils, put in the eggs, and let it boil till it is as thick as cream. Dish it up with bread cut in dice.

It would be tempting to try this dish with raw egg yolk instead of hard, but it is splendid as is. The concept of pounding the hard muscle of the oyster to a pommade is brilliant; it aids the liaison and immeasurably increases the oyster flavor.

Since the book comes from Vermont, it is perhaps understandable that there are no recipes for any of the great New England chowders. More disappointing is the absence of a recipe for baked beans. It would seem that New England women long were diffident about publishing the recipes of those homey local dishes that were in fact masterpieces of culinary art.

As printed cookbooks became more and more popular, the tradition of the family manuscript gradually died out. Still, women continued to write down favorite recipes in notebooks. Some survive. A charming Yankee one in our possession is signed and dated S. C. Wightman, May, 1826. It gives this recipe for "Italian Cheese":

> A quart of good cream, the juice of four lemons and the rind of one steep[ed] the night before in a glass of brandy, add a proper quantity of sugar and whip it well together in the morning & let it stand till night to settle then take of[f] the thick froth & put it in a sieve with a piece of gauze under it let it stand till the next morning and turn it out just before you use it.*

There is also a delicious recipe "To Stew Pigeons"; they are stuffed with their livers, a little thyme, parsley, chives, breadcrumbs, mace, salt and butter, and stewed in only one spoonful of water, with papers pasted under the lid so that none of the aroma escapes. "Derby or Short Cakes" calls for 1 lb. butter, 2 lb. flour, 1 lb. currants, 1 lb. "good moist sugar," 1 egg, and ½ pint milk. "Roll it thin" and bake like cookies.

A recipe "To Cure Hams" calls for 1 lb. Bay Salt, ½ lb. Common Salt, 2 oz. Salt petre, 1 oz. ground Black Pepper, and 1 lb. Treacle [molasses] to a Ham. Bay, or sea salt, was considered vastly superior to common salt, but since it was also more expensive, it was often eked out in just this way.

In 1824 appeared one of the most important cookbooks ever published in America. *The Virginia Housewife or, Methodical Cook*, by Mary Randolph (1762–1828), is not only one of the finest; it may also be called the first truly American cookbook in that all the strands of influence in Virginia cookery were beautifully worked into place. In her preface, she says, "The greater part of the following receipts have been written from memory, where they have been impressed by long continued practice." She was con-

---

* The brandy in which the rind is steeped is of course added to the other ingredients.

sidered the best cook in Richmond at the time; her heyday
was the last decade of the eighteenth century.

The warp was solidly English, but it was the cooking of
the English gentry and had little in common with that of
the Puritan dissenters who founded the Massachusetts
colony, for instance. Here we have the soups, "A NICE
BOILED PUDDING," crumpets, "NICE BUNS" ("make them in a
quick oven—do not burn them"), a very fine "PIE OF
SWEETBREADS," "TO DRESS DUCKS WITH JUICE OF ORANGES,"
and that most English dessert, "APPLE PIE."

Woven in among them is the French influence in Virginia. This was primarily the contribution of the Huguenots, who fled France around 1700 and settled in various
parts of America. Most of them came from the Languedoc, and brought with them their ways for numerous
à la daube dishes, "TO HARRICO MUTTON," and so on.

Interestingly, the more elaborate French cuisine that so
enchanted Jefferson seems not to have greatly influenced
Mrs. Randolph—except perhaps for the ice cream recipes,
of which she gives no fewer than eighteen. So far as we
can ascertain, each is the first of its kind in America, and
they are of a quality to shame modern Americans.

Mrs. Randolph was a genuine cook, and a perceptive
one, noting that "the strawberries must be very ripe" and
"if rich cream can be procured, it will be infinitely better—the custard is intended as a substitute, when cream
cannot be had." Other kinds of ice cream include raspberry, peach, coconut, chocolate, coffee, almond, lemon,
and "Lemonade iced" (a sherbet). The most curious one
is for a frozen oyster soup.

Mrs. Randolph had a lively, intelligent interest in foreign cooking. Recipes for "Olla," "Ropa veija," and "Gas-
pacho" appear among her Southern dishes, always carefully
described as Spanish. She tells us how "To make a dish
of curry after the East Indian manner" (and how to blend
a curry powder) far more authentically than thousands of
curry recipes in modern gourmet literature. There is a recipe for "Gumbs—a West India dish" and also "To caveach

fish," which is, of course, *escabeche*, the ancient Arab pickling dish. Caveach was a familiar item in earlier English cookbooks,* but the other recipes would seem to be first appearances in American print.

There are, as might be expected, any number of fine Southern recipes, such as "To barbecue a shote" (young Pig), "To corn shote," and "To toast ham," to name a few. This last is a forerunner of what we call Virginia baked ham; it is noteworthy in that it did not have the present sweet spicy glaze. There is also "CATFISH SOUP, *An excellent dish for those who have not imbibed a needless prejudice against those delicious fish.*" And there is—

CHICKEN PUDDING, A FAVOURITE VIRGINIA RECIPE.

Beat ten eggs very light, add to them a quart of rich milk, with a quarter of a pound of butter melted, and some pepper and salt; stir in as much flour as will make a thin good batter; take four young chickens, and after cleaning them nicely, cut off the legs, wings, &c. put them all in a sauce pan, with some salt and water, and a bundle of thyme and parsley, boil them till nearly done, then take the chicken from the water and put it in the batter pour it in a deep dish, and bake it; send nice white gravy in a boat.

TO MAKE WHITE SAUCE FOR FOWLS.

Take a scrag of veal, the necks of fowls, or any bits of mutton or veal you have; put them in a sauce pan with a blade or two of mace, a few black pepper corns, one anchovy, a head of celery, a bunch of sweet herbs, a slice of the end of a piece of lemon; put it in a quart of water, cover it close, let it boil till it is reduced to half a pint, strain it, and thicken it with a

* *The Experienced English Housekeeper* by Elizabeth Raffald (1769) has several recipes, and Hannah Glasse gives recipes for it under "The Jews way of preserving Salmon, and all Sorts of Fish." Very possibly the Jews, fleeing the Inquisition, brought the dish with them from Spain.

quarter of a pound of butter mixed with flour [else-
where specified as 2 teaspoons], boil it five or six
minutes, put in two spoonsful of pickled mushrooms,
mix the yelks of two eggs with a tea cup full of good
cream and a little nutmeg—put it in the sauce, keep
shaking it over the fire, but don't let it boil.

In this case, the liquid in which you poached the chicken
will do nicely for the sauce.

Following is a recipe for:

APOQUINIMIC CAKES

Put a little salt, one egg beaten, and four ounces of
butter, in a quart of flour—make it into a paste with
new milk, beat it for half an hour with a pestle, roll
the paste thin, and cut it into round cakes; bake them
on a gridiron, and be careful not to burn them.

These are beaten biscuits, and we have not found an
earlier version. The Indian name is difficult to account for,
because the ingredients are thoroughly English. Since it
would have been black women who beat them, it is possibly an African technique for achieving tenderness.

Baking soda makes one appearance, as a substitute for
the natural leavening of yeast or eggs, and pearl-ash (potassium carbonate) is similarly used in an interesting recipe
for "Plebeian Ginger Bread." Mrs. Randolph seemed perfectly aware that these would cheapen the product; they
are quite out of character with the rest of the book. These
chemical leaveners give lightness but an inferior texture
to cakes. They also leave faint metallic traces of bitter-
ness—a taste that, unfortunately, Americans grew to love.

These are the only flyspecks in an otherwise impeccable
baking section. The bread recipe is fine. Flour, water,
yeast, and salt; not a trace of sugar. "In winter," Mrs.
Randolph counsels, "make the bread up at three o'clock,
and it will be ready before bed time. In summer, make it
up at five o'clock."

Doubtless the most American aspect of *The Virginia*

Housewife is the extraordinary number of recipes using tomatoes. As mentioned, they began appearing in recipes by 1792, but by the 1831 edition, they are integral parts of twelve dishes. Many must be considered American firsts: tomato ketchup, tomato marmalade, tomato soy, "ochra and tomatas," stewed tomatoes, scalloped tomatoes, and the Spanish dishes mentioned earlier. There are also two recipes for eggplant, the first we have found in American sources. Like tomatoes, they had long been grown in those parts, however; Mrs. Randolph says, "The purple ones are best; get them young and fresh." How often does one see such advice in a cookbook today?

It is sad to report that Mrs. Randolph likely gave many Americans their first macaroni-and-cheese recipe. She directs that the macaroni be boiled in milk and water until "quite tender" (God help us), then drained, put in layers with cheese and butter and baked in "a quick oven" for twenty to thirty minutes. It started out as a misconception of an Italian dish. As long as it involved only good cheese and butter, it wasn't too bad, but in the latter half of the nineteenth century it began turning up in its present horrid form—overcooked factory macaroni, floury white sauce, and process cheese. The cheese has no more taste than the macaroni, and if it did, the library paste would blanket it. But it has become more American than apple pie.

We have a particular affection for a little cookbook called *The American Frugal Housewife, Dedicated to Those Who are Not Ashamed of Economy*. It was first published in Boston in 1832 by Lydia Maria Child, one of that race of New England women who somehow found the time and energy to care for home and family, to write prolifically, and to promote abolition and other social reforms. She was not a brilliant cook, but many of her ideas are sound, and are the more significant because they were addressed to women of humble means. Thus, she discusses various substitutes for coffee, but advises that "the best economy is to go without." Like any good housewife of her time, she knows that coffee "should be ground soon after roasting, and used as soon as it is ground." She warns that pearl-ash "injures the flavor of the meal."

Salt fish "should not be boiled an instant; boiling renders it hard." To go with it, you cut salt pork into small bits "and try* it till the pork is crispy. It should not be done too fast, lest the sweetness be scorched out." This is a very old New England dish that Mrs. Child does not dignify with a title—it is just one of the many ways to fix fish. There is an attractive contrast of textures and tastes that demonstrates how well those New England women worked with unpromising materials.

The American Frugal Housewife presents a very early recipe for New England's classic dish.

> Baked beans are a very simple dish, yet few cook them well. They should be put in cold water, and hung over the fire, the night before they are baked. In the morning, they should be put in a colander, and rinsed two or three times; then again place in a kettle, with the pork you intend to bake, covered with water, and kept scalding hot, an hour or more. A pound of pork is quite enough for a quart of beans, and that is a large dinner for a common family. The rind of the pork should be slashed. Pieces of pork alternately fat and lean, are the most suitable; the cheeks are the best. A little pepper sprinkled among the beans, when they are placed in the bean-pot, will render them less unhealthy. They should be just covered with water, when put into the oven; and the pork should be sunk a little below the surface of the beans. Bake three or four hours.

Note, again, the absence of sweetening. Nowadays, it is taken for granted that Boston baked beans are sweet, but it was evidently still a novelty in the middle of the nineteenth century, when Mary Cornelius noted in *The Young Housekeeper's Friend*: "Many persons think it a decided improvement to put in a large spoonful or two of molasses. It is a very good way."

* Try: render, i.e., fry gently.

James Beard, in *American Cookery*, declares that the dish was originally made with maple sugar, which was replaced by molasses. He adds, "my palate cannot reconcile the sweetness of syrup or molasses and the simple hardy flavor of pork and beans," but his recipe includes half a cup of maple sugar or syrup. He felt that it would not be authentic if it was not sweet. His palate here was better than his scholarship.

7

Eliza

Cat-fish that have been caught near the
middle of the river are much nicer than
those that are taken near the shore where
they have access to impure food. The small
ones are the best.

Eliza Leslie

THE MOST popular cookbook of the nineteenth century
first appeared in Philadelphia in 1837. It was *Directions for
Cookery*, by Eliza Leslie, which in our view ranks with
Mrs. Randolph's *Virginia Housewife* as one of the two
best all-American cookbooks ever written. James Beard,
be it said, has rendered a service in making Miss Leslie
better known to modern cooks. Why does he say, however, when he quotes one of her recipes for scalloped
tomatoes, that it is "a very good one even now"? He surely
does not mean "even now when tomatoes are no longer
fit to eat," so presumably he means "even now when
cooking has become sophisticated." In truth, American
cookery reached its highest level in the second quarter of
the nineteenth century, with Miss Leslie as its guide. From
then on, it was downhill all the way.

Miss Leslie was sufficiently sophisticated to have written
Domestic French Cookery (1832), which she described as

a translation. But her classic *Directions for Cookery* is thoroughly American. It shares with earlier cookbooks a concern for quality that now seems almost alien, and abounds in such critical assessments as her remarks above on choosing catfish, and "The Portuguese pork, which is fed on chestnuts, is perhaps the finest in the world." Miss Leslie advises that oysters "may be kept for a week to a fortnight" in a tub of salted water, fed with cornmeal, the water being changed every day. (An old merchant in the Fulton Fish Market told us that this was still done early in this century, in tank barges along the South Street docks. He said clams had to be fed "on the tide" or they would not eat and the water would spoil. This sort of folklore is unhappily disappearing.)

The recipe for Cat-Fish Soup in Leslie calls for ham (good old country ham, of course), a head of celery, milk, and butter, and is thickened with the yolks of four eggs— in other words, a sort of elegant chowder. (She notes that eels or chicken may be handled in the same manner.) Indeed, the whole soup section is remarkable. Miss Leslie truly understood the construction of these dishes and went out of her way to let the reader in on what she had learned. Note the grasp of technique in this excerpt from the recipe for Fine Beef Soup:

> ...Pour on the water, hang it over a moderate fire, and boil it slowly: carefully skimming off all the fat that rises to the top, and keeping it closely covered, except when you raise the lid to skim it. Do not, on any account, put in additional water to this soup while it is boiling; and take care that the boiling goes steadily on, as, if it stops, the soup will be much injured. But if the fire is too great, and the soup boils too fast, the meat will become hard and tough, and will not give out its juices.

The soup is then strained and put in a cool place (if properly made, it will jelly in the pan, Miss Leslie notes) until the next day, when the fat and any sediment clinging to it are scraped off. She then adds parboiled vegetables, explaining that too much recooking of the soup would "destroy the flavour, and render it flat and insipid." "Many persons prefer boiling all the vegetables in the soup on the first day, thinking that they improve the flavour," Miss Leslie writes. "This may be done in common soup that is not strained but is inadmissible if you wish it to be very bright and clear." This is very nice French technique. Of another soup, Miss Leslie says it should be "of a fine clear amber colour." She tells how to clarify it with egg white if it is not clear, adding, "But it is better to have the soup clear by making it carefully, than to depend on clarifying it afterward, as the white of egg weakens the taste."

Two recipes, Rich White Soup and Milk Soup, use almonds as integral ingredients. They are direct descendants of the medieval *blanc mange*, versions of which appear in the oldest English cookery manuscripts (from about 1380). Long before the time of Miss Leslie, however, the name *blanc mange* had been applied to a sweet pudding made with almonds. Our 1826 Wightman manuscript gives such a recipe, which demonstrates admirably the change this dish was undergoing:

Blanc Mange

Take two ounces of Isinglass cut very small. Pour rather better than half a pint of milk upon it dissolve it over the fire the night before you make it then put a quart of cream to it not too thick three or four laurel leaves & three or four teaspoonfuls of rose water sweeten it to your taste boil it about ten minutes then strain it for use. You may use almonds pounded instead of laurel leaves if you please.

Isinglass is the prepared bladder of sturgeon, which gives a high quality of gelatin. In another connection, Miss Leslie observes that a prepared gelatin was coming into use as a substitute for calves' feet in jellies, and says, "Its greatest recommendations are convenience and expedition."

Corruptions were creeping in. Of her own three recipes for *blanc mange*, one is made simply with milk and arrowroot, the ignominious end of a great and ancient dish. Today it is accurately called cornstarch pudding.

There are other interesting omens of the approaching decline in our cookery. One is the gradual disappearance of the shallot. Even the admirable Miss Leslie makes only rare use of it, and after her, it virtually disappeared from American cookbooks for a century—a great pity. Our own hypothesis is that the pervasive flavor of the tomato drove out the shallot as bad money drives out good. Supporting this is the fact that the great variety of ketchups that characterized early American cooking was gradually replaced by the ubiquitous tomato ketchup. Miss Leslie, in 1837, published recipes for eight kinds: anchovy (two), lobster, oyster, walnut, mushroom, lemon—and tomato. (Be it noted again, there was no sugar in any of them.) Anyone familiar with Chinese cooking will recognize the original source of ketchups, but they came to us from England. (The Oxford English Dictionary says the word apparently derives from Amoy Chinese *kétsiap*, meaning brine of pickled fish. The Malay *kēchap*, often given as the source, may be from the Chinese as well.) Until about 1850, when an American recipe called for a spoonful of ketchup, it most likely meant mushroom, walnut, or oyster. These interesting condiments did continue for some decades, but mostly because Miss Leslie's works continued to be best sellers.

Her lobster ketchup uses the flesh and coral from a three-pounder, reduced to a pommade in a mortar, flecked with cayenne, and gradually mixed with a bottle of sherry. She recommends that it be added to melted butter as a fish sauce; it should be delicious. Another calls for anchovies, shallots, horseradish, mace, sliced lemon, whole cloves, peppercorns, a pint of port, and a pint of Madeira, all boiled down until reduced by half. Used discreetly with rich butter, it would make an admirable steak sauce—if you go for that sort of thing. Doubtless the nasty bottled steak sauces of today, such as President Ford poured on his cottage cheese, were originally based on such formulas; they are now so hyped up with bad vinegar and chemical preservatives that they ruin the taste of anything they are put to.

Miss Leslie's bread was still an honest loaf, made only of flour, salt, water, and yeast (either from the brewery or homemade). But the cake and quick-bread sections are beginning to look very American: our sweet tooth is becoming more evident and the use of chemical leaveners is increasing. The recipe for Washington Cake cautions, "Take care not to put in too much pearl-ash, lest it give the cake an unpleasant taste." Usually, Miss Leslie's good judgment prevailed. Here, she gives the classic recipe for a Sally Lunn:

> Sift into a pan a pound and a half of flour. Make a hole in the middle, and put in two ounces of butter warmed in a pint of milk, a salt-spoonful of salt, three well-beaten eggs, and two table-spoonfuls of the best fresh yeast. Mix the flour well into the other ingredients, and put the whole into a square tin pan that has been greased with butter. Cover it, set it in a warm place, and when it is quite light, bake it in a moderate oven. Send it to table hot, and eat it with butter.

Miss Leslie's New Cookery Book, published in 1857, gives the same recipe but, as noted in an earlier chapter, finds it necessary to warn that sugar or spice would spoil the cake. Americans were beginning to hoax things up with sugar.

An earlier Leslie edition gives an exceptionally fine recipe for Boston Cream Cakes. It calls for a batch of individual cakes, made with ½ pound butter and 8 eggs, filled with a custard made with 12 egg yolks, flavored with "a vanilla bean and a stick of the best Ceylon cinnamon," and a glass of rose water.

Perfectly typical of today's updated recipes for this

old American sweet is one given by Judith Jones in
American Food, by Evan Jones. It is a banal two-egg cake
spread with a filling that has been thickened with one-
third cup flour and two miserly eggs. *Sic transit gloria.*
James Beard gives a one-egg version of the cake, and
asserts, "Old recipes *invariably* called for sour milk or
buttermilk and soda." (Emphasis ours.) Not Miss Leslie's
old recipe.

The point is not just that Miss Leslie's recipe is richer—
although since sweets can hardly be defended on any
ground but sheer gourmandise, they ought to be of the
finest quality, or shunned. It is a question of the contrast
of textures; the slightly dense, golden-crusted *madeleine*
type cakes full of buttery goodness have a surprise filling
of a beautifully flavored, rose scented, silken custard, un-
cheapened by flour. The comparison of Miss Leslie's cakes
with the miserly modern version is a perfect illustration
of the decline in taste and cooking skills of the past one
hundred and fifty years.

Mrs. Jones, who, incidentally, is editor of the Julia
Child cookbooks, appears to be responsible for a recipe in
Evan Jones' book that she calls "Miss Leslie's Indian
Pound Cake." The ingredients: 6 tablespoons butter, 1 cup
sugar, 4 eggs, 1¼ cups flour, ¾ teaspoon baking powder,
¼ cup white cornmeal, ⅛ teaspoon grated nutmeg, ¼
teaspoon ground cinnamon, ½ teaspoon vanilla extract,
and 2 teaspoons applejack.

Shall we turn to Miss Leslie? Her ingredients for *her*
Indian Pound Cake: ½ pound fresh butter, ½ pound
sugar, 8 eggs "beaten as light as possible," ½ pint wheat
flour, 1 pint fine yellow Indian meal, 1 nutmeg, 1 tablespoon cinnamon, a glass of white wine, and a glass of
brandy. (This recipe appears in *Directions for Cookery.
Miss Leslie's Seventy-five Receipts*, 1832 edition, gives a
virtually identical recipe.)

That Mrs. Jones roughly halved the recipe is understandable. But why did she reverse the proportion (and

then some) of wheat flour to cornmeal? Why did she
specify white meal instead of yellow? (Elsewhere, Miss
Leslie was quite firm about that.) Why did she add baking
powder, which did not yet exist? Why did she change
the method? Why did she use two teaspoons of applejack
instead of generous amounts of white wine and brandy?
Why in short, did she call it "Miss Leslie's Indian Pound
Cake"?

Occasionally an old recipe may benefit from modernization, but surely the reader should be so informed. It is sad
to be obliged to point out flaws in what is in many ways
an admirable book. Mr. Jones writes with love and enthusiasm about the regional cuisines of America, but there
is no bibliography and one is left feeling unsure of his
sources.

Although *Directions for Cookery* was first published in
Philadelphia, the Pennsylvania Dutch influence is barely
discernible. Scrapple and shoofly pie do not show up, but
Miss Leslie does say of cottage cheese, "This is that
preparation of milk vulgarly known as Smear Case
[spreading cheese]." There is a Moravian Sugar Cake
and a fine recipe for Pepper Pot, which uses peppercorns
rather than the long pod some purists insist upon. There
is also what may be the earliest printed version of what
came to be pure Americana, *cole slaw*. (Amelia Simmons
mentions *slaw*, made with red cabbage, but gives no
recipe.) Miss Leslie calls it Cold Slaw, a typical linguistic
substitution of a word of similar sound for another that
is not understood. *Cole* is the old English word for cabbage (*kohl* in German), still surviving in words like
cauliflower and kohlrabi. (From Latin *caulis* and Greek
kaulos. Cabbage, by the way, comes from French *caboche*,
meaning head, and the word still survives in certain
patois.) *Slaw* is a simple corruption of salad. It may have
come through either German or English. Miss Leslie
recommended an old-fashioned boiled dressing, the likes
of which was to continue as the dressing for cole slaw

and potato salad well into the twentieth century—when it was displaced by commercial mayonnaise.

In the same year of 1837 when Miss Leslie's classic appeared, Sylvester Graham issued his tract on the evils of bolted flour—that is, flour with most of the nutrients removed. The message evidently spread. By 1845, Graham flour appeared in *The Improved Housewife*, "by a Married Lady" (Mrs. A. L. Webster), published in Hartford, Connecticut. It is sad to note that one of our earliest "health"-bread recipes is also one of the earliest to call for sweetening—a pattern that has only intensified since. It is also ironic, because it was precisely the impoverishment of ordinary flour that inspired the addition of sugar.

Mrs. Webster's book also has news for Beard, who says in his *American Cookery* that before the late nineteenth century, cream pies were not pies at all but "really simple cakes, made in two or three layers with a cream or custard filling." Well, Mrs. Webster's cream pie is a sure enough pie, with a filling made of five eggs, a pint of "sweet thick cream," sugar, seeded raisins, nutmeg, and a bit of salt. Beard's cream pie filling has seven tablespoons of flour, two eggs, and milk or light cream—"for a rich flavor, use part milk and part evaporated milk"—and he suggests topping it with "gelatinized whipped cream."

Mrs. Webster's Connecticut Thanksgiving Chicken Pie is worth a look:

> In sufficient water to prevent burning, stew old or young fowls, jointed, all but tender enough for the table. Pour all into a dish, and season with salt and pepper to the taste. When about cold, place the parts in your pudding dish, lined with a thin common paste, adding about half a pound of butter to three pounds of fowl, in alternate layers. Take more of the paste; roll it *nine times*, studding it each time with butter (it must be very rich;) be careful to roll out, each time, from you, and to roll up towards you, leav-

ing it, at least, an inch thick. Add the upper crust; cut a lip in it; and ornament it with some of the reserved paste, having first lightly sprinkled the chickens with flour, after almost filling the dish with the liquor in which the chickens were stewed. Pin tight around the rim of the dish a cloth bandage, to prevent the escape of the juices; and bake from an hour to an hour and a half, in a quick oven. If the top burns, lay a paper over it.

One more interesting development was taking place. Most cookbook writers up to and including Miss Leslie measured dry ingredients by weight rather than volume, in baking. Mrs. Webster now announces, "For most preparations, it is easier to measure than to weigh." But it is not as accurate, dear lady. Flours and for that matter many other ingredients vary enormously in bulk. As if to emphasize the danger, Mrs. Webster's table of measures contains a blooper that may have caused many a tear: "Butter, when soft—one pound is one quart." It is, of course, one pint, and anybody who finds measuring butter in a cup easier than weighing it is a ninny.

Mrs. Webster was, at best, what one would describe as a good plain cook and yet she, too, reflects some of the superior virtues of her time. On making coffee, for instance, she states firmly, "Old Java and Mocha are the best kinds." It should be roasted "till the color of chestnuts...the day it is to be used....Do not let it boil; the perfume will be lost by evaporation. Do not make the coffee in a tin vessel. Make it in China, delft-ware, or in silver." Compare her directions with those in any gourmet cookbook today....

We have remarked earlier the sensual and knowledgeable approach to flour and bread and beans in Mary Cornelius's *The Young Housekeeper's Friend* (1845). The book is interesting on other counts as well. Her *Directions Respecting Fish* are to the point: "Purchase those which have just been caught. Of this you can judge by their being hard under the pressure of the finger. *Fish lose their best flavor soon, and a few hours make a wide difference in the taste of some sorts.*" (Our emphasis.) In the 1871 edition Mrs. Cornelius gives this fine recipe for Marblehead Chowder:

> Fry three or four slices of salt pork, soak a dozen hard crackers, cut up four or five onions. When the pork is fried brown take it out, and lay in half of the crackers, and half the onions. Cut up the cod, and lay the pieces next, then the rest of the crackers and onions, season it with pepper and salt, pour boiling water enough into the kettle to cover the whole. Let it stew moderately an hour.
>
> The fish should be fresh from the water. Cod's heads and sound bones make the richest chowder.

Another chowder of hers, which also appears in the earlier edition, ends thus: "Some people add a cup of milk just before it is served." This is the first mention we have come across of a milk chowder.

Chowders seem so thoroughly American that it is worthwhile to look backward for a moment. Mrs. Randolph, in *The Virginia Housewife*, published a recipe for "Chowder, a sea dish":

> Take any kind of firm fish, cut it in pieces six inches long, sprinkle salt and pepper over each piece, cover the bottom of a small Dutch oven with slices of salt pork about half boiled, lay in the fish, strewing a little chopped onion between; cover with crackers that have been soaked soft in milk, pour over it two gills [1 cup] of white wine, and two of water; put on the top of the oven, and stew it gently about an hour; take it out carefully, and lay it in a deep dish; thicken the gravy with a little flour and a spoonful of butter [kneaded together], add some chopped parsley, boil it a few minutes, and pour it over the fish—serve it up hot.

At first glance, the white wine and *beurre manié* might suggest a derivation from the French *chaudrée*. That is not to be ruled out; certainly the word chowder also derives from *chaudron*, or cauldron. However, recipes for chowder were fairly common in English cookbooks; here is one from *The Art of Cookery* by Hannah Glasse (1789 edition):

To make Chouder, a Sea Dish

Take a belly piece of pickled pork, slice off the fatter parts, and lay them at the bottom of the kettle, strew over it onions, and such sweet herbs as you can procure, take a middling large cod, bone and slice it, as for crimping, pepper, salt, all-spice, and flour it a little, make a layer with part of the slices, upon that a slight layer of pork again, and on that a layer of biscuit and so on, pursuing the like rule, until the kettle is filled to about four inches cover it with a nice paste, pour in about a pint of water, lute down the cover of the kettle, and let the top be supplied with live wood embers. Keep it over a slow fire about four hours.

What is likely, is that the New England chowder derived directly from the primitive "sea dish" rather than the fancied-up versions. The French and English had fished for cod for centuries and the New Englanders took to it immediately.

By way of curiosity, we give a recipe that appears in the Albany edition (1796) of *American Cookery* by Amelia Simmons:

Chouder

Take a bass weighing four pounds, boil half an hour; take six slices raw salt pork, fry them till the lard is nearly extracted, one dozen crackers soaked in cold water five minutes; put the bass into the lard, also the pieces of pork and crackers, cover close, and fry for 20 minutes; serve with potatoes, pickles, apple-sauce or mangoes; garnish with green parsley.

The recipe is not only curious but unclear. As it stands it is not a chowder at all in that there is no liquid, but that does not make much sense either because the ingredients are for a classic inland chowder and the method does not follow any known early New England procedure. The book is rife with editing errors; perhaps she intended that the poaching liquid be added and the dish stewed for twenty minutes, rather than fried.

Mrs. Cornelius gives us two recipes for clam chowder, one of which, she says, is made with "long clams":

Fry in a deep kettle two large slices of fat pork. Add three large potatoes, sliced thin, and two quarts of hot water. Boil until the potatoes are not sufficiently done to break; then put in pilot-bread [crackers], half a pint of milk, a piece of butter large as an egg, a little salt and pepper. When it again boils up, add a pint of clams, with their liquor. Boil one or two minutes, and serve.

Just to balance the picture, we should include a clam chowder with tomatoes—anathema to New Englanders but popular in New York. Pierre Blot, a French chef in New York, gave this one in his *Hand-Book of Practical Cookery* (1867):

It is generally admitted that boatmen prepare it better than others, and the receipts we give below came from the most experienced chowder-men of the Harlem River....

Put in a *pot*...some small slices of fat salt pork, enough to line the bottom of it; on that, a layer of potatoes, cut in small pieces; on the potatoes, a layer of chopped onions; on onions, a layer of tomatoes, in slices, or canned tomatoes; on the latter a layer of clams, whole or chopped (they are generally chopped), then a layer of crackers.

Then repeat the process...till the pot is nearly full. Every layer is seasoned with salt and pepper. Other spices are sometimes added according to taste; such as thyme, cloves, bayleaves, and tarragon.

When the whole is in, cover with water, set on a
slow fire, and when nearly done, stir gently, finish
cooking, and serve....

By mid-century, the trickle of new cookbooks had
become a stream. Most of those published in the first
half of the century did not survive much beyond the
1860s, although they were shamelessly cannibalized by
the new wave of authors. Mrs. Randolph suffered particularly from this plagiarism; for example, her recipe
for Hare or Rabbit Soup turns up word for word in
Mrs. Porter's New Southern Cookery Book (1871), without credit, of course.

The reason for the apparent need for new cookbooks
was the revolution taking place in our foodstuffs and
technology—notably, the introduction of steel-rolled flour
and the generalization of the newfangled kitchen range.
Neither development aided the cause of gastronomy—
on the contrary—but the cast-iron stove was unquestion-
ably a real improvement in working conditions for
women.

Before we leave fireplace cookery, a word about the
miracles achieved there for millennia by womankind.
They fashioned a museumful of brilliant contrivances to
ease the back and control the heat. Basic was the swinging
crane that brought the pot near to or farther from the
fire. In *Grandmother in the Kitchen* (1965), Helen Lyon
Adamson describes one ingenious device she says she
found in an (unfortunately unidentified) eighteenth-century source:

Roasting Meat on a String

Drive a peg into the mantel directly over the center
of the fire. Tie to this one end of a stout worsted
string. Truss the thing to be roasted and fasten it
in the middle of the string; tie a stone at the other
end to hold it down. Depending on the fire, hang the
roast near or away from blaze. Set it turning slowly

by twisting the string as taut as the catgut on a fiddle; the meat will turn as the string unwinds and then re-winds under its own momentum. The string must be twisted when it runs down (about 5 minutes) and it is work that any child can be set to do and work he will enjoy. In roasting meat this way, it is well to up-end it when half done so that the juice does not gather in one end. Place a dripping-pan under the roast and, before you start, rub the roast with fat and sprinkle it with flour or cornmeal. Baste from the drippings in the pan.

To this day, great numbers of women around the world cook beautiful food over open fires. At an auberge in the hills of Quercy, in France, where there was no stove, we once partook of an eight-course feast that no French restaurant in America could duplicate. We recall espe-cially a fragrant omelet of truffles, cooked in a long-handled skillet over a fire of vine cuttings. In the moun-tains of Corsica, people still hang hams and sausages from the rafters, where they gradually acquire from the fireplace the taste and texture that only these ancient methods obtain. Where the stove has come, people tend to stop smoking meats.

The new iron oven, while satisfactory for many purposes, did not bake bread and pastries nearly so well as the old brick ovens. Saddest of all was the virtual disappearance of roasted and broiled meats. Ideally, meat and birds should be roasted on the spit. What we call roasting today used to be more properly called baking. Mary Randolph (*Virginia Housewife*, 1824) says in her recipe for roast turkey to "spit it, and lay it down a good distance from the fire, which should be clear and brisk ...if it be of a middle size, it will require one hour and a quarter to roast." (The turkey was, if anything, larger then than now; we may safely assume that it was 12 to 15 pounds.) By the time we get to Fannie Farmer, it is baked for three hours and she pours 2½ cups boiling water into the pan, which is not our idea of roasting. Julia Child, also, gives a true home economist's recipe in

From Julia Child's Kitchen (1975): bake a 12- to 16-pound turkey for 3½ to 4½ hours at 325°F with an additional margin of 30 minutes! (She also claims that frozen turkey is "delicious.")

Lacking a fireplace, one of our main preoccupations has been to bake a turkey so that the flavor and texture approach that of a roasted bird as nearly as possible. We had occasion to print our Thanksgiving turkey recipe in *The Times.** The principle is to roast the bird at a high temperature for a relatively short time; we have yet to roast a 16- to 18-pound turkey more than two hours. Readers wrote in to say that they tried this "unorthodox" method with "trepidation"; they all pretty much said they would never again roast a turkey the "old" way. But the high-temperature way is the "old" way and, for that matter, the French way.

What it lost in subtle aroma and flavor, the stove gained in ease of temperature control. But along with these developments, as noted, came the chemical leavenings, and the craving for sweetness. The new ovens were great for cakes, and women were baking them like mad —big, sweet, fluffy ones with gooey frostings—and they wanted new recipes.

These changes did not come overnight, but the pace was remarkable. Women leaders, who were active in campaigns for abolition of slavery, for women's rights, for education, and for child-labor laws, were doubtless persuaded that all change was progress, especially if it seemed to cut corners in the kitchen. Alas, they were deceived; the overwhelming majority of women remained as enslaved to their households as before, but their families ate worse.

Interesting evidence came in the form of a new genre of cookbook: the collection of favorite recipes of local ladies, often published for charitable purposes. They lack the cohesiveness of a work by a single serious cook, but in some ways they are more revealing of how people

* See Appendix.

cooked. Among the best-known of the period are *The Kansas Home Cook-Book* (Leavenworth, 1874), *Housekeeping in Old Virginia* (Louisville, 1879), and *Buckeye Cookery* (Minneapolis, 1880). The Kansas and Minnesota books are hardly regional; the number of oyster and clam recipes is astonishing. The sodden macaroni baked with floury white sauce and cheese was spreading, but perhaps the cheese was better. Sweet pickles now outnumber sour, and tomato ketchup now calls for a pound of sugar to a peck of tomatoes. Salad dressings are mostly sweet. Desserts, especially layer cakes, occupy an inordinate space.

While some of the debasing influences were at work in Old Virginia as well, it produced the best of the three books; cooks there had a great heritage and tended to be more conservative. There is a splendid Sauce for Cod's Head that calls for the meat of a freshly boiled lobster pulled in bits, ½ lb. drawn butter, 1 spoonful walnut ketchup, 1 slice lemon, 1 or 2 slices of horseradish, a little pounded mace, salt, and cayenne pepper, all heated together, with the lemon and horseradish nicely taken out before serving. It is signed Mrs. R— and is lifted, virtually word for word, from Mrs. Randolph's recipe of 1824. Many of her other recipes appear under other names. Mrs. Tyree, of Lynchburg, advises that "Shoat (which I must explain to the uninitiated is a term applied in the South to a young pig past the age when it may be cooked whole) should be kept up and fattened on buttermilk, several weeks before being killed, as this makes the flesh extremely delicate."

North and South, however, still cared about coffee, which had to be lovingly blended, roasted, and freshly ground. "Be particular and not allow the coffee to boil," writes Mrs. Sarah E. Jacobus of Kansas, "as this destroys the peculiar aroma which is the charm of a good cup of coffee."

What is important about these books is that they reflect what Americans thought was good eating a century ago. For comparison, consider the cookbook prepared by the Republican National Committee for the 1972 campaign, with recipes contributed by members of Congress. The reader can consult these in the Appendix; we haven't the stomach for them here.

8

Fannie

All civilized nations cook their food, to improve its taste and digestibility. The degree of civilization is often measured by the cuisine.

Opening of Mary Lincoln's Boston Cook Book (*1883*)

Food is anything which nourishes the body Thirteen elements enter into the composition of the body: oxygen, 62½%; carbon, 21½%; hydrogen, 10%; nitrogen, 3%.... The thirteen elements named are formed into chemical compounds by the vegetable and animal kingdoms to support the highest order of being, man.

Opening of Fannie Farmer's Boston Cooking-School Cook Book (*1896*)

THE ADVENT OF Fannie Merritt Farmer was an historic watershed. Before her, women wrote of cooking with love; she made it a laboratory exercise. She embodied, if

that is not too earthy a word, all the major ills of twentieth-century culinary teaching. She was the maiden aunt
of home economics.

Miss Farmer is often thought to be the founder of the
Boston Cooking School. In fact, she *studied* there, was
graduated in 1889, immediately began to teach, became its
principal in 1891, and published a new textbook for it in
1896, which became the bible of American kitchens. She
may have been the first person who learned cooking in a
school and promptly began to teach it to others. This became standard American practice.

The Boston Cooking School had a solid foundation. Its
first principal, Mary Lincoln (1879–1885), and a co-
founder, Maria Parloa, were excellent cooks. Mrs. Lincoln's *Boston Cook Book* (1883) and *Miss Parloa's Kitchen
Companion* (1889) were influential in their day but are
now virtually forgotten. A pity. We shall try to remedy
this by giving them a major share of the space in comparing them with Miss Farmer's work, which is unfortunately
widely available. They are also more fun. They were almost the last sensualists among authors of major American
cookbooks.

Mrs. Lincoln was one of the last of a long line of
women writers who learned cooking from their mothers.
In an earlier chapter, we quoted her warning about the
overuse of baking powders, and her concession to the use
of a little sugar in bread to make up for the deterioration
of flour. She is much better on kitchen techniques:

> It requires practice to make puff paste well; and as
> there are so many other dishes more easily made and
> vastly more important, it is better not to waste time
> and strength on it. Let your ambition as a house-
> keeper soar higher than perfection in making puff
> paste. But those who *will* have it may observe the
> following directions.

They are much the best directions we have read. Most
writers adequately describe the technique of producing a

sheet consisting of hundreds of alternating layers of dough and butter, but they neglect to explain a secret for success: "The number of folds or layers of butter and paste makes the paste flaky, *but the amount of air in it makes it rise and puff in baking.*" (Our emphasis.) That is the reason for the old-fashioned advice to roll lightly and always *away* from the body; a back-and-forth motion is more likely to force out the air.

Mrs. Lincoln was similarly perceptive about whipping cream. Rich cream "should be diluted and well mixed with an equal quantity of milk." *Eheu, fugaces.* As Beard correctly notes, even "heavy" cream today will hardly whip; he recommends the electric mixer. We prefer a whisk. Mrs. Lincoln favors a whip (paddle) churn as giving a better consistency than the newfangled egg beater.

To a modern reader, Mrs. Lincoln is remarkable for her honesty and her respect for the work of other craftsmen. She gives the sources for scores of her recipes; this scruple was never widely held but it virtually disappeared from American food writing with the arrival of Miss Farmer. Some of Mrs. Lincoln's recipes were already very old, and because they reflect our New England culinary heritage, we will reprint some of them here.

Forefathers' Dinner

Succotash is the great dish in Plymouth at every celebration of Forefathers' Day, December 22. Tradition says it has been made in that town ever since the Pilgrims raised their first corn and beans, and it is supposed they learned to make it from the Indians.

Strangers are rather shy of this peculiar mixture; but it is a favorite dish with the natives, and to this day is made by some families many times through the winter season. Although the dish has never been made by the writer, it has been tested by her in that ancient town many times, and the excellence of the following receipt is unquestionable. It is given in the name of *Mrs. Barnabas Churchill*, of Plymouth, a lady who has made it for fifty years after the manner handed down through many generations.

One quart of large white beans (not the pea beans); *six quarts of hulled corn*—the smutty white Southern corn; *six* to *eight pounds of corned beef*, from the second cut of the rattle rand; *one pound* of *salt pork*, fat and lean; *chicken* weighing from *four* to *six pounds*; *one large white French turnip*; *eight* or *ten* medium-sized *potatoes*. Wash the beans, and soak over night in cold water. In the morning put them on in cold soft water. When boiling, change the water, and simmer until soft enough to mash to a pulp and the water is nearly all absorbed. Wash the salt pork and the corned beef, which should be corned only three or four days. Put them on about eight o'clock, in cold water, in a very large kettle, and skim as they begin to boil. Clean, and truss the chicken as for boiling, and put it with the meat about an hour and a quarter before dinner time. Allow a longer time if a fowl be used and keep plenty of water in the kettle. Two hours before dinner time, put the beans, mashed to a pulp, and then hulled corn into another kettle, with some of the fat from the meat in the bottom to keep them from sticking. Take out enough liquor from the meat to cover the corn and beans, and let them simmer where they will not burn. Stir often, and add more liquor if needed. The mixture should be like a thick soup, and the beans should absorb all the liquor, yet it must not be too dry.

Pare, and cut the turnip into inch slices; add it about eleven o'clock, and the potatoes (pared) half an hour later. Take up the chicken as soon as tender, that it may be served whole. Serve the beef and pork together, the chicken, turnip, and potatoes each on separate dishes, and the beans and corn in a tureen. The meat usually salts the mixture sufficiently, and no other seasoning is necessary. Save the water left from the meat, to use in warming the corn and beans the next day, serving the meat cold. This will keep several days in cold weather; and like many other dishes, it is better the oftener it is warmed over, so there is no objection to making a large quantity.

The white Southern corn is considered the only kind
suitable for this ancient dinner.

Notes: We suggest white kidney beans or cannelini.
Rattle is an old term for shank or brisket, and *rand* is a
dialect word for a long piece of flesh. Clearly, the dish is
a blending of Indian and other influences, but pure Yankee
withal, in that it had been made since early Plymouth
times.

Mrs. Churchill is a frequent contributor to the Lincoln
book. Here is her recipe for Indian Meal Pudding:

Rub a tablespoonful of butter round the bottom and
sides of a smooth iron kettle,—granite or porcelain
will do; when melted, add *half a cup* of *boiling water*.
This will prevent the milk from burning. Add *one
quart* of *milk*. Let it boil up, and almost over the kettle; then sift in *one pint* of *fine yellow granulated corn
meal*, sifting with the left hand, and holding the meal
high, that every grain may be thoroughly scalded.
Stir constantly; add *half a teaspoonful* of *salt*, and set
away till cold. Then add *half a pint* of *New Orleans
molasses* and *one quart* of *cold milk*. Put it into a
well-buttered deep pudding-dish, cover with a plate,
and bake very slowly ten or twelve hours. Put it in
a "Saturday afternoon oven" where the fire will keep
low nearly all night. Let it remain over night, and
serve for Sunday breakfast.

Mrs. Lincoln suggests adding a teaspoonful of mustard
with one-quarter cup of molasses to a mess of baked
beans, explaining, "The mustard gives the beans a delicious
flavor, and also renders them more wholesome." She goes
on to say: "Much of the excellence of baked beans depends upon the bean pot. It should be earthen, with a
narrow mouth and bulging sides. This shape is seldom
found outside of New England, and is said to have been
modeled after the Assyrian pots.... Many a New England
bean-pot has been carried to the extreme South and West,
that people there might have 'baked beans' in perfection."

Mrs. Poor, another of Mrs. Lincoln's faithful contributors, gave this recipe:

An Old-fashioned Boiled Dinner

Notwithstanding that this dish has fallen into ill-repute with many people, it *may* be prepared so as to be both palatable and nutritious for those who exercise freely. It is more suitable for cold seasons. The most healthful and economical way, though perhaps not the old-fashioned way, is to boil the beef the day before.

Four pounds of *corned beef, two* or *three beets, a small cabbage, two small carrots, one small white French turnip, six* or *eight potatoes* of *uniform size,* and *one small crooked-neck squash.*

Wash and soak the corned beef in cold water, and put it on to boil in fresh cold water; skim, and simmer until tender, but not long enough for it to fall to pieces. Let it cool in the liquor in which it was boiled. Put it into a flat shallow dish, cover it with a board, and press it. Remove all the fat from the meat liquor, and save it to clarify for shortening. Save the meat liquor, but do not let it stand in an iron kettle or tin pan. Boil the beets the day before, also, and cover them with vinegar. The next day prepare the vegetables. Wash them all, scrape the carrots, and cut the cabbage into quarters; pare the turnip and squash, and cut into three-quarter-inch slices, and pare the potatoes. Put the meat liquor on to boil about two hours before dinner time; when boiling, put in the carrots, afterward the cabbage and turnip, and half an hour before dinner add the squash and potatoes. When tender, take the vegetables up carefully; drain the water from the cabbage by pressing it in a colander. Slice the carrots. Put the cold meat in the centre of a large dish, and serve the carrots, turnips, and potatoes round the edge, with the squash, cabbage, and pickled beets in separate dishes; or serve each vegetable in a dish by itself. This may all be done the same day if the meat be put on to boil very early, removed as soon as tender, the fat taken off, and the vegetables added to the boiling meat liquor, beginning with those which require the longest time to cook. This will depend very much upon their freshness. But whichever way the dish is prepared, boil the beets alone, remove the meat and fat before adding the vegetables, and serve each as whole and daintily as possible. The next morning use what remains of the vegetables as a vegetable hash.

It is interesting to note the diffidence with which Mrs. Poor introduced this recipe; it explains why these old dishes so rarely appeared in printed cookbooks. Yet it is a magnificent dish. Mrs. Poor was clearly an excellent cook who took pains to tell exactly how *she* made it, but felt compelled to indicate that it was not always made that carefully.

Here is another of her recipes:

Bean Porridge

Five pounds of *corned beef*, not too salt, or *four pounds* of *beef* and *one* of *salt pork*; *one pint* of dry *white beans*, *four tablespoons* of *corn meal*, *pepper* and *salt* to taste, *one pint* of *hulled corn*. Soak the beans over night. In the morning parboil in fresh water with a pinch of *soda* till soft. Put the corned beef and pork in cold water, skim carefully, and simmer four or five hours, or till tender. Take out, and cut into two-inch pieces, and remove the bone and gristle; also the fat from the liquor. Put the meat and beans into the meat liquor, and simmer very slowly three or four hours, or till most of the beans are broken. Half an hour before serving stir in the meal, first wetting it in cold water to a smooth paste. The meal should thicken the porridge to about the consistency of a thick soup. The meat should be cooked till it falls apart. Season to taste with *salt* and *pepper*. Add the hulled corn, and when hot serve with brown bread. Sometimes the vegetables usually served with a boiled dinner are cooked with the meat, then removed, and the beans cooked as above, in the meat liquor.

"This old-fashioned and very nutritious dish was one of the chief articles of winter food at my grandmother's farm in Northern New Hampshire eighty years ago. When cooked, it was poured into bowls or basins holding from a pint to two quarts. A nice tow string was laid in a loop over the edge, and the porridge was placed where it would freeze. By holding the dish in hot water it would cause the porridge to slip out; then it was hung up by the loops in the 'buttery,' and was considered 'best when nine days old.' At early dawn the 'men folks' who went into the forest 'chopping' would take the skillet, or a little three-legged iron kettle, some large slices of 'rye and Indian' bread in their pockets to keep it from freezing. The porridge was hung, wrapped in a clean towel, upon the sled stakes. Their spoons were made of wood. The hay that lay on the floor of the ox sled was of use to keep their feet warm, and given to the oxen for 'bait' at noon. When it was twelve o'clock 'by the sun,' they kindled a fire by the aid of a 'tinder box,' warmed their porridge, and with their brown bread enjoyed this strong food as no modern epicure can his costly French dishes."

It is to be remarked that this recipe was given to Mrs. Lincoln prior to 1883, so we are being permitted a glimpse of daily life around 1800, and there is every reason to believe that the dish is much older. The pinch of soda is interesting; it means that the water in northern New Hampshire was hard. (One of the bits of lore that an assiduous reader of old cookbooks learns is that dried peas and beans must be cooked in soft water; old French books specify river or fountain water, *not* well water. On the other hand, *fresh* peas and beans are to be cooked in hard water; it preserves color and texture better.)

It is interesting also that Mrs. Poor felt obliged to put in quotation marks the word "Indian" when referring to cornmeal. As noted, while the early settlers learned a

great deal from the Indians—cornmeal, parched corn, hoecake, and much more—all the so-called Indian pudding
and bread recipes we know were clearly adaptations of
English recipes using Indian meal. An example is Maria
Parloa's recipe for Indian Waffles in *The Kitchen Companion* (1887).

Maria Parloa was an interesting writer who reportedly
studied with Pierre Blot in New York, headed her own
cooking school there, and wrote several books before
helping to found the Boston Cooking School. She must
have influenced a whole generation of cooks and cookbook writers, but she seems to be totally forgotten today.

She seems to have had a better knowledge of French
cuisine than do many of our modern "gourmet" cooks.
She understood the role of the Seville orange in her sauce
for duck; if it is unavailable, she says, grapefruit might be
tried because "it has a little of the peculiar bitter flavor
that makes the Seville orange desirable." Of the new
bleached asparagus she says, "it is an unfortunate fashion,
for the vegetable does not compare in flavor or tenderness
with the old-fashioned green asparagus." Like Jefferson
seventy-five years earlier, Miss Parloa offers a market list
that includes all the common vegetables and herbs, and
many that may be hard to find in a friendly neighborhood
supermarket today: salsify, *kohl-rabi*, *egg-plant*, okra, cel-
eriac, shallots, rocamboles, Spanish onions, escarole, Monk's
beard (endive), garden and water cress, sorrel, lamb's lettuce or corn salad, chervil, borage, and tarragon.

But she is not a lifted-pinky gourmet. She is not above
giving us an admirable recipe for a plebeian Yankee dish,
such as this one:

A Salt-fish Dinner

Outside New England a salt-fish dinner is hardly
known, and even in that section it is rarely served in
such perfection in the interior as it is in the towns
bordering on the coast. To the uninitiated it may

seem to be a very insignificant meal; but to those who know what it really is, few dinners are more attractive. The preparation of a salt-fish dinner calls for care and skill. The materials should be of the very best. Codfish is the only suitable fish to use, and dunfish is better than white; the process of curing the former being preferable to that of curing white fish, and the result being a darker and richer fish.... The fish never should be cut before cooking.

Preparation of the Fish

A genuine salt-fish dinner is composed of a whole salt cod, beets, carrots, onions, potatoes, salt pork, butter, hard-boiled eggs, flour, salt, and pepper. The night before the dinner is to be served, wash the fish carefully.... Put the fish into a large pan, skin side up; and soak it over night in sufficient water to cover it.

The next day place the fish, skin side up, in a fish-kettle or in a large pan. Place on the fire where the water will heat slowly to the boiling-point without actually boiling; then set back where it will keep hot for five or six hours. If care be taken not to let the fish boil, it will break into soft, rich, gelatinous flakes when served; but if it be boiled, it will be dry, thready, and hard.

Miss Parloa goes on to describe in great detail the cooking of each vegetable, and the slow frying of the cubes of salt pork until they become brown and crisp. Now here is her recipe for the obligatory egg sauce that goes with it:

Egg sauce is made by beating together half a cupful of butter and a table-spoonful of flour; adding half a pint of boiling water; setting the saucepan on the fire, and stirring until the sauce begins to boil; immediately drawing the saucepan back, and adding half a tea-spoonful of salt and half a salt-spoonful of white pepper; chopping two hard-boiled eggs rather fine,— doing it with a plated knife or spoon,—and adding them to the mixture already prepared.

These homey dishes are part of our heritage, yet recipes for them are surprisingly rare. Miss Parloa's instructions for boiling the salt cod are most perceptive, and characteristic of her entire repertory. In preparing the vegetables, she says, "Beets may be boiled without washing. When they are washed, the little roots are apt to be broken, and the juices escape. This impoverishes the vegetables and spoils the color." It is a splendid dish, lovingly and intelligently presented. While the egg sauce, purely English in origin, cannot be compared to the *aiolli*, the dish stands up in its own way to the great boiled salt cod dinner of Provence, which is also called *aiolli* because of the obligatory accompaniment of that redolent amalgam of garlic and fruity olive oil.

Mrs. Lincoln and Miss Parloa, then, were good cooks, who with some embarrassment yielded to the decline in produce and standards of their time. With Fannie Farmer, embarrassment disappears, and with it the love of food.

We began this chapter with the opening lines of the Lincoln and the Farmer textbooks. Mrs. Lincoln puts taste first, Miss Farmer chemical composition. (All of our schools of home economics do the same today.) Miss Farmer's first recipe tells how to detect the presence of starch ($C_6H_{10}O_5$) by the addition of a weak solution of iodine; it will turn "an intense blue." Scrumptious.

As noted, Miss Farmer's book early became, and still remains, the bible of the American kitchen; now in its twelfth edition, it has sold more than three million copies.

A certain mythology has grown up around it. In the current paperback edition, for example, it is claimed that she "invented" precise measurements of ingredients by volume rather than by weight. This would be a dubious honor, if it were true.

As early as 1845, Mrs. Webster was counseling her readers to measure by volume, and we learn from her chart that "sixteen Spoonfuls are half a pint." Mrs. Lincoln, in her *Boston Cook Book* (1883), spent three and a half pages on how to measure accurately. "An *even* or *scant teaspoonful* means the spoon filled lightly, and levelled off with a knife." The measuring cup, we learn, had been accepted for decades as containing one-half pint, and was marked to show one-quarter and one-third cups. She maintained that, with her table of measures, "the cup and spoon may be used as accurately as the scales." So while Miss Farmer did ban forever the rounded measure and "butter the size of an egg," (an old-standby direction, translated by Mrs. Lincoln as one-quarter cupful or two ounces), she introduced nothing new.

We repeat that, where accuracy is necessary, weight is more precise than volume. Any real cook knows that eggs are not identical, that flours vary astonishingly, that baking powders are not all alike, and that even salt varies in saltiness; blind dependence on accurate measurements is naïve. Finally, one must depend on feel and taste. This Miss Farmer did not allow; it was, perhaps, too sensual.

Her attitude became the law for American food editing. When the singer Pearl Bailey wrote an earthy, loving cookbook about the art her mother had taught her, the question of measurements arose. "Can you measure life?" she retorted. "How can I tell you—I don't know how much you want to put in." The trouble is that many people no longer know how much they themselves want. A woman in a New York publishing house complained, "I never know what they mean when they say, 'season to taste.'"

While Mrs. Lincoln attributed many of her recipes to the donors, including Miss Parloa, "Mrs. Towne's Matilda," "an unknown friend," and so on, the only source credited in Miss Farmer is an unidentified "French Chef," to whom she assigns several exotic recipes such as mulligatawny soup. Clearly, she did not create hundreds of recipes out of the blue. She learned cooking from Mrs. Lincoln's book (the textbook at the Boston Cooking School at the time), but did not acknowledge it in any way. Now, recipes that have many sources need not be attributed; Miss Fannie, however, exaggerated in this regard. She was by no means the first to appropriate other people's recipes as her own, but as the patron saint of American housewives she put her seal of approval on it, and contributed to the moral climate of the cookbook world today, where plagiarism is the norm. Among other things, this practice cuts us off from the past, so charmingly revealed by some of the Lincoln recipes quoted earlier.

We have mentioned how Miss Farmer hyped up her breads with ever-increasing amounts of sugar. She poured it on with a heavy hand in whatever she was doing. Take salad dressings: In the original 1896 edition, there are thirteen recipes, of which ten have sugar—including the mayonnaise. By the 1914 edition, the last one that Miss Farmer edited, fourteen out of seventeen salad recipes have sugar, and the amounts have increased. She has, for example, added sugar to her tomato aspic. By the 1965 edition, we have this horror:

> For a special variation, put in a jar ½ cup [commercial] mayonnaise, ½ cup lemon juice and ¼ cup sugar (more seasonings if you like) and shake well.

This American fixation on sweet salads, so well documented in the succeeding editions of Fannie Farmer, was, shall we say, firmly set by the invention of Jell-O in 1897, a fitting close to the late nineteenth century with its steady decline of taste. Sugary, gummy messes, chock full of synthetic flavors and colors, blanketed the country.

Fruit salads, each less believable than the preceding one, dominated the salad section of the 1914 *Boston Cooking-School Cook Book*. Lemon Jell-O now was the popular substitute for aspic. There is a *Brazilian Salad* that begins, "Remove skin and seeds from white grapes and cut in halves lengthwise," and goes on with pineapple, apples, celery, Brazil nuts (whence the name of the dish), lemon juice, and a sweet mayonnaise. Another recipe pours the syrup from a can of peaches into the Jell-O....

Miss Farmer had already, in 1896, given us this gem:

> Remove one section of skin from each of four bananas. Take out fruit, scrape, and cut fruit from one banana in thin slices, fruit from other three bananas in one-half inch cubes. Marinate cubes with French Dressing. Refill skins and garnish each with slices of banana. Stack around a mound of lettuce leaves.

It must have made a charming display.

That is pure women's-magazine gourmet cookery. Insane "fancy" combinations of ingredients without regard to balance of taste and texture are commonplace now; a favorite of ours is a published recipe for a hamburger with chopped peanuts and bananas, including the instruction: "Mash bananas with mustard to taste." But it was unusual in Miss Farmer's time.

It is clear that the dour spinster had at least one vice: a craving for sugar. This may have been the secret of her success, which is otherwise inexplicable. Americans were eating baked goods of poor flour and were turning to sugar, and Miss Farmer was there to give it to them. In her 1914 edition there are five recipes involving marshmallows; soon, they would be added to salads....

Her sauces were so full of flour they could nearly stand up alone—her *Bordelaise Sauce* calls for 3½ tablespoons of flour for 1 cup of stock. She calls for eight minutes of simmering in this recipe, an unprecedented concession to finesse (Escoffier calls for some 4½ hours, minimum, and uses less than one tablespoon of flour). Her other sauces call for no simmering whatsoever, even the *béchamel*. The lady was a very poor cook, and singlehandedly was responsible for a great deal of what is wrong with modern American cooking. It is a mystery how James Beard was able to say for the jacket of the facsimile 1896 edition: "Fannie Farmer remains one of our gastronomic deities!

She was equally at home with the traditions of American cooking and the intricacies of French cuisine."

Before we leave the nineteenth century, let us take a brief look at the history of sauces in America. On the frontier, of course, the sharpest sauce was a good appetite; the foods were good, in the main, but there was neither time nor ingredients for such refinements. The well-to-do colonists, as noted, relied on English cookbooks from the golden age of English cookery. The sauces were most often formed in the cooking process, as in fricassees and stews. The older ones were not thickened at all, but simply served with sippets (dry-toasted bread) to sop up the broth. Occasionally, bread and sippets were allowed to soak and simmer imperceptibly until they were integrated into the sauce—what the French call *mitonner*, a process still used in country soups.

Elegant kitchens used egg yolks, butter, and cream for liaison of sauces; this was still most often recommended by Hannah Glasse as late as 1805. Amelia Simmons (1796) treated sauces only in passing. Water fowl requires onion sauce, she says. This would be a sort of *soubise*: onions cooked until soft, seasoned, pureed, and mixed with thick cream. Miss Simmons suggests that a fowl have "a pint of stewed oysters, well buttered and peppered."

Gravy meant the natural meat juices and was often simply "buttered and a spoonful of catsup added." Until the second half of the nineteenth century, ketchup usually meant a pickle of mushrooms, oysters, or walnuts. Mrs. Randolph gave a recipe for tomato ketchup in 1824 and it quickly became popular, but it was specified as such. A sophisticated and elegant cook, Mrs. Randolph most frequently called for a sauce of melted butter and parsley. Occasionally, she added a spoonful of mushroom ketchup. Sometimes she used butter or yolks to thicken a sauce, but the butter would likely be first rolled in flour—2 teaspoons of flour to ¼ pound of butter—a sort of *beurre manié*. The proportion of flour to butter is about one-

fourth the classic formula (equal amounts by volume), so
it can be seen that butter was the main liaison.

Miss Leslie's classic *Directions for Cookery* (1837) devotes an entire chapter to sauces. Most of them have no
flour whatsoever but a few call for *beurre manié*. There
is a section on Store Fish Sauces, meaning sauces that keep
well. Here is an interesting one:

General Sauce

Chop six shalots or small onions, a clove of garlic,
two peach leaves, a few sprigs of lemon-thyme and
of sweet basil, and a few bits of fresh orange-peel.
Bruise in a mortar a quarter of an ounce of mace, and
half an ounce of long pepper. Mix two ounces of salt,
a jill [½ cup] of claret, the juice of two lemons, and
a pint of Madeira. Put the whole of these ingredients
together in a stone jar, very closely covered. Let it
stand all night over embers by the side of the fire. In
the morning pour off the liquid quickly and carefully
from the lees or settlings, strain it and put it into small
bottles, dipping the cork in melted rosin.

This sauce is intended to flavour melted butter or
gravy for every sort of fish and meat.

It was a common practice to add such homemade sauces
to melted butter; if they were well made and used with
discretion they must have been excellent. At least, they
had character; the butter gave richness and texture, and
there was an interesting tang and aroma from the better
of those "Store" sauces.

What came later had all the charm of library paste.
White sauce, or *béchamel*, became the rage. It was believed to be very French. Indeed, the quality of French
sauces also declined in the nineteenth century, but the
French would never have recognized the *béchamel* and
Espagnole recipes that began to appear in American cookbooks, and clog them to this day.

From the beginning, they demonstrated our infantile
desire to achieve dazzling results with no expenditure of

time or effort. We wanted to do "fancy cooking" without learning the techniques required.

In this effort, Fannie Farmer was a trailblazer. Beginning with her, the home economists, nutritionists, and instant chefs pushed aside the cooks, and cookbooks became sets of idiot directions for other noncooks. No longer were taste, texture, freshness of produce lovingly discussed. Nor would technique be sensual, and individual. From now on, things would be measured by the one-eighth teaspoon and the milligram of riboflavin. Welcome to the twentieth century.

Fannie reigned unchallenged until the *Joy of Cooking* by Irma S. Rombauer appeared in 1931. The first edition was privately printed; it was an immediate success and it is claimed to be the best-selling cookbook of all time. The book's prime virtue is its chattiness; Mrs. Rombauer wrote about cooking with enthusiasm if not discernment. Indeed, it is said that she wrote the book in protest against the antiseptic, loveless approach of Fannie Farmer. There are good things in Rombauer; she tells us how to churn butter, how to make cheese, how Janka made strudel, and how the sausages were seasoned at butchering time in their valley. Unfortunately, the book has many of the flaws we have been discussing, such as sugar in the bread recipes (the one for French bread calls for milk, shortening, and 5 teaspoons of sugar for a small batch—the French permit only flour, yeast, salt, and water). There is the usual appalling collection of sweet gelatin salads and dressings.

The 1943 edition devoted eight pages to canned-soup combinations; one of them is for Mongole Soup:

> I should like to sing a paean of praise about this and the following soups made with a basis of pea and tomato. If there is anything better in the hurry-up culinary art I don't know what it is. Rich? Yes, but you may plan to serve simple food afterward. This is worth adding a fraction of a pound to your avoirdupois. Only don't fall in love with it and serve it too often.

The ingredients for this masterpiece of hurry-up culinary art are: 1 can condensed tomato soup, 1 can condensed pea soup, 2 cups top milk, salt, paprika, sherry, and grated cheese.

This recipe does not appear in the 1975 edition but a variation does: Quick Crab or Lobster Mongole. You simply add canned crab or lobster to what is essentially the same mixture as above, with the interesting substitution of *3 tablespoons dry white wine* for the sherry. Nothing could be more "gourmet" than this undiscriminating use of "dry white wine," and no recipe could better illustrate the lack of understanding of basic culinary principles and of plain good taste that prevail in American fancy cooking today.

9

The Recipe Racket

...If all the writers upon Cookery had acknowledged from whence they took their receipts, as I do, they would have acted with more candour by the public. Their vanity to pass for Authors, instead of Compilers, has not added to their reputation.

Mrs. Mary Cole, in The Lady's Complete Guide *(1791), which we hasten to add was brought to our attention by Judith Herman and Marguerite Shalett Herman in* Cornucopia.

A CAREER GIRL confided recently that she had been engaged to write a cookbook. A friend of ours, who was raised in a Protestant school, asked, "Whatever gives you the right to do that?" The author said, "Why not? Everyone does."

And indeed, everyone does. Short of hard-core pornography there is, we think, no branch of publishing more cynical than that concerned with food—so much so that honest writing seems unprofessional to the trade. Not long ago, when one of the authors submitted a requested article to *The New York Times Magazine* on the history of a dish, she was asked to "change the recipes a little bit" so that the two books she had quoted need not be credited. She refused.

From *The Delectable Past* (1964) by Esther B. Aresty	From *The Hellfire Cookbook* (1975) by John Philips Cranwell
MUSTARD SOUP	MUSTARD SOUP TISEL [*sic*]

2 tablespoons butter	3 tablespoons butter
3 tablespoons prepared yellow mustard	3 tablespoons flour
2 tablespoons flour	3½ cups hot chicken stock
2½ cups thoroughly skimmed chicken stock, heated	2½ cups milk
1¼ cups rich milk, heated	½ teaspoon salt
½ teaspoon salt and a dash of white pepper	½ teaspoon white pepper
½ teaspoon onion juice	1 tablespoon grated onion
2 egg yolks	3 egg yolks
2 to 3 tablespoons sweet cream	4 tablespoons heavy cream
	5 tablespoons hot prepared mustard
	24 slices pepperoni (optional)

Melt the butter, stir in the flour and blend smoothly. *Add the hot chicken stock and milk, and whisk until smooth. Add salt, pepper* and onion juice. *Simmer for 10 to 15 minutes. Cool slightly. Combine egg yolks and cream and add to the soup, custard style—that is, temper first with a few spoonfuls of the warm broth.* Last, add the mustard.

Melt the butter and stir in the flour. Blend smooth. *Add the hot chicken stock and milk, and whisk until smooth. Add salt, pepper,* and grated onion. *Simmer for 10 to 15 minutes. Cool slightly. Combine egg yolks and cream and add to the soup, custard style—that is, temper eggs first with a few spoonfuls of the warm broth.* Add the mustard last, and mix it well into the soup before serving.

(Our emphases)

Note: Both recipes purport to be from *Le Viandier* (c. 1375), long credited to one Guillaume Tirel, *dit* Taillevent. Taillevent's *Soupe en Moustarde* (manuscript in Bibliothèque Nationale, Paris) involves eggs fried in deep fat served in a soup of wine, oil, water, and fried onions all simmered together with toast, with mustard added before serving. The recipe could hardly be more different from the one presented by Aresty and Cranwell.

If we may steal the old joke about the Hungarian recipe that begins, "First you steal a chicken...", then the first direction for writing a cookbook is, first you steal a lot of recipes. This goes back a long way. The earliest extant cookbook of the Western world bears the name of one Marcus Gavius Apicius (circa 25 B.C.–30 A.D.). According to Bertrand Guégan, a French scholar, the recipes were apparently collated around 230 A.D. by an unknown cook, and many of them appear to have been lifted from the Greeks.

The earliest known French cookbook, *Le Viandier*, is always credited to Guillaume Tirel, called Taillevent, chef to Charles V and Charles VI. It was thought to have been written around 1375 and at least by the time of François Villon (1431–1463?) the name Taillevent had become a synonym for chef. Unfortunately for the accepted tradition, a rolled parchment called the Sion manuscript turned up some years ago in Switzerland. Paul Aebischer, in the scholarly *Vallesia*, reprints it and says, "What we have here is a *Viandier* by Taillevent before Taillevent." He goes on to present irrefutable proof that it was written about a century before Guillaume Tirel's copy.

An interesting aside on the Taillevent work. The French have always been faintly embarrassed by the actual recipes; they find them bizarre—too many spices. To a Moroccan cook they would not seem strange at all. There certainly is a Saracen aroma. And why not? The Moors had been as far north as Poitiers and were still raiding now and then in the Midi. Also, the lunatic Crusades were a very real memory; the Arabs were still preeminent in medicine and they had controlled the spice trade for centuries; spices were a luxury and therefore *de rigueur* in the kitchens of the king.

Mrs. Mary Cole, in 1791, complained that cookbook plagiarism was much practiced in eighteenth-century England and cited such illustrious borrowers as Hannah Glasse and Elizabeth Raffald. In the nineteenth century, it was rampant. The cannibalization of Eliza Acton's remarkable work, *Modern Cookery for Private Families* (1845), is difficult to believe. A small example: "Mademoiselle Jenny Lind's Soup," carefully credited by Acton to the "great singer's cook" and "obtained through the kindness of a Miss Bremer," becomes in Mrs. Beeton's *Household Management* (1861) *Soup à la Cantatrice*, with the measurements ever so cunningly changed. Mrs. Beeton's work, a tome of over 2100 recipes and hundreds of items of household information, had to have been lifted. She bore four children and died at the age of twenty-eight. It seems doubtful that she had time even to try the recipes.

Elizabeth David discusses why Mrs. Beeton's book (and others such as Cassell's *Dictionary of Cookery*) eclipsed the superior work of Eliza Acton. "The English public had become accustomed to cookery-books put together by syndicates of editors and recipe compilers rather than written as the expression of one author's experience and beliefs. In other words, housewives and cooks did not read cookery books, *they merely looked up recipes.* [Our emphasis.] A book such as Miss Acton's, written as a coherent whole, is essentially one to be read as written, with intelligence and understanding and application." Hear, hear.

Let us turn to America. In *Mrs. Porter's New Southern Cookery Book* (1871) may be found, word for word except for an obvious error in copying, the unattributed recipe for "Hare or Rabbit Soup" from *The Virginia Housewife* (1824) by Mary Randolph. Fannie Farmer, in much the same way as Mrs. Beeton in England, plagiarized and outsold superior books.

American women seem to be so insecure about cooking that they buy only books that bear the seal of approval of a well-known institution. It matters little whether it be the Boston Cooking School, *Good Housekeeping*, *McCall's*, *Time–Life*, or *The New York Times*; it will sell so long as it is spelled out in big fat print on the cover. In contrast, the finest cookbooks of recent years have remained *succès d'estime*. One thinks of Marcella Hazan, whose *Classic Italian Cuisine* never strays far from the food she loves and grew up with in Northern Italy. ("Buy a piece of cheese and grate it," she implores, knowing full well that most of her readers will buy stale, dusty grated cheese that never saw Italy.) Or Diana Kennedy, who spent years of study in Mexico before coming up with what is considered a definitive work, *The Cuisines of Mexico*. Or the remarkable book by Paula Wolfert, *Couscous and Other Good Food from Morocco*, which evokes the wonderfully exciting sounds and smells of the *souk* (market) and the *attarine* (spice stall)—the Eastern fragrances of a highly sophisticated cuisine. Or take Richard Olney's *Simple French Food*, a fascinating book about not so simple French cooking, written by a discriminating cook for intelligent readers. Or take Madeleine Kamman, whose serious work, *The Making of a Cook* (1971), was politely received and had a modest sale while her more recent *Dinner Against the Clock*, which she herself puts down as "good quality trash," was enthusiastically reviewed, won awards, and is selling at a better rate than the first. One can only conclude that cookbook buyers do not really want to learn to cook—they want to look up a fancy recipe, and presto!, dazzle their guests.

Where do the recipes come from? Peg Bracken, who qualified as an authority by the wildfire success of her *I Hate to Cook Book*, writes in *Family Circle* (October 1974) that one of the best sources of recipes is the back of the package "because a manufacturer would have to be awfully dumb to put a bad one there." She added that recipes out of magazines were "exceptionally reliable because the magazine's Home Ec staff is too busy cooking and tasting and experimenting to answer all the bad tempered letters they would get [if they weren't good]... whereas a cookbook writer might have skipped the country long ago."

Publishers, food manufacturers, and the public labor under the misapprehension that home economists and nutritionists are qualified to test and devise recipes. Actually, cooking is not a required subject in colleges that grant such degrees (who, indeed, would teach it?) and where it is taught at all, it is usually a brief optional course in the chemistry of food preparation. Consider the tale of Nikki Goldbeck, holder of a degree in nutrition from Cornell University's Home Ec school, now called the School of Human Ecology—which hasn't used a stove since its cafeteria was replaced by vending machines. Ms. Goldbeck is the young author of several well-intentioned cookbooks aimed at the Granola generation. In one of them, she confesses that on graduation she had been hired to develop "recipes for unflavored gelatin, a product [I] had never even heard of." She had evidently entered the recipe racket thinking that gelatin came in six horrible, sugary synthetic flavors.

A secretary in an advertising agency on Madison Avenue confides that she was ordered to whip up a list of recipes for a client, a cracker manufacturer; she went to the library, copied a dozen recipes, and doubled the amount of cracker meal in each one. And that, Peg Bracken, is where recipes on packages come from.

As for magazine recipes, here is one chosen at random from the same issue of *Family Circle* that carried Bracken's advice: Chocolate Pudding Cream Pie. It's cream cheese, milk, and instant chocolate pudding all gucked together and dumped into one of those horrible store-bought pie crusts. Or one may invite Bracken to savor this lovely recipe from the package of a best-selling plastic chicken heavily promoted on television: 1 chicken, 1 bottle Russian dressing, 1 envelope dehydrated onion soup mix, 1 jar (10-ounce) apricot preserves. *Bon appétit.*

Many of the cookbook authors we know do not really care about food; such people will put out a book with scissors and paste. How could it be otherwise? He (or she, as the case may be) will crib recipes from here and there, changing the amounts ever so slightly, and if he goes so far as to test the recipes himself, he will consider it a job well done.

Publishers are addicted to trends, and natural foods are one of the latest. One only has to dump in a spoonful of wheat germ and honey here and there to publish. Even sadder for the cause of good food are the authors who dump into standard recipes a lot of wine or a glug of spirits and call it *Cooking with Wine*. A book of that genre was committed by Ruth Ellen Church (also known as Mary Meade), described as "the award-winning food editor of the *Chicago Tribune*." She tells us that the French set the following rules for wine with cheese: 1. *Never serve cheese with a sweet wine.* She has never heard of Château d'Yquem with Roquefort. 2. *Always serve red wine with cheese.* The French usually do, but in white-wine districts they drink what they produce. Also, many French gastronomes maintain that the finesse of a great red wine cannot hold up against a blue cheese, for example: you are better off with the coarser reds, the whites, and even sweet wines, as noted above. 3. *Any cheese will do, except cream cheese or goat milk cheese.* What does she think the French drink with goat cheese? Coca-Cola? If you have the good fortune to shop for white wine in the Sancerre, the *vigneron* is likely to flatter his wine and your palate with a bit of homemade goat cheese, inelegantly called *crottin* (turd). The great Ali-Bab, French gastronome, notes: "Goat cheeses bring out remarkably the bouquet of wine."

(Before we leave advice on cheese, though, we must quote from an ad for *The Cheese Handbook* by T. A. Layton. The ad reproduces part of a page on which Manchego, a Spanish sheep cheese, is described as follows: "Butter fat content very high, production very uneven in quality as it is made by peasants.")

Among what Miss Church describes as "very special, gourmet recipes," she puts 8 oz. of tomato sauce, oregano, and basil in Burgundy Pot Roast, she puts sugar in *Coq au Vin*, and she uses bouillon cubes nearly everywhere. Her salads are mostly viscous sweet messes, but "Seafood Mousse Louise" has cachet: 1 tablespoon gelatin, ⅓ cup sherry, ½ cup water, 1½ cups mayonnaise, 1 cup chili sauce, 1 tablespoon lemon juice, ½ cup heavy cream, 1 cup flaked cooked or canned crabmeat, 1 cup finely cut shrimp, 6 hard-cooked eggs, grated, 4 oz. chopped ripe olives, 2 teaspoons each of parsley and pimiento, grated onion, lemon peel and Worcestershire sauce, a dash of Tabasco, salt, and pepper. Poor Louise.

Now that "ethnic" food is fashionable, there are pitfalls for the unwary borrower. In Rebecca Caruba's *Cooking with Wine and High Spirits*, we find a recipe for *Bouillabaisse à la Caen*. Olive oil, tomatoes, garlic, and saffron in the heart of Normandy? She says, "Only the eel has been eliminated and if you care to add it, you will have an authentic *bouillabaisse* as served at Caen." It would hardly be less authentic if served in Marseilles.

An authentic recipe, clearly, is one that is true to its basic principles. From time to time, a talented cook may devise a delicious variation on a regional specialty, or a borrower who is forced to work with different ingredients and tools may add an original and useful dimension. Such variations should, however, be noted.

It is not only morality that is at issue in crediting the source of a recipe. (We do not propose a list of sources for such common recipes as pancakes, for instance, although many everyday recipes become more interesting if one knows their provenance.) We all stand on the shoulders of our forebears. It's rather like archaeology; recipes are part of our culture, and they will tell us a great deal about ourselves and our past if we but exercise intellectual honesty. As we have suggested before, and will show again, good food writers are scrupulous in such matters, while snitchers are invariably botchers. They are slovenly thinkers and poor craftsmen who do not understand the construction of a dish, and they will destroy its balance and harmony because they are intent on disguising the fact that it is stolen property.

Among chefs there are very few secrets. They are highly trained professionals, and anything new doesn't stay so very long. Among housewives, however, it is very different. Many years ago, at the Methodist Church in Housatonic, Massachusetts, we ate the best baked beans we ever hope to eat. Could we have the recipe? The dear lady was pleased to give it. We were not too surprised when, on trying it, the dish, while delicious, was not exactly the same as the one she had served. A village woman who is noted for making the best beans in the township may be excused for keeping her secret.

There is a story in France (surely apocryphal, and told in different versions) about the aged Bressane woman on her deathbed who had never divulged her secret with fricasseed chicken. (She had only sons, and one does not give such secrets to daughters-in-law.) As she lay, waxen and motionless, surrounded by a large and loving family, she beckoned to her favorite granddaughter and whispered hoarsely in her ear; "Three drops of juice"—a pause, and gathering herself together with a mighty effort, she hissed, "*de citron*" (of lemon), and expired.

A secret was kept in another way by Craig Claiborne in *The New York Times* (June 13, 1974). "We recently contrived a splendid sauce for smoked fish...made with horseradish, sour cream and ground walnuts. It is to feast." It calls for 1 cup sour cream, ¼ cup heavy cream, ⅓ cup grated horseradish, 1 4-oz. can walnuts, 1 tablespoon sugar, and salt to taste. Escoffier's standard text, *Le Guide Culinaire* (1921 edition), publishes such a contrivance on page 49: 9 oz. grated horseradish, 9 oz. walnuts, 1 teaspoon salt, 1 tablespoon sugar, and nearly 1½ cups thick cream. (Transcribed to American measures.) In Claiborne, the proportion of walnuts and horseradish has been somewhat reduced, and sour cream has been substituted for *crème fraîche*. Elizabeth David has translated Escoffier's account of his being served this sauce with *omble chevalier* (a fish found in certain Alpine lakes) while on a hunting trip in the Savoy. He ends the piece with: "For my part, I have never forgotten the sauce of horse-radish and walnuts." Escoffier, be it noted, did not claim to have contrived this sauce.

Only five weeks earlier, Claiborne had bragged, "We can quote chapter and verse about the world of Georges Auguste Escoffier, the man who is to the Gallic table what games are to Hoyle." (Surely he meant what Hoyle is to games, but never mind.) He went on to confide that he had only just then heard of Edouard Nignon, a famous contemporary of Escoffier, regarded by many French gastronomes as a finer cook and certainly a far more interesting writer on food.

Claiborne credited one recipe, *Truites Farcis (sic) Fernand Point*, but Point would not have been pleased. The recipe came from the hand of one Jean Banchet, who claimed to have gotten it from Point. Perhaps. Point's famous recipe for *Truites Farcies* appears in his post-humous book, *Ma Gastronomie*, and in fact, we were ourselves given the recipe many years ago by Mme. Point and have made the dish a number of times. For the stuff-ing, Point took carrot, mushrooms, truffle, and a stalk of celery, chopped them, simmered them briefly in butter, added a bit of flour, stirred in two egg yolks, added salt and pepper, and allowed the mixture to cool. The braising ingredients for the trout were aromatics, butter, and about a cup of port, and that is all. To finish the sauce, he added three good spoonfuls of thick cream, a bit of *beurre manié* (kneaded butter and flour, the size of a hazelnut), and a good chunk of butter to the pan juices. The recipe that appeared in *The Times* called for the mushrooms to be boiled (!) in ¼ cup cream; yet another ¼ cup was added, plus the murderous amount of five tablespoons of flour. In the cooking liquid appear shallots, leeks, garlic, one cup white wine plus about one cup more that had been included in three cups of fish broth. Not *one* of these ingredients appears in the original recipe. Almost as serious as the presence of white wine, which totally changes the balance of flavors, is the fact that the amount of liquid is nearly quadrupled. This changes braising into poaching, quite a different process. Banchet-Claiborne now add two more cups of cream to the cooking liquid, which is then heavily reduced, and the sauce is "finished" with hollandaise sauce.

"On doit la verité aux morts," Voltaire said. (One owes truth to the dead.) If there is anything worse than garden-variety plagiarism, it is such vandalism practiced on established works by translators and editors.

In French classic cuisine, nomenclature is highly codified. The bible of today's haute cuisine is *Le Guide Culinaire* (1902) by Escoffier. Chefs can be exasperatingly vague about the amounts of the ingredients, which are often left to one's discretion, but the presence or absence of a single herb may change the name of the dish. Thus, one may hear a chef say, "It's a sort of *Genevoise*," meaning that it is a red-wine *fumet* from braising fish, suitably reduced, seasoned, and whipped up with butter. It puts you on notice that he did not follow the consecrated formula in some way; it may be an improvement, or it may not. If the chef is famous enough, the variation may bear *his* name. This is essentially what happened with Escoffier. He often changed dishes that antedated him while retaining the designation—some of which were created by Carême (1784–1833)—but the Escoffier version has become the definitive one, and any variations must be carefully attributed.

Esther B. Aresty, in *The Delectable Past* (1964), mangles masterpieces with an almost charming innocence. For "Apician Ham and Figs" she starts out with a canned ham, missing the point that the enzymes in the figs helped to tenderize the ham, which was probably pretty tough. More serious is her addition of cheese to *Veau Villageoise*, a recipe by Menon, the great eighteenth-century French cook. She should have heeded the advice of Archestratus, classical Greek poet and gastronome, whom she had quoted earlier:

All other ways
Are quite superfluous, such as when cooks pour
A lot of sticky clammy sauce upon it,
Parings of cheese, and lees, and dregs of oil,
As if they were preparing cat's meat.

In *The New York Times Magazine* (February 11, 1973) under the heading "Fernand Would Have Liked Naomi's *Marjolaine*," Raymond Sokolov gave a "translation" of Point's famous *gâteau*. What's Naomi to Fernand or he to Naomi that he should need her help? Sokolov explains: "Recipes for the rich dessert, with its three cream fillings, are in print but are unworkable, because *they aren't entirely authentic*. [Our emphasis.] To the rescue came Naomi Rubenstein, who had tasted *marjolaine* chez Point, then set about creating this practical set of directions in her Brooklyn home."

He neglects to tell us that one of the recipes in print is from the hand of the master himself and appears in *Ma Gastronomie*. It would be difficult to question its authenticity and it is a perfectly clear, workable recipe. There are a number of differences between the two *marjolaines*, the most serious of which are the following: For 8 egg whites, 8 oz. almonds, and 5¼ oz. hazelnuts, Point calls for 21 tablespoons sugar and only 2½ tablespoons flour; Naomi calls for 1 cup sugar and 4 tablespoons flour. (Conversion to American measures.) Point bakes his *marjolaine* for three or four minutes at 392° F; Naomi bakes hers for *40 to 50 minutes* at 300° F. (She specifies that it should "solidify and dry out," a crucial difference.) Point works the butter for his cream filling to a pommade; Naomi *melts* it, something no classically trained *pâtissier* would do. Finally, Point strews his cake with chocolate sprinkles; Naomi does not.

Point seems to be a favorite victim of the manglers. His *foie gras en brioche*, more than the *marjolaine*, demonstrates the essential qualities of his lovely cuisine. Women of the Lyonnais and surrounding areas (Point was from the Bresse, and his mother and grandmother were very fine cooks) have for centuries been tucking the wonderful local sausage into *brioche* dough and baking it. Marvelous food. Point did it with *foie gras*. He was likely not the first to have done so, but he brought it to sublime heights. There is no secret about it, however. The fact is that Point did very little cooking in his last years and, according to his disciples, he was not secretive about his recipes. Here are the essentials of Point's recipe as given in his book, omitting only certain details of preparation: take a beautiful *foie gras* (fresh) and marinate it for 24 hours in port, armagnac, and aromatics. Insert a fresh truffle, wrap the liver, coat it with chicken fat (melted, but not hot, he warns—a fine point showing his awareness of pitfalls for less experienced cooks), cover, and cook in a *bain marie* at 212° F for 30 minutes. Cool, and place in a timbale lined with *brioche* dough (no sugar, he specifies) and cover with the same dough. Allow to rise, and bake for about 40 minutes. Unmold and serve hot or cold. *Voilà*. For a chef, it is a remarkably clear and precise recipe.

If you have the courage, let us turn to *The Chef's Secret Cook Book* by Louis Szathmáry. He tells us that Point "took to the grave the secret of a *brioche* filled with goose liver," so the young chef who took over the kitchen at La Pyramide "invented a perfect substitute." Szathmáry gives us the "secret" recipe: 1 loaf sliced white bread, 1 long round or triangular can *pâté* imported from France or a good quality smoked liver sausage (Braunschweiger), 1 cup canned chicken broth, 1 envelope unflavored gelatin, 3 tablespoons water, 1 teaspoon lemon juice, ½ teaspoon sugar. You slice the *pâté*, cut matching holes in the bread slices into which you fit the *pâté* and, finally, coat the ghastly mess with the sweetened rubbery lemon gelatin. A travesty.

In the cookbook industry, a major problem is that

most cooks cannot write and most editors and cookbook writers cannot cook. Charles Virion, a French cook who lives in America, once allowed a magazine to publish his recipe for chocolate soufflé. Years later, the editor asked him to let her include it in a book. At that time, he was preparing his own book and so he refused—in writing. The editor's book appeared with the recipe, nevertheless. Not only did she ignore his request, but adding insult to injury, she tacked on the instruction: shake the soufflé to see if it is done. Under *his* name. Virion was as shaken as his soufflé.

As the Italian saying goes, to translate is to betray. Chefs are exceedingly difficult to translate because they are imprecise about amounts and, since they are speaking to fellow professionals, they may leave out whole operations. It takes experience and care to give the readers a faithful rendition. The problems of produce and substitutions are even more vexing. In some cases it would be wiser to say that there is no way to do that dish in America, and just offer the recipe for intellectual enjoyment.

Let us glance at *The Escoffier Cook Book*, which purports to be a translation of *Le Guide Culinaire*. It gives no hint of which edition was used and has capricious omissions and some ludicrous errors: entry #1027, for instance, gives us "English Brandade of Salt Cod." English *brandade?* The good citizens of Nîmes would be astonished.

The long-awaited American edition of Ali-Bab's great *Gastronomie Pratique* (translated by Elizabeth Benson for McGraw-Hill) promised to be such a great event that one would like to give it only praise. But the reader is misled as to which edition was used (it was the ninth), whole sections were summarily omitted, and the recipes were ruthlessly culled from more than 1100 to some 530. No responsibility is taken anywhere for these excisions— nor is there any admission that they exist. The fact is that some of Ali-Bab's most interesting and practicable recipes are missing. To cut out lentil soup, oxtail soup, and a giblet soup while retaining the turtle and mock turtle soups seems poor judgment. What were the criteria?

What of the translation itself and the knotty problems of converting rational metric measurements by weight into our higgledy-piggledy system of sixes and sevens? On a fine metric balance scale, the weight of a cup of flour (of various types, one French) hovered between 160 and 170 grams. Let us say that one tablespoon weighs 10 grams. So when Ali-Bab calls for 20 grams of flour for a sauce, it is excessive to translate it as 3 tablespoons (30 grams), especially since few people level off carefully. Also, a liter is appreciably more in volume than a quart, and this did not always seem to have been taken into consideration. The question may seem niggling, but the difference in the sauces is enormous; one will be library paste, the other will still be somewhat runny. We are only too aware that most American food writers prefer library paste, but it does seem that it is the original author's preference that should rule.

Only one reviewer of this important book wrote as if she had ever even seen the French original, let alone studied it. There is blame enough for everyone.

Annemarie's Cookingschool Cookbook gives a recipe for "Chocolate Mousse Normandy" which she calls a "variation" on a recipe by the late Dione Lucas. Among other changes, Annemarie Huste actually specifies margarine instead of the original butter—a whole cupful—thus murdering the recipe and destroying the already tenuous relationship with Normandy. In the introduction she states, "in any recipe where the taste of butter is unimportant, margarine functions identically." One is forced to question not only the sensitivity of her palate but the soundness of her observations on the behavior of butter in cooking. In the same book, she gives this recipe for Beef Stock: 2 cans of beef broth (Campbell's), 1 teaspoon Bovril, water, and aromatics. Making your own stock, she claims, results in a "liquid that tastes and looks like dishwater." The use of brand names is always questionable; only in special circumstances can it be countenanced, yet Annemarie specifies Campbell's frequently.

Very well, French cooking is badly understood in America and not well suited to our produce. But how shall we explain a similar mangling of our own heritage? Just leafing through *Thomas Jefferson's Cook Book*, edited by Marie Kimball, one spots the most curious bowdlerizations and errors. In her introduction, to show how quaint the recipes were, she remarks that a chocolate cream was poured over chicken gizzards. This is remarkably interesting; evidently gizzards contain rennet just as calf's stomach lining does. Mrs. Kimball publishes the recipe itself with two junket tablets instead. Clearly, this might have made a useful footnote for modern cooks, but the change in the recipe deprives us of knowing how colonial women coped with such problems as that of rennet. And by implication, we do not know what historical information is missing from all the other recipes. Mrs. Kimball also tells us that Jefferson probably "wrote the notes that here follow" in December 1784. Among the items that follow is a "Soup of small roots" with a footnote that reads: "Soup of small roots is attributed to Carême, the great French cook." Carême did, indeed, give a recipe for similar soup, but, unfortunately, 1784 was the year of Carême's birth, and his great work on cuisine (1833) did not appear until some seven years after Jefferson's death. The fact is that such soups were made in France long before Carême.

In *The Virginia Housewife* (1824), Mary Randolph gives this remarkably fine recipe

TO DRESS DUCKS WITH JUICE OF ORANGES

The ducks being singed, picked, and drawn, mince the livers with a little scraped bacon, some butter, green onions, sweet herbs and parsley, seasoned with salt, pepper, and mushrooms; these being all minced together, put them into the bodies of the ducks, and roast them, covered with slices of bacon, and wrapped up in paper; then put a little gravy, the juice of an orange, a few shallots minced, into a stew pan, and shake in a little pepper; when the ducks are roasted, take off the bacon, dish them, and pour your sauce with the juice of oranges over them, and serve them up hot.

Note: The gravy was natural meat juices and the oranges were the bitter Seville variety.

The much admired *American Heritage Cookbook* (1964) gives Mrs. Randolph's duck recipe using the following ingredients:

1 large duck	¼ cup orange liqueur
Salt	Grated rind of 1 orange
Pepper	¼ cup orange peel, cut in
½ cup sugar	thin strips
1 dessertspoon red wine	Fresh lemon juice (op-
vinegar	tional)
Juice of 2 oranges	Parsley

The vinegar and sugar are caramelized, and the parsley is tucked in the tail before serving. Why invoke the name of Mary Randolph in presenting what is actually a banal, overly sweet *Caneton à l'Orange?* Where is the duck liver? Where are the mushrooms and sweet herbs? Where is the stuffing? Where are the shallots? Where, in short, is Mrs. Randolph's recipe?

A book we were beguiled into buying by an attractive brochure is *The Early American Cookbook* by Hyla O'Connor. Out of some 280 recipes "gathered from original colonial manuscripts and rare printed cookbooks," not one is attributed, nor is there any bibliographical information. No dates are offered, and only rarely is the region mentioned.

O'Connor, a home economist, apparently has never milked a cow. Where a recipe for Buck-Wheat Cakes, which we were able to identify (from a photograph of the original typography used as decoration) as having come from Susannah Carter's *The Frugal Housewife* (1772), calls for "milk-warm water" in the original, she writes "two cups of milk." She also complains that the mixture is "very bland" and suggests adding ¼ cup molasses. She talks about Washington and Jefferson making ice cream and then proceeds to give us a recipe calling for "2 tablespoons all-purpose flour"! Jefferson's recipe is in his papers; there is, of course, no flour. Nor does flour seem to have appeared in American ice cream recipes until Fannie Farmer and the home economists.

O'Connor gives what turned out to be Simmons' recipe for Apple Pye from *American Cookery* (1796), again identified by a pretty reproduction. The original directs the reader to use Paste No. 3, for which O'Connor gives quite a different method and leaves out the egg whites called for. In Miss Simmons' recipe for A Whipt Syllabub, similarly identified, which calls for cream, white wine, egg whites, and says "sweeten it to your taste," why did O'Connor add *three cups of milk* and *twenty-two tablespoons of sugar*? It makes a sugary, milky froth out of what was an elegant mixture. Be it remarked that none of the reproductions were attributed.

Standards of food writing are such that when members of academe try their hand at it they forsake scholarly discipline. A medievalist professor, in a feature story in *The New York Times*, translates the word *melle* in a recipe as soften, where it could only mean mix; the word comes from Old French *mesler* and the modern *mêler* is so used to this day. (A common Middle English form is *meddle*.) For what she describes as a fifteenth-century *blankmangere*, she calls for chicken breasts, quartered almonds, cream of mushroom soup, and one hundred pastry shells!* In no early English manuscript were we able to find prototypes for some of her recipes. Another professor gives a recipe from *The Forme of Cury* (about 1390) for "Gourdes in Potage" which instructs: "Take pork

---

* *Fabulous Medieval Feasts* by Madeleine Pelner Cosman (n.d.).

soden. Grynde it, and alye it therewith and with yolkes of ayren." She "modernizes" this recipe by taking ground pork (apparently raw), browning it, and dumping it into the soup; we never again hear of egg yolk.* (There is only one possible reading: Take boiled pork. Grind it, and bind it with egg yolks. It is likely that a copyist's error omitted a direction to form dumplings to be simmered in the soup; that is speculation, but it makes sense from a culinary point of view.) There are so many imponderables in trying to recapture the taste of medieval food that to change the entire structure of a dish where the language permits no misunderstanding is inadmissible. As we have said earlier, old recipes may occasionally benefit from some modernization, but changes should be carefully noted and discussed.

There is only one way to publish compendiums of recipes from the past, and that is to give each recipe as found (with bibliographical notes, please), followed by any pertinent information or suggestions. In that regard, *The Cornucopia* by Judith Herman and Marguerite Herman is exemplary.

What would be delightful would be to have beautiful facsimile editions of the originals. The difficulty of getting access to old cookbooks and manuscripts is staggering. Often it is prohibitively costly. We cannot understand why museums and libraries are not more active in publishing the treasures that repose in their collections. It would save wear and tear on the originals, make money for the institutions that own them, and make our patrimony available to people who must otherwise depend on the manglers.

Even so literate a publication as *Natural History* has Raymond Sokolov saying that eggplant is "an altogether late arrival in the English-speaking world," continuing, "Indeed,· no European botanist mentions it before the beginning of the seventeenth century and the first mention of it in English did not come until 1767, only 208

* *To the King's Taste* by Lorna J. Sass (1975).

years ago." John Gerard's well-known *The Herball*, published in 1597, describes eggplant in great detail under the name of Madde Apples. Gerard notes that "This Plant grows in Egypt almost every where..." and that it bears fruit "of the bignesse of a Swans egge.... In the duke-dome of Millain it is called *Melongena*; and of some, *Melanzana*: in Latine, *Mala insana*: and in English, Mad Apples. In the Germane tongue, *Dollopffell*: in Spanish *Verangenes*.... The people of Toledo eat them with great devotion, being boiled with fat flesh, putting to it some scraped cheese, which they do keep in vinegar, hony, or salt pickle all winter, to procure lust." Clearly, the Moors brought it to Spain (Gerard mentions Barbary) and it seems safe to place this before 1492.

The late Clementine Paddleford, who was food writer for *The New York Herald Tribune*, wrote a valuable book on regional cookery, *How America Eats*. In an interview with Horace Sutton of *Saturday Review*, Claiborne said: "I had been to school in Europe, and I knew all the sauces.... Clem knew not one thing about food." Well, Claiborne did not then, nor does he now, know all his sauces. As for Clem, whatever her short-comings, she was a good reporter. Her New England Clam Chowder was authentic (unlike Claiborne's—imagine not using salt pork!) and she credited her sources. Also, she liked people and she had a good ear. She quotes, for example, a Dr. Coffin saying, "You must know the history of every lobster you cook. But if you must pick your lobsters at the local market, the only alternative is to get them lively. Cook in Maine sea water." She goes on to give his recipe for Maine Lobster Stew, one of America's truly great dishes. She tells also of a Miss Sue, no longer young, who "used to cater two flossy events in a day and cook everything myself.... I'm old-fashioned with my cooking, never use store stuff and I want lard in pie crust and fresh apples. Now Addie here uses all the new fangles and she has good luck, but I couldn't, never will." Alas, Clem's ear was better than her editor's taste; there is no mention of lard in the recipe that follows—it must have gotten kitchen-tested out by the home economists.

The book is now out of print but the publishers have put out a new version; they changed the name, dropped the attractive regional approach, took out every word of Clem's wonderful chitchat with the friends she made everywhere. What did they want to do that for?

10

The Gourmet Plague

Yes, the French love good eating. . . . Their
skill in combining simple raw materials to
produce superlative dishes grows out of the
idée fixe that anything eaten, even the daily
potato, humble carrot and turnip and less
tender cuts of meat, must be well prepared.
Gourmets are not made by eating occasional
party fare or company meals or by infre-
quent excursions to famous restaurants.
Good food must be eaten every day, every
meal with each dish carefully prepared and
suitably seasoned.

Louis Diat, in French Cooking for Americans

Iᶠ wᴇ Americans are ever to eat well again, we shall have
to declare "gourmet" a dirty word.

It started out as a perfectly valid borrowing from the
French, a noun meaning "a connoisseur in eating and
drinking; an epicure," according to Webster. One could,
perhaps, defend the attributive use of the word if indeed
the attributions had anything to do with epicureanism,
but the word is applied indiscriminately to anything

edible, or nearly so, that has been fancied up. Gourmet cooking has nothing to do with the excellence of basic materials, the artistry of the cook, or a discriminating palate. *Poulet de Bresse*, France's finest chicken, perfectly roasted, would not qualify as gourmet. Nor would an old hen lovingly simmered with onions and carrots. Not fancy enough. But take the breast of an American chicken (the most tasteless and cottony part of a tasteless and cottony bird), blanket it with a pasty white sauce (calling it *velouté* makes it so very French, *n'est-ce pas?*), arrange it prettily on a bed of spinach (frozen, chopped, and bound with that same horrid sauce—you may now call it *à la Florentine*), strew slivered almonds or grated cheese about, glaze it, and you have a gourmet master-piece. Or stuff it with rice, *foie gras*, and truffles. The *foie gras* and truffles will surely be canned and of poor quality, but they make everything look fancy and terribly expensive, which is finally the name of the game. It is then sauced with pretty much the same old floury glop, but now it is called *Espagnole*, is a muddy brown, and will taste of tomato paste, mediocre Madeira, and canned bouillon.

A recipe given by Craig Claiborne and Pierre Franey is for a *velouté* to be served on fish fillets. It calls for 8 (yes, eight) tablespoons of flour to thicken just two cups of fish broth to be added to one cup of pan juices and one cup of heavy cream. The reduction of those juices with the cream would have made a heavenly sauce; adding two cups of library paste made it a catastrophe. Claiborne's recipe for another fish *velouté* in *The New York Times Cook Book* calls for 24 (twenty-four) table-spoons of flour to five cups of stock, which may be a gourmet record. (It is very nearly 5 tablespoons per cup of liquid.)

Claiborne claims to know his Escoffier inside out. In his *Guide Culinaire*, the great chef notes at the very beginning:

The *fonds de cuisine* [stocks] represent the basis, the most necessary elements, without which nothing serious could be undertaken.... The most skillful worker cannot create something from nothing; and it would be most unrealistic to insist that he present a work done according to the rules of the art if he has been furnished with only defective produce.

Escoffier goes on to say that it would be just as absurd to expect that "a *piquette* [a thin acidy wine], on bottling, be transformed into a great wine." Yet, this is exactly what gourmet cookbooks would have you do. Pick up any writing on French cooking for Americans—Julia Child, Simone Beck, Beard, Jacques Pépin, Claiborne—and you will find canned bouillon listed among the ingredients. Among those who write in English on French cooking, only Elizabeth David and Richard Olney, to our knowledge, remain true to the most elementary flavor principles in this respect. Anyone who writes recipes is sadly aware that many readers will substitute canned stock, but the readers should know that they are cheating and so understand where the dish failed.

It has been said that Campbell's soups have done more to debase the cooking of Americans—and their palates—than any other single factor. Women simply do not make soups anymore, and the stock pot has disappeared. Only a few old cranks seem to appreciate the difference that a well-made stock makes in a sauce.

"...at one time, a badge of shame, hallmark of the lazy lady and the careless wife, today the can opener is fast becoming a magic wand." The writer is Poppy Cannon in *The Can-Opener Cook Book* (1951). She was one of the early gourmet writers, and her frank espousal of canned soups had incalculable influence on that movement: her enthusiasm and her position in the world of fashion gave the tin can a cachet that it would otherwise not have had. "Armed with a can opener, I become the artist-cook, the master, the creative chef....It is easy to cook like a gourmet though you are a beginner. We want you to believe just as we do that in this miraculous age it is quite possible—and it's fun—to be a 'chef' even before you can really cook."

Something must be said about the extravagance of gourmet cooking. We are not now referring to fresh butter, heavy cream, or other beautiful produce; in our society, such things are expensive when available at all. We are referring to the use of costly ingredients *because* they are costly. Food pages dominated by caviar, truffles, *foie gras*, chicken breasts, and filet mignon were always absurd; they became downright offensive when inflation and recession struck the country.

One trouble is that Americans have forgotten how to be poor. Not that hard times ever were fun, but people coped better. In fact, the history of cookery is largely the triumph of housewives making do with what the gentry wouldn't touch. Eating high on the hog meant eating the fancy marketable cuts; the poor would get the jowl, the chitterlings, the feet, the tail, and with them would make fine food. All the great tripe, snail, and sausage dishes are their inventions, and all the chowders. What is *bouillabaisse* but a chowder that Marseilles women made of the trash fish that their husbands couldn't sell? (Now the gourmet cooks add lobster to it, which does nothing for the lobster and nothing for the *bouillabaisse*.)

Most of the fish, the hog, and the steer now are processed into convenience crud, and housewives wouldn't know what to do with the cheap parts if they had them. During the 1973 beef famine, reporters sought to learn how people were coping. Most were like this young couple at a supermarket: the husband was unemployed, the wife pregnant, and their cart held a sack of candy bars, a TV dinner, and a coconut pie. "You've got to treat yourselves once in a while," the husband explained. As for middle-class women, most admitted that they had no idea what to do, but some thought they were being pretty smart by leaning hard on "casseroles." " 'Lots of macaroni and cheese' is the battle plan of a New Orleans housewife," said a *Times* roundup. " 'I've gotten down to basics.' " Another housewife, of Brooklyn, boasted, "I put in everything I can think of, peas, beans, scraps of meat left over." In Missoula, Montana, a member of the League of Women Voters made a discovery: "I find that if you use half as much meat as usual in a casserole and double the other ingredients, it will go for two meals."

When Claiborne and his partner, Franey, returned to *The Times* in early 1974, they marked the occasion with a feature describing a dinner for eight that would cost $900, cooked at home. (A reader commented, "It's the dawn of an old era.") The menu called for caviar with vodka, striped bass fillets with champagne sauce, stuffed squab Derby, braised endives, salad, Brie cheese, and grapefruit sherbet. The wines were a Montrachet, a Château Ausone, a Romanée-Conti, and a Dom Perignon. Claiborne and Franey allowed that if the caviar and the wines were deleted, the cost "might deflate to around $90." It is a revealing comment, for the wines had been chosen as pretty much the highest priced in each class, and there was no suggestion that a reader might drink a very enjoyable wine at much lower cost.

At that, it was a faulty meal: the fish was pasted with that floury *velouté* described earlier; the *foie gras* and the truffles in the squabs were canned and hence a pointless extravagance; instead of the classic *demi-glace*, the sauce for the squab included tomato paste and flour, and there was sugar in the braised endives.

Faced with this basic menu, it would have been better to reduce the fish juices with heavy cream, as described earlier, and simply to roast the squab, deglazing the lovely pan juices with a little Madeira and very well reduced homemade veal broth, and to serve it on a crunchy *rôtie* (toast). There are more elaborate ways of dealing with the bird, to be sure, but none that show off the natural flavor of pigeon as well.

The menu was Claiborne's and Franey's answer to the
question: "What would you command if you were allowed one last great meal on this earth?" It "is a game
we have played with many chefs throughout the world,"
Claiborne recounts in his new book, *Craig Claiborne's
Favorites.* "It is astonishing," he says, "how many chefs
say for their last great feast they would like things on
the order of tripe à la mode de Caen, cassoulet, and
breaded pig's feet—real peasant fare. P.S. To tell you the
truth, we would willingly settle for a pound of fresh
caviar and fresh buttered toast." This explains, perhaps,
how he is able to say: "We find pork...almost as appealing as caviar."

> JUST A QUIET DINNER
> FOR TWO IN PARIS
> 31 DISHES, NINE WINES,
> A $4,000 CHECK
> —*Headline, page 1*, The New York Times,
> *November 14, 1975*

The diners were Claiborne and Franey. Claiborne had
made the high bid on a dinner for two, offered by American Express, at a charity auction. They had considered
"nothing but vodka or champagne with caviar followed
by foie gras with Chateau d'Yquem—but no, any old
millionaire could do that." That would not do, so they
ordered twenty-nine more dishes and seven more wines.
    Under the heading, EDUNT ET VOMANT,* the columnist
Harriet Van Horne wrote: "...no journalistic caprice
has, in my memory, set off such a shudder of distaste....
This calculated evening of high-class piggery *offends* an
average American's sense of decency. It seems *wrong*,
morally, esthetically and in every other way." (Emphasis
hers.) The Vatican newspaper deplored the display while
millions were starving; the French press noted that the price

---

* They have eaten and let them vomit.

of the dinner represented a year's wages for many workers. (A roundup of world opinion, slated for the following day in *The Times*, was killed.)

"I never heard of anything so vulgar," a woman said to Van Horne. Few people seemed to realize that it was also ignorant. Denis, of Chez Denis where all this took place, had tactfully tried to tell our ambassadors of good will that there would be enough food for ten; that "it was not required that all foods be sampled." The sumptuous menus of the nineteenth century were served *à la Française*; more like a series of seated buffets than modern service. A diner chose what tempted him from each service or, more likely, what was nearest. Only gluttons would eat *three* soups; Claiborne found the third one "anticlimactic."

"The foods were elegant to look at, but the over-all display was undistinguished, if not to say shabby." Claiborne had other complaints: "...but the beurre blanc should have been very hot." As we discuss elsewhere, a *beurre blanc* is butter whipped into a reduction of shallots and white wine vinegar; it is an exceedingly fragile liaison and it takes a flair to make it fluffy. If it had been "very hot," it would no longer have been a *beurre blanc*.

Van Horne also wrote: "[Claiborne] has sinned against certain canons some of his colleagues in the press prefer to honor. What I am trying to say, as politely as possible, is that I do not like the jiggery-pokery by which this $4,000 dinner check was paid."

There was a storm of protest, and *The Times* printed some of the hundreds of angry letters from shocked readers. Claiborne, in his reply, regretted that many had found the dinner "obscene or decadent or a symbol of contempt for the hunger that exists in the world today." He went on to ask "those who were not amused if they seriously believe that as a result of that evening I have deprived one human being of one mouthful of food."

This may answer Van Horne's question: "Was there no remorse between the foie gras and the café filtre?" *Edunt et vomant.*

Doubtless responding to published criticism, the Claiborne-Franey team wrote, "So-called gourmet cooking does not of necessity imply truffles and foie gras. Any dish that is soaringly good to the senses...can fall into the sublime category." The prose is Claiborne, but the solution is Howard Johnson's: two gourmet meat loaf dishes. One calls for 2 pounds of ground veal and ⅔ pound of mushrooms, served with something called Sauce Alexandre, a floury *velouté* with ½ pound of mushrooms added. Another uses that great gourmet staple, chicken breasts, 2 pounds of them, with a cup of chopped watercress. This is also sauced with a *velouté* to which chopped watercress is added, thus making the same culinary error as before, that of repeating the characterizing ingredient in both dish and sauce. It is wrong in taste, texture, and color, and violates every principle of saucing. Neither of these dishes is cheap—each calls for at least 1½ cups heavy cream, for instance—and yet both manage to be hopelessly banal.

In another piece, Claiborne and Franey lead off: "While there is something excruciatingly mundane about dishes made with ground meat and noodles or macaroni (could it have something to do with their low-budget connotations?), they can also be outrageously good." (The parenthetical remark is theirs.) We are then treated to two recipes, *Beef with noodles casserole* and *Macaroni and beef casserole*. There is more difference in the titles than in the recipes; each calls for butter, onion, green pepper, tomatoes, flour, nutmeg, and lots of cheddar cheese. One calls for ground round steak and noodles and the other for chopped ground chuck (*sic*) or round steak and macaroni. The recipes may well have come from Howard Johnson's; this is gourmet on the cheap.

There are not many Claiborne features in which one cannot find one or more unfortunate errors. A recipe for *Potée Bourguignonne* calls for a chicken, stuffed with Italian sausages (!), and fresh pork (a *potée* is not a *potée* without corned pork). Burgundians would be surprised to find a chicken in their *potée*. (The dish, as presented, is a flattened-out version of *poule au pot d'Henri IV* from the Béarn.) Claiborne and Franey give a recipe for Alsatian pastry that calls for "well-chilled corn oil" and milk. Never have we seen such a recipe for pastry except, perhaps, on a Mazola label; certainly never in Alsace. Proper Alsatian pastry recipes call for butter and lard, not unlike the Danish recipes one of us grew up with. (Danish cooks say that butter is for flavor and lard for tenderness.) Some cooks add egg yolks as well. But corn oil? *Nicht.*

Another Claiborne anomaly is his recipe for Flageolets, Bretonne Style in *The New York Times Cook Book.* A *flageolet* is a bean grown around Arpajon and dried in the shade in such a way that it retains its green color and even a memory of the taste of the fresh bean. For rustic bean dishes, the earthy taste and texture of other beans make a far better choice; the elusive flavor of *flageolets* is easily masked, and every effort should be made to enhance it. But they are imported and expensive; hence gourmet. Let us see what Claiborne does with them. First, he boils them up with "5 or 6 cloves." *Poor little flageolets.* Next, he dumps them into a sauce which he apparently considers to be *Sauce Bretonne*, which consists of 2 tablespoons butter, a chopped onion (cooked until brown), ¼ cup tomato puree, 4 tomatoes, 3 cloves garlic, salt, pepper, and parsley. It reads like a recipe from a second-rate spaghetti joint. All that tomato, all that garlic, and the browning of the onions (not forgetting the 5 or 6 cloves) would effectively mask anything, even rank meat. The *flageolets* never had a chance.

It is interesting to note that Escoffier gives no recipe

for *flageolets à la Bretonne*, considering them, perhaps, too delicate for this robust sauce. His recipe for *Haricots blancs à la Bretonne* calls for cooking white beans with the "ordinary aromatics"; no cloves are mentioned. The sauce proper starts with onion cooked in butter to a "blond color" only, is then moistened with 1 cup white wine, reduced by half; 1½ cups each of *Espagnole* and tomato sauce and "one small clove of garlic" are then added.

Overseasoning, let us note again, is an American neurosis that we attribute largely to the impoverishment of our foods. This is not a view widespread in the foodwriting game. Raymond Sokolov, writing in *Natural History* magazine, reports a conversation with Simone Beck, co-author with Julia Child of *Mastering the Art of French Cooking*. Mme. Beck, he says, "told me that it was from Mrs. Child that her palate learned to appreciate the slightly higher level of seasoning prevalent in America. Is the famous 'delicacy' of French food partly due to the cultural caution of French cooks with salt?" Or could it be that our palates are simply numbed? Sokolov writes: "If I really follow my own 'taste' in salting food, I ruin dinner for most people, except for NaCl true believers like myself." Elsewhere, he says that for him, "fiery jalapeño peppers...were a test of manhood." Olé!

In a *New York Times Magazine* article entitled "Burnt Flavor at the Box Tree," praising an expensive new restaurant, Sokolov explains the special character of its sauces: "plenty of Cognac goes into his brown sauces" and they are based on a stock made from "burned scraps of filet and burned celery chunks. The burning—not browning—gives the sauce a faint whiff of singed meat that is meant to remind the customer subliminally of a charcoal-broiled steak...." Similarly, his book, *The Saucier's Apprentice*, states: "Good brown *roux* will look almost the same color as chocolate." Flour and butter cooked to the color of chocolate will be scorched and will communicate an acrid taste to the sauce.

The introduction to Claiborne's *Kitchen Primer* says: "The basis of most French cooking is butter and cream; they are called for unstintingly here and without apology. As far as I am concerned, there are no substitutes." Opening the book at random, we find "A Good Plain Yellow Cake" that calls for "8 tablespoons (½ cup) solid, white vegetable shortening." The sugar cookies that follow call for the same thing. "Pie Pastry" calls for "½ cup solid or nonliquid shortening (this may be part butter)."

Claiborne's version of mayonnaise, unlike the classic, contains mustard, and he prefers peanut or salad oil to olive oil. We love what Elizabeth David said on the subject: "...to me, nothing can replace the flavour and aroma of a genuine, mildly fruity olive oil...so it should be said that a great many people...prefer to use groundnut [peanut] oil not only because of its cheapness but because they are not accustomed to the flavour of olive oil. Groundnut oil makes quite passable mayonnaise and could certainly be used for practicing but as it is absolutely devoid of taste, it is necessary to add flavour in the form of a little extra lemon juice and perhaps mustard." For our part, any calories we eat have got to be delicious, and nothing but the best Provençal or Lucca oil goes into our salads.

A notice in Claiborne's *Primer*:

    IMPORTANT! READ THIS:

A white sauce is nothing short of miraculous for there is literally no end to its uses and variations.

The same old library paste, *ad nauseam*.

Claiborne announces that milk and cream "freeze well." But do they thaw well? They do not. Frozen cream "kernels" on thawing, and milk acquires a flat taste. They can still be used in some cooking, however. As noted, there is a page and a half on how to make coffee but not one word on quality, the importance of fresh roasting, or the desirability of grinding it at home. On paring vegetables: "Then lay out a length of waxed paper, or newspaper if you want to be economical, to catch the peelings." Condescension to the economically minded aside, any housewife knows that newspaper is ever so much more capacious and efficient, because of its absorbency.

A rather more interesting kitchen hint was given by Claiborne in the staid old *Times*: "We were enchanted to learn that we share an enthusiasm of long standing with Mrs. B———. When nobody else is around, she likes to streak in the kitchen, except when she's deep fat frying. Then she wears an apron."

Not so charming is Claiborne's advice on cooking with wine. An article of his that appeared in *The Washington Post* opens: "Some young innocents we know (including a cookbook author or two) have wild conceptions about the technique of cooking with wine." Some innocents are less young. Farther on, he says, "And heaven help the guest who dines on a dish to which a cup of such wine [uncooked] has been added just before serving. If the wine is not cooked, it maintains its raw taste and is apt to lead to acute indigestion." Now, wine is used in cooking, but not to make it digestible. The long, slow simmering of meat with wine and aromatics transfigures the dish and is, indeed, the very soul of French cooking. However, it would not be out of place here to cite Escoffier: "We counsel that any wine which is destined to give to a sauce its characteristic note should be always added *hors du feu* [off the fire] because boiling evaporates the aroma of the wine." This is almost invariable with fortified wines such as Madeira, but it is also done with table wines. We know one great chef who adds to a sort of *Bordelaise* (a long-simmered reduction of red wine, beef stock, shallots, and aromatics) a glug of good red wine just before the "finishing" with butter—to freshen the taste, as he describes it. Also, the people of the Southwest of France have for centuries been putting uncooked wine into their soup bowls—a custom known as *faire chabrol*—with no ill effect. Indeed, most of us who drink wine drink it uncooked.

For the gourmet cook, sloshing about quantities of wine and brandy is pretty much *de rigueur*. The wine is usually poor and the quantity of brandy invariably excessive. ("Cooking wine" is an abomination. An old motto in our kitchen is that there are wines that one might possibly drink that are not good enough for cooking.) To cook a great wine is a pointless extravagance, but tag ends of stale wine usually work out well, provided that they were pleasant to drink in the first place. The taste is all that is left when the alcohol is volatilized.

It is no doubt because cognac is expensive that the gourmets slosh it on so. One of Claiborne's recipes doused a pound of scallops, which have a subtle, almost elusive flavor, with ¼ cup of cognac, two cups of tomatoes, and paprika.

Flambéeing is the pinnacle of gourmet cooking. We once asked Mère Allard, Burgundian and great *cuisinière* (now retired) of the Paris bistro that bears her name, about the practice of flambéeing *boeuf bourguignon*. She made a moue and said, "Burnt alcohol tastes like burnt alcohol." A headwaiter in New York is credited with the comment, "The customers like it, and it doesn't hurt the food much."

When they are not putting the wrong thing into a dish, the gourmets are likely to be taking the wrong thing out. In Sokolov's *Great Recipes from The New York Times*, pork chops are baked in 1½ cups of wine and ¾ cup of chicken broth. The last step reads: "When chops are done, remove from oven. Drain them, discard liquid, and serve." There went most of the flavor, down the drain. Other *Times* recipes have instructed us to discard pan juices from cooking fish. Fresh pork rind, an item indispensable in many dishes—*daube* or *cassoulet*, for instance—which is not only rather expensive but usually requires a small safari to foreign butcher shops when needed, was likewise consigned to the garbage pail. (Fresh pork rind may be rolled up and frozen against the time of use. It must not be kept too long and should be quickly parboiled before using.)

Now, French women are often accused of setting an extravagant table, and perhaps they do, but there is more than a touch of frugality in their madness. No carcass of a bird, no fish heads or bones, no good meat bones get thrown out. It is not only thrifty to boil them up into lovely *fumets* and broths, but it yields flavor and texture that cannot be obtained in any other way. Since flavor is precisely what is most lacking in American produce, it seems criminal to waste it.

In fact, the greater part of America's gourmet cuisine is at best second-rate Escoffier. We are too kind. Escoffier was a dazzling virtuoso and he had produce of a quality such as we can only dream of today. It is frequently said that French *haute cuisine* was invented to mask rank produce. The truth is that everyone who had enough to eat had beautiful produce, and *haute cuisine* was invented to dazzle the aristocracy and to mark the difference of class. Lower down the ranks, people had to content themselves with the lowlier cuts that were despised by the aristocracy and the bourgeoisie alike, and this is where the fabled dishes of France originated: the tripe dishes, the *cassoulet*, the *potée*, the *daube*, etc. But these lowly cuts of meat and vegetables and aromatics that went into them were of beautiful quality. Take *le bouillabaisse*, *le cotriade*, or *la chaudrée*; they were made of trash fish and whatever else was not sold from the day's catch, but the fish were leaping fresh. There was never any question of using stale fish.

On the contrary, it is today's produce that needs masking. With modern refrigeration, food never seems to go quite rotten; it just tastes embalmed. Sadly, no amount of masking, and no matter how skillfully done, takes away that embalmed taste.

Interestingly, the young chefs in France, at least the gifted ones, are turning away from Escoffier. He himself changed his methods and refined his cuisine during his long career. It is instructive to compare his *Guide Culinaire* (1902) with *Ma Cuisine* (1934). In the latter work, he used considerably less flour in his classic sauces (about two teaspoons per cup of finished sauce), removed the tomato from his *Espagnole* (an important point that has gone unremarked), deleted flour from his tomato-sauce recipe, and included many dishes from his native Provençal.

Indeed, *la nouvelle cuisine*, if we leave aside dietetic cooking, certain exotica, and the public-relations aspect of it all, is essentially a return to a much older French cuisine: the ancient art of reduction, of *coulis*, and the liaison of sauces with butter, egg yolks, or cream instead of cheap thickeners such as flour and other starches. The flavors are at once more intense and more subtle. The effect is reminiscent of the lovely eighteenth-century dishes in the anonymous *Cuisinier Gascon* and Menon's *La Cuisinière Bourgeoise*. There is indeed a great deal of simplification going on today in French cuisine, but not the kind that requires less skill or lesser quality of produce. Quite the contrary. There is no masking possible, and the sauces are far more fragile. Flour-based sauces may be a horrible necessity in huge kitchens—they are much cheaper and they are virtually indestructible, even with long waits in hot kitchens—but there is little excuse for them in small *chef-patron* restaurants and even less in private homes.

Part and parcel of this new French *haute cuisine* is the feverish search for quality produce. French agriculture, too, is hard hit by industrialization, but it is at least two generations behind us. Also, the French love to eat well, and they are remarkably adept in arranging things so that they will be able to do so. It is amusing to note that while fancying up food is a symptom of snobbery in America, it is the beautiful simplicity of flawlessness that is the in thing in France. It is now the less affluent who feel they have to paint the lily. While one must deplore snobbery wherever it appears, it doesn't take much intelligence or even a very discriminating palate to prefer simple perfection to pretentious failure.

Now, how did we come to preferring pretentious failures? We were taken, that's how. It must be added that we were easy marks. Oddly, one reason is our addiction to shortcuts and our contempt for arduously acquired craftsmanship. We have matured a bit since the days when con artists could promise that we could learn to play the piano in ten easy lessons—"They laughed when I sat down to play"—and most literate Americans are aware that painting-in the numbered squares is not the path to creation of art. But one typical cooking school offers to make you a gourmet chef in a "Crash Course" of fifteen hours. (The nature of the emergency is not specified. Marriage?)

Our sophistication does not yet include food. We must have every ingredient measured to the last ⅛ teaspoon, and we cook by painting-in the numbered squares. When the authors were asked to supply a fish recipe to accompany a feature on the pending demise of the Fulton Fish Market, we submitted the best and simplest recipe we know:

There is a Provençal saying to the effect that a fish swims in water but dies in oil; olive oil, it goes without saying. This means that the fish must be flapping fresh. Coat the fish with good olive oil; lay it on a well oiled piece of foil or cooking parchment; salt and pepper it, inside and out; sprinkle with fresh lemon juice; close the foil tight and bake it in a hot oven until *barely* done. Fish must still be translucent along the backbone. Thyme or Italian parsley may be lightly strewn about and a sliced onion or two, lightly sautéed in olive oil, may be included if it pleases you.

Consternation among the editors. "How much olive oil?" We replied, "How big is the fish?" Not getting through, we dropped the recipe. Thereafter, recipes were incorporated in our text in such a way as to bypass the editors.

One does not become a chef, at least not in France, before spending three long years as an apprentice, followed by three or four equally hard years as a journeyman (*commis*, then *chef de parti*). This helps to explain why most books and schools promising to turn you into a French chef are frauds. An American who is confronted with produce of lamentable quality, who has little or no experience, whose kitchen equipment has been chosen for decor rather than utility, and who has no staff of assistants, can hardly hope to produce *haute cuisine*.

More serious, perhaps, is the fact that we have become downright neurotic about food. Is it polyunsaturated? How many calories? (Nevertheless, we continue to dose everything up with sugar.) Is it sterilized? Is it in or, horror of horrors, is it *out*? How much is a pinch of salt? Goodness knows there is plenty to be frightened about, what with residual insecticides, hormones, antibiotics, the additives and the subtractatives. These have been exposed by a handful of latter-day Rachel Carsons. But meanwhile, the taste and texture of our produce have deteriorated to the level of a cruel and monstrous joke. Take the tomato, or the chicken, or bread, or... This has aroused some disorganized resistance, but not from the gourmet experts. Julia Child et al., in *Mastering the Art of French Cooking*, announce that "the book could well be titled 'French Cooking from the American Supermarket,'* for the excellence of French cooking, and of good cooking in general, is due more to cooking techniques than to anything else." Escoffier starts his works discussing the quality of the produce for his *fonds de cuisine*; for the French, this is primordial. A woman giving a recipe will say, "*Prendre un beau poulet, bien dodu*" (Take a fine chicken, nice and plump), and you can just see her patting a chicken appreciatively. American women used to be equally concerned; we have quoted elsewhere the dictum of Amelia Simmons (1796) but it bears repeating:

> We proceed to ROOTS and VEGETABLES—*and the best cook cannot alter the first quality, they must be good, or the cook will be disappointed.*

An admonition that Mrs. Child would do well to heed. In her recent book, *From Julia Child's Kitchen*, we find that she is still in the supermarket:

> The other day my supermarket had some gorgeous 2-inch squares of well-trimmed, nicely marbled meat all beautifully packaged in see-through containers. A big red extra label...announced loudly: *Barbecue. Brochettes*....I grabbed up a package, rushed home, skewered it, basted it, broiled it, and was it ever tough! Blind faith in my market had made me careless.

All is technique, Mrs. Child said in *Mastering the Art of French Cooking*, but even technique gets short shrift in her recent book. She tells us: "...gather a modest variety of canned fruits, boil them a few minutes in their own syrup with strips of lemon peel and a stick of cinnamon; then while their syrup is boiling down to a glaze, you arrange the fruits beautifully in a serving dish, interspersing them, perhaps, with thinly sliced bananas and a sprinkling of sliced almonds (always on hand in your freezer for such occasions). When you spoon the glaze over the fruits, you have a lovely looking dessert that, also, has a certain sophistication of taste." She calls for "Enough ready-mix for two 9-inch pies" in one recipe and she announces that "frozen store-bought ready-made shells" are to be part of her show on *quiches*. She sits in her "little house near Grasse" pining, "...if I could just get the chicken breasts the way I could get them in the U.S." Bless her. Grasse is a hop, skip, and a jump from Sisteron, whence come the most delectable mutton and lamb we have ever eaten, perfumed with the wild thyme on which the animals graze. It is sold in no American supermarket.

How many of our leading writers and gourmets have criticized our virtually inedible American chicken? We can recall only Simone Beck, and she showed remarkable restraint. When we criticized "sterilized" cream—the cream that keeps virtually indefinitely and has an odd taste that can best be described as having been boiled to death—we got a sniffy note from a *Family Circle* food editor saying it "reacts and tastes exactly as the regular." And *she* tells us how to cook. When an American *crème fraîche* appeared on the market some time ago, the gourmet press went gaga. It sells at astronomical prices and in no way could be mistaken for *crème fraîche*; it has an unpleasant off taste and a curiously waxy texture.

What we need is not fancy gourmet items but simple, beautiful, old-fashioned double cream; the kind that Fannie Farmer back in 1896 explained had to be diluted half and half with milk to whip properly. What is called heavy cream today has less character than the cream we used to take off the top of the milk bottle not so many years ago. It tasted better, too. (The coffee "lighteners" cannot be described in polite society.)

Dr. Paul A. Fine, in the study of our eating patterns discussed in the first chapter, described the movement from immigrant and rural communities into the mainstream of American life, which is characterized by a diet of Oreos, Crisco, TV dinners, macaroni and cheese, Pepsi and Coke, pizza, Jell-O, Heinz ketchup, and instant coffee. Dr. Fine goes on to discuss those who break out of the mainstream—those "upwardly-mobile, educated, self-reliant people who are usually at least one generation removed from their ethnic origins." Here one finds the gourmets, the experimenters, the consumerists.

Dr. Fine says that "Quality consciousness lies both to the right and left; mainstream eaters tend to use commercial products as their standard of quality—that is, use, say, Campbell soup as the standard for good soup rather than homemade soup."

Where Dr. Fine errs is in assuming that the gourmets do not use Campbell's soups. Convenience foods have so debased the American palate that even those who would describe themselves as gourmets—and this includes food writers and teachers—use canned soups regularly. The grotesqueness of doing gourmet cooking using canned soup seems to strike very few people.

What is tragic is that it is precisely the taste-makers who are the easiest marks for gourmet cooking. Many of them are honestly interested in ethnic cuisines—often that of their own ancestry from which they had been alienated—but are led astray by what Dr. Fine calls "flattened out" versions. The commonest of these are spaghetti, pizza, Tex-Mex dishes, and so on. French country cooking fares no better.

Dr. Fine noted that women no longer grew up learn-ing to cook and had to learn from schools and books. Actually, this has been increasingly true for most of a century, and accounts in large part for the desperate state of affairs. A really fine cook learned to cook at her mother's side. Such women do not feel the need to make gourmet concoctions—they are secure in the knowledge that the food they cook is delicious and that it has pleased countless generations.

Interestingly, the only really good cooks we know in this country (American-born) were somehow spared the mainstream homogenizing process. They have not lost touch with their past. They have inherited a cuisine that came to them from women who had to do farm chores, help in the fields and care for large families with no labor-saving devices, not even running water. They had no more time to do fancy cooking than the modern liberated woman, but they coped better. We too would cope better if we learned the cuisine of our grandmothers, whether it be Boston Baked Beans or a French *daube*. They are dishes that simmer away for hours on end but mind themselves perfectly and actually improve on re-heating. It's a cinch with modern stoves—grandmother managed with a wood-burning stove or fireplace. The dishes are relatively inexpensive, and there are no compli-cated techniques to learn. All that is required is decent produce and the willingness to learn the construction of a few of those old-fashioned dishes so that one can do them without agonizing over measurements.

Finally, however, regional cuisine is based on the produce available, and French cuisine in America must be something of a compromise. We would like to see a revival of genuine American cooking. Traces still persist, but fewer and fewer cooks make Maine Lobster Stew, or the chowders, the gumbos, the crab cakes, the baked beans, the oyster loaves, and other great dishes of our past. The fascinating Portuguese strain in New England cookery indicates that we can assimilate a good deal of ethnic cooking without losing our essential character. We admire French cuisine, but we have failed to learn its most important lesson, so well stated by the great French gastronome Curnonsky: "Cuisine is when food tastes of what it is."

11

Vive la Différence

Women lack the instincts for great cooking. . . . They have one or two dishes they
accomplish very well, but they are not
innovators.

Chef Paul Bocuse, to Craig Claiborne,
The New York Times, *June 30, 1975*

WHO DOES Paul Bocuse think *invented* cooking?

Reporting this old canard in his inimitable style,
Claiborne described Bocuse as the King of Chefs and
"heavily macho and with a high profile sex image." The
meaning was pretty clear, but *Newsweek* spelled it out,
saying that the chef "routinely expresses contempt for
women in the kitchen. 'The only place for them is in
bed,' says Bocuse, adding that 'anyone who doesn't change
his woman every week or so lacks imagination.' " Well,
that is what women are for, isn't it?—that, and the
drudgery of housework? When it comes to creativity,
leave it to the men.

This is not sex, it is a rape of women's talents.

That a woman should say much the same thing about
women and their cooking is incredible. Yet none other
than Julia Child is quoted by Nancy L. Ross of *The
Washington Post* as saying: "French women don't know

a damn thing about French cooking, although they pretend they know everything." Among the French women who hobnob with American Embassy wives such as Mrs. Child, this may be true; among the French women we know, there are magnificent cooks. She told John Kifner of *The Times* that her new book, *From Julia Child's Kitchen*, was for "people whose hobby is food, not for housewives." Kifner explained, "The word 'housewives,' in her vocabulary, ranks with 'home economists' as a term to be disdained." It seems that the term cook is also to be disdained; she calls herself The French Chef although she is neither French nor chef.

Trouble is, most American food writers don't know the difference between a chef and a cook. Jovan Trboyevic, owner of Le Perroquet in Chicago, told us not long ago: "There are great cooks who will never be chefs and chefs who will never be cooks. A chef is an executive."

A chef is someone trained to serve a table of ten people ten different meals, all dishes arriving on time—a stunt that is brilliant, antigastronomic, and demented. In fact, he is a glorified short-order cook. If the chef is a gifted cook, you will dine well; if he has a touch of genius, you will dine memorably. But how often does that happen?

It should be explained that the title of chef is earned only after three long, hard years as an apprentice, followed by another three or four long, hard years as a journeyman. It is not a title you pick up at the local Cordon Bleu cooking school. Mimi Sheraton, who studied at the Cordon Bleu in Paris, has this to say: "That was utter baloney. The chef used red and black food coloring in everything, and everybody cheated on the exam— the chef told us what to do so he wouldn't look bad." (*New York*, November 18, 1974)

Le grand restaurant evolved after the French Revolution, when the chefs who had served the aristocracy had to find new masters. Thus, any man with the price could be a prince for the evening, complete with an obsequious retinue in livery. The occupation of chefs became *épater les bourgeois*—to knock their eyes out. It seemed necessary, because the clients had *cuisinières* at home who were fine cooks.

Balzac said, "One does not dine as luxuriously in the provinces as in Paris, but one dines better; the dishes are better thought out. In the far reaches of the provinces there are Carêmes in petticoats, unknown geniuses who know how to make a dish of beans worthy of the nod with which Rossini acknowledges a perfectly successful dish." Rossini, so the story goes, was so enamored of the cooking of his *cuisinière* that when she threatened to quit, he married her.

This theme was repeated in art form by Marcel Rouff in *La Vie et la Passion de Dodin-Bouffant*. Dodin is invited by a prince to dine and is treated to a royal feast of some fifty dishes, made by chefs and served by a *maître d'hôtel* and a host of servants. Dodin reciprocates with a dinner where Adèle, his *cuisinière*, prepares and serves a one-dish meal, the lowly *pot-au-feu*, but such a *pot-au-feu* that the prince tries to steal her away. Whereupon Dodin marries the woman. The entire book is an homage to *la cuisine de femme, la vraie cuisine de France*, with mouth-watering description of scores of dishes that Rouff attributes to Adèle, *la cuisinière*.

Leo Larguier, in *Clarisse, ou la vieille cuisinière*, says that women cooks "are naturally delicate, and gastronomes by profession would do well to study them more." He goes on to repeat a story told by Théodore de Banville wherein Sophie, the *cuisinière*, has prepared a dinner suitable for a proper bourgeois house but the master, following his nose, comes to the kitchen, and lifts a lid from a casserole. "It is one of those dishes that the artist makes for herself and never for her master, a *ragoût* of mutton, but ideal, tawny, golden, with a concentrated, translucent shimmering sauce, and potatoes that glistened like topazes." *Bref*, he devours the *ragoût* and licks the pot clean. The terrible

Sophie returns: "Don't come in here again. Me, I don't eat your slop!"

Robert J. Courtine, France's most prestigious food writer, talked about these differences at lunch a few years ago, waving a fork above his Lorraine *potée*, a hearty dish of cabbage and pork. "Cooking is naturally feminine," he said, "but when it becomes art, it is masculine. Genius apart, I prefer women's cooking. Thank God there is not too much genius around. Otherwise, you could not eat a *potée*. A great chef would put something in it—I don't know, caviar?—and it would work. But if he's not a genius... Well, I remember a well-known chef presenting a dish of *crêpes* filled with ham and *crème fraîche*, rolled in *béchamel*, *gratinées*, and *flambées*." Courtine grimaced. "Never would a woman serve a dish like that.... A woman cooks for love of her man, a chef for himself, for his pride. The genius of simplicity is the genius of woman, the genius of complexity is the genius of man."

Courtine regarded the late Alexandre Dumaine as one of the greatest of chefs. Significantly, it was not one of the elaborate dishes he was celebrated for that Courtine recalled, but a simple dish of veal sweetbreads with fresh-picked spinach. "Dumaine just stirred the spinach in the pot with a wooden fork on which he had impaled a clove of garlic. That was a woman's trick."

A similar dish of Dumaine's sweetbreads, with fresh garden peas, was a golden memory to the late Madeleine Decure, editor of *Revue de Cuisine et Vins de France*. Reminiscing, she said: "I told Dumaine that that dish recaptured the taste of the sweetbreads my mother used to make." Was he pleased? She looked surprised at the question. "Well, I should hope so. You know, my father often told me, 'I married your mother because she made *la bonne soupe*.' And she did."

Miss Decure, a fine cook of impeccable taste, had nothing but scorn tempered with pity for women who attempted to dazzle guests with cooking for which they were not trained. "Snobs," she said. "*Les pauvres*."

It is interesting to note that women's cooking in France is precisely the hearty food that men like. Unlike their misguided American sisters, they leave to chefs the confection of baubles to tempt jaded palates. *La potée, la daube, la garbure, le cassoulet, le navarin, le pot-au-feu*—all these stews and bean dishes are women's cooking. And when chefs cook for themselves or wish to please an old friend, they cook these homey dishes. Escoffier often said he preferred his wife's cooking to his own. When we shared a *lapin à la moutarde* with the late Père Troisgros, he explained, "This is not a restaurant dish; it is a dish for the *patron* and his friends."

After dining magnificently one evening at Le Vivarois, we were chatting with the earnest young *patron*, Claude Peyrot, generally regarded as the most brilliant chef in Paris. "You liked that?" he asked. "Ah, you should have known my mother's cooking." He got that dreamy look that a Frenchman gets when he talks about his mother's cooking, and he launched into a description of how she would get from the *clapier* a rabbit "nourished on the good grass of our country" and lovingly simmer it with the wine and herbs of the region, the Vivarois. "That was cooking," he said. "Ah, I lived in a time that will never return."

That American gourmets should insult women's cooking is not especially new, but one would have expected Paul Bocuse of Lyons to be more loyal to his own tradition. For centuries, Lyons has been regarded as the gastronomic capital of France, and that reputation was largely created by *les mères saintes*. These legendary *cuisinières* first cooked for the silk merchants of Lyons and, as the textile industry gradually dispersed, often opened restaurants where they served the same food they had cooked for *les bourgeois*. Many of them became famous. Gradually, the old cooks retired and were replaced by chefs, but until a few years ago, Mère Brazier, then in her seventies, was still presiding over the kitchen of one of the twelve top-rated restaurants in France. The tradition lingers in the names of the restaurants (Mère Brazier, Mère Guy, Mère Charles, Tante Alice, Chez Juliette) and in their menus: *quenelles, saucisson en brioche, volaille demi-deuil, poulet au vinaigre.*

The *cuisinières* formed the taste of the Lyonnais. Their men were connoisseurs because they ate well at home, and they insisted on eating well when they dined out. There is this sort of chemical interaction between an exigent and knowledgeable clientele and the quality of restaurants; where the customers eat poorly from childhood, they cannot very well know good food from bad. Even a good natural palate must learn to distinguish between subtlety and blandness, between clear strong flavors and raucous ones, between harmony and cacophony. The Lyonnais did.

Now, Bocuse knows all this, and he is one of the most brilliant chefs in France. But he is also an *enfant terrible* who loves to play practical jokes.* In those recipes he gave Claiborne during that antiwoman interview, could he just have been putting Americans on? Or perhaps his recipes were not faithfully transmitted. Since it was Bocuse who brought up innovation, let us examine those dishes.

The *navarin* is an ancient women's dish: mutton stewed with spring vegetables, which must include turnips to justify the name. Bocuse's *Navarin de Homards* (unaccountably translated by Claiborne as *Baked Lobsters with*

---

* An example: One mid-November weekend, Bocuse threw a surprise banquet for some forty restaurateurs, merchants, and journalists down from Paris for the annual Beaujolais tastings. It was an authentic medieval feast, except that a mystery wine was served, which the guests were asked to identify. Near the end, Bocuse revealed that he had mixed tag ends of bad wines. He succeeded in spoiling his own dinner by serving bad wine with it. (Our own response had been that we hadn't the faintest notion what wine it was, but we could not drink it. We still regret having eaten that great meal without wine.) It should be added that Bocuse is capable of extraordinary generosity to his colleagues.

vegetables although it never goes near an oven) is a chichi travesty on the original. Five different vegetables are separately blanched (the roots having been cut into fat matchsticks), then simmered with the lobster for an additional twenty minutes; the cooking liquid is then thickened with THREE TABLESPOONS OF FLOUR. The vegetables will be overdone and the sauce sludged up with flour; the dish has neither the rustic simplicity of a mutton stew nor the *éclat*, the lightness and brilliance, of his more successful creations.

When we queried Bocuse on his use of flour in this dish we received this reply: "I inform you that there must be no flour in the *Navarin de Homard.* . . . Not knowing English, I was not able to verify the recipe written by Craig Claiborne." One may be permitted to ask how many recipes have been similarly rewritten.

Poulet Sauté au Vinaigre (translated by Claiborne into "Sautéed chicken with tomato sauce") is said by the Lyonnais to be a dish of the Rhone boatmen, made with the wine that had soured en route. The fact is that nearly everywhere in France women have made *poulet au vinaigre* for centuries. The dish will vary slightly with regional differences in the chicken, the type of vinegar, the aromatics, and the fat used in the sautéeing. One of our prized recipes comes from an old woman in the *causses* of the Quercy who sautéed the chicken in goose fat with a clove or two of garlic and simply sprinkled *verjus* (unripe grape juice) on towards the last. If it were an older bird, she explained, she would put the *verjus* in right after the initial browning, thus demonstrating the origin of the dish; vinegar and similar acids have a tenderizing effect. She warned against too much; just enough to give "that little tart taste." The whole charm of this ancient dish is lost when you start mucking it up as Bocuse and/or Claiborne did with 12 cloves of garlic, ½ cup red wine vinegar, ¾ cup white wine, 1 cup fresh or canned chicken broth, 3 tablespoons tomato paste, 1 lb. tomatoes, and tarragon.

With all that tomato and vinegar, it is difficult to see much difference between that sauce and ketchup.*

It is instructive to examine a recipe, *Poulet au Feu d'Enfer* (hell's fire), from *Ma Gastronomie* by Fernand Point, under whom Bocuse worked. The recipe is clearly based on *poulet au vinaigre*, but Point wished to indicate that the presence of even a little tomato and so much vinegar was a daring departure from the classical version.

> Cut up a chicken and sauté it in butter. When nicely browned and almost done, throw in a little finely chopped garlic. Deglaze with a good glass of wine vinegar, reduce, moisten with 4 tablespoons white wine, again allow to reduce, and moisten with a little consommé and a little tomato concentrate. Decant, skim, and add *fines herbes*, tarragon, parsley, and a good chunk of butter (and more vinegar if it is not highly enough seasoned) at the moment of serving. (Our translation.)

Bocuse's final dish, *Soupe aux Truffes Elysée*, is a show stopper; *Newsweek* described it as "orgiastic." When a chef is presented with the Legion of Honor, clearly something spectacular is expected. (Others have already chided Claiborne for reporting that Bocuse was the *only* chef ever so honored.) The dish consists of butter, onions, celery, carrots, fresh mushrooms, Smithfield ham, 1 pound canned truffles, ¼ pound fresh or canned *foie gras*, vermouth, and chicken broth, all baked in individual crocks topped with puff paste. In France, truffles and *foie gras* are at their best in midwinter; in America, they are, for all practical purposes, unobtainable fresh and beautiful at any time. (The recipe was presented to *Times* readers in late June.) Canned truffles and *foie gras*, even when genuine, range in quality from poor to mediocre and cost a

---

* In his newly published *La Cuisine du Marché*, Bocuse gives a more authentic recipe for *Volaille de Bresse sautée au vinaigre*: 1 chicken, 4 shallots, ⅓ lb. butter, 1 cup good wine vinegar, salt, and pepper. Was the tomato added to the other recipe to please the Americans?

king's ransom. Do you not know how to make puff paste? Never mind. Claiborne, always ready with a puff, gives an address and the price, smack in the middle of the recipe.

The baking of a puff paste over steaming broth is something no amateur should attempt. It certainly is dazzling, but the truth is that no matter how feathery, how airy the crust, it is going to turn sodden as it falls into the soup. Buttery, crunchy croutons would provide more attractive textural contrast and retain interest even after imbibing the liquid.

The great Carême allowed that *vol-au-vent* was delightful to the eye, but warned emphatically of the "painstaking care" it required. The acknowledged master pastry chef of France was cautioning other professionals that, while it was spectacular, it was tricky and liable to end in disaster. What he said about puff pastry applies to most chef's cooking in the hands of amateurs. Carême was wryly aware that a great deal of his success was due to the razzle-dazzle of the architectural structures with which he topped his creations. But the basic food under his astonishing *pièces-montées* was often very simply cooked; one example is the lowly whiting cooked in butter, parsley, and a little lemon juice.

What is surprising about these three Bocuse recipes as presented by Claiborne is the context: they were chosen to illustrate a massive promotion of *la nouvelle cuisine*, a movement precisely away from the floury excesses and ostentatious presentations of nineteenth-century cuisine and back toward the simpler, yet more refined sauces based on reduction of meat broths and other cooking liquids. Bocuse's incorporated group, La Grande Cuisine Française (which Courtine has called "some sort of a bizenesse" promoting conserves and wines for a fee), has left the impression that it invented *la nouvelle cuisine*. This is hardly grateful to Fernand Point, who many years ago taught the philosophy to some of the most illustrious members of Bocuse's company.

When *Newsweek* (August 11, 1975) invited Julia Child

to comment on this new French revolution, she said, "They've finally gotten it through their thick heads that there are some people who don't want to be stuffed full of fat and truffles." *Newsweek* added that Mrs. Child's new book would "echo a shift she perceives among Americans toward lighter and more adventurous cooking—and one whose origins predated the 'revolution' in France." Yet, a few months later, *People* reports: "*Julia is staunchly loyal to the rich sauces and gastronomic extravagances of the old French cookery*, and its master chef, Auguste Escoffier, of whom she says stoutly, 'He's codified everything in cooking.'" (December 1, 1975; our emphasis.)

One may be forgiven, perhaps, for wondering whether Mrs. Child is for or against gastronomic extravagances and richness, so let us turn to the "lighter and more adventurous cooking" that she talked about to *Newsweek*.

In San Francisco about that time (mid-1975), The French Chef demonstrated an array of her specialties, some of which would appear in *From Julia Child's Kitchen*. For comparison with Bocuse, we'll take three: *Caneton en Aspic à la Parisienne*, Beef Wellington, and *Crêpes à la Pagode en Flammes*. Mrs. Child is exceedingly fond of aspics, which she describes as "a glistening poem ... of high sophistication" and "so dazzling you would think only a professional could execute it." True, aspic dishes may be flashy, but they are seldom delicious. Unless they are made from calf's foot, they have no gastronomic interest whatsoever. To keep the aspic from melting at room temperature, the usual solution is, of course, commercial gelatin—which is what Mrs. Child uses. A perfectly made aspic is a transparent, trembling creation that has most charm in hot weather, precisely when its presentation poses the greatest problems. People rarely take the trouble to serve it cradled in shaved ice, the only way to present it successfully. Hence, rubbery gelatin.

When it is not in aspic, a Child adventure is likely to be encased in a pastry crust. Beef Wellington (which is now passé, glory be) is tenderloin partly roasted, cooled, smeared with *foie gras* (tinned, to be sure) and *duxelles*, wrapped in puff paste, baked, and served with a truffle sauce. Mrs. Child suggests instead a *brioche* crust (with which we would not quarrel, except that the recipe she specifies is heavily sweetened), and for the sauce she suggests what she claims approaches a *demi-glace* that is made with "brown stock or canned beef bouillon." Beef Wellington is not French. Escoffier, for example, gives more than fifty recipes for tenderloin of beef, not one of which is in a crust. For good reason. Beef does not take kindly to reheating, and under a crust it acquires a steam-table taste. Lovers of good beef leave Wellington alone.

As for that flaming *crêpe* dish, *McCall's* described it as "Instant Elegance." Not bad as a definition of gourmet cooking. Mrs. Child has a penchant for rolling things in *crêpes*. A Child-like *crêpe* dish appears in *Cooking of Provincial France*, a Time-Life production headed by M. F. K. Fisher, the late Michael Field, and Julia Child. This adventure uses thirty-three ingredients in five separate operations. Courtine summed it up nicely: "It's a lot of work for such a meager result! It's the sort of dish to dazzle and beguile a foreign woman but it is false grand cuisine and as antigastronomic as can be."

As it happened, Time-Life had incautiously engaged Courtine to write the introduction and notes for a translation of its "French" cookbook, which it had the effrontery to put out in France. The notes, a blistering and brilliant commentary on the innumerable imbecilities in the book, were unaccountably printed with the translation, to the discomfiture of all concerned—except the ineffable Courtine. We picked up our copy at the coming-out bash in Paris, and our report appeared in *The New York Times* under the tagline, "The Self-Roasting Cookbook." (We were never again invited to a Time-Life party.) Courtine's corrective comments can stand as a critique of fake French cuisine as taught by our leading mentors. For example: "Classic mayonnaise does *not* contain mustard.... There is no cream in 'true' hollandaise.... You must *not* put garlic in onion soup.... Nobody would *dream* of adding croutons to tripe." Where the authors state that game is not roasted, Courtine snaps, "Except partridge, pheasant, quail, etc." Again correcting the authors, he advises that coarse rustic terrines are likely to be better in a restaurant than the fancy ones. And much more.

Speaking of terrines, and of all that fat and those truffles to which those thick-skulled Frenchmen are alleged to be addicted, Mrs. Child's new book has a recipe for a *pâté* that has 1 cup butter and ¾ cup lard in the crust and 2½ cups of pork fat and a pound of truffled *foie gras* in the stuffing. The truth is that the book abounds with recipes involving *foie gras*, truffles, and rich crusts.

Among influential American food writers, only Claiborne puts more flour in sauces than does Mrs. Child. She explains: "It is actually the uncooked or poorly cooked *roux*, in my opinion, that has given flour a bad name in sauces. But since it takes only 2 or 3 minutes to cook flour and butter together, and since there is nothing difficult about it whatsoever, there is no excuse at all for a badly made sauce." A *roux* is cooked in two or three minutes? Escoffier did not feel it necessary to tell chefs how long to cook *roux*, but *Larousse Gastronomique* is specific: a white *roux* is to be cooked, stirring constantly with a wooden spatula, for five minutes, but without taking on color. (Brown *roux* takes at least twice as long.) But Mrs. Child's recipe for *béchamel-velouté* says just cook the *roux* for two minutes, then cook the sauce for two minutes, and it is done.

" 'All this beating of poor old Escoffier over the head,' murmured Mrs. Child sadly," in that *New York Times* interview. Poor old Escoffier indeed. Let us look at the recipe for *béchamel* in his *Guide Culinaire*. He uses far less flour, and simmers it gently for one hour. He also uses veal, onions, and herbs, and this, be it noted, is already a debased version of earlier *béchamels*. In his later years, Escoffier evolved toward a more refined cooking. In *Ma Cuisine*, written over thirty years after his classic

Guide, he reduces the amount of flour to less than one tablespoon per cup of finished sauce for his *Velouté Simple* and directs: "Conduct the cooking of the *velouté* at the gentlest simmer to facilitate the skimming and obtain a transparent sauce. *Time of cooking and skimming*: One and a half hours."

From Julia Child's Kitchen makes the two-minute *velouté* seem easy: "you may want to simmer it longer, but this depends entirely on how strong and well-flavored the stock was to begin with...." Mrs. Child appears not to understand that those hours of simmering and skimming are necessary to throw off the dross—the grease and palpable presence of the flour. If it were only a question of concentrating the flavor, that could be accomplished more easily by simple boiling, instead of simmering with the *roux*. If Mrs. Child *will* use Escoffier's flour-based sauces, she should heed his advice.

Referring, presumably, to those same thick-skulled French chefs who at last are following the American example, Mrs. Child says: "A number of contemporary chefs in France, who profess to scorn brown *roux* (flour and butter) and other starchy sauce thickeners, have taken to blending a strongly reduced and concentrated meat stock into the deglazing of their roasts, and then thickening it with a liaison of butter." She finds it too strong. In a general note she says, "You need not use your own home-made brand of consommé either, of course, *but you should most certainly disguise canned consommé; a short simmer with some tasteful additions,* and it becomes your own." (Our emphasis.) (For 8 cups strong, concentrated canned consommé, she adds, among other ingredients, ⅔ cup vermouth!) No amount of simmering with whatever additions is going to make canned consommé taste anything but canned. It is the presence of "taste enhancers" and other nasty additives that is objectionable; if you reduce canned soups, the flavor becomes *more* objectionable, not less. No one can hope to succeed in making the lovely sauces of *la nouvelle cuisine* (or *l'ancienne*) who does not understand that they are based on beautiful produce, clarity and purity of flavor, and flawless technique. *Flour in sauces is the crutch of a poor cook.*

In support of flour-based sauces, Mrs. Child notes that chefs Raymond Oliver, René Verdon, and Jacques Pépin use them. They do indeed. *Hélas.* Pépin, an engaging fellow, who was Director of Research and Development for Howard Johnson's and has been known to call for "canned beef gravy" in a sauce, puts flour even into fresh stewed peas! Speaking of the chefs of *la nouvelle cuisine*, he told David McCullough in Book-of-the-Month News: "As for nonsense, take their theory that you can make sauces by reduction, by simply boiling and not adding flour. It doesn't work. You can boil all you want and won't get a sauce."

But when she cites Point, "the presumed father of the new school of chefs," as suggesting "a little *roux* moistened with milk and cream to pour over his delicate mousse of pike, his *Quenelles à la Crème*," she misunderstands. A *roux*, dear lady, is butter and flour gently simmered, to which one adds liquid. What Point proposes in this recipe is a curious *beurre manié*, an amalgam of butter and flour, further softened with heavy cream, and added in bits to thicken the simmering milk—a very different process. Out of more than two hundred recipes in Point's *Ma Gastronomie*, flour enters a sauce but four times, and only in the form of *beurre manié*. According to some of his most brilliant students, it was added in tiny amounts—"*comme une noisette*" (like a hazelnut). Most often, however, Point finishes his sauces in one of two ways: one is to add thick cream and veal glaze to the cooking juices, then boil for a few minutes to blend and reduce. The other is *monter au beurre*, to whisk in bits of butter to deglazed liquids or suitably reduced cooking juices, the method that Mrs. Child depreciates so. It is a fragile liaison of a finesse that cannot be matched in any other way, but it does take beautiful ingredients—and flair.

Mrs. Child uses flour even in something she typically

calls *"Lentilles garnies; lentilles en cassoulet"* and in *"Pot-age purée de lentilles; potage purée Conti,"* which she claims is "along classic lines, including Carême's turnip," but she adds 3 tablespoons flour to only six cups of liquid already thickened with 1½ cups of puréed lentils. No cook would add flour to lentils; they are quite farinaceous enough. We have not been able to find a single recipe in classic or regional cuisine that calls for flour with lentils—these recipes may be unique. Her "New England fresh fish chowder" should be unique; she adds 3 tablespoons of flour, sour cream, and croutons. Pilot crackers are tradi-tional, but croutons? flour? sour cream? Why does she not call it "Julia Child's Chowder" and add what she pleases?

In her new book, Mrs. Child reveals with disarming candor: "I certainly never knew a thing about yeast and dough until my colleague, Simca, and my husband, Paul, and I went through the 750 days of our great French bread spree, while we were working on Volume II of *Mastering the Art of French Cooking.* I had sometimes wondered, when I ordered a frankfurter and sauerkraut on a bun in one of those sausage snack bars, why the bun usually disintegrated into a slimy mess in the bottom of the plate." Earlier, *Newsweek* had reported: "After 200 ... bakings, 250 pounds of flour and five months of toil— Voilà! Julia Child has done it. She has made French bread out of bleached American flour." Mrs. Child is indeed an industrious woman, but when she and we were young, many American housewives used twice as much flour in baking, day in and day out, and nobody thought it re-markable.

It should be said that the nineteen-page recipe for French bread that resulted was one of the few published in the United States that stuck to the correct ingredients: flour, yeast, water, and salt. It also gives much useful infor-mation on shaping the loaves. Its most serious fault is that there is no setting of the "sponge." Most of us know that yeast is a living organism that requires moisture, food, air, and an optimum temperature (around 70° F) to grow and multiply, and that the lightness of bread is produced by the resultant gases that are trapped in the dough. What few people nowadays understand is that the flavor and texture are greatly affected by the strains of yeast and the speed of fermentation. (We leave, for the moment, the question of quality of flour, although here also, she is not fussy.) If you mix store-bought yeast with water and flour into a very soft dough and let it sit at 70° F for several hours, you will attract "wild" yeasts; the slow fermentation will allow the yeasts to multiply in a leisurely fashion and the lovely wheaty taste will have time to mature. Additional flour is then kneaded in, and the dough goes through at least two more risings. We are talking about serious bread-making.

The best bread is made from the time-honored "mother" dough; a small hank (depending on the size of the batch) of dough is put aside for the next baking. Mrs. Child states: "Sour dough is an American invention. . . . We think that our recipe will give you a tastier loaf." It may be doubted that the ancient Egyptians trudged down to the supermarket to buy foil-wrapped instant granulated yeast. While a number of societies early turned to yeasts based on ale brewing, most peoples clung tenaciously to the "mother"-dough method. To this day, bread made using a "chef" or "mother," popularly known as *pain au levain*, is highly regarded in France and commands a premium price. (In actual fact, such bread usually contains ordinary yeast as well; technically the name only means that the sponge method was employed, but the old-fashioned wheaty taste of properly fermented bread is implied.) Sour dough differs from the "mother" method only in minor details; the trick is to keep the "wild" yeasts alive and kicking until the next baking, and the precise way of doing it will depend on ambient temperature, frequency of baking, and tradition. The individual strains or races of these "wild" yeasts will give different results—we have had tantalizingly different loaves when trying out various ancient and primitive ways of attracting and assisting the growth of "wild" yeasts, although not so much, perhaps, as with various kinds of wheat and milling methods. It is interesting to note that since Volume II of *Mastering the Art of French Cooking*, Mrs. Child has heard tell of the "sponge," which she calls "yeast batter": it improves taste and texture, she tells us. But any serious baker knows this from childhood.

A food writer's opinion of another's work is occasionally as revealing as his or her own. Commenting in *McCall's*, on the new edition of Irma S. Rombauer's *Joy of Cooking*, Mrs. Child deplores the disappearance of a recipe, "perhaps now a collector's item," for Baked Bean Sandwiches. For collectors, she repeats the recipe. It seems that you mash 1 cup baked beans, add lemon juice or ketchup or chili sauce or mustard and butter and minced onion or celery. This is spread on Boston brown or rye bread, sprinkled with chopped parsley, topped with strips of bacon, and the whole mess is stuck under the broiler. "Now, that's a nice simple recipe, rather a *frijoles refritos* type of thing." So much for Mexican cooking; now let us see Mrs. Child tackle three cuisines at once, or perhaps it's four.

"Here we have rice and risotto the French and French Chef ways," Mrs. Child says in her new book. She is introducing a recipe called *Risotto garni*. It has pork breakfast sausages, onions, green bell peppers, cooked rice, chopped [!] raisins, bananas, hard-boiled eggs, herbs, and "½ cup or so chopped almonds, walnuts, pine nuts, peanuts, or whatever else in the way of nuts you have." Mrs. Child explains: "risotto is a prime repository for leftovers." She says this dish is really a kind of curry dinner, that her family first encountered it in a Chinese restaurant in Kandy, Ceylon, where it was known as "Flied Lice with Mix," and that her family likes to eat it with chopsticks. Reason begins to falter. This is French? This is risotto? *Pace*, Child, but it is pure Trader Vic.

The author treats *lasagna* in the same debonair way. She

recounts what happened when she presented her *Lasagne à la Française* on television: "I was almost lynched by the Italian anti-defamation league. 'What do you mean, using our national dish, lasagne, for leftovers. The very idea made me ill!' shrieked one letter from New Jersey." Mrs. Child does acknowledge that, on the air, she had been "a bit carried away, [and] made a few Italianesque cracks. . . ." To objectors in the audience, The French Chef sends form letters. Mrs. Child continues:

> The one on lasagne, written with great enjoyment by me, tells enraged viewers that the whole idea of learning how to cook is so that one can grab any idea from anywhere and put it to good use. Here it is the idea of lasagne that is "freed from ethnic restrictions and limitations," and is ready for improvisation. . . . And to enrage them further, the final touch, "We should be thankful to the Italians for having invented lasagne-shaped pasta, and to the French for their fine cooking methods that make such a splendid dish possible." Strangely—or should I say thankfully—I have never had any reply whatsoever to this masterful rebuttal.

To cap it off, Mrs. Child recommends serving French bread with her *lasagna.* . . . Improvisation is to be encouraged, but it requires a gift. Furthermore, nomenclature is not without meaning, or at least should not be. Mrs. Child gives a recipe for *Haricots secs garnis à l'alsacienne* that calls for sauerkraut with . . . black beans and olive oil! "I don't think this is Alsatian at all, but if the Alsatians were blessed with black beans they would surely use them in this hearty combination." (If they had olive oil. And if the Cubans had sauerkraut, would they call it a *Choucroûte Habañero?*) Mrs. Child, incidentally, adds cornstarch to her sauerkraut.

And then we get The French Chef's *Brandade à la soissonaise.* A real *brandade* is salt cod pounded to a creamy mass, made fragrant with olive oil (it is indeed a Provençal word meaning vigorously stirred, as she says), and they do grow beans around Soissons, hundreds of miles to the north. By that reasoning, Mrs. Child gives us a peculiar sort of Arabian *hummus* of white beans with sesame paste, and calls it by a French Yankee-Dixie name.

Black beans and olive oil in Alsace, sesame paste in Soissons, "Flied Lice" in risotto, and many more anomalies reflect a disregard for the inner nature of a dish and for the region and the people who created it. Finally, it would seem, a dish is *à la Française* if Julia Child, The French Chef, says so.

It is certainly not *à la Française* if French women created it. We repeat the comment she made to *The Washington Post*, referring to the fact that her cookbooks had never been translated into French: "French women don't know a damn thing about French cooking, although they pretend they know everything."

Mrs. Child herself, by friendly accounts, was a poor cook when she enrolled at the Cordon Bleu in Paris at the age of thirty-seven. (Indeed, *People* reports that "Julia cooked as if the way to a man's heart was through his stomach pump.... But Paul manfully shoveled it in because, he groans: 'I was willing to put up with all that awful cooking to get Julia.'") In no time, she was herself teaching French cooking to other Americans who found themselves at loose ends in Paris.

The instant chef is a pattern that seems to shock few Americans. There cannot be many mothers who would send a child to study the violin with somebody who had taken it up only the year before. Yet it is commonplace for Americans to whip through a fast course in cookery and take up the career of creating gourmet chefs.

It is tragic that American women, alienated from their own culinary past, should have so meekly followed the lead of the gourmet chefs in the kitchen. The cuisine they present, already second-rate Escoffier, is so corrupted with expediencies that all is travesty.

There is no question that women cooks would benefit greatly from the professional training and discipline that are required of chefs, but this they are denied by the virtually medieval apprenticeship system in France. Apprenticeship to a working chef is the ideal way to learn the trade; so far the hotel schools have yet to produce a great cook. Executive chefs they turn out by the score. It's the same in any *métier* that verges on art; not many stonecutters become great sculptors. Consider the thousands of well-trained male chefs in France. While most knowledgeable eaters would agree on the ten most brilliant, after that there would be less and less agreement. This is not a very high percentage of recognized artists. If there were anything like the same number of similarly trained women cooks, they could do no worse. Indeed, the one woman chef who managed to run the gantlet, Mme. Paulette Castaing, *chef-patronne* of the Beau Rivage at Condrieu, near Lyons, has her two stars from Michelin and the respect of her male colleagues. She is an attractive, intensely feminine person who, in spite of her smallness, was shown no favors during her apprenticeship and journeyman days. "It was not easy," she admitted.

Bocuse repeated the old routine about how "few great women architects and orchestra leaders" there are. We will leave aside as evident the biological demands made upon women in the bearing and rearing of children—just at the time when a *métier* demands all of one's energies. Also the fact that most professions were virtually closed to women. There is, as well, a deep psychological and social barrier that is just beginning to budge, ever so little, here and there. Society will NOT tolerate from women the same ego, the same dignity, the same devotion to her work (which almost inevitably leads to some neglect of her family and the concomitant feelings of guilt), the same search for fulfillment, and, above all, the same search for recognition of her work.

Until very recently, indeed, actresses and women singers were highly suspect. What passes for celebrity in a man is notoriety in a woman. This possibly explains why, among the arts, it is in poetry that women have had some individual successes—often posthumously. It is such an inward, almost secret art, that even genteel women were able to learn the craft and practice it without showing up men—the fatal error. It takes a courageous woman of great dedication to practice her art in the marketplace. It is not easy for men; for women it is nearly impossible. But there is particular irony in the fact that women are virtually barred from stardom in an art which is peculiarly theirs, and have to suffer the indignity of loutish attacks from a Bocuse.

We have already mentioned the *daube*, the *cassoulet*, the *navarin*. All these long, slow-cooking dishes, *les petits plats mijotés*, are women's dishes, as are Boston Baked Beans, Brunswick Stew, New England Boiled Dinner, or whatever. They are dishes that make the best possible use of local produce, and they were invented by women who had to help in fields, milk the cows, tend the chickens, have the babies and mind them, do the housework, and still come up, day after day, with delicious meals for a hungry family, often from sparse and unpromising materials.

No intelligent woman is altogether enchanted with being a housewife, but women, even the most militant feminists, should take pride in the womanly craft of cookery, and respect those who created it. Further, women's cooking is certainly better suited to the needs of career people, men or women, than is chef's cooking. All those great long-simmering dishes were created precisely to mind themselves while women occupied themselves with other work; today, with new aspirations and modern conveniences, it is more important than ever that we not depreciate this cuisine. Instead of foolishly aping the antics of French chefs, real or pretend, with all the expediencies and infinitely time-consuming froufrou that such cuisine demands, women would do better to learn and understand the cooking of their grandmothers.

Not all women's cooking is rustic. Women in prosperous regions who had time to fiddle with such things made dishes having a finesse and charm that a male chef would be hard put to equal. *Beurre blanc*, for instance, invented by the women of the Loire to go with the shad and pike that used to be so abundant there, is the loveliest of sauces. The great Curnonsky, who was from Angers (on the Loire), claimed that only women could make it; he exaggerated, but it does illustrate "the genius of simplicity" that Courtine praised. This sauce does not mask the taste of the fish; the memory of shallot and white wine vinegar adds just the right aromatic note, and the fluffy butter supplies the richness that is desirable with these fish, which have a tendency to be dry. Mère Allard, one of the great women cooks of France, points out that it is finest with poached fish, somewhat less effective with plain grilled fish, and should never be served with sautéed fish. Male chefs, and those who pathetically try to emulate them, could learn lessons about harmony, basic lines of a dish, and the general rightness of things from such a cook.

Mère Allard taught Fernande (her daughter-in-law and successor) how to make *beurre blanc* and Fernande told us. We give it here for the edification of Claiborne who, after tasting it a few years ago Chez Allard, ecstatically announced to his readers that French butter was so wonderful that this sauce "consisted simply of whisking the butter with a little water." This from a man who had boasted, in knocking the late Clementine Paddleford, that he "knew all the sauces." He has always had difficulty with *beurre blanc*. He later published George Verrier's recipe with a typical chef's complication: 2¼ cups heavy cream, heavily reduced. As with any regional dish, there are numerous variations, but the addition of even a little cream is considered heresy up and down the Loire. Cream sludges up the wonderfully clear yet subtle taste and silken texture of a classic *beurre blanc*. Far stranger was the recipe that Claiborne gave in *The New York Times Menu Cookbook*. It called for 6 tablespoons butter, 1 cup heavy cream, 1 egg yolk, 2 tablespoons lemon juice, and Tabasco. *Sacre bleu!*

Beurre blanc is thought to be a very difficult dish, but

we find it mainly a matter of beautiful produce and a little love. Buy the best butter you can find—we make ours, but decent cream is getting more and more difficult to find. American shallots are the coarse-tasting red ones and are often rancid as well; since the superior gray ones are unobtainable, we frequently use scallions instead—they work, and give a fresh taste. Unless you have best white wine vinegar from France, you are better off with good cider vinegar; it is often used in Brittany. As for the fish, catch it—even in our port cities, fish markets go from bad to worse. Any handsome white-fleshed fish is fine; besides the classic shad and pike, there is striped bass or red snapper, for instance. We will not go into the poaching of the fish except to warn you that the sauce will require your rapt attention for about fifteen minutes and will not stand, so until you have made it several times, it is prudent to set the poached fish on a rack over the fish kettle and to have all in readiness before you start in on the sauce.

Mère Allard's Beurre Blanc

Take three or four shallots and chop them fine. Put them in a heavy pot (not aluminum) with a quarter cup of best white wine vinegar, ½ teaspoon coarse sea salt (omit for now if butter is salted), and several peppercorns. Reduce over a brisk flame until virtually dry, watching carefully because it must not even begin to turn color. Have a good pound of best butter (very cold, Fernande stressed) cut roughly into tablespoon-size chunks. Take the pan off the fire for an instant, put in a piece or two of butter, and stir with a wooden spoon until well incorporated. After a couple more such additions, change to a sauce whisk and place on the gentlest possible heat. Whisking madly all the while, add the butter, a chunk or two at a time. Check for seasoning (you may add a few drops of lemon juice if it pleases you), and strain into a warm (not hot) sauce dish, or over the fish. Strew with finely chopped parsley. Steamed potatoes are the traditional accompaniment.

If you are successful, you will have a fluffy, aromatic

sauce. You will be able to tell very quickly if it is going to "take"—it takes on a slightly gluey look, rather like a mayonnaise. Failure is due to excessive heat; if it threatens to separate, you can sometimes rescue it by carefully setting the pan in cold water for just an instant, then continuing on lower heat. If worse comes to worst, firmly announce it as *beurre fondu*.

12

Dining Out

Howard Johnson's—
the Taste of America!

Television jingle

Nᴏᴛ ʟᴏɴɢ ᴀɢᴏ, the New Jersey Turnpike Authority
canceled the Howard Johnson's concession after seventeen
years. It explained that the clientele had become tired of
the food—not of its awfulness, but of its sameness. An
official said the new concessionaires would provide "gourmet foods, international cuisine, chafing-dish service." We
waited two months to let the new management break in,
then tried one of Marriott's gourmet caravanserais. A
truckdriver had told us that the food was "basically the
same" as before, and indeed it was, though it came from
a different commissary. We tasted a factory fruit salad;
canned, thickly floured bean soup; salad with iceberg lettuce and a quarter of a cotton tomato, laced with industrial dressing; a tasteless, dry chopped beefsteak; frozen
shrimps dipped in a sweet crumb batter, fried, refrozen,
and reheated; cardboard pies; and poor coffee with a
nameless whitener.

In short, the taste of America.

When we asked a waitress about the history of the
shrimps, she said, "I don't know what they are—I only
serve it." The manager more graciously acknowledged

that he had no cooks, and indeed regarded "these convenience items" as a costly substitute for real food; he himself, he confided, cooked from scratch at home. "But we've been getting a lot of good comments," he said. Perhaps a public that has been educated to mistake fancy for good will accept the false promise of a chafing dish as an improvement upon the reality of thawed glop.

There is, in fact, about as much difference in taste among our feeding chains as there is among makes of American cars. As measured by business success, however, perhaps it is McDonald's that should claim the Taste-of-America title. Back in 1973, *Time* dedicated a cover story to Big Mac, "The Burger That Conquered the Country." The piece was couched in that breathless admiration which billion-dollar successes inspire in business writers. But it did mention the objections of some effete elitists:

> Pop Sociologist Vance Packard laments: "This is what our country is all about—blandness and standardization." Novelist Vance Bourjaily extravagantly views McDonald's popularity as a sign that America is "a failing culture." He explains: "This country is full of people who have forgotten what good food is. Eating in most countries is a basic pleasure, but people in the U.S. don't eat for pleasure. To them, eating is just something done in response to advertising."

Time went on to mention that some aesthetes regarded a McDonald's outlet as a neighborhood blight, and that the nutritionist Jean Mayer of Harvard warns that a steady diet of its hamburgers, French fries, and synthetic milk shakes could bring back scurvy. But *Time* retorted: "Since no one is forced to eat at a McDonald's, the chain must be giving multitudes exactly what they want." True, they can eat at Howard Johnson's, or Burger King, or any other McDonald's under another name.

As for the taste of McDonald's, *Time* brought up the big guns of gourmet food writing to rebut Bourjaily. They are worth quoting in full:

Craig Claiborne: "The hamburgers are quite swal-lowable. There is a highly compatible onion flavor. The French fries are first-rate; they are made in fresh fat and are crisp. I do think they could put more pickle on the hamburger. Overall, I would rank them on a par with Howard Johnson's hamburgers."

James Beard: "McDonald's is a great machine that belches forth hamburgers. The whole thing is aimed at the six-year-old palate. They don't salt things enough, and the malts taste like melted ice cream. But the place is efficient and clean, and the help is pleas-ant. The packaging is damned smart because it insu-lates. The food may be more honest than some things you get at higher prices."

Julia Child: "The buns are a little soft. The Big Mac I like least because it's all bread. But the French fries are surprisingly good. It's remarkable that you can get that much food for under a dollar. It's not what you would call a balanced meal; it's nothing but calories. But it would keep you alive."

Gael Greene: "When I want meat, I want a steak. But when I want a hamburger, I want a Big Mac. It has all those disreputable things—cheese made of glue, Russian dressing three generations removed from the steppes, and this very thin patty of something that is close enough to meat. It's an incredibly decadent eat-ing experience. And I love the malts—thick, sweet and ice-cold. They're better than if they were real."

The foregoing judgments tell us less about McDonald's than about their authors: the feckless condescension of Claiborne ("quite swallowable"); the generous effort of Beard and Child to find something positive to say without losing the gourmet franchise (the packaging, the prices, the frozen fries); the East Side porno-chic of Greene, founder of the erotic school of food writing.

To tell the truth, we had thought Greene was the only member of that school, until we read an essay in *The New York Review* about the new wave of porn novels by women, a genre we are unfamiliar with. The critic N. A. Straight remarks that in these oeuvres, "it is hard to figure

out which is more important: food or sex." One gathers
that there is little sensual pleasure in either. Pending the
publication of Greene's new sex novel, here is another
sample of her clever and brittle food-writing style: "Imagine an evening cuddling with a confirmed virgin. That
was the '52 Mouton-Rothschild. It just wouldn't give. It's
not ready to be loved." It is to be doubted that that 1952
wine was too young (any more than was that ageless Mc-
Donald's shake that Greene affected to adore), but how
many readers would know, or care? Horace Sutton quotes
Clay Felker, the publisher of *New York* magazine, as
boasting: "Gael never had a hot meal until we gave her
the restaurant job." Like most other American food writers, Greene by her own account made the leap from a
badly fed childhood (she was raised in a Velveeta cocoon,
she told Sutton) to haute cuisine à la Dione Lucas and Le
Pavillon without ever having encountered good home
cooking.

In identifying its experts, *Time* omitted to mention
their commercial associations. Beard, who was an actor
before he got into the food game, has toiled for such clients as Planters peanut oil, Green Giant, Nestlé, Restaurant Associates, and Pillsbury, the owner of the Burger
King chain. Claiborne, as we have noted, is only half of a
food-writing team, the other half being the executive chef
of Howard Johnson's. So Claiborne's rating of Big Mac
as "on a par with Howard Johnson's" was praise indeed.

It was, in fact, according to Mimi Sheraton, "like con-
doning Hitler because he was on a par with Ivan the
Terrible." Sheraton, one of the few food writers who do
honor to the trade, was contributing valuable shopping
advice to *New York* magazine at the time. (She has since
moved to *The Times.*) In the definitive piece on Mc-
Donald's, she commented, "Howard Johnson's burgers are
worse than McDonald's. . . ."

Sheraton demonstrated that the Big Mac was a rip-off
in price as well as nutrition and taste. At the time of her
survey, she found that McDonald's was effectively charg-

ing from $3 to $4.20 a pound for beef worth 80 cents.
The product, she said, was higher in price and poorer in
quality than competing burgers. Ditto for the French fries
and synthetic shakes. As for the taste, we cannot improve
on Sheraton's findings:

> McDonald's food is irremediably horrible, with no
> saving grace whatever.... [The meat] is ground,
> kneaded and extruded by heavy machinery that
> compacts it so that the texture is somewhat like that
> of baloney sausage, and it becomes rubbery when
> cooked. Once cooked, the burger is insulated in a
> soggy bun, topped with pickle slices that seem re-
> cycled, or dehydrated onion flakes, or shredded let-
> tuce that is more like wet confetti, and one or an-
> other of the disgusting sauces. All is wrapped in pa-
> per, then closed in a sturdy, airtight box, "cooked to
> inventory" as they say in the trade, and set aside until
> ordered. Potatoes may be crisp, but they have no
> taste. The shakes (significantly not called *milk* shakes)
> are like aerated Kaopectate.

Sheraton said she would never eat a McDonald's "filet,"
having tasted one at the mill in Gloucester, Massachusetts,
where blocks of frozen fish are sawed, fried, and refrozen. "We sell more fish now that it doesn't taste like
fish," a sales manager told her. "As I took a sample of the
results, my host said proudly, 'Tastes crisp, doesn't it?'
How could I be the one to tell him 'crisp' is not a taste?"
How could she, indeed, contradict the judgment of those
gourmets who so admired the crisp French fries (Claiborne and Child), the pickle and the onion powder
(Claiborne), the insulation (Beard), and the secret sauce
they identified as a mayonnaise remoulade "not to be
thrown overboard" (that's Beard again). Sheraton called
that last an oily, sweet-sour emulsion that "should be
thrown, if not overboard, then down the toilet."
If, as Sheraton suggests, "what McDonald's is guiltiest
of is perverting the tastes of children," then the gourmets
may fairly be taxed with perverting the taste of grown-

ups. But it may be argued in their defense that the fast-food chains succeeded with little direct help from the lifted-pinky brigade. True, when they are not working at the trade, gourmets often reveal themselves to be charter members of the mainstream. A prominent collector of fine wines confided to us that, in privacy, his favorite beverage was Pepsi. Julia Child told Sheraton that she loved "those cute little goldfish crackers people serve with cocktails, and then, of course, hot dogs and hamburgers with onion, pickles and ketchup." Beard called himself "a hot dog fiend," even eating them for breakfast, and confessed to a passion for raw marshmallows. And Sheraton continued: "Almost any hot dogs and hamburgers 'dripping' with ketchup, and Hershey almond bars, are also among Craig Claiborne's junk food fancies."

But in their writing for pay, the gourmets have seldom shown much interest in what ordinary Americans eat. Rather, like their colleagues on the women's pages and in the women's magazines, they entertain ordinary Americans with the fashions and foibles of the rich.

The affluent themselves are of course easily persuaded. Critics of McDonald's are accused of being elitists—i.e., snobs. But what could be more snobbish than the following defense by David S. Sampson, an aide to Nelson Rockefeller's Commission on Critical Choices for Americans: "I like McDonald's. I don't like the food. I don't like to eat there. I feel uncomfortable when I go in. But I like McDonald's because they seem to care a little [for the poor]. Maybe it's all business and they really don't. But they seem to, and even that's rare enough these days."* The implication is that good food is too good for the common people, and if they are happy with their swill, why should we object—as long as we don't have to share it?

But the joke is on the affluent. When they step out to dine by candlelight, the chances are growing that they

* Op Ed page, *New York Times*, July 18, 1975.

will eat the same thing they and the common folk are eating at home—TV dinners. The only real difference is the price.

The dirty secret of American luxury dining is precooked frozen food. It will remain a secret, because the industry has no intention of allowing the public to know that it is getting vending-machine food at luxury prices. When San Francisco considered an ordinance to require that restaurants disclose which items had been frozen, it was shot down by the massed artillery of the local industry. Victor Bergeron, founder of the Trader Vic's chain and a dedicated foe of authenticity in cuisine,* called the bill "the damndest, goofiest, craziest thing I've ever heard of" and insisted that there was nothing wrong with frozen food. Then why didn't the owners want to label their offerings as frozen? A fairly desperate explanation was offered by Roland Gotti of Ernie's, which was rated by *Holiday* as "one of the world's few truly great restaurants." He testified that it would add to costs if restaurants had to change their menus "every time a frozen item is temporarily substituted for an unavailable fresh item." The clinching argument, however, was that a Truth in Dining law would sap San Francisco's gastronomic reputation and thus reduce its convention business. As Jack Shelton, an independent restaurant critic, put it bitterly, delegates must not be told that the Chicken

* *Trader Vic's Book of Mexican Cooking* recounts that when the author was asked to open a Mexican restaurant in San Francisco, "I knew as much about Mexican food as my great-grandmother in the Pyrenees." So he went to Mexico. "I ate Mexican food until it almost gave me an ulcer. In Mexico it was pretty greasy. The finest Mexican food I have enjoyed came from what is known as Texas-Mex. Now, I know I'm going to make a lot of Mexicans sore as hell—you have to understand that I am an American, not a Mexican, and I eat what pleases me most." What pleases Trader Vic most is canned brand-name soups and sauces. Reading his recipes nearly gave *us* an ulcer.

Kiev they eat in San Francisco is the same as the one they eat in Duluth.

"There are many restaurants using frozen food, but no one is going to admit it," Pierre Franey told *The New York Times* in an interview. Franey, the Howard Johnson's chef and a partner of Claiborne's, said that virtually all the fancy restaurants now used freezers, if only to tuck away leftovers. "Nobody's going to admit that," he said, "but they don't throw it away, either." He saw nothing wrong in this. In fact, he said, if he were still cooking at Le Pavillon, which in its heyday was regarded as the best restaurant in the country, he would use the freezer.

"I would make sauces in large batches and freeze them," he declared. "The technique has improved. There is nothing wrong with this—and there is nothing wrong with frozen dough, frozen brioche dough, for instance. If you have a good freezer and keep it at 10 below zero all the time, it is going to be beautiful."

It may be doubted that the late Henri Soulé would have allowed Franey to do anything of the kind. Soulé was a notorious perfectionist, who closed the Pavillon when help and produce became inadequate to maintain his standards. While a meat stock might survive freezing, any butter sauce, or any other emulsion, would break down. In fact, sauces threaten to break down even at kitchen temperatures. That is why restaurant chefs cheat by adding flour, to escape the fragility of the pure, concentrated juices. All American "gourmet chefs" follow their example. But any cook who respects the craft would regard freezing a sauce as vandalism.

We doubt also that Franey's frozen brioche dough does quite as well as the fresh. One may forgive a baker who resorts to freezing dough so that he may sleep nights, but he should not pretend that it is just as good.

Even where they have not surrendered to buying food that has been cooked elsewhere, most fancy restaurants now cook large batches and freeze them, to save time and enable them to offer a large menu with a minimum of waste. The practice is not new, nor exclusively American. Back in 1965 we ran into a young Philadelphian who was working as a student saucier in a famous restaurant in the South of France. We observed that the food was not up to its rating, and he confided, "They play games with the freezer." He announced that when he got home, he was going to open a very expensive restaurant that would make no compromises. Eight years later, we visited his place (one of the two better French restaurants in Philadelphia) and asked him what he had since learned. "That compromises are essential," he replied.

Another Howard Johnson's executive, Frank M. Barrett, told *Fast Foods* magazine: "I think anybody who's not using convenience foods is out of it. And some of the prepared food around today is top quality. You'd never know the difference. We're going to open a restaurant a week this year [1973], and where could we get cooks and chefs for this kind of expansion? Even if we could get them, we couldn't train them fast enough."

To say that there aren't enough good cooks is a breathtaking understatement. But when restaurant operators use that justification, they are like the proverbial defendant who has killed his parents and pleads for mercy as an orphan. (A reader wrote us that his wife had applied to Stouffer's for a job and had been told that it hired no cooks, only "thawer-outers.") The New York industry, mounting a crash course for cooks, devoted eight class hours to Reconstituting Convenience Foods. The operators *prefer* to employ unskilled labor; many of their employes, among the lowest paid in the city, must draw on welfare to support their families. Convenience is for owners. It spares them the hassle of going to market for the best or cheapest available produce, and of supervising its proper preparation. Even unskilled help can peel and fry potatoes, which are better to eat and cheaper than the frozen product, but it's a nuisance, and, as the operators repeat ad nauseam, the public doesn't know the difference.

For the fast-food chains, the profit margin is such that putting out the real McCoy is not worth the bother. *Food Processing* magazine reported that a sack of frozen French fries cost a chain 5 cents and sold for 20 cents. "Only soft drinks yield a greater percentage of profit," it said. For the restaurant of pretension, a frozen "gourmet" dish that cost it $1.38 could be sold for $7.50, whereas traditionally, operators have figured on food costing 30 to 40 percent of the bill to the customer. Many restaurants now "slush down" a day's supply, which means that they allow the dishes to thaw to about 40°, and on order, pop one into the microwave or convection oven. At the end of the day, the unused portions go back into the freezer, of course.

The food processors have made restaurant owners an offer they cannot refuse. Some produce as many as two hundred "gourmet" dishes, enabling a hostelry without a cook to boast a menu as fancy as Delmonico's. Meats come partly precooked, with grill marks burnt in, and there is also the now popular abomination of Surf 'n' Turf, which combines the extravagance of both steak and lobster with the taste of neither.

"Breaded shrimp, oysters, crab meat specialties, lobster Newburg and pompano are packed in attractive packages with four-color illustrations and tend to make a chef proud of preparing a gourmet entrée," the magazine *Quick Frozen Foods* reported.

That was in 1973, which one supplier of equipment to the industry described to us as "the year of the breakthrough." The magazine said its survey had found that a majority of restaurants already used some prepared frozen foods and planned to use more. Not surprisingly, up to 80 percent and more of the fare served by chains and industrial feeders was precooked. More disturbingly, the independent restaurants—the last holdouts and our only hope—were either folding up or joining the frozen-food parade.

The demise of small business is an accepted by-product of a misguided modernism. Even in France, the expressway has been the death of some fine inns on the byroads, and no turnpike authority would dream of renting its valuable concessions to *Maman et Papa*. A Parisian banking syndicate, which landed the first such feeding concession in that country, warned in its opening announcement, "One does not take the autoroute to practice gastronomy." In the States, urban blight and urban renewal combine to make life impossible for Mom and Pop. We had the occasion, during one summer in New York, to write the obituaries of two good fifty-year-old family restaurants, evicted to make way in the one case for a parking lot, in the other for a skyscraper. Even if the restaurant operators could have afforded the skyscraper rents, no building promoter would have them, because investors want to see long-term leases signed by corporations with top credit ratings. Like the autoroute, the skyscraper rents its captive clientele to an enterprise that installs feeding stations at several levels, their prices rising with the altitude, all being supplied from a central thawing station below ground.

We visited some of these stations in the line of duty, when the male half of this writing team served a hitch as food critic of *The New York Times*. One of them was Top of the Six's, a gourmet tourist heaven operated by Stouffer's, which long ago was a family enterprise famed for its chicken pies and pastries. Here is our report:

The press release said that sometime in July this 15-year-old landmark would serve its ten millionth meal, and the lucky diner would win a Bermuda holiday for two. That called for a visit, at $35 with wine and tip, for two. We didn't win.

People who like Muzak and the Radio City show may well like the Top of the Six's; in fact, many diners were evidently pleased. What was remarkable about our food was the lack of taste, in both senses: no taste to the shrimp cocktail, nor to the beautiful-looking tomatoes, the zucchini in tomato sauce, the filet mignon, bland, tenderized and quite cold, as were the "French fries." The last were reheated on request but preserved that unmistakable mushiness of frozen precooked and reheated fries. My "beef Stroganoff" was a Swiss steak on noodles reminiscent of a hundred airline meals.

We passed up a wonderful dish that, if the menu was accurate, combined veal, crabmeat and whipped cream. We also ducked the orange sherbet with chocolate sauce, but tasted the "chocolate souffle," a whipped pudding concoction. The coffee was indifferent, the wines (a Pouilly-Fuissé and a Médoc) good and reasonable.

We asked to see the kitchen whence these wonders came and were told that it was closed to the public and anyway was 40 floors down. We returned, cognito, and were courteously received by Martin Brody, the general manager, who showed us the various production stations with their steam tables, pressure cookers and ovens.

"We don't have a chef system," he explained, "we have a food management system, with dieticians who are either home economists or A.D.A.–trained." (That's the American Dietetic Association.)

The specialists who devise the menus work in Cleveland, headquarters of the Stouffer's chain, which formerly was a division of Litton Industries and now is in the Nestlé family.

Mr. Brody described Stouffer's as a middle-of-the-road operation, as between custom cookery in chef restaurants and electronic mass-feeding stations that do practically no cooking at all. He showed with pride the ovens where puffy small loaves, made from frozen dough, are "proofed" and baked daily.

Asked why pies and cakes were not on the dinner menu, he replied that they weren't selling, whereas the "distinctive things," like the chocolate thing and the orange sherbet in chocolate, were.

Who needs cooks?

We met those sweet loaves in scores of restaurants around the country, and saw some on sale at the counter to take home. "Reconstituted, these have the appearance of homemade bread," *Quick Frozen Foods* reported. "When brought to table on a cutting board, along with a sharp knife and generous amounts of butter or margarine, the loaves serve as an 'icebreaker' in gaining the patron's confidence in the restaurant's food and service."

What was even more distressing for us than Top of the Six's was to follow the advice of *Holiday* magazine and make "a gastronomic pilgrimage" to Stonehenge Inn in Ridgefield, Connecticut—and meet the same sort of meal. This shrine was built by the late Albert Stockli, who, as we wrote, was "a sort of P. T. Barnum of American cuisine who dazzled the expense-account yokels with such stunts as truffles in artichoke with mustard (*flambé, naturellement*), Wild Fowl of Samos (chicken) in sherried tomatoes, *und so weiter*." Gourmet Continental cuisine, if ever there was.

It is said that Stockli made up for the bizarreness of his menus by the quality of his foodstuffs. We are not convinced, all the more because in a 1970 interview he predicted that all restaurants soon would be serving precooked frozen dinners. Anyway, we got Stockli recipes, frozen and reheated, at $40 for two. There were among other things a soup of cherries whipped with cheese and cinnamon, a veal chop drowned in a mess of mushroom, chestnut, and perhaps carrots, and a rack of lamb that arrived cold. The headwaiter said haughtily that lamb ordered rare (that is, pink) *had* to be cold. It does if it's precooked. . . .

There was a time in the memory of Americans still living when travel in our country could be a gastronomic adventure. Railroads, river boats, and steamships vied with one another in food and service. Menus changed with seasons and regions: jambalaya in Louisiana, Brunswick stew in Georgia, scrapple and crab cakes and shad in the Mid-Atlantic states, wild mountain trout in the Rockies, lobster stew and chowders and baked beans with ham and brown bread in New England. And if the hotel menu palled or was too dear, the locals might direct one to a tearoom kept by two spinsters who served good plain cooking and superb pastries, or a boardinghouse where, on Thursday nights, the housewife served a stewed hen with dumplings that was memorable....

No more. For the food lover, travel in America today is an unmitigated ordeal. Whether he goes by car, rail, or air, all he can hope for is gourmet glop à la Marriott or Howard Johnson's. Amtrak, seeking to revive railroad travel by subsidizing the same companies that destroyed it, has not tried to revive the old culinary standards. It now proposes one nationwide menu of "international" junk such as Tournedos Mexicana, an affront to an inoffensive neighboring country: two tenderized frozen fillets broiled and covered with Swift's Knorr "sauce Béarnaise." Or a tomato bisque made, according to the official instructions, of a can of tomato soup and "a half-can of chicken stock (if available) or water" and half-and-half cream. The food is, in short, not distinguishable from that served in the air, the only differences being that on the train, the diner eats in relative comfort, drinks real, if indifferent, coffee, and is billed separately for the meal.

Soon after our family moved East in the late 1940s, we adopted what we called Moses' Law: Don't eat at park concessions. It was named after Robert Moses, who was then New York's commissioner of parks and everything. But this turned out to be unfair. The rule was actually universal. A young scientist in the family eventually revised it to read: The quality of food and service is inversely proportional to the captivity of the clientele. In other words, when a concessionaire draws patronage because it has nowhere else to go (e.g., airports, airliners, expressways) or because of the beauty of the site (e.g., atop skyscrapers or the Eiffel Tower or on a sightseeing boat), he tends to skimp on the merchandise.

When we mentioned this in a column once, an airline public-relations chief who asked to remain anonymous wrote to say that its clients were not captives, because they could always switch to another line, and in any case, there was a bloc of unfortunately silent patrons who did like the food. True, they can change airlines, but they cannot change the food—not since the great sandwich war of the early years of jet travel, when airlines, which had sensibly agreed to serve only sandwiches on short flights, cheated by offering ever-fancier spreads. When the caviar began to nibble into the profits, they agreed to moderate their generosity. Now they may *advertise* the voluptuousness of their fare and of their stewardesses (Fly me!), but the reality of the fare never corresponds to the promise.

(This applies, incidentally, to Air France, despite the raves of gourmet writers who have been regaled with special dinners in its commissary at Kennedy International Airport. Moved by the protest of French travelers, the home office has wisely begun to serve, on short flights within Europe, snacks based on good French bread and cold meats and cheeses.)

It is unhappily evident that a silent majority of passengers do find the food at least edible, whether because they have been tranquilized by liquor or because they eat no better at home, or both. In restaurants, the majority are not silent; on the contrary, there is a happy hum in a successful restaurant that normally adds to the pleasure of dining. A well-known promoter in Paris once confided to us that he had instructed his architects to install mirrors and other hard surfaces precisely to encourage this sound. But when bad food is being served, that hum of contented diners is more painful, to a food lover, than canned music.

We withstood that discord for nine months of professional dining. With some pleasant exceptions, our eating ranged from bad to mediocre. And this was mostly in New York, which, no doubt because it is the most foreign of our cities, still provides the most interesting food in America.

Does that sound New York–provincial? Unpatriotic? Well, where are the *American* restaurants? So impeccably American an institution as the 1974 Mobil Travel Guide gave its top rating to six restaurants in the United States, of which five were "French" and one Chinese. *Holiday* conferred its Distinctive Dining Awards on 163, of which 97 were "French," 19 "Italian," and the rest a potpourri of exotica including old Englishe (*Holiday*'s spelling), Franco-Oriental, Franco-Russian, Continental, and pseudo-Polynesian. ("Trader Vic's," a San Franciscan boasted to us, "is the only Polynesian restaurant where you can get lentils with sauerkraut.")

The quotation marks around "French" and "Italian" are of course our own. A large majority of employes of "French" restaurants in this country never worked in a French restaurant. Most of those with French passports are Bretons, many of whom come from a village near Brest that is not noted for gastronomy. A former aide at the French consulate in New York recalls registering them. "One listed his occupation as 'coiffeur or cook.' I look for hair in my soup." We once saw employes of a "French" restaurant in New York eating asparagus drowned in ketchup.

Even among the professional French cooks to be found in some of our better restaurants, few if any have completed the long, hard climb from apprentice to helper to sous-chef to chef of a serious restaurant in France. Why would a successful chef, working with French assistants and French produce in his own country, want to come here?

During World War II, some refugee chefs gave a lift to our cuisine, as other refugees were enriching our music, arts, and sciences. With such a pool of talent,

Henri Soulé made Le Pavillon into a great restaurant. But one by one, his key people left, and comparable replacements could not be found. Standards suffered. The late Charles Masson of La Grenouille, who was one of Soulé's original team, told us: "I remember the way *pommes noisettes* were started continually, twenty minutes before being served. In the last years, they were made at three p.m., and reheated...." Finally, Soulé closed Le Pavillon. "What happened to Soulé will happen to me," Masson said. "The day my best workers leave me, they will be irreplaceable."

In Paris once, we attended the cooking finals of the annual contest for the best graduate apprentice of the year. A restaurant owner from Cape Cod offered the winner a job as "chef" at three times the wages he could expect as a young journeyman in France. The boy was tempted, but turned the job down when he learned that the restaurant served nine hundred meals at a sitting. "That's not cooking," he said. "That's feeding." Some youngsters do, however, make the leap, choosing sure employment at high pay in the United States over the slow and competitive climb to master craftsmanship in France. These are our French chefs.

One who opened an expensive restaurant here not long ago confided: "You come here figuring on making a little money, having a good time, and then going home. But you get married, and buy a house and a car, and then it's too late."

The sense of having abandoned a craft may help account for a touching phenomenon. Expatriate chefs here, on their days off, head for colonies in exurbia where they spend much of their free time gathering mushrooms, fishing, and otherwise assembling good fare, making sausages and pâtés, and proving to one another that they can cook the good, earthy food that their mothers used to fix—*la vrai cuisine, quoi!*

If our "French" restaurants are not very French, our "Italian" restaurants are even less Italian. A second and third generation of cooks and clients have drowned a great culinary tradition in a red tide of canned tomato sauce on limp factory pasta. When we hinted, at a popular trattoria in Brooklyn, that such a meal was not precisely authentic, the young owner retorted, "This is Italian-*American* cooking."

A similar thought was conveyed to us once at Sabatini, an overrated restaurant in Florence. Perhaps from force of habit (we lived in France then), we had ordered our meal in French. As we were leaving, the headwaiter asked us if we had enjoyed the food and service. "*Ni l'un, ni l'autre,*" one of us replied. "Ah, monsieur," the man said with a commiserating grimace, "you must come back some time when there are not so many Americans." We never did.... We doubt that Sabatini is much better when the Americans are not there, but it's a fairly sound rule that a "foreign" restaurant maintains its standards only to the degree that it caters to clients of its own nationality.

In the restaurant field as in home cooking, the gourmet hacks have persuaded the public that foreign and fancy are synonymous with good. This is not a total loss, in the rare cases where the foreign is authentic or the fancy is well done. But it has been nearly fatal to our own culinary heritage.

An extraordinary example of this was the dinner thrown by President Cottage-Cheese-and-Ketchup for Comrade Brezhnev at the White House. The menu was printed in mangled French, and the recipes seemed to correspond. The plate of resistance (if we may) was *Supreme of Lobster en Bellevue*, an aspic unknown to haute cuisine. It baffled even the French, who were, however, delighted with the Franglais. A writer in a hotel trade paper in Paris chortled, "J'attends d'être invited at the White House. J'y speakerai english with M. Nixon without difficulties!" For his turn, Brezhnev had an all-Russian feast flown in from Moscow: caviar, sturgeon, Kamchatka crabs, cucumbers, an assortment of game, strawberry mousse, Soviet wines. The Kremlin won the match hands down.

Why didn't Nixon serve Maine Lobster Stew? It took Frenchmen to explain. Those globetrotting food writers Henri Gault and Christian Millau of the Guide Juillard have said in another context, "Americans suffer from an inferiority complex in this regard, and there is not, as far as we know, a single American restaurant that has achieved glory with oyster pie, snapper soup, ham steak, or even fried chicken, shad roe, clam chowder and other authentic American dishes. And it's too bad."

This would not have been their finding as recently as the 1930s, before the present generation of gourmet snobs took over. Even today, a well-heeled and well-directed traveler can with luck run across an occasional sample of our ancient culinary glories. But if Gault and Millau are largely correct, their diagnosis is incomplete. The primary reason why restaurants don't serve glorious Americana today is that their produce and their skill and their motivation have declined.

The gourmets were only the flacks who tried to persuade the public that the food was getting better. What gives hope is that, in spite of the fact that they have dominated the media since the war, they have not entirely succeeded.

We must now get into the act, briefly. As we have mentioned, one of the authors yielded to an urgent appeal to take over the critic's job at *The New York Times* in early 1973, with the understanding that he would not have to stay longer than a year. We threw in our napkins after nine months, sick of the gourmet plague that had marked our first meal for pay, and our last, and most of those in between. This was not much of a surprise to us. But what was extraordinary was the response of hundreds of readers who wrote that they felt the same way, but had thought that it was they who were out of step.

For a sample of what we were eating and what we

were writing about it, the reader might now look up our first and our last reports, reprinted in the Appendix. It may now be revealed that the hotel where the chef apparently could not make a soufflé with bits of fruit suspended in it was the Waldorf-Astoria. The occasion was a gourmet society's dinner, and our review ended:

> If we were appointed by a club of food lovers to arrange a gastronomic dinner, we'd send out scouts to scour the city and the countryside for fresh fish, garden produce, chickens that scratch in the dirt and eggs laid by such fowl, and maybe some wild mushrooms, and we'd hire a cook who knew how to fix such things so they taste as they are.
>
> The food and wine societies would also serve the cause of good eating and drinking if they encouraged those few farmers, bakers and other artisans who preserve what is left of old traditions of quality. Each of them deserves a certificate of honor, and a price for their work to make it worthwhile.

Sadly, the gourmet society never took up our appeal. As we wrote later, just about every organization of nature lovers fights to defend nature against the encroachments of loggers, strip miners, and polluters, but who ever heard of a gush of gourmets protesting the erosion of our food supplies? Since the function of these groups is chiefly to establish that they eat better—that is, fancier—than other Americans, the disaster that has hit our common tables only enhances their sense of superiority. It is status, not food, that they love. Rather than consider the foregoing appeal as a call for help, the leaders of the food fraternity took it as a declaration of war—on them. Perhaps it was.

13

The Hustlers

Some emoluments fall on all those who
practice journalism.

*Horace Sutton, defending travel writers against
the charge that they are whores*

Groucho Marx once said he would not join any club
that would accept *him* as a member. On the same wise
ground, we should not elect anybody who *wanted* to be
President, nor take the advice of anybody who *enjoyed*
being a food critic. Catch 22.

To put it another way, nobody who loved good food
and had a long experience with it would want the job,
not in America today. This has not, sadly, penetrated
the consciousness of many editors. We received an appeal
from a cub reporter who had just been appointed as
restaurant critic of a major newspaper in the heartland.
He asked us for a quick fill-in on "saddle of lamb and all
that stuff." We advised him not to take the job. He
never replied.

No responsible editor would dream of assigning someone to review a concert who did not know the difference
between Bach and Gershwin, or didn't care. But it is
routine to assign anybody who happens to be available to
review restaurants. The assumption seems to be that
everybody eats, and that should be enough. The critic of

a major publication, a man who is the soul of probity, confides to friends that he doesn't care much about food, and has even indicated as much to readers, in a laudatory review that began: "Restaurant reviewers and food buffs who are more deeply involved with their taste buds than we are with ours, may disagree, but..." He proceeds to rave about a Mexican pepper dish that is "pure green fire." Readers are told: "For a new taste sensation that may leave you numb for the next 24 hours, try this. Quite wonderful, and accompanied by saffron rice and pinto beans, at $4.50." How did he taste the saffron?

One of the burdens of serious dining for pay is that the critic, when panning a restaurant, is also panning the taste of those who like it, including, quite often, friends and colleagues who have tipped the critic off to this find. There is, of course, inherent in any criticism an assumption that those who disagree are mistaken, but the literary critic who gives the back of his hand to a shlock best-seller lives in a class that shares his values at least in part. Not so with the qualified restaurant critic. To cite that comment in our Stouffer's review, many cultivated readers despise Muzak and the Radio City Music Hall but would find nothing amiss in the fare at Top of the Six's. Indeed, the state of the cultivated palate is such that, in 1976, *The Times Magazine* could declare: "Commercially grown mushrooms are actually superior to those growing wild in fields and pastures."

James Beard has harrumphed that the San Francisco restaurant critic Jack Shelton "enjoys being destructive." On the contrary. The critic has every motive to be positive. He desperately seeks places or at least dishes he can recommend to his readers—after all, that is his primary job. For our part, we never panned an *unsuccessful* restaurant (what is the point of warning the public against a danger that it is not likely to encounter?), although this meant we had to eat many an awful meal without even getting some copy from it. We panned *successful* restaurants only to sharpen perceptions of common shortcomings, and only because there were not enough pleasant experiences to fill a weekly column. Even so, there was always the danger of overpraising an only passable house, in appreciation for a relatively satisfactory dish or two. We never had occasion to regret a negative review; we did suffer remorse once or twice when hindsight showed us to have been too kind. To send a reader to a bad meal is unpardonable.

A good professional critic eats *worse* than a good amateur. The amateur hunts out one or a few restaurants within traveling distance and the range of his pocketbook, learns the strong points and the weaknesses, cultivates an understanding with the staff that will lend meaning to the question "What's good today?"—and settles down to a long relationship. The critic who wants to tell his anonymous readers what they will find must be anonymous too, and must try all the likely places, and eat what the house recommends to a stranger. We have likened this to playing Russian roulette with five bullets in the revolver.

The importance of anonymity was brought home to us one evening in Paris when we allowed some friends to lure us away from our habitual places to try a new restaurant that had been praised by Robert J. Courtine in *Le Monde*. Courtine, who in our view is far and away the best food critic in the world, had for years been lashing his country's restaurateurs to revive the woman-made glories of regional cuisine. (This passion is as notorious as his evil disposition. We once attended a luncheon for the gastronomic press at an enchanting inn in the Pyrenees, where the host had killed two sheep to make a sort of Basque haggis—stuffed stomach—in Courtine's honor. The critic sniffed around the kitchen, and disappeared. When we caught up with him in Biarritz that evening, we asked him how he had known that the lunch would be mediocre and the haggis inedible; he merely wrinkled his nose and shrugged complacently.) So when he wrote about a Savoyard meal he had savored at Le Chamonix, just off the Champs Élysées, we looked forward to following his lead. On being seated, we were handed typical, banal Parisian tourist menus. We called *le patron* and asked for the dishes we had read about. He replied, "We do not *serve* them. We prepared them for Monsieur Courtine."

With such experiences in mind, we sometimes remarked to French confrères that we readers did not eat in the same restaurants where they ate. But the rich (i.e., Americans) can afford scruples. French publishers, even when they do not tie a plug to advertising, are reluctant to pick up the tabs for critics, and on their modest space rates, the critics can hardly be expected to do so themselves. The practice of critics' charging restaurants for a plug, or at least knocking them down for a good meal, seems to be as old as restaurants themselves; it is said that Grimaud de la Reynière, the first critic, shook down the chefs of the first grand restaurants of the late eighteenth century.... A saving element is that the French public implicitly doubts the motives of journalists and politicians. Further, a large segment of that public can judge good food for itself, and has a large array of good restaurants to choose from.

That is hardly the case in our country. Yet the holiday junket, the free meal, and the puff for advertisers are very nearly as prevalent in American travel-and-dining journalism as in the French. John Wilcock, himself a travel writer, said in a *Times* article about his colleagues: "They're whores, except for the biggest names.... They don't make any criticism and the reason is obvious: Their publications would lose money.... Most travel writing —the airline magazines, the canned releases and planted stories—is just P. R. bull, paying back somebody's free trips." One of the biggest names in travel writing, Horace Sutton of *Saturday Review/World*, replied angrily that the *Times* itself was not pure, since some of its free-lance contributors solicited freebies on the strength of their assignments. "How else would the writer survive?" he

demanded. Not, he said, on what the travel section paid.
"Some emoluments fall on all those who practice journalism," he said, listing various facilities offered to *Times*
people, among others. "There may be whores among us,"
he allowed, "but no more, I would judge, than among
sportswriters, financial writers, White House correspon-
dents or political pundits." There is more truth in this,
perhaps, than Sutton had in mind.

Nonetheless, the quiz-show and payola scandals of the
1950s did make freeloading a subject of embarrassment
to the more respectable media, and with the engagement
of Claiborne in 1957, *The Times* introduced the rule that
a restaurant critic dines incognito, pays his bill, and may
criticize as well as praise. A scattering of honorable
publications have since adopted the incognito rule, but
a majority still treat food writing as a branch of advertising, and apply the same ethics to both.

"Inspectors" for the major hotel and restaurant guides
do not as a rule even eat in the places they rate, much
less pay the bill. Those of the American Automobile
Association (13.5 million copies a year) are really sales-
men, collecting $200 and up for each listing. The Mobil
Travel Guide (1.5 million copies a year) assures readers
that "quality of the food is a prime consideration" and
"Every kitchen has been inspected," but its inspectors
eat at very few of the 21,000 places it rates, and then they
call ahead. The inspection, if any, is mainly for cleanliness
—"So much so," reported Linda Scarbrough in a *Times*
review, "that field inspectors are encouraged to carry
pocket mirrors around with them—to check out the
underside of all toilet-bowl rims." She quotes Steven
Mera, the chief editor of the guide, as saying, "Some
places with really great food we might not rate at all,
because they're dirty." A responsible guide, like the
Michelin, must have a staff of able and anonymous inspectors who eat at every restaurant listed, and it must
be reissued each year. If any such guide exists in the
United States, we are not aware of it.

As for the slick food and travel magazines—even those that do not require the restaurants they praise to buy advertising—all follow the Chamber of Commerce policy: If you can't boost, don't knock. Faithful to this rule is *Gourmet*. A sample: "... for the most part the food at Sardi's is more than creditable, and it occasionally reaches an exalted level." Actually, for the most part the food at Sardi's is less than creditable, and it is *Gourmet*'s prose that is exalted. As the writer doubtless knew. The wife of one well-known professional blurted to us one evening, "You're lucky—you can criticize!"

That cry from the heart (or palate?) was not, unfortunately, typical. How the trade views itself was faithfully related by Sutton in a food issue of *The Saturday Review/World*. In his essay, Sutton leaned heavily on the wisdom of Beard, whom he described as "the doyen of America's burgeoning food fraternity." The preference for the fancy French "doyen" over the plain English "dean" is of course typical of the fraternity, just as Beard's acceptance of fees from Pillsbury, Nestlé-Stouffer's, Planters, and Restaurant Associates proves his talent, according to Sutton.

"In the American fraternity," he writes, "no one has less than a kind word for Jim Beard." Although we are not fraternity members, we too have a kind word: of the three dominant figures in the gourmet biz—Child, Claiborne, and Beard—only Beard seems from his work actually to enjoy cooking and to write well about it. But as a former actor, he doesn't mind appearing in commercials, and has absorbed some of their ethos. A food lover who writes, as he does, that iceberg lettuce is "maligned and mistreated" and has "good flavor and interesting texture" simply cannot be trusted.

It is only fair to warn the reader that the authors may be prejudiced. In addition to calling the honest San Francisco critic Jack Shelton willfully destructive and saying that Gault and Millau "too often ... go ass over teakettle about something," the Sutton-Beard piece took a swipe at John L. Hess, then food critic of *The Times*, who, it said, "is accused of being influenced by his wife." (The accusation, although anonymous, is correct.— J.L.H.)

We quote the following passage, at once flattering and insulting, only to make a general point: "John Hess wrote brilliantly from Paris, but thrust into the prestigious fishbowl food berth in New York, he is, in the words of one senior member of the fraternity, 'in a puddle he doesn't know how to swim out of.' [In Sutton's puddle or fishbowl, as the case may be, touting fancy grub is a large social cut above foreign correspondence.] His columns on such varied subjects as finding edible wild roots in New York and farming Chinese vegetables in New Jersey are offbeat and interesting, but there are those who claim that he is too conditioned to France and to French restaurants to defend American fare properly."

It is not clear here that "to defend American fare" in Sutton-Beard's view means to praise Big Mac burgers, but the context leaves no room for doubt. Beginning his piece with the salivating notion of Gael Greene that "food and sex are completely interwoven anthropologically," Sutton tells us: "Europe and the Orient developed sophisticated cultures embracing both sensualities. But the settlers who came to the New World were too busy with basic needs to bother about the niceties. In America, food initially was a matter of survival; later, it was little more than a function." Sutton abandons without explanation the problem of how the settlers procreated —presumably, not in a sophisticated manner. (Actually, the carryings on of some of the Virginia gentry, as recorded in diaries and lawsuits, were depraved enough to have interested even Gael Greene.) He continues: "It was not until the end of World War II, says James Beard,...'that Americans began to think of eating as a pleasurable thing, a sensual delight.'" Thanks to returning GI's and tourists and, of course, to the burgeoning food fraternity, "The kitchen cook in America, hired or housewife, was encouraged to embark on new cooking experiments at home. Restaurateurs were encouraged to forsake steak and potatoes for heavy forays into the world of snails and highfalutin sauces."

That is defending American fare?

That is only Beard-Boorstin history, a farrago of errors that insult our intelligence, our scholarship, and our forebears. We repeat: the earliest settlers, and the Indians before them, had a marvelous array of foods to choose from, and developed sophisticated and sensual ways of handling them. The foods were gradually homogenized by the Industrial Revolution, and good American cooking was gradually supplanted by the gourmet plague. Finally, the Pepsi generation of gourmet writers taught Americans to be ashamed of their own great food heritage.

As for restaurateurs, although few have actually forsaken steak and potatoes, most have betrayed them: the beef is usually frozen, tenderized "so you can eat it with a fork," and tasteless; the potatoes are either precooked frozen French fries (the gourmets love 'em), or Idahos —one of the few remaining glories of American produce —baked in foil, a gourmet imbecility that leaves them slightly steamed instead of deliciously mealy and crisp-skinned. The foiled spud is served with a shiny synthetic or superpasteurized "sour cream" and a sophisticated salad of James Beard's iceberg lettuce and cotton tomato, drowned in a sweet "Russian" or "French" dressing to lend them taste. The entrée is accompanied by sweet buns, and the whole is "washed down" with an iced sweet drink of cola or tea or coffee or, more pretentiously, Sangría.

From the late eighteenth century, it is true, American restaurants of pretension tried to follow the new French model, offering enormous menus of elaborate dishes. This posed the double handicap of requiring large staffs of skilled help and large supplies of fine foodstuffs. A skim through *"Oscar" of the Waldorf's Cook Book* shows that the talent for haute cuisine was seldom there, although good cooking was still common in America in his time. Oscar Tschirky, who dominated the gourmet scene in New York in the late nineteenth and early twentieth centuries, was in fact not a cook but a headwaiter. He began in Delmonico's, which, Boorstin grandly asserts, "set a standard for New York gourmets which by the mid-twentieth century made that city, next to Paris, the restaurant capital of the world." Save the mark! In *On the Town in New York*, Michael and Ariane Batterberry say that Oscar "was a punctilious gourmet and so hidebound a snob that he claimed he would rather see Mrs. Astor sipping hot water in the Palm Garden than a nameless nouveau riche devouring a ten-course dinner." Oscar's cookbook is an incompetent caricature of haute cuisine; its only value is to demonstrate that the present generation of gourmet frauds originated nothing. Snobbery and the cult of a misunderstood French elegance have always been with us.

As for the foodstuffs, they evidently suffered not only from progress but from the very nature of the food business. Jovan Trboyevic, proprietor of Le Perroquet, one of the better restaurants in Chicago, explained to us: "There is a built-in staleness in our trade. If you have deliveries A, B and C of something, the oldest must be served first." This is a curse of the fish and produce trades as well. It would seem to follow that restaurants should keep their menus short. Instead, they stock up, relying on the freezer and the refrigerator to eliminate waste. When we complimented a New York restaurateur one Wednesday on a dish of fresh whiting, he told us complacently that he had bought enough to see him through the weekend.

Trboyevic, incidentally, is an alumnus of the Swiss hotel school (the École Hotelière in Lausanne) that Claiborne attended, but he does not call himself a cook. Claiborne has called it "the best cooking school in the world." The restaurateur, who got his real training by working in France, said the school was "overrated" and mainly gave its graduates the impression that they understood food service; one-third of the eighteen-month course is devoted to service, one-third to administration, and one-third to the kitchen, which apparently specializes in "Continental" cuisine. This may help explain Claiborne's obsession with elegance of service, and the gaps in his understanding of basic French cuisine. The best cooking schools in the world have, of course, been the kitchens of great chefs such as Fernard Point, just as the greatest art schools have been the ateliers of the masters. Cooking taught by the numbers comes out like painting-in the numbered sections.

The reader may have observed that gourmet writers lean to gush and pretension in prose as in food. They may twitter like Claiborne ("smashingly palatable"..."quite swallowable"..."we were all but undone with the pleasure of"..."wonderfully versatile, if not to say sublime" ... "The vegetables with which we dipped were eminently serviceable"..."since we are enthusiastic in depth for the cooking of China, Mexico, India and so on, we find fresh coriander absolutely essential to our peace of mind.") Or they may lift a pinky with Sutton's doyens and archdeaconesses. Or they may be inscrutable, as when one archdeaconess hails a colleague for his "quirky discretion" and "a subtle enthusiasm that should be reassuring to us all." Or they may be cute and call a bartender a *mixologist*, and *wash down* their meals with wine. (That's not civilized dining; it's colonic irrigation.)

But there are good writers who write about food.

In our country, interesting food may be found in two kinds of restaurants: a tiny minority of the expensive, independent ones, and a tiny minority of cheap, ethnic ones catering to communities that have not yet been homogenized. Interesting food *writing* tends to divide into similar categories: the elegant and the blue-collar. The former requires a large expense account, the latter

a tough digestion and a penchant for travel to hard-to-
find places like the Lower East Side of Manhattan; Dah-
lonega, Georgia; Opelousas, Louisiana; and Kansas City,
Missouri. (Kansas City has been particularly hard to find
since the city fathers built an airport over St. Joseph way,
cunningly designed to discourage strangers.)

Both the elegant and the offbeat sectors are inviting
to creative writers because the typical reader of modest
means and sedentary condition is seldom able to check
their judgment. (We recall the plaint of an old sports
journalist, "Before television, we could really write up a
storm.") But the writers pay for their fun by eating a
lot of bad food. *New York* magazine, which features
both schools of food writing, once put its staff to sampling Lord knows how many pastrami sandwiches, and
then blazoned their choices as the best in town. A gentleman at a black-tie gourmet dinner confided to us that
the best pastrami was to be found, not among the ten
named by *New York*, but in a delicatessen concealed
in a loft building in the garment district. We hastened
there and sampled a sandwich, incognito. Unlike *New
York*'s journalists, we also insisted on visiting the kitchen,
a filthy cubbyhole in the basement, where we learned that
the meat came in cartons from a Brooklyn factory. A call
there confirmed our surmise: the factory supplied the
same product to a number of *New York*'s contest winners.
The plant manager was pleased at the honor but bemused
by the observations of the judges. "The most amazing
point," he said, "was that you had a number of different
comments—this pastrami was too salty, and that was not
salty enough—and it was the same item." (We await
New York's comparisons of delicatessen potato salads
and such; some of our most highly touted gourmet stores
buy the stuff readymade, but, as one manufacturer complained, "the man who makes the deliveries often sneaks
around the back door.")

To our taste, the best of the elegant food writers in
America is Roy Andries de Groot of *Esquire*, and the best

of the amateurs of the oil tablecloth is Calvin (Bud) Trillin of *The New Yorker*. Trillin is a first-rate reporter in the tradition of A. J. Liebling, and he writes so engagingly about food, among other Americana, that he lured de Groot, and later the Hesses, to Bud's home town, Kansas City

American Fried: Adventures of a Happy Eater, a collection of Trillin's food essays, opens: "The best restaurants in the world are, of course, in Kansas City. Not all of them; only the top four or five. Anyone who has visited Kansas City and still doubts that statement has my sympathy: He never made it to the right places.... Despite the best efforts of forward-looking bankers and mad-dog franchisers, there is still great food all over the country, but the struggle to wring information from the locals about where it is served can sometimes leave a traveler too exhausted to eat." Trillin mercifully tells the traveler where: the best hamburgers in the world are at Winstead's Drive-In, the best steaks at Jess & Jim's, the best chili dogs at Kresge, and the best ribs and French fries at Arthur Bryant's Barbecue, which is simply "THE SINGLE BEST RESTAURANT IN THE WORLD."

Who could resist? De Groot hastened to Kansas City and, as is his wont, reported that he had dined well there —but not, with one exception, at the places Trillin adored. He found that Winstead's had long since been taken over by a conglomerate named King Louie International. After a brave taste, de Groot wiped his Winstead hamburger clean and gave it to his dog. She spat it out.

De Groot also tried a Kresge chili dog and wrote, "The first bite convinced me that if this was the best in the world, the world left something to be desired." This matched something a native told us about another of Trillin's temples: "If Jess & Jim's is the best steak restaurant in the world, the world's in a bad state." Said another: "I've had good and bad steaks there, but for Christ's sake, don't order the frog legs."

Presumably having received the same advice, de Groot

did not visit Jess & Jim's, but he did report he had found several good restaurants, the finest being the Savoy Grill. As it happened, we were directed there too, and enjoyed the famous Western murals, the cattle-king decor, the friendly service and good beef. But the Idahos were baked in foil, there were no vegetables except iceberg lettuce and cotton tomatoes, and the only breads were sweet brown-'n'-serve rolls and cinnamon buns.

De Groot again had better luck than we did when he dined at THE SINGLE BEST RESTAURANT IN THE WORLD, possibly because he arrived when old Arthur Bryant was around. Although, as a local man put it, the place had been "urban renewaled" out of its old quarters, we found it as described: a store in the black district with oilcloth tables, soda vending machines, and a brick oven in the rear where meats well smoked with hickory were piled on slices of factory bread and doused with a sauce of Tabasco, tomato, vinegar, and unidentified seasonings, allegedly mixed in gasoline drums. To our taste, the ham was very good, the beef poor and greasy, and the famous spare ribs edible but dry and disappointing.

Midwesterners are seldom offended at having some local feature described as the best in the world, but Kansas City folk were embarrassed when we mentioned Trillin's enthusiasms and even the new sophisticated foreign spots that de Groot had admired. "There are some nice places to eat in Kansas City," a professional man allowed. "But around here, a lot of people who never had a good meal in their lives are setting themselves up as gourmets." As for the Trillin eulogy, he opined, "It was written on memory rather than reality."

Months later Thorpe Menn, book editor of *The Kansas City Star*, wrote in an open letter to Trillin that he had asked a number of knowledgeable locals to review the book, but all had refused, on the ground that they liked Bud too well. "You just cannot resist the temptation to tug a little at America's leg," Menn said. "Fine. Why not something of an ironic guide to eating? But

Calvin, you are too straightfaced about it." As a result, he reported, "unknown thousands of Kansas Citians" had been embarrassed by having to take out-of-town visitors to Trillin's temples of chili dogs, indestructible malts, and cole slaw. Shrewdly, Menn guessed that Trillin was kidding also in his dithyrambs about New York lunch counters that concealed treasures of exotic gastronomy.

To be fair, Trillin did warn the reader. In one essay, he made himself the butt of an old joke. (The way we first heard it, this man was always complaining to his wife that she didn't fry liver the way his mother used to; one day, she burned it, and he exclaimed after the first bite: "Ah! *That's* how Mother used to do it!") In a supermarket, Trillin recounts, he came across a carton of macaroni and cheese that he remembered from childhood as a Kraft dinner. It didn't taste right. Next day, he reheated some, "and realized that what I had been nostalgic for was not Kraft dinner, but day-old Kraft dinner." How can you get mad at a guy like that?

The problem is that while our daily food is absurd, it is not really hilarious. It may be described with irony and wit, but not with frivolity. Trillin is right on when he describes what is touted by forward-looking bankers and mad-dog franchisers. When he says "there is still great food all over the country," he is only exaggerating an important fact: that good, if not great, food does survive in some places in our country, if not all over it. But as Thorpe Menn says, Trillin can't resist pulling the reader's leg by sending him to places that are folkloric as all get-out, and serve day-old Kraft dinner.

De Groot, now, is a man who takes eating seriously. In the old tradition of European food writing, he announces himself well before his arrival and challenges the host to do his best. An imperious diner, he eats well, and holds that if anyone eats badly it's his own fault. He confided one day that he had received letters of complaint about his praise for Ernie's of San Francisco, but retorted, "I don't think you can say Ernie's is a bad restaurant because somebody went in and didn't take care of himself."

De Groot's writing has the substantial merit of persuading readers that dining can be a rich, sensual, and civilized experience, and there is some reason to believe, or at least hope, that his praise puts some restaurateurs on their mettle to deserve it. But it has some pitfalls for lesser mortals.

Thus our disparate observations at Kansas City's Hotel Muehlebach, made famous by Harry S Truman. Some years ago, *The New York Times* mentioned that the place had run down. De Groot phoned the hotel's executive vice president and was invited to stay in the Presidential Suite. His reception was so delightful that he told *Esquire* readers, "I could hardly escape the impression that *The New York Times* report had been some of the unfittest news it had ever printed."

A year later, we made reservations at the Muehlebach as ordinary travelers. Dumped across the street by the airport bus, we made our way with our luggage past a temporarily untended door, down stairs and half a block to the desk, waited five minutes for a bellman, were taken in a dirty elevator to a room that had not been made up, were abandoned there and finally deposited in another room whose soiled paint was peeling from the walls. This at $30 a day, in 1974 dollars.

(Considering that our guidebooks rate hotels and restaurants chiefly for cleanliness, one wonders how closely they inspect. A distinguished French couple we know recount that on arrival at the Waldorf-Astoria in New York, they noticed a champagne cork under the drawing-room couch. Intrigued, they left it there; it was there when they departed a week later. At the $30-a-day Allerton Hotel in Chicago, a peanut shell lay at our doorsill on our arrival; it was there when we left four days later. We conclude that the difference between a cham-

pagne cork and a peanut shell measures the difference
between a Waldorf and an Allerton.)

Similarly, de Groot fared better than we did at
Ernie's, which was one of the six best restaurants in
the country according to the 1974 Mobil Travel Guide
and "one of the world's few truly great restaurants,"
according to *Holiday*. Actually, we fared better than
some San Franciscans had warned us we would: the
service that evening was good and the meal well prepared
to order, except for an unsuccessful soufflé of grainy
texture. We had a nicely poached salmon in a good
beurre blanc, lamb chops done pink as requested, ac-
ceptably done string beans, and a properly roasted pigeon
with an indifferent bread stuffing.

But everything tasted bland. Even the Pacific salmon,
which we chose over the imported frozen turbot and
sole. When we introduced ourselves next day to Chef
Jean Lafont we remarked on this, and he replied, "You're
right. Salmon is not very tasty." It is possible that he had
never tasted *fresh* Pacific salmon. It is indeed hard now
to find fresh fish anywhere on either coast, short of
meeting the boats at the dock, but the insipidity of the
food at Ernie's, an expensive restaurant in the heart of a
productive region, is difficult to excuse. Its young Basque
saucier, Sauverer Meniburu, said with a shrug, "We must
change with the times. We don't have the kitchen teams
of old days." But Ernie's does have the long menu of
old days, and, as its owner told the San Francisco Board
of Supervisors, it would be expensive to change it every
time it chose to substitute a frozen item for the fresh....

Writing for the Paris edition of *The New York Times*,
one of the authors once tipped readers off to an obscure
little restaurant of remarkable cuisine. A compatriot later
confessed to us that he had brought his wife there to try
it, but finding the place nearly deserted, they had slipped
away Perhaps because we worship success, many of us
seem to prefer to go where we must wait in queues to

be fed, and are encouraged to leave before we are finished.

Doubtless the evening we dined at Ernie's was a slow one, for we were seated only thirty minutes past our reservation time. (This, locals told us, was below par for the course.) Like others, we passed the time in the bar, with an overpriced bottle of an overrated California white. Some cynics postulate that bar sales are the reason why many restaurants keep diners waiting, but our experience in The Bakery, which has no bar, suggests that the chief motive for overbooking by restaurants is the same as that of airlines: to maximize turnover.

The Bakery was, in a way, worth waiting for. Chicagoans say it used to be a good, cheap Hungarian restaurant before its boss, Louis Szathmáry, who used to be a psychologist in Hungary, decided to become a gourmet chef and a consultant to Armour on gourmet frozen foods. To describe The Bakery as a success is an understatement. *Holiday* called it "the most popular restaurant of the century!" and assured that "everything is delectable," while Mobil promised "delightful dining in intimate, unpretentious restaurant." Unpretentious, yes.

With reservations clocked on the quarter hour, we make sure to arrive on time, and are led to a tiny, drab waiting room crowded with standees. No drinks. A mild reminder that we have reserved brings the reply, "I know you have—we don't take anybody without a reservation." Forty minutes of this, and we are seated in a dining-room pantry, its walls covered with as many framed documents as those of a fake physician. We still have time to study the diplomas from *Holiday*, the honorary citizenship of Baton Rouge, and a framed article by Szathmáry in *Cooking for Profit*, a magazine of the gas industry. Under the headline "Use Psychology on Your Customers," he advises, "Make sure the person on the phone who takes reservations sounds cheerful."

The limited-choice meal, when it arrives, justifies *Holi-*

day's exclamation point: a whipped pâté tasting chiefly of cinnamon; a scorched and starchy asparagus soup; beef Wellington (the quintessence of the gourmet plague and at best a dish designed to damage good beef) coated with the same pâté and served with an incredible sweet currant sauce; a dried-out pork chop in diner gravy; salad with a nameless sweet dressing; ugh-y banana cream éclair and mocha torte, and weak American coffee. There is no wait for the bill ($11 each plus tax and tip), which comes with the coffee....

When our report on this feast was published, Szath-máry sent us an ironic letter that had been dictated, he said, "on the way to the bank." Laughing all the way, we presume. Well, it is difficult to quarrel with success, and the likes of The Bakery are proliferating all over the country. In a way, it's a hopeful sign. We'll explain that odd statement a few pages on.

We have noted that we had some pleasant experiences during our term of professional dining—but nearly all of them were in "foreign" restaurants catering to their own communities. In San Francisco there are still a few of those wonderful *Maman-et-Papa* bistros where you can eat a decent table d'hôte with the house wine for *deux fois rien*. Such as Klu's Basque Restaurant ("Headquarters for Wool Sheep Cattlemen") in North Beach, where dinner one evening included an excellent cabbage soup, splendid braised oxtails *plus* a nicely roasted chicken, all (with forgivable American salad and ice cream) for $3.50 each. Chicago's Greektown has a clutch of restaurants, each with a lamb roasting in the window, music pouring from the door, and a happy throng within feeding on reasonably authentic cooking at less than $5 for an ample meal with wine. At the Greek Islands Restaurant, we had an ouzo on the house while we waited, then a good *tarama* (roe paste), an excellent cucumber-in-yogurt salad, lamb and artichoke in *avgolemono* sauce, dried codfish in a garlic sauce, a fine baklava, fair coffee, and a bottle of Hymettus white—at less than half the price of the meal at The Bakery, and light-years better.

In New York, that most cosmopolitan of cities, the well-directed diner may visit a different country every night for a couple of subway tokens and the very modest price of a meal. Our most interesting experiences in restaurant-hopping for *The Times* came as we compared groups of ethnic establishments: the Hungarian (stuffed cabbage, goulash, noodles, cucumbers, crepes), the Indian (flat and puffed breads, curries), Middle Eastern (sesame, chickpea, and eggplant hors d'oeuvres; lamb patties; genuine shish kebab; natural yogurt), the Brazilian (*feijoada*, black or red beans and rice, codfish in many splendid dishes, sautéed collard greens), the Cuban (black beans and rice, plantains, pork, dried beef), the Japanese (whose arrival in numbers has introduced a cuisine often presented with matchless elegance, comparable to flower arrangement), and, above all, the Chinese.

Americanization was visibly taking its toll, however. As we were exploring the Hungarians, for example, their last old-fashioned baker retired and factory-sliced bread replaced the good sour rye. Iceberg lettuce, cotton tomatoes, blotting-paper chicken, stale fish, and poor coffee were common, but could be avoided. Even in otherwise poor restaurants, a cook might keep the faith with one native dish, like the German saloon in the Bronx where the pork and cabbage were fine, although many diners washed it down with steins of Coca-Cola.

Only the chauvinistic Orientals clung stubbornly to their traditions. At Fulton Fish Market in the hours before dawn, fully one-third of the buyers were Chinese or Japanese, and they were the most demanding; theirs were the only restaurants where one had a good chance of finding reasonably fresh fish. Chinatown also has the only edible chickens in the city; grown especially for this community, they are eighteen to twenty weeks old and are fresh-killed, as compared with the eight-week-old, hormone-stuffed products of our commercial freezers.

The Chinese, poor though most of them are, pay twice as much per pound for the taste of something like the real thing. They also have their own noodle makers, bean sprouters, roast shops, and truck gardens, delivering their own fresh greens the year round.

The restaurants serving this community of one hundred thousand, many of its people newly arrived from the Fast East, have little in common with the chop suey joints that serve middle America with the taste of Howard Johnson's, or with the gourmet-touted palaces that burn the palate with chic "Szechuan" or "Hunan" cooking reluctantly turned out by Cantonese and Shanghai chefs. One *can* eat poorly in Chinatown, but the visitor who insists on eating where the Chinese eat and on ordering what the Chinese order can eat better in Chinatown than anywhere else in the country. *The Times* rates restaurants from one to four stars; we conferred four stars only once, and that was on Chinatown as a whole.

But we are the melting pot; Chinatown already has its juvenile delinquents and its burger joint. As all foreign restaurants ultimately qualify for citizenship, we cannot depend forever on the exotics among us. And since the American restaurant professionals have generally opted for industrial feeding, virtually the only hope for decent dining in our future rests on the amateurs. That is what we meant when we said, a few pages back, that the proliferation of places like The Bakery was a good sign, in a curious way.

All over the country, but especially in college towns, resorts, and arty neighborhoods, pleasant cafés are being opened by enthusiastic refugees from the theater, the arts, academe, and the professions. These young people mostly come from families that have been eating badly for three generations, but they have been constructively influenced by the natural-foods movement and some foreign travel (though when abroad they tend to follow such guides as *Europe on $5 a Day* and eat where other

Americans eat). They respect crafts and hard work—indeed, they often do their own decorating, and quite often do it well. It's a nice change from Howard Johnson's Formica. But the food is almost never very good.

The gourmet hucksters have sold these amateurs on the very square notion that you, too, can be a chef in ten easy lessons, or in none at all—just the price of a book. Doesn't Julia address the reader as "chef"? The innocents actually advertise their inexperience, with a shelf of gourmet cookbooks over the bar, or a publicity handout that identifies the chef as a twenty-eight-year-old woman "who studied the French horn at the Royal Academy in London and worked for a time as a chauffeur in Palm Beach, Fla." (It's probably unfair to blame the press agents. When we remarked in a column that restaurant publicity seemed to concern itself with anything but the quality of the cooking, one of them replied that the reason was that "many editors say it is 'too commercial' to mention the food.")

That hornplayer-chauffeur-chef's place was actually one of the better amateur cafés we visited, and we rated it one star, which meant fair. At a modest price, we had a respectable beef bourguignon, a nice beans-and-sausage dish rather extravagantly called cassoulet, and a crisp Romaine salad. We also had flabby bread, a dull store-bought pâté, an awful gourmet mushroom bisque sweetened with port wine, overdone sea bass with overdone broccoli, oversweet pastries from an overrated shoppe, and poor, muddy drip coffee.

As it happened, it was the chef's day off, so we talked to her even younger substitute, a former secretary who was fixing a decent-looking omelet. She confided that she loved cooking and planned to leave soon for Europe, where she hoped to work in the kitchen of some good restaurant. "The restaurant business is dying because people in it don't care," she said. "I want to work with people who know what they're doing."

There is hope.

There is hope, too, in the letter sent us by another young woman amateur in Aspen, Colorado:

> We went into the restaurant business for one purpose, and that was not getting rich. We have dined miserably and unhappily all over the country. We wanted to know if it was possible to operate a restaurant at the level of good home cooking and decent service —profitably.
>
> We have found, as you mentioned...in many articles, an incredible proliferation of pre-packaged, machine-made foods. These are easy to avoid, as immoral, even though cooks are (a) impossible, (b) eat a lot, (c) drink a lot, and (d) receive large bi-monthly paychecks. We have also found that most ingredients that we wish to purchase fresh must be purchased frozen, and many are available irregularly or not at all. In addition, foods that are available "fresh" are available to us once or at most twice weekly. Fresh means that the foods were shipped from somewhere three days before they were received, loaded onto a truck, and eventually delivered to us. Before shipping they accumulated at a loading point for awhile, too....
>
> Judge some restaurants (those outside the distribution areas) on the basis of how well they do under the given circumstances. The owner of La Grenouille [in New York] announces in horror that some people cook omelets in oil. What other choice is there when the only butter you can get consistently has a terrible off taste? Which is the worse crime? One other thing that we can no longer get is fresh whipping cream; the sterilized kind tastes like chalk, but is still better than Cool Whip. One more decline in quality, though, and I won't be so sure.
>
> I read your articles, and because I grew up in the truck-farming center of southern New Jersey, I am ashamed. But then I say to myself, "I make my frozen vegetables as delicious as possible. I can be sorry, but I don't need to be ashamed."...
>
> Can we operate selling good food profitably? A

year isn't long enough to tell, but the answer appears
to be either *possibly* or *probably* not, at least the way
things are going. Probably yes if we raise all our
prices beyond the reach of the under $25,000 a year
man. Probably yes if we lived where people were
pleased to spend "only" $20 a person for a good meal.

The writer of this letter enclosed a menu, which
demonstrated that she was indeed caught in an impossible
dilemma: armed with a gourmet cookbook, which she
identified as her life raft, she was trying to serve chef's
food with poor ingredients and unqualified help. Her
instincts were fine: she wrote with joy about a one-time
find of fresh-picked corn and sun-ripened tomatoes and
a supper of freshly caught trout. It would be illegal to
serve wild trout, but the real solution, the only solution,
is there in her own sound instincts: Burn that cookbook
and those menus, find or grow some decent garden
produce, use the best Colorado beef and Idaho potatoes,
serve good home-baked bread and pastries (or buy them
from those health freaks down the road, asking them to
skip the molasses in the bread), and eke these out with
beans, cabbages, and onions. Buy good coffee in the bean,
preferably roasting it yourself, and grind it and make it
in a drip pot. Even if you must subsidize a farmer, assure yourself a supply of real chickens and eggs and, above
all, milk and cream, which you can churn in a blender to
make butter. Then start cooking real food; if you must
use some frozen peas and limas, it will be forgiven,
provided that they are of good quality and have not
been abused. The best way to assure *that* these days,
unfortunately, is to freeze it yourself.

What we have prescribed would not, of course, be a
gourmet restaurant, and we cannot guarantee that it would
succeed with the Aspen crowd. But if our correspondent
were to try it and fail—as quite evidently she was failing
when she wrote us—she would at least have no reason to
feel ashamed.

14

A la Mode

Can be used as Beaujolais in America.

*Legend on a vat of bad wine
in a Bordeaux warehouse*

Once a sensual pleasure, food has become a snob thing, closely allied with those other preoccupations of "women's" journalism, Society and fashions. The seasons have disappeared from our produce markets but have entered our cookery in the fashion sense—there are dishes that are "in" this season, and dishes that are "out." We learned this from *Women's Wear Daily*, an authority on such matters, which employs the peremptory language of writing that is addressed to insecure readers. ("Do the unconventional!" *WWD* orders. But dahling, if that's what *everybody* is doing this season, how can it be unconventional?)

There was some good and some bad news for us in the 1973 winter fashions. The good news was that what these same counselors were ordering us to serve a few seasons earlier were now *out*: beef Wellington, creamed mushrooms on toast, seafood gratiné in crepes, rubber cheese, duckling with sticky orange sauce, ad nauseam. The bad news was that some potentially marvelous dishes were also *out*: T-bone, porterhouse, and sirloin steaks; prime ribs of beef "especially with Yorkshire pudding"; *coq au vin.*

Pork-liver pâté, which we love, was out in favor of duck liver sautéed. Oh dear.

In place of the *coq au vin*, *WWD* said, serve (that's an order!) *poulet au vinaigre*; instead of beef, serve veal scallopini; instead of duck *à l'orange*, serve duck *au poivre* —but to serve chicken with green pepper would be like wearing last year's gown. Oddly, quiche was not listed, pro or con, which could only leave a thousand caterers and a million hostesses floundering like bits of ham in a floury custard limbo. But help was at hand. Definitely *in* that season was "Oyster cocktail Orford: Plump oysters in spiced tomato juice. Serve in mugs."

To mugs, they mean. Not a word in the article about the quality of the food to be served to guests; if you want to be *in*, you must ignore taste. To ban good beef in favor of bad chicken and veal, to ignore good cooking in favor of gourmet cuisine, is chic.

That season, a terribly chic restaurant had opened on Manhattan's East Side, and was reported in *The Times* to be serving bad food to the Beautiful People. It was a smash success, and its press agent later wrote with complacency:

> It is clear that ambiance has become more important than food and that the people who frequent La Goulue are interested in who's there, what they're wearing and what they're saying.... The readers of The Times should know what makes a restaurant "in" when everything seemingly works against it: the location (highly residential), the owner (no experience in the management of a restaurant), the appeal (highly snob) and the prices.

At home on Park Avenue, Mr. and Mrs. Frederick Winship gave their "almost annual chili dinner." The fourteen guests were Beautiful People all, and the chili was served in silver tureens, the beer in Baccarat crystal, by butlers wearing white gloves and orange jackets from Zampieri in Rome. The affair was reported by *The*

Times in that split-level style that it uses for its women's pages—loads of froth for those who crave to learn how the gentry cavort, with a knowing wink for the sophisticated. (A favorite of ours in this genre was a full-page layout headlined "Royal Wedding is Hardly Topic A in New York.") Besides thoroughly describing the clothing of the guests, *The Times* gave us the recipe for Mrs. Winship's almost annual chili. It was based on six 15-ounce cans of red beans in chili gravy, and laced with "1¼ cups May wine or light Beaujolais."

After reading about this high living, we understood why *ratatouille*, a dish we were glad to find on the table of every *in* hostess in the early sixties, had disappeared a decade later. As the French say, nothing is so out of fashion as fashion; nothing would persuade a smart hostess to serve a *ratatouille* now. We have always wondered what people with this year's breed of dog have done with last year's.

Now if, as Dr. Paul A. Fine says, we Americans are neurotic about our food, then we are positively bonkers about our drink. Nobody, for example, regards it as even a little odd to find airline stewardesses hustling booze in the middle of the morning. It does, to be sure, make the lunch that is to come more endurable. But suppose the passenger makes it to town, and wants a quick bite. He knows a stand where the pizza or the souvlaki or the chili is not bad—that is, it would not be bad if he could have a glass of beer or wine with it. No such luck. He must either take a ghastly chemical soft drink there, or head for a relatively expensive restaurant, or a saloon with a steam table.

In most states, licenses to sell alcoholic beverages are limited, ostensibly to curb drinking but actually to preserve monopolies that date from Prohibition days. When we lived in half-dry Utah, the stuff was sold only by the bottle, and a sinner had to get a license to buy one; the saying there was that you could buy a drunk but not a drink. We ban the importation of liqueur-filled chocolates. . . .

Our ethos is torn between abstinence and alcoholism; there is no middle ground. The idea that a mild ferment of grapes or hops or apples is a normal part of civilized dining is un-American. When we wrote once that we did not consider a meal complete without wine, a lady reader accused us of encouraging drunkenness. Poor soul, she might better have addressed those hotels that advertise "free guest ice" on every floor.

A great French chef once confided to us his distress at the fact that many American clients, including food writers who sing his praises, insist on taking setups to their bedrooms. It was not the whiskey and ice that bothered him, but the solitary drinking, and the worry that too much liquor would dull their appreciation of his cooking. That would be the view of any fine cook. Mère Brazier, the most famous Lyonnais cook of her time, once offered us a Scotch, as a courtesy to Americans. When we refused, she snapped, "Good! It smells like crushed bedbugs." The late Fernand Point of La Pyramide at Vienne, a master teacher as well as a master chef, wrote in his notebook, "After absorbing a cocktail, not to mention two, the palate can no longer distinguish a Château Mouton Rothschild of a great year from the contents of a bottle of ink."

This is notoriously not the view of our resident gourmets. When *House & Garden* polled a passel of liquor merchants and writers on what wines they drank before meals, as aperitifs, it reported, "Craig Claiborne likes a Tequila Sunrise: 2 ounces of vodka, 1 ounce tequila, 1 cup orange juice and enough grenadine to give a sunrise color wash." This from a man who writes of serving only the most expensive wines. What the professionals actually drink is problematical. When *New York* magazine staged a tasting of diet soft drinks, its own wine expert and an immigrant French chef-writer, Jacques Pépin, served on the jury. Curiously, the only harsh criticism came from the amateurs; the pros were loyal to the business principle that you don't knock the product. They did find a couple of the diet drinks "little"—the saccharin equivalent of "a small wine."

In our view, hard alcohol tends to dull all the senses, and mixed drinks, especially sweet ones, coat the palate with a lingering taste that quarrels with the food to come. (By the same token, we deprecate spicy "appetizers," which belong in snacks.) To be sure, French sophisticates have taken to whiskey, because it's British and hence snob, and more traditional Frenchmen remain addicted to aperitifs such as the anise-flavored pernod or herb brews such as vermouth; these were anciently taken for medicinal reasons, a notion that persists in the word *digestif* as applied to a liqueur taken after the meal. We prefer as an aperitif a dry white wine such as Sancerre, or a good champagne on festive occasions, but can see no gastronomic harm in starting with whatever wine one plans to drink with the meal, or in starting with good beer or "hard" cider.

Alas, real cider has almost vanished from our ken, American beers are not fit to drink, and even imported beers have been thinned, pasteurized, and in some instances apparently sweetened for the American market. A Midwestern braumeister explained, "We don't make beer, we make flavored water for people who don't like beer." It was encouraging to hear, not long ago, of an organized campaign of resistance in Britain to the new beers, which *The New York Times* reported were now being "watered down, injected with agents to produce artificial foam, filtered and pasteurized . . . [and] pressurized with carbon dioxide." But Britons remember what they call "real beer." Americans don't.

That leaves us only wine as a decent accompaniment to food. While most of what is on sale at a moderate price

is poor, the careful shopper in most cities can find some
that pleases the palate. But for many Americans, the
pleasure of drinking wine has been spoiled by the fear of
doing the wrong thing—a snobbish terror inflicted upon
them by the gourmet gang.

A clever attempt to exploit this neurosis was the Electronic Wine Steward, a computer gadget for liquor shops,
which was unveiled at a trade show in New York. The
customer pushes the buttons, and the printout tells him
what wine to buy to serve with what food. Sheila Hoffman, a marketing consultant who developed the machine
in cooperation with wine merchants and supermarkets,
told dealers in a leaflet, "It eliminates consumer reluctance
to ask questions lest they appear uninformed."

We engaged in a dialogue with the computer and were
advised that, with lobster Newburg, we should serve a
pink or a white Anjou. Four brands were listed; all happened to be on offer at nearby booths. The machine also
provided us with a recipe, which Hoffman candidly said
she had clipped from some magazine. The printout announced: "THIS GOURMET RECIPE HAS BEEN CREATED FOR YOU
BY THE PET MILK SPECIALIST." It called for one can of Pet
Milk, a bottle of Wesson oil, a cheap brandy, a cheap
sherry, and chicken stock, all to complete the ruin of two
pounds of frozen lobster tails.

Only snob-induced fear makes such food, such wine,
and such marketing tactics possible. Compare this with the
attitude of people who really enjoy food and wine for
what they are. At an Italian feast of the *Vigilia di Natale*,
Christmas Eve, before a table laden with spaghetti with
clam sauce, mussels, codfish, smelts, shrimps, octopus, and
a huge lobster, our host, Len Tredanari, raised a glass of
his homemade wine and said, "You know, at this moment
my mother would tense up, because she knew what was
coming. She always set a new tablecloth, and my father
would hold up his glass and pour it on the table. He told
everybody that eating was for fun, and now they could

relax." We cannot endorse the gesture, but for the sentiment, *benissimo*!

Aside from sex, we know of no agreeable subject about
which more nonsense has been written than about wine.
As with sex, a swarm of self-elected experts has thoroughly intimidated a naïve public only too easily convinced of its own impotence This is more true, we fear,
with Anglo-Saxons than with Latins, who seem to possess
more confidence in these matters (whether justified or
not).

Consider, for example, the advice of a man who was
long Britain's most influential guide to gastronomy, and
whose name we'll omit here because he has since died. In
The Sunday Times of London he decreed that claret (an
Anglicism for Bordeaux) be served "at mouth temperature." At the time, we suggested that His Nibs was one of
those gentlemen of whom it used to be said that butter
wouldn't melt in their mouths.

As with many other things, the optimum temperature
of wine is a matter of personal taste—within limits. If as a
consenting adult His Nibs got his kicks from drinking
Bordeaux at body temperature, that was his affair. When
he tried to impose that peculiar predilection on the public,
it became another matter. We must reproach the British
pooh-bahs and their American followers for the idiotic
rule that red wine must be served *chambré*—that is, at
room temperature. What room? What temperature? The
British, who abandoned central heating when the Romans
departed, keep their homes at the temperature of a Bordeaux cellar, so no harm's done. But when Americans try
to obey the diktat, we find waiters cooking a bottle on
the radiator before serving it.

Wine is an organic miracle in delicate suspension, a
living complex that, as vintners like to point out, will
"flower" in the spring with the vines. It suffers from the
shock of bottling and transportation, and must rest to re-
cover. It is shattered by extremes of heat or cold, or by

sharp swings of temperature. So the common abuse of
fine wines in our country is saddening. Often in expensive
restaurants, we have been served white wine that has been
stored for days and weeks on end in the refrigerator. The
damage is often compounded by the silly pretension of
serving it in frost-coated glasses. When we protested
about a Pouilly-Fumé so destroyed at Delmonico's, Thomas
Ghilardi, the septuagenarian wine steward, replied, "I
agree. But Americans like it that way."

Here misinformed snob advice joins a national addiction
to drinks (and foods) that are either ice cold or scalding
hot. In either case they tend to numb the palate and probably damage our innards. On both the East and West
coasts and in between, we have been served beer that, by
a triumph of barroom cryogenics, has formed a skim of
ice on the surface. Considering the taste of the brew, this
may have its value; nations that make good beer prefer it
at temperatures that permit drinkers to savor it. For that
matter, people who like the taste of fine whiskey (they,
and it, are rare) don't put ice in it. On the other hand,
most connoisseurs prefer white wines (and white liquors)
chilled, and red wines *cool*. No matter what the wine
guidebooks say.

A confession: in a Lyonnais restaurant one summer long
ago, we sent back a *pot* of Morgon (one of the *grands
crus* of the Beaujolais) because it had arrived at table in a
bucket of cold water that had several ice cubes floating
in it. Later, we were embarrassed to learn that the good
bourgeois of Lyons, who were literally weaned on Beaujolais, liked their wine that way—that is, at the chilly
temperature of the Beaujolais cellars—and were, of course,
right. For a decade thereafter, we toured the vineyards
every mid-November, tasting cups in hand, to lay in our
annual supply of Chiroubles or Morgon or Fleurie or
Julienas and, always, Côte de Brouilly. One of the first
things we learned was that Beaujolais reaches the peak of
its fresh, fruity flavor during the winter after its harvest,
and then starts to decline. Always. Growers have proudly

served us Beaujolais that was years old and still fit to drink, but never pretended that it was as good as when it was young. André Allard, whose bistro on the Left Bank is famous for its Beaujolais, says that, ideally, the wine should all be used before June. It follows that, since wine is not ready to travel before it is several months old, and is said to age six months from the shock of crossing the Atlantic, Beaujolais can never be tasted at its best here. Yet Beaujolais, genuine or fantasist, is often sold here when it is years old, and we have heard merchants and "experts" alike say of such a bottle that it has not yet reached its peak.

In getting advice on wine, it's not always easy to tell the merchants from the experts. Following a complaint by a major importer, *The New York Post* dropped a wine columnist who had criticized some labels, and replaced him with a writer who just happened to be the publicity man for a number of wines. His enthusiasm for the product was as unbounded as it was uninformed. But, while only a few other wine writers are directly in the selling side of the business, most depend on the merchants for their tastings, and their information. This is sometimes good, sometimes bad, always self-serving. Thus, when a columnist wrote that it was okay to keep fine wine on a rack in the living room, he should have added that it was okay for the dealer. He would serve his readers better if he advised them not to *collect* wine unless they had storage space of reasonably cool, stable temperature. He would serve them even better if he exposed the conditions under which most dealers keep their wine. The consumer who cannot be sure that his "big" wine has been properly stored by his supplier, and who cannot put it to rest in a cool place at home for at least a few weeks, is simply throwing his money away—unless all he wants is to impress his guests with the label. Fortunately, there are many sturdy "little" wines that the consumer, once free of his snob advisers, can drink with pleasure.

The notion that wine improves with age has enough

truth to be dangerous. In the nineteenth and early twentieth centuries, fine Bordeaux were made to keep, with
strong doses of tannin from the grape stems and storage
in barrels for at least three years before bottling; they
were seldom ready to drink before they were ten years
old, and some took much longer. In old age, they deposited a brown sediment; hence the ceremony of carefully carrying the bottle half reclining, to avoid stirring
up the sediment, and of gently pouring it into a decanter,
stopping near the bottom when the trickle turns cloudy.
It is amusing to see these ceremonies still practiced, often
ineptly, when the reason for them has disappeared. It is
sad to see once beautiful wines gone to perdition in the
cellars of misinformed collectors.

Today, even the greatest châteaux have cut the tannin
and the aging in the barrel in order to turn over their
stocks quickly. The prime drinking age varies from château to château and from year to year, but few wines
indeed are still improving after a decade. Nearly all other
dry wines have shorter life spans than the big Bordeaux.
The Troisgros at Roanne, often called the best restaurant
in the world, serves its fine house Burgundy only eighteen
months or two years old—and chilled, at that.

Another myth of wine snobbery has been immortalized
by the story of the drunken writer who threw up at the
table of a Hollywood mogul. "That's all right, Sam," the
writer said, "the white wine came up with the fish."
White wine with fish, red with meat and cheese—right?
Certainly, if that's what you have, and above all if that's
what you like. But *must* you serve a white wine with, say,
a fish stew, or eel *à la meurette*, cooked with Burgundy?
If you do serve a white, as is your right, then you are
violating another "law," which orders you to serve the
same wine that the dish has been cooked in. Now, that
law is not a bad one, unless you've been cooking with port
or Madeira or cognac. Or unless your palate proposes
some other wine.

For people in wine-growing regions, the question of

what wine to serve does not arise; they drink what they make, and find it good. Over the centuries, the art of women cooks has fashioned a cuisine in harmony with the products of their soil. The outsider does well to follow their example when he can, and drink the regional beverage with the regional food. The Rhineland and Alsace make no red wines to speak of, and *feinschmeckers* there drink flowery whites with *choucroûte* and even venison. That great Burgundian connoisseur Père Troisgros, on the other hand, held that white wine was a hussy to be encountered in a bar but not in a restaurant; he liked to set up blindfold tests to prove that a nice cool red wine goes better than white with fish. A majority of connoisseurs, though, prefer a dry white with most fish dishes, red with beef, lamb, and game, and either red or white with pork, veal, or chicken, depending always on the manner of cooking, the availability of the wine, and personal preference.

This said, there are a few taste principles that are common among people who drink wine with every meal, for pleasure and not for snobbery. There is a saying in the trade, "Buy over apples, sell over cheese," reflecting the fact that fruit acid tends to kill the palate for wine, while cheese incites thirst and "flatters" wine. Even so, a sweet wine such as Sauternes may go very well with a fine pear, or with a meat dish cooked with fruit. (Incidentally, a Château d'Yquem or other fine Sauternes with *foie gras* is a revelation.) Further, any sharp cheese, like a blue, will murder the taste of a delicate wine; the advice of the Time-Life gourmets to serve a big Bordeaux with Roquefort properly shocked Courtine, and will shock the reader if he tries it. A Sauternes or a champagne would be fine.

Curnonsky, *le Prince des Gastronomes*, used to say he had never found a wine that could be drunk with salad (i.e., with vinegar), so he never ate salads. At any rate, wine drinking can be suspended during the salad course. Artichokes, by the way, have the curious effect on the

palate of making other foods and wine taste sweet. More
generally, strong seasonings fight all other tastes (which
is why we do not care for spicy appetizers), so subtle
wines should be saved for subtle foods. Put another way,
strong, "coarse" Mediterranean wines stand up best to
strong Mediterranean dishes. As for fiery curries or chilies,
it might be best to stick to beer. For those food writers
who claim to like them so hot that they burn for days,
we'd recommend a fire extinguisher.

With such dishes as bouillabaisse, the fashion now is to
serve rosé. Pink wine has become cheap snob, because "it
goes with everything," thus avoiding the imagined obliga-
tion to switch from white to red. Like an amphibious
plane, it can either sail or fly but does neither very well.
We are among a minority who get little pleasure from
pink wines, and have been pained to see farmers in Sancerre plowing up good white-grape vines and replanting
to meet the rosé fashion. As for the American cold duck
fad and its successor, Sangría (lemonade and sugar with
bad wine, long used as a hot weather drink in Spain but
served here with meals) ... Ugh.

We have put off mentioning American wines because,
frankly, we regard them as too expensive for what they
are. This is said not in prejudice but in sorrow. California
jug wine was the first we ever drank, and in those days it
was good value. Even now, Italian-Americans who buy
California grapes in the market make a pretty decent wine
at home. But once these same grapes pass through the
industrial refineries and arrive pasteurized and screw-
topped, we are glad we can buy something better in an
imported wine.

We have no doubt that California and other parts of the
country can make as good wine as anybody. Some day, no
doubt, they will. But right now, to quote a young woman
who grew up in France and moved to San Francisco,
"California wine has no pizazz." We suspect that good
vintners who go to California make a wine without char-

acter for the same reason that good braumeisters who come here make a beer without character, because they think that's the American way.

The fact that more and more Americans are fooling around with making wine, and beer, and cider, is wonderfully encouraging. Those early Virginia settlers were right: surely, in this great continent, there are regions that will produce great wine when, in the old manner, we find the right combination of grape, cultivation, and vinification. Meanwhile, we must learn to drink for pleasure, and for pleasure alone.

15

Home Ec

First, a home economist is not a cook!

A professor of Home Ec at Queens College

THE FLAP began with a casual remark during a radio interview. It was an old observation in our house: that any country that teaches cooking under the title Home Economics has got to eat badly.

A New Jersey listener wrote in to suggest that somebody give the new food critic of *The Times* a bop on the head.

"You certainly have put your foot in the molasses and I fear you will have sticky walking from now on," she continued. "I happened to catch the Martha Dean program, and I heard your sweeping statements about Home Economists, Nutritionists and frozen foods. Shame on you. . . .

"I am a professional Home Economist. I worked for the two largest food companies, General Foods and Standard Brands. I have great respect for Home Economists, Food Companies and frozen foods."

At this point, in early 1973, we did not realize quite how baleful the influence of Home Economics had been. In a column, we published the good lady's complaint and commented:

Ah, well, if you can't stand the heat, stay out of the kitchen, as the man said.

In that period of time (as they say in Washington) when foods and words were precisely what they purported to be, if you called Grandma a Home Economist she'd have bopped you on the head with a mixing spoon. She was a cook, and not ashamed of it.

A home, in those days, did not mean a conglomerate. It must have taken a heap of economics to make General Foods a home.

Now, an economist may be a good cook, just as a physician may run a four-minute mile; it happens, but one occupation must get in the way of the other.

The same holds for the nutritionists, chemists and health faddists of all kinds. (They have made some important contributions, which will be acknowledged in another context, but if one is making enemies, one might as well go whole hog.)

At a national symposium of nutritionists the other day, and in the flood of diet literature that overwhelms this desk, all the talk was about riboflavin, amino acids, polyunsaturated fats and calories. What is missing is the taste, the sensuality of good food.

Does anybody remember Henry Fonda as young Abe Lincoln judging a pie contest in Illinois? That's sensuality. And the oyster scene in "Tom Jones"—far sexier, in this viewer's opinion, than anything Marlon Brando might do with butter.

A young woman in the publishing biz confided recently that most of the food writers she knew (not all, most) didn't seem to care much for food. It shows.

If, as our New Jersey correspondent implies, the Home Economists, nutritionists and food companies are responsible for the way Americans eat—the TV dinners and other "convenience" foods, the synthetic dairy products, the diet colas, the flannel chicken, bread and tomatoes—they have much to answer for.

They answered. What surprised us was that a majority of the home economists who responded agreed with the main thrust of our remarks. But let us quote the defenders first. A professor at Queens College wrote: "First, a home economist is not a cook! Home economists come in all types, none of them 'cooks,' few of them are gourmet foods specialists, *nor do they pretend to be* [our emphasis].... I am a home economist, a textiles and clothing specialist, but... I also teach home economics teachers-in-training.... We in the field have, for many years, been fighting the image of 'cooking' and 'sewing.' " The home economist for the Green Giant Company in Minneapolis wrote: "Contrary to Mr. Hess' accusation that we are puppets of our companies' marketing departments, we are proud of the opportunity given us to initiate new product ideas and work with them through package photography and introduction to the consumer." Another professional demanded that we "stop tearing down everything" and asked: "How come in today's issue the news of Sara Lee selling ice cream is tucked way back in the Advertising News? I think that is news that should be put on the food page." And a Brooklyn home economist wrote about her struggle to teach cooking to children on a minuscule budget. "However," she went on, "I'm not complaining. Every once in a while a kid comes back and tells me he 'always makes that Macaroni and Cheese recipe he learned in class.' That makes me feel awfully good."

It should have made her feel awful, period. Those children's mothers, who learned cooking from *their* mothers, were fixing cheap, nourishing, and delicious dishes such as beans and rice, and greens with hog scraps and pot licker, until they were taught by television commercials, home economists, and their own children to be ashamed of real food. A male reader wrote us:

My West Indian mother made the most wonderful pigtails in rice and peas, thick split pea soup with dumplings, plantain and ham hocks; delightful codfish cakes with no potato or flour; delicious souse (pig feet, snout, ears); lamb kidneys, and many, many other things which she did *routinely*. She just did them because that was the way to do it. No intent to be fancy or frilly or other culinary pretensions. Just good food.... As my mother said—"What doesn't kill, will fatten."

The same sensible and sensual approach to food marks the cookery of American black, Puerto Rican, Italian, and Slavic women. But a home economist trained by a textile specialist can teach their children only how to fix a carton of factory macaroni with factory cheese.

As the Queens professor wrote, home economics has for nearly three-quarters of a century been "fighting the image of 'cooking' and 'sewing.' " (We wonder whether her textile graduates defend today's shoddy synthetic clothing, the way so many nutrition graduates defend today's junk foods.) Actually, the fight began even earlier, in the age of Fannie Farmer, when the teaching of household crafts was taken out of the home and into the schools. Quite soon, the subject got the euphemistic title of Domestic Science, which gradually gave way to the even euphonier one of Home Economics and is now being topped by Human Ecology, whatever that is.

It must be said emphatically that this tragicomic history arose from a noble motive. Women did not win the battle for education in order to learn how to become household drudges, nor even to learn how to pour tea, arrange flowers, decorate the home, and manage servants. The first schools for girls were dedicated to just those ends, and women rebels properly resisted them. To meet such resistance, academic bureaucrats first sugared the pill, then changed the content, but never suggested the obvious solution, which is to eliminate home-career or "women's" courses altogether.

What Home Ec means today, God knows. A Baltimore member of the sorority tried to tell us. She quoted the founders of the movement as having defined it in 1902 in this way: "Home economics in its most comprehensive sense is the study of the laws, conditions, principles and ideals which are concerned on the one hand with man's immediate physical environment and on the other hand with his nature as a social being; and is the study specially [sic] of the relation between those two factors."

Our correspondent said: "The definition remains valid

today except for the fact that today there is greater emphasis on interaction rather than relation. Please note that cooking and sewing are not mentioned in the definition. It does not necessarily follow that the best cook on the street is the best mother, marriage partner, career woman and citizen." Okay, but just what does it take to make the best mother-wife-careerist-citizen? ... Perhaps anticipating that we would make neither heads nor tails of the 1902 definition, the Baltimore lady gave us another, from the founder's credo of the American Home Economics Association:

> Home economics stands for the freedom of the home from the dominance of things and their due subordination to ideals and the simplicity in material surroundings which will most free the spirit for the more important and permanent interests of the home and society.

That could be read as a defense of TV dinners. But the only thing that is clear from this gobbledygook is that home economics is not about cooking and sewing. Still, that Queens professor who declared that home economists were not cooks and "few of them are gourmet foods specialists, *nor do they pretend to be*" was evidently out of touch with her graduates. Most of those who find jobs are forced to pretend that they know cooking.

Certainly, many of their employers and most of the public *think* these young women are experts. Not long ago, an executive of a major publication confided to us that she was having trouble finding a suitable food editor. "I'd promote X to the job in a minute," she said, "if she could only write." Now, X was the publication's home economist, who "kitchen-tested" its recipes and wrote about them; she had already earned a fortune as a cookbook author on the strength of that connection. It was rumored that her stuff was ghost written for her, and certainly it was shamelessly lifted from other books. But what the executive did not realize was that X was a bad cook, even after years of on-the-job training, and her work showed it. If she had pretended to be an expert writer, the executive would have nailed her as a fraud, but her incompetence in the kitchen has gone undetected to this day.

Many home economists are, however, quite honest and clear-eyed about the problem. After that column of ours, one telephoned: "I'm a home economist and have always wanted to say such things, but it would be professional suicide." Another wrote: "After graduating from a Canadian university with a degree in home economics, I realized the awful gap in my training. I couldn't cook.... The professors don't know how to cook, so they perpetuate the dreary emphasis on nutrients." And, as we have mentioned earlier, Nikki Goldbeck charmingly recalled that when she was graduated from the School of Home Economics at Cornell, her first job was to devise recipes for unflavored gelatin—a product she had never heard of before! Yet some corporation thought her qualified to invent recipes for its packages and its news releases, which in turn would be published in newspapers and magazines, and finally in cookbooks.

As a food editor, one of the authors was on the receiving end of a flood of those releases. Many arrived all prepared to be set in type electronically, with no editing needed, and we saw several published in major newspapers under the bylines of their food writers. To avoid embarrassment, the companies promise each newspaper exclusivity in its area for its canned recipes.

This public-relations mail frankly assumes that editors are both venal and stupid. On taking office as editor in June, the author received a letter from the Carnation Company that opened, "It was a pleasure to read your May columns. With your help, readers everywhere are learning what nutrition is and how to serve it." Each succeeding monthly letter used a variation of the same theme. In November: "As usual, your October columns were timely and informative. Your readers keep getting the critical information they need to put current see-saw commodity and nutrition information into perspective." That this faith was often earned was suggested by a release from American Business Press, Inc., which said, "Who's making the money when we pay 98¢ for a two-pound bag of onions? Who's getting rich when we pay 69¢ a pound for chicken? The men who should know—the journalists covering the huge U.S. food industry—say no one.... The editors agree there is little the consumer can do about spiraling food costs other than shopping carefully and selectively." With honorable exceptions, the men and women who give consumer advice in newspapers and in government tend to echo this sentiment, and when they depart from it, may run into trouble with their publishers. *The Columbia Journalism Review* and *Media & Consumer*, among others, have amply documented the prostitution of food pages. But they are concerned with the threat to consumers' pocketbooks and health, while we are here concerned with the assault on our palates.

Underpaid and understaffed as well as underqualified, the women who edit our newspaper food sections say they use canned copy because there is no other way to fill the space between those pages and pages of ads. And several home economists properly chided us that, if women are white slaves, they have been forced into it by male panders. One wrote:

> Having been in the food and garbage business for over forty years, I feel compelled to ask you, are you aware as to whether or not the home economist makes the marketing decision on putting such products in the market? During the 26 years I was employed by one of the companies you mentioned this was not the case. The home economist could come up with a superior product only to be told the ingredients were too expensive. Who then decided the quality of the ingredients to be used? In my experience, the product managers, the production people, market researchers, in short, marketing had the last word and men not home economists made those decisions.

The New York chapter of Home Economists in Business (HEIB), which has a remarkably high proportion of anticollaborationists, commented in its newsletter that members were often hired simply to meet consumer complaints. "How many of us," it demanded, "could actually go into the president's or general manager's office and say that our company is making a lousy product?"

The typical career of a Home Economist in Business is seldom rewarding, in any sense of the word. That lady from Green Giant mentioned a common chore: "to initiate new product ideas and work with them through package photography and introduction to the consumer." A television director told about using half a dozen of them to prepare Wuffins for a commercial, Wuffins being muffins made of Wheaties. A photographer described home economists as food cosmeticians, who learn how to use glycerine on canned peaches and frankfurters, and liquid soap on apricots and cheese, and how to handle any of them under hot studio lights.

The big market for home economists is in the public schools. There is hardly a district in the country that does not have a graduate Home Ec to supervise its food programs, yet the junk that is served is a national scandal. Mountains of candy and soft drinks are peddled to pupils; some teachers use sweets as rewards for good behavior. A glance through the slick journal of the American School Food Service Association finds it chock full of ads for thawing equipment, dried eggs, textured protein additives, and canned and frozen foods, such as pizza. A seven-year-old boy we know went to school in New Jersey with a lunch consisting of a hard-cooked egg, an orange, and a banana; his teacher, shocked, sent him across the highway to buy a pizza and a drink. We mentioned this to three young home economists at a nutritional guidance center in East Harlem. All thought the teacher had done the right thing. They had majored in nutrition at three different colleges. None had taken a class in cooking. (One said proudly, "We are trying to make Puerto Ricans

realize that beans and rice can be a meat substitute."
Heaven love her, how could we tell her that Latins had
always known that? The girls were also teaching the
women about casserole dishes, such as "how to feed six
people with one can of salmon and leftover bread."
Heaven help us.)

Here and there, mothers who know real food have
led revolts. In Bloomington, Indiana, Mrs. Jean Farmer
learned that her child's school, with 530 pupils, sold them
500 soft drinks and 300 candy bars each day. After a
two-and-one-half-year fight, the vending machines were
thrown out. In Swarthmore, Pennsylvania, Mrs. Bernice
Sisson was shocked at the way cooking was being taught,
so she undertook a survey of schools in eastern Pennsylvania. She found one evidently well-planned program
in Chester, where a real cook seemed to have sneaked
in, but most other districts were assigning pupils such
horrors as Hot Dogs in the Blanket ("Follow instructions
on can"), Tuna Shortcake ("one can cream of celery or
cream of mushroom soup . . ."), and Choco-Scotch Clusters
(Rice Crispies, chocolate bits, peanut butter). Eastern
Pennsylvania is not at all unusual. A reader in Topsham,
Maine, said the girls there were required to make
Pillsbury-mix doughnuts and milk shakes, while an
Arizona district put on the dog in a syllabus in French,
with translations: "Pot au feu (pot on the fire; vegetable
soup)" . . . "Chauflour [sic] au gratin (cauliflower and
cheese casserole)" and "Blanquette de veau aux cham-
pignons (veal pastry shells served with mushrooms)."

Mrs. Sisson got the notion that cooking was not being
taught in the Home Ec schools. She checked out the
nearby Drexel Institute of Technology, and confirmed
her fears. So she prepared an outline for a model class
in cooking for children and sent it to Drexel. Then she
telephoned a professor there. She wrote us about the
conversation:

> Her tone of voice made it clear that I had a lot of
> nerve to have gone into the schools at all and then

write about it.... I said that I wrote the paper because I was unable to find anything in the literature
about curriculum planning or any organized approach
to the teaching of cooking. "Well, that's the way
it is."

"Besides, dear, the new approach to food is through
understanding the chemistry. Drexel students can't
begin to deal with food until they have a solid back-
ground in chemistry. As you beat air into an egg
white the molecular structure of the protein
changes...and that's what the Drexel student un-
derstands." "But can she make a soufflé?" I asked
innocently.*

She continued by saying that cooking is a science
and that the very word "cooking" is demeaning and
should be changed. I said that while there was science
in cooking, there also was art, and that there should
be pleasure associated with both cooking and eating.
She said that the food companies provided plenty of
pleasure, and she didn't want to fight the food companies, but join them.

I said I perceived a conflict of interest there—by
turning out both the home economists who go to
work for food companies and inadequate cooking
teachers, she was in a way insuring a pool of customers for the food companies. She indicated that
my comment was a little deep, so I illustrated...
[with] a package of French Toast Mix, saying that
since I couldn't see any time saving in using it, I
believed that the only people who would buy it
were people who didn't know how to make French
toast. She said that if a product didn't sell, it would
be taken off the market. (I felt that her remark
rather proved my point, but was too exhausted to
say so.)

Mrs. Sisson's experience could have been repeated at
any school of home economics, even if it is called Human
Ecology as at Michigan State and Cornell or Human

---

* We would have asked if she could make an omelet or scram-
ble an egg, but the point is still valid.

Development as at Penn State, where a dean boasted, "The pots and pans courses have gone into the College of Education." The Times quoted a student at Cornell as saying, "It wasn't until after I arrived that I found out it was a home economics school, and I was shocked." But if it was cooking she feared, she had no reason to be shocked; there have been no stoves in the School of Human Ecology at Cornell since the cafeteria was replaced by vending machines. A sociologist on the faculty mourned, "With all this, you can't get a good meal on the campus." "All this" referred mainly to the great agricultural-research complex at Cornell where, another teacher observed, "They developed the standard cauliflower not to stink up the house. Trouble is, it doesn't taste like cauliflower." But the first prof was also referring to the Cornell School of Hotel Administration, which is worth a digression here.

Chiseled on the entry is the school motto: LIFE IS SERVICE—HE WHO SERVES BEST, PROFITS MOST. A student explained to us: "This school trains food managers, not cooks. They're just interested in making money." Professor Vance A. Christian told a Times reporter: "This little school has changed the hospitality industry throughout the world. I don't know if it's for better or for worse as far as the guest is concerned. We took them out of the art era and put hotels into the business era." No doubts were expressed by Graham Kerr, a television performer who calls himself the Galloping Gourmet, presumably to suggest that any viewer can be an instant chef, and who occasionally lectures at the school. He said of the hotel trade, "It's a super, warm human business to be in and everybody will come to you with a fistful of dollars." But Dean Robert A. Beck worried aloud, "Sometimes it seems that the hospitality's gone out of the hospitality field."

We enjoyed the hospitality of the school's Statler Inn for a couple of days, and found it a well-run, clean, and comfortable facsimile of all the Statlers, Hiltons, and Holiday Inns run by its benefactors. The food was student

Howard Johnson's, the coffee if anything worse. The catalogue offers a major in Food and Beverage Management, but cooking even there is only elective, under the headings of Specialty Food Preparation and Survey of Convenience Food. The authorities declined to let us borrow the cooking textbook, but a student later told *The Times*: "From the practical point of view, I didn't acquire too much. The first recipe I saw at Cornell was for onion soup, which had been a specialty at the hotel I came from. The instructions here said, 'Step one—open the can. Step two—heat it up.'" Professor Christian commented: "We have to deal with reality. If we're to be professional leaders, we can't be philosophers or historians."

The philosophers and historians are presumably a can-opener's throw away, at the College of Human Ecology. It does offer a major in Nutrition, with such courses as Physichemical Aspects of Food, Experimental Food Methods, Volume Food Production Practices, and Carbohydrate Chemistry. So we learn that while a home economist (or human ecologist) is not a cook, she may very well be a nutritionist. Now, then, let's look at nutrition.

16

The Nonfoodists

The word *nutrition* often is used synonymously with the word *food* which by definition also must consider color, flavor, and texture. It is wiser to consider nutrients as the chemicals in food that feed our biochemistry and/or alter our physiology in such a manner as to affect the bioavailability of nutrients.

Dr. Paul A. Lachance, professor of
nutrition at Rutgers University

OKAY, so a home economist is not a cook but may be a nutritionist. And nutrition is not about the color, flavor, and texture of food, but about whether it is good for you. Yet by their own standards and by their own admission, nutritionists have failed to improve the American diet. In fact, as all of them acknowledge, the nutritional quality of our diet has been declining for a generation—although most of the world's nutritionists are to be found right here. It is our contention that they have failed because, among other reasons, they do not believe in taste.

Professor Lachance of Rutgers, a panjandrum of the profession, has discussed the issue in a series of articles entitled "Nutrition for Food Executives." He does not conceal his contempt for the palate as a nutritional guide, explaining that man is a creature of habit and not instinct:

> He has no inborn physiological or instinctive urges to keep him on the safe side of malnutrition. He has food tastes, but food tastes alone cannot be relied upon as a sound guide to nutrition, especially in a technically sophisticated community such as ours, in which fallacious ideas, prejudices and superstitions about food abound.
>
> The traditional answer to this problem has been nutrition education, with particular emphasis over the past 20 years or more on teaching school children the concepts of a balanced diet.
>
> In my opinion, this type of nutrition education has failed.... Food sales—and therefore food marketing and food production—have been geared to satisfy the customer's social being, particularly his food habits.... But it is evident that when combined with convenience, potential effect on well-being, and product qualities approximating those of a previously acceptable product—for example, low calorie beverages taste almost as good as regular soft drinks—such food products can and will have a market....
>
> Food processing practices that emphasize nutrition will decrease the public's aesthetic concern for the source of such nutrients. Let's face it: an amino acid is an amino acid whether it is synthesized chemically or microbiologically or is contained in a vegetable protein or a fish protein....
>
> Meanwhile, what is the industry doing? The momentum is encouraging! The industry has readied nutrified donuts, pastries and flavored beverages for breakfast and nutrified puddings, cakes, brownies, ice cream sandwiches and chocolate bars for the snack and lunch market. These coupled with prefrozen preplated dinners nutrified to assure one-third of the RDA nutrients for the one remaining meal at home —dinner, with fruit and vegetables—mean there is a real chance that a balanced diet may for the first

time in the history of man become a reality rather than a mere goal.*

This may be wisdom for food executives. It is pernicious folly for people. Even animals tend to know what is good for them, which is why a cow will lick salt and a cat will eat grass. As for humans, if they had lost this instinct, they would be extinct. The ancients understood the principles of nutrition; left to their own empirical ways, people sought a nice balance of grains, fruits, greens, gourds, beans, and meat or seafood, and this balance characterizes the diets of most civilized societies, whether Greek, Chinese, Italian, or what have you. The affluent, to be sure, had a tendency to overeat, and the poor, to be sure, seldom got the food they wanted and needed. But only in our modern society do affluent and poor alike suffer an unbalanced diet.

Real nuttiness about nutrition appears to have grown with the industrialization of our food supply. We have mentioned how the removal of the wheat germ from flour, beginning in the 1840s, promoted the sugar sickness that afflicts us today; the resultant obesity and sense of dissatisfaction may also have inspired a neurosis about nutrition. As early as 1896, Fannie Farmer, the maiden aunt of home economics, published a table in her *Boston Cook Book* listing the precise amounts of protein, fat, and minerals in each of thirty varieties of fish. One can envisage a young lady on Beacon Hill totting up the comparative values of mackerel and cod while her Yankee cook waits with pursed lips. . . .

Today, the charts are far more complicated and even sillier, driving conscientious housewives to distraction. What nutritionists know but ignore, with their growingly complex Recommended Dietary Allowances, the folk wisdom knows very well: "Jack Sprat could eat no fat, his wife could eat no lean." No two people have the same metabolism, or the same needs. Without benefit of charts,

* In *food product development*, December–January 1973.

some people at any table will salt their food more than others. It is possible that their palates know what they need—or at least that they need *something*, which unfortunately today leads many people to eat too much of what they don't need in an effort to get what they do need.

It is curious to consider that, according to the current expertise, Miss Farmer was poisoning her readers, with her sugar and eggs and salt pork and what-all. But ignorance has never dampened the enthusiasm of nutritionists, nor their contempt for folk wisdom. Dark-skinned people around the world have known for millennia that they could not safely drink unfermented cow's milk. Until recently, nutritionists didn't know it, and wouldn't believe it. We have seen a study of dietary habits among the Southern poor, by two well-meaning Yankee ladies.* Repeatedly, blacks told them, "Sweet milk don't set so well on my stomach," while buttermilk was all right. It never occurred to them that the repugnance was physical; they put it down as a cultural aberration, with undertones of sexual taboo. Dr. Lachance might have added it to his "fallacious ideas, prejudices and superstitions." This obtuseness caused thousands of illnesses and many deaths among African children on whom our aid missions inflicted milk, until the recent "discovery" that it wasn't good for them. (A discovery, like that of the sources of the Nile, often occurs when accredited scientists confirm what "inferior" people have known for centuries.)

The appalling slump in the American diet, and the failure of the food scientists to combat it—nay, their collaboration with it—emerged from a symposium held in 1972 by the American Medical Association, in cooperation with the Department of Agriculture. Virtually all of the papers† warned that "too little is known" and

---

* *'Twixt the Cup and the Lip*, by Margaret Cussler and Mary L. De Give (Twayne, 1952).

† Published in *Nutritional Qualities of Fresh Fruit and Vegetables* (Futura, 1974).

"more research is needed," but they said enough. They noted:

—The only broad comparable studies of the American diet, done by the USDA, found that 40 percent of families were deficient in one or more major nutrients in 1955, and this had risen to 50 percent by 1965. Consumption of fruit and vegetables declined 9 percent and dairy products 8 percent, while meat-poultry-fish rose 11 percent and soft drinks 79 percent. Predictably, the city poor ate the poorest. Less predictably, women ate worse than men.

—The average American ate 414 pounds of *fresh* fruit and vegetables a year in 1925–1929; by 1971, this was down to 239 pounds. Meanwhile, consumption of *processed* fruit and vegetables rose from 84 to 293 pounds. Eating of fresh potatoes fell from 168 to 82 pounds, while sweet potatoes, formerly a major source of our Vitamin A, had then virtually disappeared from the American diet.

—Processing destroys nutrients. Freezing, for example, kills Vitamin A. Early picking, mishandling, and packaging all reduce food values and some introduce poisons. (Sulfur dioxide, widely used in drying and packaging, has been found toxic to rats.) Even for canning, food is picked "firm ripe—i.e., not quite ripe enough for table use."

It is part of the survival scheme of nature, we have said, that fruits enrich themselves in flavor and nutrients as they finish ripening, so that birds and mammals, including man, eat them and propagate the seed. Drs. Tung-Ching Lee and C. O. Chichester put it this way: "Early man recognized that his survival depended on proper food choices based on appearance, odor, texture and taste. Although an attractive food is not necessarily a nutritious food, the harvest time of fruits and vegetables does relate to organoleptic [taste] qualities." They went on to observe that modern research and practice are directed instead toward a premature picking.

Although none of the symposium papers said so directly,

a major cause for the decline in consumption of fresh produce is that it has declined in quality and taste as its cost has risen. For one thing, our soil has been losing good trace minerals and gaining bad ones, such as lead, in dangerous amounts. We don't know much about these trace elements (which is one reason why the claim that enriched junk is as good as a balanced diet is reckless pseudoscience), but we have learned a scary amount. Dr. Richard Doisy, a biochemist at New York's Upstate Medical Center, has commented on the growing evidence of chrome and zinc deficiencies in the population. The former is linked to diabetes, the latter to glandular deformity, dwarfism, and loss of taste. A Denver study found that nearly half of children of all income groups were getting less zinc than they needed. The reasons given are depletion of the soil and the effect of food processing; in sugar refining, for example, 90 percent of the chrome is removed. And these are only two of fourteen trace elements that scientists know are needed by man, with twenty more under study.

Dr. Frank S. Viets, Jr., of Fort Collins, Colorado, a retired USDA researcher, pioneered in the study of zinc deficiency in the soil, which has caused serious losses to farmers. When we asked him whether this also helped account for the blandness of our produce, he replied, "I don't doubt that there's been a decline in flavor, but I think it's the varieties of plants, mostly. Certainly, as we put more and more nitrogen on grapes, they don't produce as much acid and sugar. The same is true of sugar beets. We do things, and don't know the consequences."

At the A.M.A. symposium, wide variations were reported in nutrients of a given crop, depending on where it was grown: California Valencia oranges have three times as much Vitamin A as Florida Valencias (and taste three times better, too). Little is known about the nutritive value of new varieties bred for commercial farming, but the tasteless iceberg lettuce has only *one-seventh* as much Vitamin A as the old-fashioned loosehead lettuce it has supplanted. Iceberg from some areas of California was also found to have a worrisome concentration of cadmium. Some new sweet corn has a "low-digestible" starch. A potato introduced for its "superior processing qualities" turned out to have "an unusually high content of glycoalkaloids," which would seem to be as harmful as they sound. "More research is needed."

Perhaps the most discouraging paper for the food lover was read by Dr. Dale S. Anderson of the USDA station at Beltsville, Maryland. It recounts what happens to produce from the moment of its harvesting by machine (" 'Hand-picked' products are rare today") to its arrival on our tables. It starts immediately to deteriorate; unchilled beans lose 60 percent of their Vitamin C *overnight*. Shredding and packaging cause damage too. The hauls to market get longer and longer, and refrigeration of freight cars and jumbo trailers is faulty, with "cold spots" and "hot spots" and poor ventilation. Terminal markets are a mess, conditions of delivery are worse, and handling at retail stores "leaves much to be desired." Dr. Anderson concludes, "When the produce reaches its final destination —the home of the consumer—it may have little freshness left, even though it appeared acceptable when it was purchased." More abuse awaits in the kitchen (Dr. Anderson's own refrigerator showed quick swings from 40° to 70°) and poor cooking finishes off much of what nutrition and taste are left.

(The microwave oven, incidentally, is exposed as being just as deadly to vitamins as is boiling vegetables atop the stove. Despite its endorsement with only minor reservations by an imposing roster of gourmet "chefs," its usefulness is limited to reheating foods, and even that is offset by the radiation danger. No serious cook would bother with one. If you've already been conned into buying one, you might consider also buying a pocket Geiger counter that has been put on the market just for testing the safety of microwave ovens.)

Dr. Anderson's paper goes far to explain the decline

in consumption of fresh produce. It also jibes with what a woman from upstate New York wrote us: "It is ironic that here in Warwick we are next door to the fabulous black dirt produce, yet a majority of us eat onions from California, hard green rock tomatoes from Florida, etc., purchased from Grand Union, while the local fresh stuff is shipped to Boston and Chicago. It is a perfectly ridiculous distribution system." A spokesman for Grand Union told *The Times* that it did not buy tomatoes from local growers because "they can't supply us with enough, and because the local tomatoes are too tender to be sent to a distribution center and then out to the branch stores." Taste makes waste.

"Until we change our marketing system, nutritional quality will remain the hope of idealists," Professor W. H. Gabelman of the University of Wisconsin told the symposium. He did not, however, propose such a change. Wistfully, he appealed for nutritionists and plant breeders to work together to beef up the product. But Dr. Edwin A. Crosby, the agricultural director of the National Canners Association, summed up the prevailing view with brutal directness:

> If we move to nutritional labeling, we may well have a large number of consumers awakened to the realization that vegetables are *not* generally good sources of nutrients from an economic viewpoint, and if consumers are truly concerned about insuring that their families receive enough vitamins and minerals, the easy, economical route to insure this end is to purchase them in pill form. . . . If tomorrow's housewife becomes a nutritional bug with a calculator in her pocket when she goes to the supermarket and thinks only in terms of nutrition, she will avoid the purchase of fruits and vegetables. . . .
> It is evident that through genetic engineering, improved cultural techniques and careful attention to storage and marketing practices, the nutritional qualities of fruits and vegetables can be improved. The real question, however, is whether improved nutri-

tional value from fresh fruits and vegetables is truly important to the public welfare. Should this area of research be given priority or should we look to vitamin pills or fortified processed products as [*sic*] may be desirable to improve nutrition?

The canners, to be sure, have reason to be concerned about any effort to improve the fresh product or to inform the public about what is in theirs. A nutritionist at the Rockefeller Institute, evidently a cat-lover, complained to us that the thiamin (Vitamin B¹) in commercial pet food was destroyed by canning, and said Tabby is better off eating table scraps. But, with honorable exceptions, academic leaders of nutrition have taken the same line as Dr. Crosby. One of them, Dr. George M. Briggs of the University of California at Berkeley, told *The Times* that there was no significant difference between eggs laid by barnyard fowl and those laid by battery hens—only a difference in color and taste, and in minerals and vitamins "worth at most half a cent a dozen—more or less." Elizabeth M. Whelan and Dr. Frederick J. Stare, perhaps the most widely read of the academic nutritionists, go further: they say that additives make food taste better, that natural foods may be loaded with natural poisons, and that our food chemicals are "both safe and functional."

In one survey, a *Times* reporter found a consensus in the profession. She told housewives: "While the price varies a good deal, nutritionists agree that there is not enough difference among the various kinds of orange juice to matter. Even the fresh-squeezed is not appreciably richer than frozen, chilled or canned when it comes to nutrients, and some authorities think that, when there is a difference, it is in favor of the frozen. What's more, man-made products don't show up badly either."

Better than fresh, as the commercial goes. What authority these authorities have for making such statements is not specified. Nearly all research papers on nutrition, as we have said, warn how little is known, especially about trace elements and the more obscure, or even not yet discovered, vitamins and other organic compounds. But no profession (and that goes for journalism as well) likes to admit to the public the limits of its expertise. The article does quote Dr. Lachance as acknowledging that "if you get the oranges right off the tree, you might get a little more nutrient value," and it grants that synthetic orange juice is "likely to contain more sugar and to have fewer minerals." But it adds that "anyone can learn what is going into the man-made . . . by reading the label."

Not true. Exempted from labeling requirements are many common additives, including artificial colors and flavors used in nearly all processed foods. As for those that are listed, the ordinary housewife is hardly qualified to judge their safety or even their usefulness; the iron that enriches bread, for example, may be in an indigestible form, even if it meets the Recommended Dietary Allowance.

(The orange-juice article does raise the question why anybody would buy the synthetic product. The answer given is that originally it was cheaper than real juice, and then people got so used to the taste that they came to prefer it, even after prices were equalized. It took a long time, and a lot of propaganda, to bring us to this.)

Like Dr. Crosby of the canning industry, Professor Lachance of Rutgers has complained that nutritional educators are only confusing the consumer:

> One can take any one of several college level textbooks in nutrition to learn that the good sources of protein, several vitamins, and minerals are organ meats (e.g. liver), egg, milk, cheese, etc., only to advise in a separate chapter or article that to avoid heart disease one must limit the intake of—you guessed it—organ meats, milk, eggs, certain cheeses, etc.* To make matters worse, the same nutritionists

---

* Successive bulletins by the USDA home economists give precisely these conflicting counsels. See next chapter.

have on occasion written a separate article about all the junk or empty calorie foods that Americans are eating. I ask—just what choice did we leave them?

The professor went on to say, as previously quoted, that the industry with its fortified munchies was putting the teachers to shame. That was in April 1973, before a meeting of cereal chemists. Fashions change, and so do audiences. Addressing a seminar on nutrition at the end of the year, Dr. Lachance was less enthusiastic. "Currently," he said, "the food industry is catering to the American way of life but not to the 'betterment' of the consumer." But he followed this remarkable understatement with a rhetorical question: "Can the situation be improved without necessitating radical changes in food habits?" The answer is of course no, and since radical change is ruled out by definition, his solution is still fortified junk.

The defensive tone now taken by Dr. Lachance may have been the effect of reactions to his research program. Following a suggestion by one of his associates to a reporter that spinach might be made to taste like potato chips, one food lover wrote him (with copy to the authors):

Who said kids won't eat spinach? My 13-year-old son and his friends all like it. Not the overcooked or canned variety at the school cafeteria but when it is raw, or poached and chilled and served with garlic, olive oil and vinegar, or when it is poached a few minutes with braised meat. It is people like you who deal with test tubes or experiment with rats that have loused up the taste of good old yellow sticky potatoes and converted it to a starchy mess, loused up chickens, tomatoes and nearly everything else in this country.

I think the best way to make people eat better is to restore the natural flavor of foods, instead of screwing up what took generations of experimentation to discover. . . . And if there are those who don't like the natural taste of food, then they can eat shit.

We must hope that nutritionists mean well, but a more sleazy motive was suggested by an editor for a publishing house who wrote us: "For the past year or so I have been involved in editing a college textbook on nutrition; I have tried to persuade our author to modify some of her endorsements of overrefined and processed foods, but it is possible that she has received grants for her own education or research from one or more of the big food processors."

Now, if the nutritionists have failed to put us on a nutritionally balanced diet, they have certainly succeeded in putting a lot of us on a mentally unbalanced one. Here we use the word nutritionist as meaning any health expert, since all health experts are by definition nutritionists, and, for that matter, vice versa. A young Manhattan professional confided to us that her nutritionist, who was formerly her chiropodist, had put her on a tough diet. "It's so boring!" she said. "You feel great, but you must find other goals than eating." We were glad that she felt great, but worried that it might last only as long as the fashion that inspired it. Presumably, her nutritionist had made her feel great when he was a chiropodist, and *that* evidently did not solve her problems for long.

We have made a fair amount of progress, it would seem, in overcoming the Puritan notion that pleasure in sex is sinful. But this woman's willingness to put up with a boring diet reflects the fact that many people still believe that pleasure in eating is wrong. We have mentioned the housewife who wailed, "Why must food taste good?" She is not alone. Dr. Alex Comfort, who made a fortune selling people on *The Joy of Sex*, does not mind earning a dollar by warning people against other carnal joys. In an article denouncing the eating of meat, he wrote: "About 50 percent of adult male deaths in the United States are probably precipitated in whole or in part by animal fats, a fatal number second only to those precipitated by cigarette smoking."

Well, let's see now: 50 percent die from eating fats, and let's say 50 percent plus X die from smoking, so that leaves... Ah, the hell with it. Not being scientists, we should leave the diet-health issue to physicians like Dr. Comfort. But we cannot avoid the paranoia they have spread and its devastating effect on our food.

We wrote a column once that opened: "Among the foods we are being warned against these days are sugar, salt, solid fats, proteins and carbohydrates. The heart people are down on yolks, and the cancer people are worried about egg whites. Now the latest under indictment are peanut oil and coffee." We went on to quote Drs. William B. Kannel and Thomas R. Dawber in *The New England Journal of Medicine*, challenging a recent study blaming coffee for heart attacks:

> We are faced with a formidable enough task in having to engineer physical activity back into daily living, change cigarette-smoking and modify the national diet. We should not complicate the problem further by advocating premature restrictions of other pleasurable habits unless there is equally good evidence that such a change is warranted.

One result of this column was a number of letters from worried readers asking what was wrong with egg whites and peanuts. They were only too ready to strike two more foods from their diets—doubtless already so stricken they could hardly suffer more. In fact, if they stopped eating Egg Beaters, their lives would be a little less bleak.

Ironically, it's just possible that they might live longer, too. M. K. Navidi and F. A. Kummerow of the University of Illinois fed Egg Beaters to part of a litter of newborn rats, and whole eggs or ordinary laboratory feed to the rest. At the age of three weeks, they said, the Egg Beater rats weighed less than half as much as the others, and in the fourth week, all of the Egg Beater group died. However, *Consumer Reports* called Egg Beaters "a passable substitute" though neither as nutritious nor as tasty as real eggs. The substitute cost 20 to 50 percent more. Its ingredients, if you are interested, read like the poet Howard Nemerov's "Eggs Maledict": egg white, corn oil, nonfat dry milk, vegetable lecithin, glycerides, propylene glycol monostearate, cellulose and xanthan gums, trisodium and triethyl citrate, artificial flavor, aluminum sulfate, iron phosphate, artificial color, vitamins.

Supporting the paranoia that causes millions of Americans to swallow such a mess is the curious structure of our medical research. It is dominated by foundations whose primary purpose is, like that of any bureaucracy, to perpetuate themselves. At a considerable cost in overhead and tax-exempt fund raising, the system has produced some tremendous achievements, such as the virtual elimination of polio, but it has some unattractive aspects, as when the March of Dimes, having lost its *raison d'être*, switched from polio to arthritis. The foundation that owned that ailment loudly asserted its claim, and the March veered. Now it shakes its cans for birth defects.

One of the hottest properties in the trade is the war on cholesterol. It has made fortunes for the manufacturers of Egg Beaters, margarine, and vegetable oils, and saved the fish industry in the nick of time from the mercury scare. It has also made the fortune of the American Heart Association, which holds the unwritten patent and defends its turf vigorously.

Naturally, there are carpers and naysayers. Professor Kurt A. Oster, a prominent cardiologist, accuses the association of "false premises, poor observation and insufficient experimentation." He cites the notoriously low rate of heart trouble among the Masai, who live on milk, fatty beef, and blood. The association says that's because the Masai walk twenty-six miles a day. Dr. Oster asks why, then, do the lumberjacks of eastern Finland, who work at least as hard as the Masai, have the world's highest rate of heart attacks? (We Americans are only second.) Dr. Oster went to the Masai and learned that they drink only *soured* milk. He developed a theory that the homogenization of milk permits a harmful enzyme called xanthine oxidase to pass through intestinal walls, whereas in ordinary milk it is normally evacuated, and suggested that this might be the cause of high rates of heart attack in the United States. Dr. Oster recommended that we boil or curdle our milk.

Why not return to nonhomogenized milk? Because the industry would not care to reveal to consumers how little cream was left in it. When the government last lowered the required butterfat content, in 1975, it said consumers would not be hurt. But one New York dairy official—who asked not to be identified—told *The Times*: "Taste and food values will be lowered, except for weight watchers. What this means is that even more consumers will be driven away from milk, and dairy farmers will lose out eventually. Nobody gains and the consumer will lose."

Dr. Michael De Bakey, the heart surgeon, reported in *The Journal of the American Medical Association* (August 1, 1974) that a study of 1700 patients had "revealed no definite correlation between serum cholesterol levels and the nature and extent of atherosclerotic disease." And Dr. Roger Williams, the nutritionist credited with the discovery of Vitamin B, said, "Anyone who deliberately avoids cholesterol in his diet may be inadvertently courting heart disease." He urged that people instead "concentrate on the quality of foods" and eat milk, eggs, fish, and vegetables. Bless him.

As lay people, we must leave the merits of the debate to the experts, but each of us is forced to make a decision several times a day, as between butter and margarine, for example. So we must among other things consider the prejudices of the protagonists. It was amusing to watch the medical chiefs of the heart association squirm when asked about the cancer scares concerning egg whites and peanuts, and the allegation that refined sugar, and not fat, is the major dietary cause of heart disease. Egg whites and sugar are, of course, among the few foods that the heart association has left us, and peanut oil is one of its dietary mainstays. Take them away, and we'd starve to death. Well, the association brushes aside the cancer issue as not in its jurisdiction, and says the damage of sugar is not proved. Although all physicians agree that obesity is certainly a major cause of heart failure, many followers of the association actually prescribe a daily dose of polyunsaturated fats, taken straight. (They exclude olive oil, the most delicious of the common vegetable oils, as being merely neutral. Ironically, the polyunsaturated oils turn saturated at prolonged high temperature, as in normal kitchen use.) And their recommended diet is loaded with sugar, as shown by *The American Heart Association Cookbook*, a money-making promotion confected by two nutritionists. Please do look up our review in the Appendix; the book is a caricature of American home-economics cookery in general and diet cuisine in particular. We promise you'll enjoy reading about the pretzel dip of Mock Sour Cream, the canned peach-ginger ale-lemon Jell-O aspic, and the Spinach-Avocado-Orange Toss.

Under the slogan "Be a gourmet low-fat diet chef!" the National Foundation for Ileitis and Colitis (which we suppose is actually *against* ileitis and colitis) is teaching how to cook with medium-chain triglycerides. So what we have said about cholesterol can be applied to many of our diet hangups. Individuals *do* have problems that call for diets prescribed by physicians, but there is no reason why these should be inflicted on the rest of us, nor why the dieter should be led to suffer needlessly. Most Americans doubtless are overweight, but that is no excuse for the dreadful low-calorie guck peddled by Weight Watchers,* nor does it justify the University of Chicago's nutritionists commending the use of synthetic sweeteners "if you want to avoid sugar." If you want to

---

* Among the unspeakable Weight Watcher recipes we have come across are *coq au vin* made with sickly sweet synthetic grape soda and *Filet Fontaine* made with sickly sweet synthetic lemon soda. They even add sweetener to sauerkraut.

avoid sugar, avoid the bloody thing, and make industry restore the range of natural flavors it has taken out of our foods.

For the dieter, there are solutions. For example, many people may have to cut down on sodium intake, but that does not justify Morton's Lite Salt. This is one of a whole range of products aimed to tap the diet market—at a premium, of course. A reader asked us why a "diet" pack of tuna cost more than the regular pack, although the listed contents were the same. Others wonder why unsliced bread of a premium brand cost more than the sliced loaf, and why a given item costs more in the gourmet department of a supermarket than the same item in another aisle. The answer is that if you insist on being different, you should pay for it. But it does seem especially unfair to clip people because they have diet problems.

Selling Lite Salt to the hypertense is something like selling lite beer and lite whiskey to alcoholics. The product is half salt and half potassium chloride, calcium polysilicate, magnesium carbonate, and dextrose (sugar). It tastes faintly bitter and medicinal, which may be a selling point. For the patient ordered to shun sodium, why not use just half as much real salt? And why not (if the doctor approves) use pepper, other spices, herbs, or a squirt of lemon or lime juice, to replace or assist the role of salt in heightening the flavor of food? Also, one should use real salt, saltier in taste than our table variety, which is doctored to run free. *Ye are the salt of the erthe, but and if the salt be once unsavery, what can be salted ther with?** Serious cooks use French sea salt if available.

* Mathew V 13, in the Tyndale version. Note how clearer this is than the King James version: *Ye are the salt of the earth; but if the salt have lost its savor, wherewith shall it be salted?* It is often said that the King James version is the only committee project that ever sang, but it leans heavily on Tyndale, and where it departs it is not necessarily better. Anyway, until recent times, everybody has known that some kinds of salt are tastier than others. Now, we have hardly any choice.

In this chapter, we have been harsh about the nutritional profession, and neglected the minority of its members who have bucked the tide. So let us end with a jingle sent us by Dr. Edward Pinckney, a food-loving physician and writer. It was composed back in 1956 by the prophetic biochemist Dr. David Kritchevsky of the Winstar Institute:

> Cholesterol is poisonous
> So never, never eat it.
> Sugar, too, may murder you,
> There is no way to beat it.
> And fatty food may do you in,
> Be certain to avoid it.
> Some food was rich in vitamin,
> But processing destroyed it.
> So let your life be ordered
> By each "documented" fact,
> And die of malnutrition,
> But with arteries intact.

17

Manicured Chickens

With exceptions ... that are both few and
extreme enough to be called outrageous, no
information has come my way during many
years of searching for it to suggest that our
normal microbes do our neighbors or our
intimate companions any harm at all.

Dr. Theodor Rosebury, in Life on Man

A DEPARTMENT store in New Jersey was offering a
demonstration of how to make chocolate mousse. When
the cook licked some mousse from her finger, everybody
laughed approvingly except one woman, a home economist, who complained to the manager. ... Another home
economist, in Long Island, told a friend that it was
dangerous to handle raw pork, that she hadn't used butter
in five years, and that she wouldn't think of cooking a fish
with its head on. ... A Cornell graduate who is a health
official in Lexington, Kentucky, ordered a restaurateur
to switch from real cream to synthetic coffee whitener,
because germs wouldn't grow in synthetic. ...

Now, we have established that home economists are
not cooks, and that as nutritionists they are confused
about a lot of things. But on one thing they are perfectly
clear: germs are bad.

We should revise that to read: *people's* germs are bad. When germs (or dangerous chemicals) are added by *industry*, many authorities hold that this is a "socially acceptable risk." Thus, on the one hand, a report published by the National Academy of Sciences and the National Research Council warns that "radical departures from the time-honored practices in production, processing, preservation, distribution and serving of foods have raised new questions concerning microbiological contamination of products now reaching large segments of the public." But on the other hand, Secretary of Agriculture Earl L. Butz told the food industry in a speech: "We must...as never before...assume responsibility for public education on the fact that we have a safe industry. [We must] be very careful that we don't add to the cost of food by completely outmoded regulations, by unreasonable exercise of police power."

So it is no surprise that the department's home economists are as enthusiastic about the blessings of food processing as they are panicky about the germs on a housewife's hands. These twin preoccupations guide their weekly *Food and Home Notes*, which are sent to editors around the country as fillers for food pages.

In recent years (we digress again), the department has been busy indeed in defending farm chemicals, additives, convenience foods, and food prices. Some of the copy verges on the vapid: Why did food prices go up in 1974–1975 while farm prices went down? " 'This is unfortunate,' says Secretary Butz, 'but it is fairly typical. When farm prices go up, they usually come down later. When other prices go up, they usually stay up.' " A *Food and Home* note during a cherry glut: "People who like to munch on fresh sweet cherries may not know it, but they're following a very old human inclination." Advice by Nancy Harvey Steorts, Special Assistant for Consumer Affairs: "The key to wider acceptance of prepackaging by consumers is to offer a wide range of choice in packaging." That's just what we need, more garbage.

When the USDA copy is not tautological, it may be specious. Butz and his minions repeat incessantly that Americans spend only 16 percent of their incomes on food, but *Food and Home Notes'* model budget menus for low, low-middle, and moderate incomes add up to from 30 to 50 percent of average earnings in each bracket (the poor, of course, spending the highest proportion of income on food). The same publication assured the public that, more often than not, convenience foods were cheaper than foods prepared from scratch. Marian Burros, food editor of *The Washington Post*, found that the department was comparing names, not nutrition. As reported by *Media and Consumer*, she measured the ingredients and got a different picture. Homemade beef stew, for example, had much more beef, carrots, and potatoes per serving than the canned, which made up the difference with fat, broth, starch, sugar, tomato paste, coloring, and flavoring. The real thing had peas, onions, butter, and good taste, none of which could be found in the canned. There was one-tenth of an ounce of chicken in a serving of canned chicken chow mein. Etc....

The department offers local clubs a set of color slides on "how chemicals make today's foods nutritious." Issues of *Food and Home Notes* in 1974–1975 also hailed its progress in such heady areas of research as obtaining human food from alfalfa juice; one suggested use is in whipped topping for desserts. It trumpeted gains in "extending" beef with fatty tissue, blood, soy flour, cottonseed flour, fishmeal, whey, and cowhide collagen—the last traditionally used in glue. Of this triumph, it says, "If some of the other protein products affect the texture of meat when blended in sizable quantities, a little added collagen can be expected to restore the natural texture." Extenders are used for fish, too, including varieties not popular with Americans. One subsidized researcher explained: "Comminuting machines produce a minced flesh which can be reconstituted in many forms, with flavors added and texture altered by such binders as carrageenans, alginates, succinylated proteins and vegetable gums." (We don't know what a comminuting machine is, but we're against it.)

The department boasted also of its research into the best proportions for feeding manure back into chickens (up to 12.5 percent of total feed) and cattle (up to 30 percent) and of its development of dehydrated orange-juice crystals, sugar-free and presumably flavor-free; of a speeded-up technique for making cheddar cheese, and of a way to make factory-frozen French fries by *boiling and mashing* potatoes and molding them into shape, as is now widely done for potato chips and cheap cigars. No waste, and no taste.

The department does extend its filler copy with handy hints for homemakers, but its home economists reflect the state of the art in the schools that produced them. Hints:

"Thickening custards or puddings? Two egg yolks or two egg whites have the same thickening power as one whole egg." (And a pound of beans weighs as much as a pound of rice. Don't they notice the difference in texture, taste, and behavior in cooking?)

"Lasagna freezes well." (Maybe *their* lasagna, made with collagen and silo juice.)

"Watching calories? Use low-fat white sauce—in place of standard sauce. It's made with skim or reconstituted nonfat dry milk." (Watching calories? Lay off the floury white sauce. In fact, lay off it even if you're not watching calories.)

"Lamb [is] meat from young sheep usually less than a year old." (Usually??? If it isn't, it's a fraud, and it should be *much* less than a year old. The great Elizabeth David has noted that the English, like us, can't find real lamb or real mutton any more; all we get is over-age lamb.)

Our Government home economists progress from ignorance to hysteria when they confront the microbe. (Our digression has just ended.) Here are some actual warnings circulated as fillers for the nation's press by *Food and Home Notes*:

"*Don't hold any broth or gravy more than a day or two.*"

"*Don't hold leftovers more than a day or two.*"

"*Use cracked or soiled eggs only when thoroughly cooked.*"

"*Don't use cracked or soiled eggs.*"

"*Even baked beans should not be allowed to stand out for more than two hours at room temperature.*"

"*Salmonellae and Clostridum perfringens may not leave any telltale signs that they are around. Avoid them.*"

Well, the perfringens were never welcome at our table anyway. The foregoing demented advice recalls a letter to *The Times* that urged readers to boil any canned goods for ten minutes. A food lover from New London, Connecticut, wrote us, "I hope I am never invited to her house for dinner."

The housewife who heeds these government experts will also cook poultry to death, approach picnics with dread (use frozen chicken cubes in the salad, they suggest), and spend most of her time in the kitchen scrubbing work surfaces with soap and hot water between each chore. More likely, she will give up cooking, and switch to those lovely, economical convenience foods.

It may shock the home economists to be reminded that they started out as germs, and like the rest of us could not survive except in a lifelong relationship of mutual aid with bacteria—not only the bacteria that make our bread, our cheese, and our wine, but the other friendly ones in our bodies. Anybody who presumes to advise the public on hygiene should be required to learn this message. A delightful way would be to read *Life on Man*, by Dr. Theodor Rosebury, emeritus professor of bacteriology at Washington University.

He observes that the goal of an antiseptic environment is unwholesome as well as absurd. "Germ-free animals of various species have been found to be more susceptible than conventional animals to experimental infection," he says. "We don't know why this should be so, but it is undeniable that experience with certain bacteria in early life helps protect animals—and doubtless man as well—not only against those particular bacteria but against more active pathogens and against certain viruses in addition."

Grazing animals get most of their proteins from the bacteria in their stomachs, and there is evidence that we, too, get similar help from ours. Dr. Rosebury does not ignore the harmful roles of a few varieties, but he notes that purification of water, pest control, improved housing and factory conditions, and vaccines have brought many of these under control. At issue here is not the principle of hygiene, but the notion that the home and the workshop should be as antiseptic as an operating room. We recall a little factory in Vermont that used to make a mild but delicate cheese that was prized by connoisseurs all over the country. Some years ago, it was bought by a schoolmaster who fumigated and repainted the place a gleaming white. The cheese has never been the same.

A sensuous man as well as a scientist, Dr. Rosebury deplores the paranoia that has arisen concerning normal dirt and smells. Alluding to our TV-induced addiction to deodorants and reodorants, he suggests that "maybe we ought to stop at times to wonder why we like to smell like flowers or coconuts or little Asiatic deer or the guts of a sperm whale; couldn't we learn to love the smell of healthy men and women?" And again: "We have erected a god of plumbing.... Puritanism has all but disappeared, but hucksterism has moved in with new taboos, new fetishes, a new orthodoxy with a new motive.... We are being led into turning Freud's anal compulsion into a national neurosis."*

---

* Surely that explains why J. Howard McNee, a farmer near Monroe, Michigan, was fined for using sludge from the city sewage as fertilizer. No evidence was offered that the sludge

How neurotic we are was brought home one day when we published a mild objection to plastic envelopes of sugar (and of synthetic sweetener) on restaurant tables. A number of readers reproached us for our indifference to hygiene, and one insisted that if sugar bowls were brought back, "They" would slip LSD into them.

But let us consider a real health danger.

Salmonella is bacterium that is all around us, in barnyards and in homes. It is killed in normal cooking, and doesn't seem to bother most people, but some do get sick from it, and some die. At least one authority, noting how ubiquitous the bug is despite all efforts to eradicate it, advised a public-health conference in Washington some years ago that the best way to fight it was to let the public get used to it. But he was laughed down. The war went on.

We first met up with this epic struggle in New York's Chinatown. We were admiring the big, twenty-week-old chickens, which we have described as the only market poultry that is fit to eat. Not great, just fit to eat. Buying one, we noticed that the toenails had been clipped. The butcher explained that it was done on order of the state because chickens walk in dirt and their feet pick up salmonella. For the same reason, duck feet, highly prized in Chinatown, are banned altogether. Further, the butcher admitted mournfully, the birds had to be soaked in running ice water after they had been plucked, reducing their flavor and adding water to the flesh.

Further inquiry revealed that New York State had been fighting for years to eliminate live poultry from the city. (Live cattle and fresh rabbits were long gone.) The only pockets of resistance left were the live-poultry markets of the Chinese and Orthodox Jewish communities,

---

was a health hazard, and he won an appeal. But the city meanwhile was considering building a $3.5 million plant to burn its sludge, at a cost of $300,000 to $400,000 a year and enough fuel oil to heat every house in town. (Source, *Organic Gardening*)

which had obtained injunctions on the ground that the state was infringing their religious rights. An official in Albany deprecated their rejection of nice frozen chickens from factory farms. "Freezing doesn't change the quality —it just preserves it," he said. As for the water chilling: "They do absorb some moisture. We do not consider that adulteration, within roughly six percent. Some housewives *like* watered products. Some like water-added ham." Similarly, R. Paul Elliott, the USDA's chief specialist in meat inspection, insisted that in standard American frozen chicken "we have a very low-priced, fine meat." He said people who preferred old-fashioned chicken might just be nostalgic for the "gut flavor" of juices seeping from the intestines into the flesh.

Despite a federal and state war on salmonella that has gone on for more than two decades, a Congressional report in 1974 said the bug was as widespread as ever. One study of nine federally inspected poultry plants, published in 1969, found that while the ice-water chillers did cut down the count of salmonella, they did not reduce the number of birds still carrying the live bacteria, which would multiply on their way to the kitchen stove. Elliott commented that the government was therefore considering adding chlorine to the slush. This long-standing proposal has not yet been adopted, however; it may be that the industry is not yet ready to market chlorinated chicken.

So the USDA has directed the main fire of its effort at the housewife; Elliott told us that "eighty percent of salmonella poisoning can be traced to the kitchen." Yet several studies, summarized in a report of the APHIS Task Force on Salmonellosis (August 1973) concluded that "Errors in food handling at *food service establishments* and homes [our emphasis] account for about 80 percent of all foodborne disease, including salmonellosis." In our interview, Elliott did not mention the food establishments or the report's warning that salmonellae are *spread* by equipment used in processing chickens and hogs.

It is no doubt a good thing to advise housewives to cook properly and keep the kitchen reasonably clean, although the department should make up its mind whether housewives should cook those cracked eggs or boycott them. What it cannot or will not do is stop industry from misusing those very eggs. Our own retail supplier tells us that all cracked eggs are returned and sold to bakeries. Yet back in 1964, the pamphlet of the National Academy of Sciences and National Research Council, previously quoted about the microbiological hazards of new food technology, reported:

> For example, the incorporation of contaminated egg products into dry cake mixes and into commercial bakery products has resulted in several outbreaks of salmonellosis. Packaging of nonsterile products under pressure or in a vacuum may extend their shelf life by inhibiting growth of aerobic spoilage micro-organisms, but may thus permit the multiplication of, and toxin produced by, food-poisoning organisms such as Colostridum botulinum or Staphylococcus aureus.

And those, be it said, are a lot more dangerous than salmonellae. But we have not noticed that this warning has inhibited the industry from putting foods in airtight packages. Most consumers think these are more sanitary than the old-fashioned market with its occasional flies. . . . A butcher showed us a large piece of choice beef that had arrived in a Cryolite plastic pack. "It cuts down on the *shmear*," he said, referring to the surface browned by exposure to air, which must be trimmed away. "But the smell that comes out!"

The basic tool of food inspection is the microbe count. By a simple technique, the inspector can compute the number of bacteria per milligram; over a given number, the food is ruled contaminated. From the beginning, biologists have noted the obvious flaw in this procedure: it does not distinguish good or harmless bacteria from bad. But the inspectors have defended it as the only tool they have.

As early as 1961, Elliott was acknowledging the criticism. Noting in passing that studies had "shown grossly mishandled precooked frozen foods to be truly dangerous," he wrote that "some pathogens, such as Salmonellae or Staphylococcus, have been shown to be so ubiquitous that their presence in some commercial foods is unavoidable" and the "Enterocci and the coliform group ... have been shown to be ubiquitous and therefore should not be used alone to indicate fecal contamination." It would seem, then, that in commercial foods the bacteria count made little sense. But in May 1970, Elliott was writing that "microbial level can be related somewhat indirectly to health hazard." He argued also that keeping the microbes down was helpful in slowing the loss of flavor. "This is not a problem of the regulatory agencies," he wrote, "but the industry should recognize this as an advantage in competition."*

It is indeed. When the United States bans the import of fresh unpasteurized cheeses, or of other foods that may have a high content of harmless bacteria, that certainly is an advantage in competition, to the domestic industry. It is not an advantage to the consumer—as anybody can tell who compares a real Brie in France with the tasteless product imported here.

The ban has no legal or scientific justification. The National Academy of Sciences–National Research Council report noted that there was a high natural bacteria count in fermented foods and said it was "premature" to set legal microbiological standards for anything except milk and water. Referring to the fact that such standards were nonetheless used to block imports, it observed: "The exact

* *Applied Microbiology*, September 1961, and *Journal of Milk and Food Technology*, May 1970.

level at which a hazard begins to exist would be difficult to prove in court."

Curiously, Elliott of the USDA, in our interview, was not much concerned about the illegally high bacteria counts that consumerists had found in hamburger sold in supermarkets all over the country. He explained, "The high plate count is related more to spoiling than to illness."

A newspaper filler distributed by the American Dietary Association reads, "American consumers are protected by the most stringent food laws in the world." That would be correct only if the word "consumers" were replaced by "producers." And even that should be modified to read "big producers." We have seen that the main new danger of contamination now comes from the highly concentrated food industry, just as alarming perils of poisoning arise from the massive use of chemicals in farming and processing. Yet the main weight of the government health effort hits the consumer and small business.

It is in the nature of any regulatory effort that it will tend to go lightly on the big company, which at worst can put a modest fine down as a business expense. But the application of health measures designed to protect us against industrial hazards has sped the elimination of thousands of independents from the food field, and with them the elimination of tasty food from our tables.

Thus a pastry maker in New York confides that the health people give him an especially hard time because he uses real cream and real eggs instead of powders and synthetics in his éclairs. Fresh game and rabbits have disappeared, and organ meats come in frozen and tasteless. (Sweetbreads, for example, come in ten-pound blocks, so few butchers care to handle them. Once thawed, they should be used immediately. This poses a grave health risk, but never mind; sweetbreads have an extremely delicate texture and flavor that only a well-advised cook can handle, and no well-advised cook would bother with the frozen.) Natural sausage casings are practically outlawed, to the satisfaction of big manufacturers and the distress of old-time sausage makers, who know that the synthetics are wrong. They're a dying craft, anyway.

Nearly every research effort subsidized by the government has been directed toward easing the task of agribusiness, thus speeding the extinction of small farming and small processing. When the USDA finds ways to shortcut the production of cheese, it endangers the few surviving artisans who make the real thing. When it develops new species and processes for machine harvesting of produce, it forces farmers to expand acreage in order to finance the necessary equipment, or to sell out; it makes the survivors managers instead of craftsmen. When it requires factories to install enormously expensive hygienic equipment in an effort to reduce the perils that big processing brings, it is the small processor who goes under.

The effect of this century-old government effort upon our ecology, our social structure, and our health has been brilliantly exposed by the consumer movement. Regrettably, this movement has only dimly, if at all, perceived the key role of taste in all this—probably because most of its young leaders are two generations removed from any experience with good food. They are tragically vulnerable to the gourmet phonies, the home economists, the nutritionists, and the hygienists.

A sad example is *Health Foods: Facts and Fakes* by Sidney Margolius, a pioneer in consumerism. While he may be performing a useful service in exposing some of the charlatans who have exploited the diet field, he has fallen for the line of the Food Establishment. He is ambiguous about the use of additives, complacent about the effect of chemicals on the soil, and indifferent to how things taste.

Margolius actually suggests, for example, that propionates, which give shelf life to store bread, may be "preferable to the dubious molds which develop in bread or cake"; apparently, he does not think of *fresh* bread as a viable commodity. He also appears to prefer processed cheese to real cheese, doubts that tomatoes are truly better if picked fully ripe, and lives in fear of poisoning, not from synthetics but from natural foods. This last, incidentally, is part of the argument of the Establishment against the organic movement. It amounts to saying that, since Nature herself is dangerous, there is nothing wrong with adding a few thousand artificial hazards to our foods. Margolius admits that "not much is really known about nutrition," but accepts without skepticism the claim of nutritionists that battery eggs are as good as barnyard eggs. He is also terrified by salmonellae; on page 30 he tells us that they cause "thousands of illnesses a year," and by page 33, "the danger is real and clear: some two million cases of salmonella a year." Neither figure is documented.

Margolius has picked up these arguments from the academic nutritionists, who have picked them up from one another and from their colleagues in government and industry. Gertrude Armbruster, who teaches nutrition to Home Ecs at Cornell, wrote in a campus publication that additives had made possible foods that "have the convenience and storage advantages, which meet the needs of the consumer today." Citing a USDA study, she held that Americans eat only 163 different kinds of food additives, with boys ages nine to nineteen consuming the most in total amount, while infants less than one year old eat the most in relation to their own body weight. On the basis of safety levels set by international conferences, Professor Armbruster concluded, "The present use of food additives may be endorsed as safe in total amounts of each individual additive consumed." Note that this skirts the concern of scientists that a *combination* of additives and other factors may be deadly even if each component seems safe. The professor is more concerned about *natural* foods, which may be toxic "if consumed in sufficient quantity," and asserts that "additives are more closely monitored and controlled for quality and safety reasons than many foods to which they are added." This is also the position of the textbook writer Dr. Frederick Stare and his co-author, Elizabeth Whelen. Miss Whelen wrote to *The Times* that "food additives keep our food supply plentiful, attractive, inexpensive, nutritious and pleasing to the palate," adding blithely, "Years of accumulated medical knowledge point to the fact that the chemicals added to our food are both safe and functional."

So go ahead, graduates, and teach the children that junk food is safer than real food. Sell books like *Arts and Crafts You Can Eat* by Vicki Cobb (Lippincott, 1974), which urges mothers to get the kiddies to make sweet munchies, paint them with *artificial* colors, and then eat them. Miss Cobb, who also conducts children's programs on television, explains: "The natural colors of foods are often dull and not easy to extract for use in coloring other foods. Although they are artificial food additives, there is no evidence to suggest that they are harmful in any way."

One begins to wonder whether we are not, as a society, being poisoned both morally and physically. There are members of organized crime who, it is said, draw the line at pushing drugs on children. Such a scruple should, it would seem, apply also for educators, publishers, and editors.

Neither Margolius nor Stare-Whelan nor Armbruster nor Cobb pays any mind to the work of Dr. Ben J. Feingold of the Kaiser-Permanente Medical Center, who has indicted artificial colorings and flavors as causing hyperactivity in children, and who suggests they may similarly affect grownups. Nor do the defenders of additives warn their readers that the quality of government testing has been under fire for years in the scientific community. Where industry complains that the criteria are too strict, many researchers claim that they are inadequate. Dr. Jacqueline Verrett of the Food and Drug Administration is only one of many who charge that their findings have been systematically delayed or suppressed.* She recounts the long struggle of the scientists against Red Dye No. 2† (used in many foods and drinks and said to cause cancer, abortion, and birth defects), monosodium glutamate (common in most precooked sludge, and until recently in baby foods, although linked to several disorders including brain damage in infant animals), DES (the fattening hormone, banned by many other countries as carcinogenic), and other additives recognized by our government as safe.

Who, then, are the quacks—those who defend feeding Red Dye No. 2 to children, or those who cry alarm? When the late Rachel Carson published *The Silent Spring* in 1961, the Establishment called her a crackpot. Her critics have not entirely subsided, and doubtless they will not as long as there is a chemical industry, but it is comforting to observe that, today, it is the defenders of DDT et al. who are widely recognized as dangerous and unprincipled quacks.

The hired physicians of the tobacco industry long fought the cancer scaremongers as crackpots; forced to beat a retreat, they now recommend filters and low-tar cigarets. Similarly, the hired scientists of the food industry are now fighting on the ground that their chemicals are safe or at least a "socially acceptable risk," but they have prepared a third line of defense: a slogan of the American Health Foundation, an industry-subsidized organization that is influential in shaping government health policy, is, "We must develop a safer cigaret"—cigaret here being used as a metaphor for processed food!

Margolius and others note that there are a lot of rip-offs in the diet biz. Correct. They should be stopped. But where else than in a health-food store could a mother get food for her children that was free from Red Dye No. 2? Where else can anybody who prefers the taste of real

* *Eating May Be Hazardous to Your Health*, by Dr. Verrett and Jean Carper (Simon & Schuster, 1974).
† Banned since these lines were written.

food find sea salt, barnyard eggs, unhomogenized milk?
(The term health food is indeed ironic, as Adeline Garner
Shell observes in her useful book *Supermarket Counter
Power*: "Shouldn't *all* our foods be healthful?")

The health-food and organic movements, and the counterculture generally, have made some small but enormously
promising steps toward reviving the taste of our food.
They are, for example, responsible for the restoration of
unbleached flour to our market shelves. They have helped
—along with inflation and recession, to be sure—to inspire a resurgence of baking, of gardening, and of organic
farming, and are painfully developing a parallel network
of real-food marketing independent of the agribusiness
complex.

They are our hope. But their biggest handicap is that
they are cut off from our past, which after all was one of
organic farming and good home cooking and baking. It
is desolating to see thousands of middle-class youngsters
trying to farm, trying to cook, as if they had to reinvent
the wheel. The technology is nearly all there, cunning
crafts built up over thousands of years, but they don't
know it, and they don't know whom to ask.

A good example is Nikki Goldbeck. She and her husband, David, grew up in New York innocent of the taste
of good food; they tell us that *her* mother's rice was
gummy and *his* mother didn't know how to prepare fish
that was fit to eat. They moved to Woodstock, where she
wrote a vegetarian, natural-foods cookbook. (Don't laugh.
We prefer their naïveté to the cynicism of the gourmet
hacks who have turned from fondues, chafing dishes, and
wine cookery to exploit the demand for natural and cheap
food.) Then the Goldbecks wrote *The Supermarket Hand-
book*, a consumer guide to shopping and cooking.

At first glance, a book on how to buy in a supermarket
might seem as much needed as one on how to tie your
shoelaces. But a stroll down the aisles, a perusal of labels,
and a study of the junkpile in your neighbor's cart at the
checkout counter should persuade you otherwise. The ad-

vice is needed. We were a little startled to read in Goldbeck, "As we all know, fish come from the ocean (deep-sea
or saltwater fish) and from lakes and streams (freshwater
fish)." But perhaps a lot of young Americans *don't* know,
and think fish come in frozen packages and all taste the
same. The Goldbecks warn them that frozen and breaded
or precooked fish are costly, risky, and poor eating, but
they have no advice for the use of any part of the critter
except the fillet. (It's only about 35 percent of the fish,
and not the most tasty, either.) David, who says he never
ate any fish that tasted good until he met Nikki, should
learn about stews and chowders. The Goldbecks are not
alone, though. Most of the nourishment that enters our
fish stores goes out in the garbage can.

The Goldbecks give sound advice on additives and synthetics (they won't have margarine in their house), on
baked goods and cereals, on dairy products, on jams and
jellies, on baby foods (blend your own), on how to buy
produce, and on how to read a label ("all meat" franks,
for example, may be only 55 percent meat). But they also
reflect the weaknesses of the movement. To hold that
additives are guilty until proven innocent is fair enough,
but to boycott wine on the ground that substances other
than grape are used in its care and treatment is, as W. C.
Fields might have put it, carrying hygiene too far.

A curious anomaly: the Goldbecks note that our beef,
pork and chickens have been shot up with hormones and
enzymes. They have also been told by foreign visitors that
American chicken tastes like flannel, and they explain
why. Yet they advise against buying pork—which may
have some flavor—while recommending chicken as a good
buy. Presumably, the Goldbecks as vegetarians had to rely
on outside opinion. But they too often swallow the advice
of leaden-palated nutritionists. They like Instant Postum
and ketchup, they think cornmeal is more nourishing than
spaghetti (Which meal? Which spaghetti? So what?), and
they put more faith in freezing than we would. They
seem never to have eaten homemade ice cream: "Don't

panic! We wouldn't even begin to suggest that you make your own ice cream!" Well, we didn't panic, but we were a little alarmed. We do make our own ice cream, and we suggest that David and Nikki try some. It might introduce them to a brave new world.

When they are concerned with reviving folk music, members of the counterculture—at least, some members—are intelligent enough to go to the sources. They seek out old jazzmen and old mountaineers who made music before the advent of radio and rural electrification, and they tap the treasure of their memories. There is just such a treasure among those grandmothers who learned good cooking from *their* grandmothers, unpoisoned by convenience foods, home economists, and gourmet frauds. Since most teachers of cooking today are patently unqualified, it would be a blessing to put these women to work in communities and schools—all the more so in that our neglect of the elderly has become a national scandal. But to obtain this help, we will have to overcome our prejudice against old age, our ignorance about food, and the indifference or hostility of bureaucracies. This emerges from a letter we received from an elderly reader who lives about fifty miles from New York. Note her love for food, her intelligence about it, her eagerness to spread the word, and the sad ending:

> I am one of your "elderly women who learned to cook lovingly from their grandmothers." . . . What they always emphasized was the quality of the ingredients. . . .
>
> It requires considerably more time and effort to maintain quality cooking (esthetically and nutritionally) these days. [Here she lists some of her sources, a flour mill, a farm, etc.] In spite of the additional cost of many of the items I buy, my weekly food bill is lower than those of many of my friends. . . .
>
> A much needed fish store was finally opened in my town by a young couple who know little about fish but are anxious to learn. I was appalled to see the waste in the filleting they do and quite depressed to observe the women of all ages, who pay the exorbi-

tant prices for whole fish and then allow the heads, which often weigh as much as two lbs., and the meaty skeletons to be discarded. My fish lady saves all this for me from which I make superb fish soups and chowder at very little cost. The meat scraped off the bones and heads then goes into fish cakes or whatever I'm in the mood for. I always have fish stock in the freezer and can whip up a delicious soup in a very short time.

However, the preparation of the stock does take a lot of time and I do have to air out the house afterwards—and the good bread that goes with it takes time and there are times when I wonder if it's all worth it. But I do enjoy preparing good food most of the time and enjoy eating it all of the time and love sharing it with friends who also enjoy good eating. (Some ask for recipes but, if they are not discouraged by the work involved, will make quality substitutes and then wonder why it never tastes like mine.)

In today's paper you ask: Can't the schools and community groups set up clubs where elderly people who know how to cook can teach others? At a meeting of the retired, the Coordinator of Adult Education in our school district asked for volunteers to teach various courses. I offered to teach a course with a possible title of Cooking for Pleasure, Nutrition and Economy. She seemed utterly confused.... Do you do gourmet cooking, she asked several times. Have you ever called the Pathmark number given on their commercial for enonomical recipes? Have I consulted the Dep't of Agriculture booklets? When I realized that I was not getting through to her at all, I suggested that we might possibly start with bread baking and if enough interest is developed, we might continue with soups and so on. She still seemed skeptical and asked me to write up a proposal. At that point, I decided to stick to my own kitchen.

Clearly, this woman knows more about food, nutrition, and economical homemaking than all the home economists combined. But the consumer movement is not yet aware of that.

Another aberration that has handicapped the movement is the sense of guilt that it has associated with good eating. It is sinful, many good people say, to eat well while people are starving, and it is suicidal to waste resources on tasty foods in a world that will soon be covered with humanity. So they prescribe a diet for a small planet, a diet loaded with protein extenders. They actually welcome the successes of agribusiness and its government-subsidized researchers in feeding manure back into livestock, extracting nutrients from petroleum, and adulterating our meat and bread with multisyllabic horrors.

They are right to feel guilty about poverty, and right to be concerned about the environment. But their approach is self-defeating. In the first place it is utopian to expect any country or any class to voluntarily sacrifice its standard of living. Saints may heed the appeal, but there aren't enough saints to make a dent in the problem.

Think of all the splendid environmentalists who spend their spare time collecting old newspapers and smashing bottles. Together, these thousands of our most dedicated citizens recycle about as much garbage in the whole country as is generated by one shopping center at Peoria. If they were to devote the same energy and passion to hassling our lawmakers, they might well stem the flow of garbage that seems to be the main function of our industry —the demented multiplication of throwaway packaging.

Much as we hate to agree with Earl Butz, we must concede that if every saintly American were to stop eating meat, it would not feed a single starving Asian. There is a way, there has got to be a way, but if it is to succeed it will surely have to promise us all a richer, more sensually satisfying life, and not a poorer one. In exchange for blood, sweat, and tears, Churchill promised victory. In exchange for giving up our beefsteaks, the Zero Growth school offers us only Hamburger Helper.

18

The Green Revolution

Never before in the history of agriculture has a transplantation of high-yielding varieties coupled with an entirely new technology and strategy been achieved on such a massive scale, in so short a period of time, nor with such great success.

---

*Dr. Norman E. Borlaug, accepting the
Nobel Peace Prize in January 1971*

LOS BANOS, the Philippines—Such overused terms as "miracle rice" and "the Green Revolution" are voiced these days by the experts of the International Rice Research Institute with the kind of irony that used to be reserved for the "light at the end of the tunnel" in Vietnam.

Joseph Lelyveld, in The New York Times,
October 5, 1973

A<small>LAS</small>, when the foregoing dispatch was filed, we were still in the tunnel of Vietnam, and more than a year later Dr. Henry Kissinger—who like Borlaug won a Nobel Peace Prize—was pleading for one more injection of dollars and bombs to avert disaster. Just so, the fomenters of the Green Revolution are still pleading for another shot of American know-how and chemicals to clinch what they still call a victory.

Since hunger is a far greater menace than a falling row of dominoes, history may well record that the Green Revolution was a greater disaster than our Vietnam intervention. The two failures shared a common assumption, that what is deemed good for the United States is good for the world, and a common inability to consider the opinions of the natives. In addition, the Green Revolution was crippled by the lack of a palate among its engineers.

That last criticism may seem frivolous, but it is the easiest to illustrate. The first miracle rice, IR-8, was resisted by the masses of Southeast and Southern Asia because, among other things, it was mushy. Dr. Max Milner of the United Nations, an admirer of the program, told us, "IR-8 had ideal qualities, except that consumers didn't like it very well." Progress has its price. Nutritionists of the Rockefeller Foundation, which has sparked the Green Revolution, tried enriching rice with protein pellets; they turned yellow on cooking, and people picked them out and threw them away. A new high-protein corn has been rebuffed by the famished Colombian peasantry because it does not taste good to them and is more vulnerable to drought and pests than their own corn. New enriched food compounds marketed by American companies as part of the aid effort have been rejected by the Latin poor because they taste odd and/or because they are too expensive.

When Dr. Borlaug got the Nobel Prize because of the

Mexican miracle wheat that started the Green Revolution, nobody mentioned that the Mexican poor weren't eating it, and were if anything poorer because of it. In the first place, the poor in Mexico live on corn and beans, not bread. In the second place, Dr. Borlaug's wheat cannot be made into ordinary bread because it is too low in gluten, so it is used for flat breads or fed to livestock and poultry—which the poor can't afford to eat. (When this shortcoming was mentioned to an official of the Rockefeller Foundation, he replied that it was a matter of taste—"If you took a nice loaf of Bond Bread to the Philippines, people would not like it.") To be sure, the miracle wheat, grown by rich farmers on costly irrigated land in Sonora, has permitted Mexico to become a grain exporter. But as with other monocultures—sugar, cotton, bananas, and coffee, for example—it has only helped drive millions of poor farmers off the land, and worsened the problems it was supposed to solve.

When Dr. Borlaug went to Mexico in 1944, a homegrown research group was trying to improve the productivity of the native variety of corn, raised by small farmers without irrigation or chemicals. He eventually persuaded the government to drop the project, and the Rockefeller Foundation developed a high-yield, irrigated corn that, like his wheat, had "a strong responsiveness" to "heavy doses of fertilizer."* In a 1970 interview, he said, "You have to be brutally frank with some governments; you have to push them into using it." The line was quoted by Marvin Harris, a Columbia University anthropologist, in a critique of the Green Revolution in *Natural History* (March 1973). He said:

> The main problem with the miracle seeds is that they are engineered to outperform native varieties only under the most favorable ecological conditions and with the aid of enormous amounts of industrial fer-

* See *The Fields Have Turned Brown*, by Susan DeMarco and Susan Sechler (Agribusiness Accountability Project, 1975).

tilizers, pesticides, insecticides, fungicides, irrigation and other technological inputs. Without such inputs, the high-yield varieties perform no better—and sometimes worse—than the native varieties of rice and wheat, especially under adverse soil and weather conditions.

It is no accident that anthropologists, geographers, and other field workers were the first to warn of the perils of the Green Revolution; they were talking to the people most concerned. For an example of peasant wisdom, consider the anecdote told by Efraim Hernandez, a Mexican botanist. The professor met an old Indian working in his field in Tlaxcala, and learned that he planted three varieties of corn—yellow, cream, and white....

When asked which yielded the most, he informed Hernandez that the yellow-corn gave a little, the cream more, and the white-corn was the best. Hernandez then asked him...why didn't he plant the best corn? The old man smiled and said: "That is the question my son, who works at the factory, asks. Tell me, Mr. Agriculturist, exactly how much and when will it rain next year?" Hernandez responded that he could not divine the future. The old man said: "Exactly! Therefore, I plant all three, so if there is little rain, I always have some yellow-corn to eat. If there is more rain, I'll have enough with the cream-corn, and if it's a good year, with plenty of rain, I have white-corn to sell." He added drolly, "Usually, it isn't a good year."*

Even more revealing is the story of the high-protein sorghum now being studied at Purdue University. Its researchers found the grain in the uplands of Ethiopia, where farmers roast the seeds and eat them like nuts. "But only small amounts of these strains are grown," *The New York Times* reported, "because landlords, who get a share of what the farmer sells but not of what he eats, dis-

* Recounted by H. Garrison Wilkes and Susan Wilkes in *Environment*, October 1972.

courage their cultivation. The varieties have been maintained largely because the tenant farmers plant them hidden in the middle of strands of other sorghum varieties."

The Green Revolution had not yet hit those uplands. Where it has, tenant farmers have been driven from the land in large numbers, and malnutrition has worsened. "As cereal yields have increased, their production has become increasingly profitable relative to legumes, with the result that the latter are being increasingly replaced, particularly on more productive rain-fed or irrigated land. Per capita pulse [legume] production in India alone dropped 27% between 1964 and 1969."* The reason was spelled out by Professor Donald Q. Innis, a geographer from Geneseo College who has done much field work in India and Jamaica. He reported: "The miracle wheats of northern India, grown with the aid of tractors and fertilizer, grow too thickly for chickpeas to be grown between the wheat plants in the traditional way. Green Revolution areas not only become more dependent on increasingly expensive gasoline and chemical fertilizer, but people there begin to suffer an increasing lack of protein in their diet." (He might have added that in the traditional Indian rice paddies, the bullocks graze on the stubble after the harvest, but they cannot feed on the short stalks of miracle rice. Anyway, tractors feed on fuel.) In Jamaica, Innis said, farmers who have been let alone grow coffee, taro, sweet potatoes, and bananas in the same fields, but where an aid program has been installed, the landowners grow only bananas. He continued:

> When all other factors are equal, the total yield of an intercropped field is greater than that of a field with only one crop. The intercropped field has to be harvested by hand, but there is no shortage of labor in most developing countries.... Western experts know how to make a few peasant farmers into middle class

* David L. Call and F. James Levinson of Cornell, in *Nutrition, National Development and Planning* (MIT Press, 1973).

people. We don't know how to benefit all the peasants because, almost by definition, the farmer with
machinery will have to get rid of tenants and share-
croppers in order to have enough room to operate his
machines efficiently and profitably.... In the western
world we usually salve our consciences for the havoc
thus created by saying that only the more progressive
farmers are able to understand the benefits of the
modern way of doing things. In fact many small
farmers who used to feed themselves by intercropping
are driven to urban slums where they are fed American wheat.*

The Communist Chinese say that by planting wheat
and corn in alternate rows in the same field they have
increased yields by 40 percent. But there is nothing new
or exotic in interplanting. All cultures seem to have
practiced it; in our own South, black-eyed peas used to
be called cornfield peas. Robert Beverley in *The History
and Present State of Virginia* (1705) said the Indians
"plant a Bean in the same Hill with the Corn, upon whose
Stalk it sustains it self," and also "sow'd Peas sometimes in
the Intervals of the Rows of Corn." But they were
primitives....

Like Dr. Kissinger, Dr. Borlaug seems to have gotten his
Nobel Peace Prize just in time; in another year or two it
would have been unthinkable. A number of the critics
cited have noted that the rains came to Pakistan and India
in 1967 and in 1969, breaking a long drought, and weather
conditions were also excellent in the Philippines. Triumph
was proclaimed for the miracle grains. President Ferdinand
Marcos of the Philippines announced, "The rice revolution
has been permanently won." Then disaster struck.

IR-8 had been imposed on a reluctant Filipino peasantry by a combination of army encouragement, subsidies,
and the services of Esso Standard, which provided the

* *State University of New York NEWS*, March 1975.

chemicals and the advice. A virus borne by the green leaf hopper swept the paddies of miracle rice, while sparing those of the backward peasants who had clung to the traditional varieties. In Pakistan, according to the Wilkeses, yields of the new wheat fell 20 percent in one season, while farmers who had clung to the old varieties increased their yields by 11 percent. Michael Allaby, in the *Ecologist* (May 1973), quotes a Pakistani joke that the miracle rice had produced a miracle locust to eat it. Despite the reckless use of insecticides (said to have exterminated fish in Indonesian ponds and rumored to have killed children and water buffalo), the new strains quickly showed vulnerabiltiy to various pests. The decline in the grain crop and the rise of rural discontent helped finish off democracy in the Philippines, and doubtless in India and Bangladesh as well.

Not only the social but also the environmental effects of the Green Revolution have alarmed many scientists. Uncontrolled pumping from wells in India and Pakistan, to irrigate the miracle grain, has begun lowering water tables and raising the salinity of the soil. Deficiencies of phosphorus and zinc are appearing in the Indian Punjab after a decade of heavy use of chemical fertilizer. The Wilkeses and Allaby are especially concerned about the extinction of the world's reservoir of plant species as we move to massive sowings of single varieties.* A single variety bred for high yield may quickly become vulnerable to a pest, such as the Irish potato blight of the early nineteenth century, the rust that destroyed most of the American durum wheat crop in 1953 and 1954, and the corn blight that wiped out one-fifth of the American crop in 1970. The peril is exacerbated because the pests can feed on vast acreages of their preferred food, unmenaced by natural enemies that live in other crops. French specialists have reported that the plowing under of hedgerows to encourage efficient, mechanized plant-

* See *The Genetic Vulnerability of Major Crops*, a report of the National Academy of Sciences.

ing of wheat in large fields has made a major pest out of
a rust that never seriously damaged small fields where
crops were rotated. Dr. Robert van den Bosch of the University of California has reported that spraying to kill
the alfalfa weevil also had killed predators that had been
keeping aphids under control, resulting in "the biggest insect problem in California in 20 years." It was a problem
for growers, but not for the chemical companies, which
sold a lot of new pesticides.

When a plant variety turns vulnerable to a pest, which
often happens quite suddenly, the time-honored solution is
to go back to the reservoir of similar varieties and breed
a resistant substitute. But the reservoir is being drained.
Most of our crops are steadily being concentrated in
a few favored varieties. (The same, according to Allaby,
is true for our livestock and poultry, bred for high production in indoor factories and fed antibiotics to keep
them alive. He asks whether a plague of fowl pest in
Britain in 1971 may have had a genetic factor.) Where
will we find the new genes to replace the stricken ones?
Many geneticists warn that our bright new world is
wiping out the stock of wild and locally domesticated
varieties, which is why Purdue had to go to the Ethiopian
highlands to find that high-protein sorghum. As noted, if
the Green Revolution gets there, that resource will disappear.

The dramatic rise in the price of petroleum in 1973
wrecked what was left of the argument for the Green
Revolution. Poor countries like India had to cut back
on chemical fertilizers, insecticides, and fuel for tractors
and pumps. Suddenly, hand labor was not so uneconomic,
after all.

By this time, even the foreign-aid bureaucracy was beginning to realize how demented it had been to impose
labor-saving ⸗machinery on countries where 30 to 50
percent of the labor force was chronically unemployed.
As early as 1969, *Foreign Affairs* magazine was reporting

some fears that the Green Revolution was "opening a Pandora's box." A year later, Wolf Ladejinsky of the World Bank said about India, "Now that Green Revolution land is practically invaluable (sometimes quadrupling in value), the owners would like to get rid of tenants altogether." He feared that this was "courting a great deal of trouble." Failure is not, however, conceded by the miracle-seed developers, the chemical industry, and governments that, for one reason or another, are dedicated to the new technology. Secretary Butz is, of course, one of these. "The world eats far better today than it did 20 years ago," he said in a belligerent reply to proposals that we cut down on meat. "Americans are not going to eat one *less* hamburger per week. They are going to eat one *more* hamburger per week. Furthermore, they need have no sense of guilt as they do so." It has been said that only the innocent feel guilty.

Practitioners of the Green Revolution are not as ebullient as Butz these days. They don't claim that the world is eating better than it did twenty years ago, but they insist that, despite bad weather, corruption, and a shortage of chemicals, their program has been a success. Unfortunately, they say, its gains have been swallowed up by the Population Explosion, so that, as one put it, "We've been running hard for 30 years and we're still at the starting line." In other words, if the poor insist on having babies, it's their own fault that they go hungry.

An important segment of the aid establishment now proposes to cut off food to those countries that are too poor or too obtuse to solve their problems—such as countries so improvident as to have no petroleum. The chaste name for this policy is *triage*, from the sorting of wounded in military medicine, giving priority to those who stand the best chance of getting back to the battlefield. It implicitly disclaims moral responsibility on the part of those who do the sorting.

Certainly, the cancerous growth of population has become a frightful menace, not only to mankind but to all living species. At first glance, it appears belatedly to confirm the Malthusian dogma that population increases geometrically, while the food supply increases only arithmetically. The Reverend Thomas R. Malthus concluded that it was therefore wrong to feed the poor. His doctrine was discredited by the experience of the nineteenth century, but has now been revived by some preachers of the new computer religion. Taking off from the visible havoc being wreaked on our society and our environment by a misdirected technology, some argue that economic expansion should be halted, and some add, the devil take the hindmost. This philosophy has been stated in the most arrogant and brutal form by Jay W. Forrester, a professor of management at the Massachusetts Institute of Technology.

First, the arrogance:

> Until recently, there has been no way to estimate the behavior of social systems except by contemplation, discussion, argument, and guess work. To point a way out of our present dilemma about social systems, I will sketch an approach that combines the strength of the human mind and the strength of today's computers.

Now, the brutality:

> Any change which would otherwise raise the standard of living only takes off the economic pressure momentarily and causes the population to rise enough that the standard of living again falls to the barely tolerable level. . . . "Raising the quality of life" means releasing stress and pressures, reducing crowding, reducing pollution, alleviating hunger, and treating ill health. But these pressures are exactly the sources of concern and action aimed at controlling total population to keep it within the bounds of the fixed world within which we live.

Malthus with a computer. The electronic mystique has allowed a considerable number of soothsayers to pretend to scholarship. The noble discipline of economics has been supplanted by econometricians, who have totally missed the last disastrous turns of the world economy, while cliometricians are trying to substitute computers for history, their most notable result being a now discredited best-seller purporting to prove that slavery was more efficient than free farming. There are only two things that a layman needs to know about the computer: that it is only a fast adding machine and that it's only as good as the figures and assumptions that are fed into it. As they say in the trade, garbage in, garbage out. Stripped of his incomprehensible charts, the MIT management professor is saying no more than what the good Reverend Malthus was saying: Let the poor starve. He does grant that they ought to be taught contraception but, stuck with his own formula, he admits that, like any other welfare program, it may defeat itself by relieving the pressure that brought it on. He is, in short, not much help.

Population control has failed in most poor countries because it assumes that people have babies by accident. It just isn't so. The poor of Egypt (to cite a country where we briefly looked into the question) insist on having lots of children because they have a high infant mortality rate, because they need the children's labor, and because they hope that the survivors will support them in their old age. Egyptians who are prosperous and relatively secure tend to have fewer babies. This is pretty universal; in the affluent West, the postwar baby boom has subsided and there is now a downtrend in population, offset only by improved medicine and immigration. Human societies appear to have an instinct toward keeping their numbers in line with their needs. When the Hebrews were told not to cast their seed upon the ground, it was evident that they had been practicing birth control, and it would seem that their leaders desired a larger population for reasons of policy that transcended private needs. France has also—unwisely, we think—tried to subsidize large families, with indifferent success.

The relationship of population to food is too complex for MIT's computers, at least when directed by business-management types. It's not a problem of technology. Ancient Egypt, with a population of five or six million, was able to build her temples and feed Rome as well. Today, Egypt can no longer feed her own masses, now past 35 million and growing with frightful speed. Equally "primitive" agricultures, from the Celestial Kingdom to the Inca Empire, were able to feed vast populations, keep great armies in the field, and build monuments to their gods and their rulers. If people went hungry, it was not because of lack of technology or a surplus of population, but because of the greed and folly of their masters.

Dr. Moises Behar, a Guatemalan physician who is chief of nutrition for the World Health Organization, says the Mayans of pre-Columbian times apparently had "no serious nutritional problems." They ate corn and beans, fruits, vegetables and game. They cleared patches of jungle, farmed them briefly, and moved on, letting the land return to jungle. The ecology remained in balance, and the population remained within bounds. Then the Spaniards came. Their slaves cleared the plains to grow cotton, sugar, coffee, and beef for export. Surviving Indians moved to the hills, where the land was poor and soon eroded. Malnutrition, Dr. Behar concludes, "is primarily a manifestation of social injustice."

Many scholars say the same of the Third World in general. But an official of the Rockefeller Foundation told us, "If we waited for land reform, it would take decades." Well, the Indian subcontinent has been a field of the Green Revolution for decades, and it is still ravaged by famine, while by all reports there is no serious hunger in China, whose agriculture has scarcely been touched by Western technology. This backwardness would seem, however, to result more from historical necessity than from deliberate choice. The Chinese are introducing

tractors, chemical fertilizers, and their own variety of
high-yield rice as fast as they can. They have solved their
food problem for the time being by discipline and manual
labor. If, like the Soviet Union, they become bewitched
by American know-how, they may yet revive food
shortages. Certainly, the taste of their food, which enchanted so critical a visitor as Joseph Alsop, will get
poorer.

The Kremlin is investing billions in Pepsi-Cola, the
battery production of chickens and hogs, and the chemical farming of dry lands—the Green Revolution following
the Red. Yet it must import grain. It is notorious that
what variety is left to the Soviet diet comes mainly from
the private gardens of collective farmers. Though cultivated by hand, these plots are far more productive than
the great fields tilled in common. This is not to suggest
that farm technology is bad of itself, only that it should
be directed toward improving the lot of the farmer and
the quality of the produce.

The alert reader will have remarked that all we've been
saying about the Green Revolution in the poor countries
may be applied (allowing for differences in scale) to the
United States. Put another way, if the Borlaugs had understood what was going on here, they would never have
tried to impose our mistakes on the rest of the world. Let
us take another look at our own Green Revolution.

It is curious that we Americans consider the farm family
as the very embodiment of our national virtues, yet take
the decimation of our farm population as a sign of progress. Thus an official statement of our agricultural goals
declares:

Although agriculture has been and will continue to be
the economic and social base of rural America, our
rural population is becoming largely a nonfarm one.
By 1980, only one rural resident in seven or eight may

live on a farm. It is generally agreed that it is neither socially desirable nor economically feasible to try to arrest or even slow down this trend.*

Socially desirable? According to the work cited, the number of farms has dropped by more than three million since 1950, and continues to decline at a rate of two thousand a week. The number of black farmers fell from 272,000 in 1959 to 98,000 in 1970. And these rural poor flee to our decaying cities. . . .

Economically feasible? Here we get the boast that one American on the farm feeds 47.8 people, or some such figure, that we spend less than one-sixth of our income on food, and that no other approach is as efficient. These claims have been repeated many times by no less an authority than Earl L. Butz, former dean of Purdue University, former director of Ralston Purina, Stokely Van Camp, and the International Minerals and Chemicals Corporation, and at this writing United States Secretary of Agriculture.

"Without the modern input of chemicals, of pesticides, of antibiotics, we simply could not do the job," he has said. "Before we go back to an organic agriculture in this country, somebody must decide which 50 million Americans we are going to let starve or go hungry."

Before we tackle these statements, a word of caution: scholars and laymen alike often say "statistics show . . ." as if numbers had a validity all their own. Just as phony nutrition and phony cuisine have replaced real food and real cookery, so econometrics has replaced classical economics. But the econometricians have been having a bad time lately; their soufflés have collapsed, and they have no recipe for a chicken in every pot. In this age when a Nobel Prize (again!) is awarded for that pyramid of

* *A National Program of Research for Agriculture*, sponsored by USDA and the National Association of State Universities and Land Grant Colleges (1966), quoted in Jim Hightower's *Hard Tomatoes, Hard Times*, which is also the source for the figures on farm population.

surmises called the Gross National Product, it is distressing that some of its key components from time to time turn out to be false. In July 1974, the Commerce Department revised its statistics for the growth of inventories during a nine-month period from $28.2 billion to $57.6 billion. At the same time, USDA announced that farm income in 1973 was not $26.8 billion, as it had reported a little earlier, but $38.5 billion. A Congressional study later said that the department's boners on the size of the wheat and corn crops, the carryover from 1972, and the market demand had cost the government $1.67 billion in subsidies mistakenly paid to hold down production.

Recent scandals have exposed the manipulation of figures for grain actually in elevators or on ships. We ourselves once ran into a more innocent distortion. We cited USDA figures showing that deliveries of produce to New York were declining sharply, which indicated among other things that city officials had miscalculated in building the new market. Our chart came from a mountain of tables gathered by teams of USDA employes, the figures skillfully weighted to allow for the difference between grapes and potatoes, and between different sizes of trucks and box cars. When it appeared, a USDA station chief complained that we had overlooked how hard it was to count boxcars and trucks by telephone, how dependent his staff was on the goodwill and alertness of freight clerks, etc. In short, the statistics were there to fill those tables, not to draw critical conclusions.... In a report on the waste of energy in food production, Dr. R. Stephen Berry of the University of Chicago remarked that, according to census figures for 1967, "there were 7.8 million automobiles produced, and only 7.2 million automobile engines, implying that there were 600,000 automobiles on the road with no engines."

If even such data as inventories, crops, freight loadings, and engine production are unreliable, we should be leery indeed of the sophisticated structures that the computer jockeys build upon them. This is not to suggest that

statistics have no value at all; our figures on the number
of jobless, for example, should not be taken as absolute,
but they do reflect trends. With this warning, we can
proceed.

First, a devastating statistic from the USDA: the productivity of American agriculture has come to a dead
halt. From 1954 to 1960, it rose at a rate of 3 percent a
year, but from 1965 to 1970, it was virtually zero.* For
a variety of reasons, it is likely that the curve has since
turned downward. One is pretty obvious: it takes more
and more chemicals simply to get the same crop each
year from our abused soil. According to the study called
The Fields Have Turned Brown, it took five times as
much nitrogen fertilizer to grow a bushel of corn in
Illinois is 1968 as it did in 1949. Since then, the prices of
fuel and chemicals and machinery have soared, while
labor costs have declined in real terms. Further, the rising
cost of distribution, including the senseless proliferation
of packaging, has added enormously to our food bill. Another USDA confession: "Sagging productivity in food
marketing is a matter of serious concern."†

Butz's boasts are contradicted by the statistics of his
own department. We have mentioned that Americans of
modest income would spend not 15.7 but 30 to 50 percent
of income on food, if they followed the model economical
diets of USDA. The Toothman study, published by
USDA, reported that the proportion of our income that
goes for food went *up* in 1973, while the volume of food
sales *declined* for the first time since the Depression.
Toothman figured that a family of four with take-home
pay of $5200 would have had to spend *more than half*

* *Changes in Farm Production and Efficiency* (USDA, 1972),
quoted by Dr. Philip M. Raup in *Corporation Farming in the
United States* (Minnesota Agricultural Experiment Station).
† *Food Marketing Costs and Trends*, by James S. Toothman
(USDA Extension Service, Pennsylvania State University,
1974).

its income on food, if it bought the amount consumed by average Americans. The Bureau of Labor Statistics has estimated that Americans of low and middle incomes actually spend 24.5 to 30 percent of take-home pay on food. And that food is not cheap—our prices are, in fact, among the highest in the world. According to a Cornell study (Pimentel, cited below), a calorie of food energy costs 3.8 times as much in the United States as in India.

As for one American feeding forty to fifty others (depending on who is doing the boasting), we are overlooking maybe two more Americans who service the farmer with machines and chemicals—not to mention all those in processing, packaging, distribution, and advertising. As one scholar put it:

> The food industry and mass media in the United States are one and the same. Over 50 per cent of television's revenue comes from the grocery industry. The child who watches a moderate amount of television in the United States today has seen 80,000 food commercials by the time he is 16. Mother and grandmother can't compete with that kind of brainwashing.... Today we are practicing malnutrition over television.*

In totting up the cost of our Green Revolution, we must also include the cost to our health, and the cost of supporting the millions who have been driven off the farm. But Butz says that before we knock off those efficient chemicals that have given us so many blessings, "somebody must decide which 50 million Americans we are going to let starve or go hungry." Well, that's already been decided; certainly, fifty million Americans are now going ill-fed, if not hungry, and the rest of us are not eating well.

Dr. Borlaug has declared that if we were to ban all pesticides, our crops would be cut in half. As for chemical

* Robert Choate at international symposium, "Nutrition, National Development, and Planning." (MIT Press, 1973).

fertilizer, J. Philip Campbell, Undersecretary of Agriculture, has called it "one of the great bargains in the United States over the past 50 years." He added: "The farmer adopted commercial fertilizer...for a very basic reason. He found he could make money using it. There has never been and never will be anything like net profit to stimulate production."

The claims for chemicals have been contradicted both in theory and in practice. To take theory first, a number of scholars* have estimated that if all chemicals were eliminated and if idle land were returned to cultivation, output would decline by only 5 percent, farm prices would rise 16 percent and farm income would rise 25 percent, because farm costs would decline. Actually, most of the scholars propose only to curb the use of chemicals, not to eliminate them.

David Pimentel of Cornell shot Dr. Borlaug down with ease. He reported that while the use of insecticides on corn had multiplied thirty times in two decades, losses from corn insects had tripled. More generally, he said: "Despite the large increase in insecticide use, crop losses due to insect pests are also increasing and are now estimated by the USDA to be nearly 13%. In part, these trends are due to the practice of substituting insecticides for sound bioenvironmental pest controls (e.g., crop rotation and sanitation) and also to higher consumer standards." The latter refers to a preference for "pretty" fruits and vegetables, unmarked by harmless bugs. As an old Italian truck farmer we knew used to say, "If the bugs won't eat it, it's no good."

Pimentel and his colleagues also found that, while the production of corn per acre rose 2.4 times from 1945 to 1970, the input of fuel rose 3.1 times. "Therefore," they said, "the yield in corn energy, compared to fuel input,

---

* See especially David Pimentel et al. in *Science*, November 2, 1973; Dr. John S. and Carol E. Steinhart in *Science*, April 9, 1973; Dr. C. E. Butterworth in the *Journal of the American Medical Association*, February 25, 1974.

declined 26 percent." Put another way, 1 calorie of energy put into growing corn in 1945 produced 3.7 calories of corn, whereas 1 calorie of input in 1970 produced only 2.8 calories of corn. "It is estimated," Dr. Butterworth wrote in the *AMA Journal*, "that it costs four times as much to produce a kilocalorie of food energy in the United States as in India. It is important to remember that these calculations do not include the relatively enormous cost and energy involved in the preparation of refined, processed, and convenience food items." (He noted, incidentally, that even the farmer is now "dependent on the supermarket for his groceries, just as he is dependent on an intricate web of supporting industries to produce his crop.")

The Steinharts wrote:

Perhaps even the idea of a reduction of labor input is a myth when the food system is viewed as a whole.... In "primitive" cultures, 5 to 50 calories were obtained for each calorie of energy invested. Some highly civilized cultures have done as well and occasionally better. In sharp contrast, industrial food systems require 5 to 10 calories of fuel to obtain 1 food calorie.

All these scholars were alarmed at the enormous waste of energy in a time of fuel crisis. "To feed the entire world with a U.S.-type food system, almost 80 percent of the world's annual energy expenditures would be required just for the food system," the Steinharts said. Pimentel noted that our high-yield hybrid corn has a higher moisture content than earlier varieties, and often must be dried in fuel-fired ovens. He suggested a return to a corn that demands less fuel and is more resistant to insects. He and others also urge a revival of crop rotation and more frequent tilling to cut down weeds. Where herbicides *are* used, he computed, a switch from tractor to hand spraying would increase labor costs four times, but would cut energy consumption by more than 98 percent.

Environmentalists are appalled by the damage to the

soil in our one-crop chemical farming. Our livestock is estimated to produce 1.7 billion tons a year of manure, but little of it reaches the most intensively cultivated regions. Instead, it poses a pollution problem around our feedlots and chicken factories. Government scientists are feeding some of it back into the livestock.

That unreconstructed food lover Waverley Root was fulminating in the *International Herald-Tribune* one day about chicken that "tastes like a wrung-out dishmop" and steers being fed on recycled ("Gawd! recycled!") manure. He had read an article explaining that manure had a lot of nourishment that the critter has failed to sop up the first time. "Well," he said, "we old farmers knew that, and the way we got it back into the nitrogen cycle was to spread it over the fields."

Pimentel said one dairy cow or two steers or 84 chickens produced enough nitrogen fertilizer for an acre, along with organic matter that, as any old farmer knows, "increases the number of beneficial bacteria and fungi in the soil, makes plowing easier, improves the waterholding and percolating capacity of the soil, reduces soil erosion, and improves the ratio of carbon to nitrogen." He and others urge that feedlots be deconcentrated and spread out all over farming country and that farmers rotate their crops and plant and plow under "green manure," such as clover and vetch.

What they are prescribing, of course, is a return to old-fashioned farming. But this is not simply theory; there are still some old-fashioned farmers around. From Washington University in St. Louis, *The New York Times* reported (July 20, 1975): "Research scientists here have found that a test group of organic farmers who used no inorganic fertilizers or pesticides made as much money last year as a comparable group of conventional farmers who used those substances." The study involved 32 similar farms scattered over the Midwest. The 16 organic ones produced crops that were worth 8 percent less, but their costs were nearly one-third less than on the other farms. The organic growers said their soil, their crops, their animals, and even their families were healthier because they used no chemicals. One of the conventional farmers in the study looked at the results and decided to cut his use of chemicals in half. He said he couldn't afford to go all the way—meaning, presumably, to buy cattle and vary his farming technique—"because he owed a large debt for land he had bought."

George Warner, agronomist for an organic milling company in Hereford, Texas, told us that its spring wheat was measuring a phenomenal 17.8 percent protein. "It doesn't cost any more to raise it right," he said. "That hot fertilizer is not farming—it's mining the soil. And they burn the stubble!" Rich cotton planters in the Mississippi Delta, long since converted to the Green Revolution, have been having second thoughts. They complained to a *Times* reporter (August 31, 1975) that prices for machinery had doubled in two years, while the price of cotton held unchanged; that the heavy equipment packed the soil so hard it had to be plowed more deeply by even heavier equipment; that it required specially trained operators; and that when it broke down, it had to be sent away for repairs.

The complaints about rising costs have become so loud that they have been heard even by the *American Vegetable Grower*, a militant proponent of the chemicals and equipment that dominate its advertising. It reported in January 1974 that some farmers were switching over to hand labor to save fuel and chemicals, and were using pesticides on a "need" rather than a "preventive" basis. It quoted a Cornell agronomist as opining that a small cut in fuel use would actually "improve operating efficiency" for "up to 70% of growers." It does not explain why, but one should not look a gift horse in the mouth.

These are encouraging signs. We have a long row to hoe, however, if we are to get back to a sane agriculture. Our national policy has long been to encourage, and even force, farmers to get big or get out. In a conservative study,* Dr. Philip M. Raup of the University of Minnesota observed:

> "Expand the size of your farm business" has been the advice to farmers for over 50 years, from agricultural universities, experiment stations, extension services and their supporting agencies in the U.S. Department of Agriculture. The market development of farm equipment manufacturers and supply industries have been at least as effective.... Up to a point, the argument has had merit.
>
> It is being increasingly questioned in recent years. Virtually all current studies of economies of size in agriculture yield the same conclusion: In all but a few types of farming, well-managed one- and two-man farms can obtain most of the gains to be had from increased size, as measured by decreases in cost per unit of output.

Dr. Raup noted that farm subsidies and capital-gains tax shelters had encouraged a rise in corporation farming, as had the heavy investment required by mechanized agriculture. But he added that big corporations had found that absentee management leads to a loss of efficiency. Jim Hightower quoted an official of Ralston Purina as saying that "the individual farmer or family corporation can meet, and many times surpass, the efficiency of the large units that operate with hired management."†

As a result, many companies like Ralston Purina have turned to contract operations; they persuade farmers to invest in such businesses as broiler factories, where the corporation provides the chicks, feed, and chemicals and buys the broilers at its own price. The *Des Moines Register*, interviewing Alabama chicken growers who had been caught in a tragic cost squeeze, reported one of them saying that they were "the new slaves."

* *Corporate Farming in the United States*, Minnesota Agricultural Experiment Station Scientific Journal.
† In *The Washington Monthly*, September 1973. See also Hightower's *Eat Your Heart Out* (Crown, 1975).

Contract chicken-farming seems such a brilliant idea to Nelson Rockefeller that his International Basic Economy Corporation has been promulgating it in the Third World, where the poor can't afford chicken and the rich can afford better. If this succeeds, God forbid, nowhere in the world will one be able to find a chicken that does not taste like a wrung-out dishmop.

The USDA has so low a regard for small farmers that in 1975 it changed its statistical definition of farmers to exclude many who do not quite earn a living from the soil. This will surely improve average farm income, in the same way as raising the permissible level of nitrate would increase the safety of our water supply. It will also help confirm the prediction of Assistant Secretary Robert Long: "As agriculture progresses to fewer and fewer units, those remaining will find it easier to work together in the search for a new formula for a more profitable return."*

Long, a former vice president of the Bank of America, is talking about financial muscle. This has nothing to do with efficiency. On the contrary, by a sort of Gresham's Law, the inefficient dinosaurs of business buy out their most efficient competitors, and drive out the rest. Usually, the clout is enough. Only big companies can afford much television time, yet the big buyers get a break on TV rates, as they do on interest rates and everything else. When a small entrepreneur (Pepperidge Farm, for example) succeeds in spite of the obstacles, a bigger one will make it an offer it cannot refuse. The big ones have the political clout, too. When the laws are not written expressely for them, they can be evaded. It is noted that the great California irrigation projects were supposed to limit farms to 640 acres, but Tenneco owns 350,000 in the San Joaquin Valley and Anderson, Clayton, has 52,000 more. Our research stations work primarily on *their* problems: chemical and mechanical methods for taking

* *The Washington Monthly*, September 1973.

the taste out of our foods, and packaging and store
lighting techniques to make them *look* tasty.

All these factors have joined to give America a diet
of conglomerates. Hightower offers a Sunday dinner:
"The turkey is from Greyhound, and the ham is from
I.T.&T.; the fresh vegetable salad is from Tenneco, with
lettuce from Dow Chemical; potatoes by Boeing are
placed alongside a roast from John Hancock Mutual
Life; the strawberries are by Purex, and there are after-
dinner almonds from Getty Oil." He could have added
mushrooms by Clorox and pudding by R. J. Reynolds, and
washed the whole mess down with orange juice from
Coca-Cola, beer from Philip Morris, or tea from Unilever,
but no matter. It all will taste perfectly awful, if it has
any taste at all.

Things will get worse, if the Establishment has its way.
A press release by General Foods boasted that we would
all be vegetarians in the relatively near future, eating delicious steaks made of guck. It is saddening to find do-
gooders joining the conglomerates in this dreary prospect.
On National Food Day, sponsored by the Center for
Science in the Public Interest, throngs of fine citizens
picnic on soyburgers and such, to reproach the rest of us
for eating cornfed beef. That's not our idea of a bright
new world, and, thank goodness, it will never sell in
Peoria. Thank goodness, too, that it is not the only
alternative to hunger. The tastiest beef in the world is
raised in fat meadows in France and the British Isles, and
does no harm to the ecology whatever.

We have established, we think, that quality in our diet is
indissolubly linked to the survival of small-scale farming
and small-scale food handling. But if that meant simply to
turn the clock back, the situation would be hopeless. The
small farmer has nearly always been at a disadvantage in
modern societies: he sells cheap and he buys dear. Even in
so rich a country as France, the sons of peasants have
been fleeing the land for the relative ease of city jobs. At

a village *fête* once, we were struck by the fact that local farmers looked ten years older than classmates who had moved to town and were back on holiday. The farmers get no holidays. So fewer and fewer remain to produce the myriad cheeses, fruits, meats, and wines that have adorned the tables of the best-fed country in the world.

One cannot force their sons to stay. But farm life can be made more attractive. We once visited a farm in Burgundy, affiliated to a small cooperative movement of Roman Catholic inspiration. Eight families had merged their holdings; one now took care of the cows, another tended the chickens, a third did the paper work, and all took turns at chores. A member told us that it was working very well, and for the first time the farmers could go on vacation just like factory workers.

He added what seemed a pregnant thought, that the ideal size for such an enterprise was eight to ten families. More than ten invites the afflictions of large organizations: loafing, cheating, intriguing, faction. Fewer than eight is hardly enough to achieve the benefits of the division of labor. We mention this as only one possible way of improving the lot of small farmers. Surely there are others.

Critics of our society err when they seek to turn the clock back all the way. In revulsion against the corruption of our time, some opt out for the cottage crafts. We have mentioned the dropouts who try farming in the hills; nearly all fail, as they must. We have noted also the surge of home baking, weaving, and pottery making. They are fine, but they are no solution for society as a whole. Except as a hobby, women will not in any great numbers return to milking goats, weaving cloth, sewing clothes, baking bread, hewing wood, and drawing water. Nor should they. There should be a good bakery in every neighborhood, and a good tailor, a good dairy, a good delicatessen, a good produce market, and a good restaurant—and all should make good livings for their operators.

The original Adam Smith opened his *Wealth of Nations* with these words of wisdom: "The greatest improvement in the productive powers of labour, and the greater part of the skill, dexterity and judgment with which it is any where directed, or applied, seems to have been the effects of the division of labour." He did not foresee that, beyond a certain point, the division of labor in large operations would begin to lose efficiency. But with the advantage of hindsight, perhaps we can begin to devise ways of arranging our work to improve the quality of life, and not wreck it. Perhaps we are already finding such ways.

19

Hope

I knew from home the food was going to be good here—it's all different. Take macaroni. Here it tastes delicious. I guess spices are different. Everything seems home-cooked.

Sam Recenello, age thirteen, visiting Rome with the Newark Boys Chorus, as quoted by The New York Times

THE palate is not dead. Young Sam, presumably exposed from birth to American television and glop, could still taste the difference. No doubt his mother deserves much credit, for Sam associated "delicious" with "home-cooked." Yet millions of Americans who, unlike Sam, had no acquaintance whatever with decent food in their childhood are now trying to rediscover it through gardening, baking, and cooking.

To be sure, people have turned to these ancient crafts in large part because of inflation and recession, and also because they provide a sense of creativity that is lacking in their daily jobs. But this does not explain why growing numbers of city dwellers have been growing herbs and tomatoes—tomatoes!—on their window sills. And while snobbery has played a major role in the gourmet movement, certainly a hunger for sensual food was present too. There is hope.

Our commercial food system is subverting itself. Inflation, and especially the rise in the cost of fuel, has destroyed what economic logic the system appeared to have. Its pollution of the environment and of the food supply has caused our more intelligent citizens to question the established wisdom—pollution, and urban decay, and Vietnam, and Watergate, for our society is all of a piece. We are indeed what we eat.

The erosion of small farming and small business and the growth of the conglomerates have caused our society more and more to resemble some features of Soviet society, whose leaders have been striving to emulate some of the worse features of ours. It is Marxist doctrine that every society bears the seed of its own destruction—though this is seldom applied to the "classless" state—and surely one sign of it is the persistence of the peasants' free markets in the Soviet Union. Just so in our country, a revival of a sort of peasants' free market is under way, short-circuiting the approved state-capitalist network of agribusiness.

One of the most enlightening examples of this movement has arisen in the conservative city of Syracuse, New York. It is, or was, a thriving industrial center, laid waste by the epidemic of highway building and urban renewal of the 1960s. Two major interstate roads, each occupying six lanes, with dividers, borders, and cloverleafs, slashed a broad + across the heart of the city. Bulldozers knocked down much of what was left, including some fine buildings from the days of the Erie Canal. Some high-rise offices and apartments went up, but much of the cleared area is still vacant after more than a decade. Syracuse looks like a European city flattened by bombing and only partly rebuilt on a harshly modern plan.

In 1972, the city fathers seem to have awakened to the fact that all that federal building money had been a poisoned gift. The population had declined from 210,000 in

1960 to 197,000 in 1970. As everywhere else, the downtown business district—what was left of it—was losing
clientele to suburban shopping centers, and some middle-
class neighborhoods were decaying into new pockets of
slum. A delegation of bankers and businessmen went to
Europe to look for alternatives. They were enchanted by
the flower and vegetable markets they saw, and returned
asking, "Why can't we?"

Actually, like every other American town, Syracuse had
had a downtown farmers' market, but it had been razed to
make way for a piece of interstate highway and a parking
lot. But the city now decided as an experiment to close
off a city block in the very center of town and install a
farmers' market there every Tuesday from late spring
through fall. Monty Euston, a young Chamber of Commerce aide, was named manager. At the scene a year later,
he recalled:

"When we started, the Agricultural Extension people
said it would never work. Some of the farmers doubted
they'd have enough business, and the regional market kind
of lobbied against it. It took us nearly three months to
get enough farmers interested. We opened with twenty-
two, and by the middle of the season we were up to
sixty-two.

"We figure prices here run thirty to fifty percent below
the supermarkets. The Traffic Department did a count
one day, and we figure we run about twelve thousand
visitors. We get a big lunch crowd of office employees,
and a mix of slum dwellers and middle-class people that
never used to visit farmers' markets. As a result, the downtown stores have had increases of eight to fourteen percent in volume on Tuesdays. And business has gone up at
the regional market, too, where there are farmers' markets
on Thursday evenings and Saturdays."

The Parks Department had set up picnic tables on a
small lawn, for shoppers to enjoy a pickup lunch of local
goodies. On the day we were there, a throng circulated
among the two rows of farm trucks and stands, buying

not only produce but also home-baked goods, homemade candies, and handicrafts. A candidate for governor was spieling through a microphone—politicians have learned to make the Syracuse market a Tuesday stop. At one end, an accordionist was playing; nearby, peaceniks were collecting petitions beside a Vietnamese "tiger cage."

The day before, one and one-quarter inches of rain and hail had battered the countryside. Thousands of acres were flooded, the produce muddied and bruised. At dawn on Tuesday, Charles Zicciardello gathered a truckload of lettuce and cucumbers from his muddy black fields and drove to the market. A tall, bronzed, crewcut man, he was stripping the bruised outer leaves from the lettuce as fast as he could while his wife and daughters were selling it.

"That storm really did a job," he told us. "This market is the only thing that saves me from starvation. Our stuff is number one quality, but the commercial buyers will not take it if it's spotted or dirty—we'd get maybe nine cents a head. We're getting twenty-five cents here. In the supermarket, it'd be maybe forty-nine cents, and not picked this morning, either."

A red-haired factory worker who was shopping during his lunch hour said, "Where I live, it's sixty cents."

"Remember when they used to say you gotta be big to make money?" Zicciardello asked. "Well, it's the reverse. A year like this, if you've got a lot of machinery, you go bankrupt.

"In 1953, I bought my first small farm, ten acres. I was told that if I didn't get bigger, I wouldn't survive. So in 1963, I bought two farms—sixty acres—and I thought I could really make a go of it. I'm still in debt.

"I made a mistake. If I had that ten-acre farm and these markets, where I can make $350 to $450 each time, I'd make a go of it—and not rushing around, like I do now, with nine men. I say, a small farmer coming to the markets will survive."

A streetcleaning foreman nearby said, "This is the best thing ever happened to Syracuse." Its success has inspired

a number of nearby towns to do likewise, and drew in-
quiries from civic leaders as far away as Vancouver, British Columbia (though Syracuse was not the first city to
revive the farmers' market, and some of the old ones
never quite died). The success also encouraged Syracuse
to promote other imaginative programs. One was to offer
a free bus touring the downtown area, ending at the market. Another was to turn a length of the main shopping
street into a pedestrian mall on Saturdays, with flowers,
music, an art show, a portable swimming pool, and a
movie. A third was the Adopt-a-Lot program. The city
cleared and plowed thirteen abandoned lots, and assigned
them to community groups and individuals for gardening.
In its first year, an official said, it had already improved
community pride and enhanced the city's appearance, and
one group already had applied to buy its lot. What a
marvelous program for the wastelands of our cities! And
what a great way to revive the memory of what real food
tastes like!

When we visited it, the Syracuse market was a curious
mixture of the commercial and the home-grown, and of
organic and chemical production. Commercial, because
the promoters had assigned one segregated section to dealers who brought in outside produce in order to provide a
wide selection, including such imports as bananas. Also,
"to keep the place smelling nice," as Euston put it, no
chickens or rabbits or meat or fish were sold. This was a
shortcoming, he granted, and he added that if there were
more space, the problem might be resolved. There were,
however, stands from two of the last cheese factories in
these parts.

Among the farmers, there was much sympathy for organic principles, but also much confusion. For example,
many were still picking their tomatoes "mature green" instead of red-ripe. Mrs. Esther Paine of Fulton, New York,
who was selling eggs, berries, carrots, beets, and flowers,
said, "If you don't feed the ground, you only get half a
crop." But she complained, "Last year, we gave $75 a ton

for fertilizer. This year, it was $150. They tell us it will be $250 next year. This is the roughest year we've had. Maybe it's our last year." Mrs. Paine was one of the little people who are being pushed out of farming—she had 500 laying hens, as against the 150,000 of a farmer at a neighboring stand. And both compete with much bigger egg factories in the South and West.

Mrs. Mary Fatchric of Millus, New York, was selling organic string beans and homemade cakes. "Cow manure softens your earth," she said. "Commercial fertilizer makes it clayish, and in melons and squash, you get more seeds than meat. My winter squash, people accuse me of putting sugar in it." But Mrs. Fatchric had been caught up in the cholesterol panic; her cakes were made with margarine. This, in a dairy country.

Officer Charles Patchett, who was keeping an affectionate eye on the market, was a former dairyman and still lived on the farm. He was sad that the superhighways had paved over much of the best bottom land, and was glad that the farmers' market was giving people "a sense that they're cutting out the middleman."

"Farm prices have dropped to the farmer but they haven't in the market," he said. "Somewheres along the way, there's a little discrepancy. My uncle just sold a six-week-old calf at forty cents a pound. You know what veal's selling for. . . .

"One thing that scares me is that the old people are dying out and there's nobody to take their place. The papers are full of auction notices for dairy farms. Yet land values are out of sight. They're just going to have to upgrade the standard of living for farmers."

This very problem has stirred some imaginative proposals by regional planners. These include tax and zoning reforms that would take into account the fact that farmers make a positive contribution to the environment, while real-estate developers make a negative one. Suffolk County in Long Island has been gingerly experimenting with a radical solution: to buy farms and lease them back to their

operators. But counties do not have the resources to buy
what is left of the greenbelt or to subsidize farmers, even
where the politicians have the will to resist the developers.
What is required is a national policy of reviving and
protecting small farming. This would include the repeal
of those tax privileges that encourage absentee ownership,
and a redirection of our agricultural research and marketing policies.

It is hard for a farmer who is making only a modest
living to refuse a fortune offered him by a developer—
all the more if he must run a farm in the midst of suburban sprawl, overrun by dogs and thoughtless children.
It is still harder if he must hurdle official hostility to
market his crop.

Most city governments still regard the farmer as a nuisance. Builders and supermarket operators have a stronger
voice in city councils, and boosters object to the clutter
of the markets that choke the streets and occupy land that
should be supporting high-rises. New York, for example,
has worked for half a century to eliminate them. By 1973,
there was only one farmers' market left, and its days were
numbered. This was the Bronx Terminal Market, near
Yankee Stadium. When we visited it before dawn one
day, there were only 25 farm trucks there, where there
would have been 150 a few years earlier. The city had
leased the area to a promoter, who had quadrupled the
rent to the farmers and pushed them into a corner, pending construction of a stadium garage and a highway access
road into it.

"They're eliminating us," said an apple grower from upstate. "It's happening all over." A truck farmer from Suffolk, who was unloading the only red-ripe tomatoes we
have seen in a New York market in recent years, said that
when this market closed, "I'll shut down, I guess."

The prospect did not faze E. C. Fabber, the commissioner of ports and terminals. "Certainly the area is going
to be developed," he told us. "I don't know why it sur-
prises people that everything in New York is not a

brownstone. After forty years, everything has to be re-built." In an interview punctuated by telephone calls, the young commissioner continued: "Hunts Point [the new $200-million complex in the Bronx] is more effective and more sanitary.... A farmer's market is almost inconsistent with a terminal market.... We are becoming a mega-lopolis, from Boston to Washington, and real estate is too valuable.... The small guy can't make the same use of the efficiency of large organizations—the fork lift, vertical storage."

On the wall of Fabber's office was a poster reading: "Earth, this is God! I want all you people to clear out before the end of the month. I have a client who is in-terested in the property."

At this writing, the client is no longer interested. The city is virtually bankrupt, and certainly the hundreds of millions of dollars it spent to eliminate the old markets and redevelop everything were a contributing factor. Des-ultory investigations are under way into the city's deal-ings with the promoters at Bronx Terminal Market and Hunts Point. Fabber himself estimated that rents at the new Hunts Point fish market would be ten times as high as those at the old Fulton Fish Market; the small merchants revolted, and the project was abandoned after millions of tax dollars had been spent.

The crisis of our society, we repeat, is all of one piece: corruption and pollution, rural decline and urban decay, alienation and cynicism, malnutrition and phony food. We cannot solve any of them without resisting all of them. This requires a new dedication to the quality of life, in all its rich aspects. It should be a happy fight, not a sad one. Let us enjoy our food again. Enjoy, enjoy.

A Co-Author's Note

When I used the editorial "we" in writing about food for
The New York Times, some readers took it for an affec-
tation. It was in fact an effort to indicate the counsel I
was getting from my wife, without whose expertise I'd
never have taken the job. As it was, I agreed to become
food editor and critic only after several urgent appeals,
and only for a limited time, because like any well-fed
husband I'd rather eat at home.

I don't know anybody better qualified than my wife to
write about food. *Newsweek* once called her the best
American cook in Paris. This pleased but bemused our
French and American friends, because in Paris (1963–
1972) Karen cooked in French, with French produce. In
the States, our diet was more eclectic—that is, American.

Karen learned to cook as a little girl in a Nebraska farm
kitchen, perched on a stool to help Grandmother with
such chores as beating a *beurre manié*. At ten, she won a
prize for baking at the county fair; at seventeen, she was
cooking in the home of a cultivated family to earn her
way through college; in her twenties, she was learning
Chinese and Italian cuisine from neighbors in San Francisco. I have eaten well since I met her, and our travels
together for more than thirty years have added to our
common dedication to good food.

From time to time, while I was writing mostly about
people and politics and economics, we would do a piece
about dining or cookery. They were well received, all
except two: an article in the late 1950s that decried the
state of American food and the gourmet nonsense, and
another about 1965 that rebutted the slander that women
were incapable of genius in cooking. They were good

337

articles, and were turned down by all the best magazines. Nevertheless, many of the ideas in this book were first aired, under my name or Karen's or both, in *The Times*, *Atlantic*, *Harper's*, *House and Garden*, and *Organic Gardening*.

The bylines were genuine—that is, I wrote what I signed, Karen wrote what she signed, and we each wrote parts of jointly signed articles. In this book, Karen wrote all that concerns cooking, cookbook writing, and our early food history—to wit, Chapters 3, 6, 7, 8, 9, 10, and 11, and most of Chapters 2 and 5. I did the rest.

John L. Hess

Appendix

---

*Following are the first and last dining reviews, and three
other pieces, written by John L. Hess during his 1973–
1974 stint as food critic of* The New York Times. *They
have been referred to in the text, and are reprinted here
chiefly because they illustrate points raised earlier. In addition to passages identified as written by Karen Hess, her
counsel was a major factor throughout.*

Fancy Is Not Always Good

We first met up with high-toned grub at Boy Scout camp
40-plus years ago, when the chef honored some visiting
state dignitaries with a banquet that included, to our child-
ish wonderment, a salad of iceberg lettuce, canned pineapple, cottage cheese and mayonnaise, topped with a
maraschino cherry.

We threw up.

That was our first critical response to "gourmet cooking"—horrid snob phrase, that. We're more controlled
now, but our palate and our prejudice haven't changed.
Fancy for the sake of being fancy is bad taste in any art.

This reflection was inspired by the very first New York
meal we have eaten in the line of our new duty as food
critic. It was a trial run for a dinner held the other night
by a society of food and wine lovers at a leading hotel.

The invitation was gracious, the company agreeable and
the food not really bad, but since we intend to accentuate
the negative in order to draw a moral, we'll not mention
names.

The trial menu:

Hors d'Oeuvres
Consommé Tortue en gelée
Mousse de Poisson tricouleur fleuron, sauce champagne
Pigeon Souvaroff, with water cress, snow peas and salsify
Selle d'Agneau glacée, with rémoulade and salad
Fromages: Gold Rich, chèvre et triple crème
Soufflé au calvados
Café brulot

(Translation: Fish and liver pastes on pastry; cold turtle broth; a three-colored fish mousse; roast pigeon stuffed with foie gras and truffles; cold saddle of lamb; an American gouda, a French goat cheese and a sort of camembert; a soufflé with two sauces of diced apple in calvados and in apricot jam; and coffee with orange and lemon peel, flamed with Grand Marnier.)

The wines were a Taittinger pink champagne (a taste we never acquired); a Meursault-Perrières, and a Beaune, both pleasant; a Grand Rue and a Richebourg, both great red burgundies of 1964, a year long since past its prime, and an undistinguished Bollinger brut champagne.

As for the food, this nonvoting juror found himself in mild disagreement with the majority on nearly every count. We all were surprised to find seafood and liver pastes served on what is tantamount to cooky dough; this was ordered replaced by an assortment of seafood and other savories. (Our own feeling is that all spicy and rich "appetizers" tend to spoil the appetite.)

All but us loved the jellied turtle soup, though one juror wished it could be hot, and was overruled. It may be that he wanted it to taste more like turtle soup. We detected a strong flavor of clove, one of those spices heavily used in this country to lend taste to foods that have lost their own.

(Clove turned up again in the café brulot, which we found undrinkable. An observant maître d'hôtel brought us an untreated cup of the original coffee, which turned out to be hardly any better. The jury ordered café royale. Why not just a proper coffee? Not fancy enough.)

There were raves for the tricolored mousse of fish and for its sauce, which we found heavily floured. The orange, tan and green layers were a showy stunt, perhaps, but we were not convinced that a decent quenelle or even gefilte fish would not be better eating.

The pigeon was very good and the lamb in aspic acceptable, though both had been mislabeled. The jurors properly expelled a melon ball added to each serving of lamb "to lend color" and deleted the rémoulade (shredded celery root in mustard sauce) because it quarreled with the lamb and wine, but kept the similarly quarrelsome salad, with walnuts added.

Just back from France, we found the cheeses beautiful but insipid, a result of the United States ban on importation of fresh, unpasteurized dairy products.

A majority of the jurors were tickled with the diced-apple sauces served with what this diner found to be an inferior soufflé. Someone suggested that fruit be incorporated into the soufflé; a hotel official confessed that his kitchen had tried but failed to perform this feat, which can be achieved by any good, practiced cook.

This guest murmured that a decent soufflé was in itself a tour de force that needed no sauce whatever—in fact, in years of serious feeding in France and elsewhere, he had never before met a dessert soufflé served with anything but its own perfume.

The objection was not heard. The jurors ordered what we are told is a common dressing for American soufflés: zabaglione sauce (an egg dessert on an egg dessert—why?), but with the apple in calvados added for novelty.

Novelty is, of course, the name of the game. It was a novel meal, and some of the things in it were doubtless good. But it was not a good meal.

The Babbitt who says "I'm a meat-and-potatoes" guy may show better taste than is generally recognized—if the meat and potatoes are good and properly prepared. He's wrong if he spurns foreign food because it's foreign, but he's right if he rejects lifted-pinky cuisine because it doesn't taste like food.

If we were appointed by a club of food lovers to arrange a gastronomic dinner, we'd send out scouts to scour the city and countryside for fresh fish, garden produce, chickens that scratch in dirt and eggs laid by such fowl, and maybe some wild mushrooms, and we'd hire a cook who knew how to fix these things so they taste as they are.

The food and wine societies would also serve the cause of good eating and drinking if they encouraged those few farmers, bakers and other artisans who preserve what is left of old traditions of quality. Each of them deserves a certificate of honor, and a price for their work to make it worthwhile.

* * *

The cook in our family, Mrs. Karen Hess, was surprised to learn that a leading hotel here could not make a soufflé with fruit. She dashed off a memo to the chef, which follows:

There should be no problem if the basic principles of a soufflé are respected—mainly, preserving the proportion of the basic mixture to the beaten egg whites and the degree of moisture that is to be incorporated.

The classic "bouillie" (a heavy pastry cream, suitably flavored) can normally support small bits of fruit providing too much moisture is not involved.

Large pieces of fruit—e.g., apple sections lightly sautéed in butter and sprinkled with calvados—are better handled like a fillet of fish in soufflé: bake roughly a third of the soufflé mixture at 475 degrees for four to five minutes. Working very quickly indeed, place the pieces on top of this, pour in the rest of the mixture and finish baking as usual.

Some fruits are more successful if they are cooked,

puréed, sweetened and reduced to a proper consistency and simply incorporated into the beaten whites, with no bouillie. Apricots are particularly successful this way. The flavor is far more intense. This type of soufflé is the only one on which I would propose a zabaglione sauce, by the way. On the more classic soufflé I find the combination of egg with egg an abomination.

Small bits of apple, lightly sautéed in butter and sprinkled with calva, may be incorporated directly into a classic soufflé mixture and are very successful—the pre-cooking is necessary to intensify the apple flavor. Above all, one must take care not to disturb the basic proportion of wetness to the beaten egg whites.

May 31, 1973

Our Last Review

A group of readers in Rockland County complained that this department never visited their fair contrée. Challenged to nominate a restaurant, they proposed Boulderberg Manor, on Route 9W at Tomkins Cove. Done.

The place is not without redeeming social significance. In fact, it is a revealing caricature of what has happened to American food over the last century.

Boulderberg Manor is a handsome American Gothic mansion commanding a magnificent sweep of the Hudson River. It is reasonable to presume that Calvin Tomkins, the entrepreneur who built it in 1858, served the same kind of food as did his neighbor across the river, Baltus Van Tassel, whose provender is sensuously described by Washington Irving in "The Legend of Sleepy Hollow."

Today, for $8 to $12 or so, the good burghers of Rockland may eat in his house a seven-course meal described in the inevitable hall placard from *Cue* magazine as "excellent French Continental cuisine." Whatever that is.

A glance at the menu establishes that no kitchen could cook such an array to order, although a waitress insisted that nearly all the dishes had been cooked within the house that week. No doubt, all of them followed the standard recipes of the gourmet cookbooks. Few could stand reheating, and none would draw a passing mark in a good sixth-grade cooking class.

We had a pathetic, underdone quiche, a dry slice of terrine on a wedge of iceberg lettuce, raw clams utterly devoid of taste (frozen?!?), onion soup with a lump of gummy cheese in the bottom, iceberg salad, and a sherbet "Intermezzo."

Doubtless mine host had read that French gourmands, in a grande bouffe, would suspend gorging for a while and "cleanse the palate" with a sherbet. But that's a dry sherbet, often flavored with champagne, not lemon extract and sugar, as here. (There was of course sugar in every course. Indeed it was often the only taste discernible, as with the green beans.)

We passed up the snapper almandine, the trout stuffed with crab, the seafood crêpe, the surf and turf and other gourmet clichés, including Victor Borge's funniest joke on the American public, the Cornish Game Hen.

What we got were a reheated duck à l'orange and a steak that was tender and had no more taste than the doilied mushroom atop it. Baked potato steamed in aluminum foil, of course.

Finally, an oversweet cheesecake and the first hard-boiled custard we have ever seen, topped with a chilled whip that may have been cream. The coffee was weak, and we'll skip comment on the wine and the bread.

In short, what we had was the work of a faithful student of American gourmet cookery, doing his awful best, at prices that could not leave much room for profit. This house should burn those gourmet books and find a good, old-fashioned American cook and baker.

The provender that made Ichabod Crane dream is no longer available, but a good steward would scour the markets, the farms and the wharves and put good, home-cooked food on the table. I'd bet that the burghers, once they overcame their surprise, would like it as much as the glop they now push down with their booze.

January 11, 1974

Heartburn

[Review of *The American Heart Association Cookbook*, edited by Ruthe Eshelman and Mary Winston (McKay, 1973).]

How can one criticize a life-saving effort?

Time was when the family doctor (yes, son, there used to be family doctors) would say: "George, you've got to cut down on the beer and hard stuff, the bread and potatoes and desserts." It was up to George's wife to nag him about his diet, and he either followed it or didn't, and that was that.

We are more advanced today. Judging from the flood of literature now pouring out, the whole country is dieting. By the same token, the whole country is mad about something called gourmet food. Which creates a paradox that publishers and other experts are only too eager to resolve. "Be a gourmet low-fat diet chef!" cries the National Foundation for Ileitis and Colitis, which is teaching how to cook with medium chain triglycerides.

Now comes the big artillery. The American Heart Association, which declared war on cholesterol 12 years ago, has brought forth a book designed to prove that we can all enjoy living longer. Insh'allah.

If we understand it correctly, the reasoning is this: The medical evidence is not all in, and some authorities are skeptical, but the probabilities are that if we put everybody—fat and lean, sedentary and active—on a low cholesterol diet, many thousands of people will be spared heart attacks.

As Dr. Campbell Moses, medical director of the A.H.A., puts it in a foreword: "When we speak of risk, we are really speaking in a group sense, since it is impossible to predict the individual's body response."

So the problem is to persuade the general public (pulse and blood pressure normal) that it isn't really much of a sacrifice. Not easy. Consider French cuisine, the summit of Western cookery: As is well known, all Gaul is divided into three parts, which cook, respectively, in butter, olive oil and goose or pork fat. Collectively, these are anathema to the A.H.A. Even olive oil, which has no cholesterol, is sniffed at because it's low in what are described as the beneficial polyunsaturated fatty acids.

The book does not give the cholesterol score for each recipe, but Dr. Moses writes: "This is not a diet book. It is a cookbook—a fun book for people who like to cook and to eat."

Well, yes and no. For this was a committee project, assigned by a board of physicians to two nutritionists and a staff who gathered recipes from a variety of sources. Inevitably, the result is mixed. Some contributions are interesting—the bread section is delicious reading—and some are just awful.

Take the very first recipe in the book: Tuna-Dill Pâté. It's an aspic of tuna, canned vegetable juice and gelatin—the archetype of those horrid ladies' magazine dishes of the Twenties that turned American men into meat-and-potatoes guys.

The second recipe is a time-wasting flower arrangement of raw vegetables. We are told to serve these with a dip, such as yogurt with curry and mayonnaise. The editors do us a service by banning fried chips and other prepared cocktail snacks, but they're big on pretzels and ersatz dips and aspics.

Their favorite dip is a Mock Sour Cream, made of cottage cheese, skim milk and lemon juice. The aspics included a canned peach–ginger ale–lemon Jell-O mold (where do they find these things?) and even an asparagus mold, embalming one of the finest of American vegetables. But they top these with a Spinach–Avocado–Orange

Toss and a Party Walnut Broccoli that are not to be believed.

The editors lean heavily also on mayonnaise, although there is no recipe for it and the commercial product (one of the disasters of the American diet) varies widely in fat composition. (Real mayonnaise, of course, is egg yolk and olive oil.)

The introduction to the fish chapter quotes: "Show me a fish-hater and I'll show you a person who has never tasted properly cooked fish." Then what are we to make of this Fish Sauce: 1 cup mayonnaise, 1 cup chili sauce, 3 to 4 tablespoons drained horseradish, dash hot pepper sauce? A real fish lover would make do with a squirt of lemon juice, and perhaps a spoonful or two of inoffensive olive oil.

We will pass the Yogurt–Gelatine Delight, the Mint Peas (with crème de menthe!) and the French Peas (with flour, broth and water chestnuts).

There is sensible general advice on food preparation. But even if all the recipes had been assembled by a cook who knew and loved good food, a cookbook could not deliver on the premise that a low-cholesterol diet can be "just as delicious" or even "scarcely less delicious." (The latter phrase is applied to an omelet made with three egg whites and one yolk. It's just not true. In fact, to make a good omelet even better, one adds an extra yolk.)

We are told, for example, to cut down on red meat in favor of fish and poultry. But we can still find good-tasting beef and lamb, while the fish and poultry generally available to Americans are sorry eating indeed. Take our butter, lard and olive oil away and eating is not going to be as much fun as it was.

For many people, this sacrifice is doubtless necessary. The cookbook's advice will be useful to them: Lay off those abominable precooked "convenience" foods and mixes, trim your meats and broil them, cut out sauces and rich desserts.

For the rest of us, there may be an alternative. If it is

generally true that physically active people can absorb a
fair amount of cholesterol without harm, then we might
all mount bicycles. Also, bring back the old-fashioned,
hand-turned ice cream freezer. The one who cranks the
most gets to lick the paddle.

July 28, 1973

Karen's Thanksgiving Turkey

*Children are conservative. Ours were raised on old-time
Middle Western rural cooking with a dash of Grant Street
Cantonese, North Beach Italian, el Barrio Cuban and Escoffier, and they came to regard all other foods as exotic
and therefore suspect.*

*Even within the approved categories, they detested ex-
perimentation. Just as with a bedtime story, whose hun-
dredth telling must not vary from the first, so it was with
Thanksgiving and Christmas dinners.*

*My wife did once venture a remarkable turkey dressing
of oysters and corn bread—made from scratch, of course
—and it was received politely, but next time she was
urgently called to return to Karen's Stuffing.*

*While she continued to gather ancient recipes, her own
became a minor institution. She has often shared it. Here
in her words is how she makes it:*

First, you must catch your turkey. Our forefathers would
never recognize the taste of most of what is sold as turkey
nowadays. You cannot expect old-fashioned flavor from
birds that have been frozen, injected with nameless oils
(guilefully called "butter ball"), boned and treated with
sodium tripolyphosphate or other allowable chemicals.

Better meat markets will be able to furnish quality birds
that were decently fed and fresh killed. These command
a somewhat higher price—$1.29 a pound in some stores—
but they may well be a better buy because they are not
full of water and injected fats. They also tend to be meat-
ier as well as far tastier.

Wild turkey may interest some people but they arrive here frozen and are very expensive—$2.75 a pound.

First, make your broth. Take the neck and the giblets (saving the liver for the stuffing) and put them to cook in about three cups of water along with a large onion, quartered, a sliced carrot, a stick of celery, some parsley stems, and a bay leaf. Allow to simmer for an hour and a half or so. If you have veal or chicken broth to hand, so much the better—just add it to the broth.

STUFFING

1 pound pork sausage	1 cup broken walnut meats
1 cup sliced onions	
½ cup very thinly sliced celery	½ cup chopped Italian parsley
½ teaspoon thyme	1 teaspoon sea salt
1 loaf good bread (homemade preferred)	½ teaspoon freshly ground pepper
1 cup sliced black olives (mild California type, pitted)	½ cup (approximately) of stock (see above), or water.
The liver, minced	

If liked, 2 tablespoons of cognac or about twice as much madeira, port, or sherry, may be added.

Gently cook the sausage meat in a large, heavy pan, stirring until it is cooked and well broken up. Add the onion, celery, and thyme. Cook, stirring frequently, until perfectly tender and pale yellow.

Toast the bread in a medium oven so that it partially dries out. Cut the slices into very small squares. Combine all the ingredients. Check for seasoning.

This makes sufficient stuffing for a 12-to-14 pound bird.

You may do all the tedious details the day before. I always use the stuffing hot; it speeds things considerably.

Once you have neatly sewn and trussed a bird with a trussing needle and heavy thread you will never again bother with all those steel pins. It is the only way you will be able to make the wings lie close to the body—simply stitch them down. Bring the legs up and together and tie securely. The bird cooks better and is much easier to handle.

ROASTING THE TURKEY

Turkey is almost invariably overdone. The breast meat, especially, takes on the texture and taste of cardboard. A bird of 10 to 12 pounds should be done to a turn in two hours; this is predicated on the old-fashioned roasting method—a high temperature (450 degrees for about half an hour and then turned down somewhat). It does involve rather more watching and basting than the low temperature methods, but the gain in flavor is worth a bit of effort.

Wipe the bird, then rub it with a stick of butter that has been allowed to soften at room temperature. Any extra butter will go into the roasting pan. Salt and pepper all over.

If you put the bird on a rack, there is no way to avoid burning the juices except by filling the pan with water, which will give the turkey a steamed taste. Instead of that, lay the bird on its side in an ovenproof platter of about the same size. This is important, as an overlarge platter risks burning at the margins.

Have your oven at 450 degrees. In timing the roasting, it is good to know that resting the bird in a warm place for a half hour before carving is recommended, and longer if possible. This will give you plenty of time to make the sauce and provides a good margin should you really feel that longer cooking time is indicated.

A bird of 15-16 pounds should easily be done in three hours. There are so many variables, however, that you will have to rely on your own judgment and taste.

After the first 15 minutes, turn the bird over on its other side. If browning is proceeding too rapidly, turn the oven down to 400 degrees. Otherwise, wait about 15 minutes, then check to be sure all is proceeding nicely and to spoon some of the fat over the bird. Repeat about every 15 minutes. The juices in the pan must not burn.

Somewhere about half way along, turn it back to its original position. If at any point you feel things are moving too rapidly, turn the heat down to 350 degrees.

The classic test for doneness is to see how easily the legs move, but I find that appearance and poking the flesh with a finger are better and easier.

When it is done, lay it on a warm platter and start on the sauce. Skim off any really excess fat but don't forget that turkey tends to be dry. Add the lovely stock you have been simmering, and place over high heat. Using a wooden spatula, dislodge all the delicious bits of brown so that they may dissolve. Allow to reduce to a nice consistency. This is a jus, not a pasty gravy.

If you wish to heighten the flavor, you may add a couple of tablespoons of cognac or ¼ cup or so of wine—red or white—before you add the stock. Let it come to a good boil before you continue. This evaporates the alcohol and improves the flavor. Check for salt and pepper. Strain, if you deem necessary, into a gravy boat and send to table with the turkey.

Save all the fat and every bone and scrap to make a delicious soup, for which there will be suggestions next week. Turkey has a lot of flavor and it's a shame to waste it.

November 15, 1973

But Let the Potato Chips Fall Where They May

Hon. Leon Jaworski,
Special Prosecutor,
Justice Department,
Washington, D.C.

Dear Honorable:
It is my understanding, and I am sure yours, that you have engaged to hunt down dirty tricks of 1972 no matter

which party cooked them up. Regretfully, I must call your attention to a ragout that has all the aroma of a job by the Other Side.

It is a document called "National Republican Heritage Groups Council World Cookbook: Featuring Congressional and Cultural Achievements," or "NRHGC Cookbook" for short. Although dated "Summer, 1972," it has just been surfaced by something named Atland Publishing, with a letter drop at 2300 Pennsylvania Ave., NW, and a price tag of $4.50, plus 35 cents postage.

The cover-up is preposterous. NRHGC is obviously a slyly mocking title for a minorities council purporting to campaign for Republican candidates for Congress. No observer recalls such a campaign from Pennsylvania Avenue in 1972. Further, had this document been published then, it would hardly have helped the Republicans.

It is not calculated to help in 1974, either.

The frontispiece is a clever parody signed "Patricia Nixon." Under the White House seal, "Mrs. Nixon" writes:

"Cooking is truly an exciting, yet so extremely practical skill! It is the basis for happy meals and sound health for your family as well as an opportunity to exercise your personal creative abilities. This cookbook is especially interesting for it is a collection of recipes that are not only delicious but also representative of our great nation's many ethnic and national groups."

And so on.

"Mrs. Nixon" submits the first recipe, Continental Salad, which is an aspic of lemon or orange Jell-O, canned grapefruit juice and canned beets, with a dressing of cream cheese whipped with more grapefruit juice, mayonnaise and sesame.

This confection gives itself away by its excess. Much better, because almost plausible, was the legend that Mrs. Nixon's husband relishes cottage cheese with catchup. If that was a Democratic canard, this one's a canard à l'orange Jell-O.

The second recipe is signed "Judy Agnew," and the hand of the Democratic Segretti here is just too crude. It is a poor man's version of the great Greek avgolemono soup, using a full cup of rice and three eggs for one chicken, where a richer and better version uses only yolks, and one-fourth as much rice.

The chicken is removed to cool in the second sentence, and never returns. The voter gets the rice soup. Who got the chicken?

"Tricia Nixon Cox" submits a "Chicken Imperial"—another sly dig—of chicken breasts, bacon and corned beef, baked in cream of mushroom soup and sour cream. Those canned mushroom or celery or chicken soups return again and again in recipes attributed maliciously to various members of Congress, including a "gourmet" witches' broth of 20 ingredients pinned to Senator Javits.

Segretti in his most prankish mood laid nothing so foul against the Democrats.

While the author of the "NRHGC Cookbook" was careful to sprinkle a number of reasonably authentic recipes representing some of the smaller ethnic groups, the Mexicans come in for a particularly hard time, with such recipes as "green chili casserole" tagged to poor Senator Gordon Allott of Colorado: evaporated milk, 2 cans cream of chicken soup, grated yellow cheese. . . .

Senator Clifford Hansen of Wyoming is accused of spreading blue cheese on his Imperial—that word again—Tenderloin, while Mark Hatfield of Oregon is said to use corn-flakes in his Deviled-Crab Casserole.

Your own boss, then Senator William Saxbe of Ohio, is smeared with a recipe for lemon cake. "1 package white cake mix, ¾ cup Crisco oil, 4 eggs, 1 tsp lemon extract, 1 package lemon Jell-O. . . ."

Note that brand names are sprinkled liberally, if you will excuse the expression, throughout the book, doubtless to implicate big contributors.

Note further that Senator Weicker is not listed in this goulash, while it smears such loyal if lower ranking Republican Congressmen as Page Belcher of Oklahoma and Norman Lent of New York. Can't you see the opposition whispering about Belcher's Peas, Pickle and Peanut Salad? And how can Lent live down his Hot Dog Stew, with its can of bean-with-bacon soup, can of tomato soup, can of mixed vegetables, can of condensed (sic) milk and "onion flakes to taste"?

The victims may deny everything, but if you throw enough mud, some will stick.

Note finally that it was a Democrat who said, "If you can't stand the heat, get out of the kitchen." This was in the White House, and there is, in fact, some reason to suspect that the Democrats never did leave its kitchen.

How else can we explain that travesty when President Nixon served Brezhnev good Maine lobsters gucked up as homard en bellevue? When Brezhnev had the Nixons in, he had real Russian grub, not pseudo-French, flown in from Moscow. The Soviets won the round hands down.

Cynics will say that you can't make an omelette without breaking eggs, and will try to shrug this off as election propaganda. But I am confident that, busy as you are chasing Republican improprieties, you will not let the Democrats get away with this. What's sauce for the improper goose is sauce for the impropaganda.

December 24, 1973

Bibliography

Extensive use was made of Eleanor Lowenstein's *Bibliography of American Cookery Books 1742–1860*, American Antiquarian Society, Worcester, and Corner Book Shop, New York, 1972. We also consulted the *Gastronomic Bibliography* by Katherine Golden Bitting, San Francisco, 1939, and the *Bibliographie Gastronomique* by Georges Vicaire, Paris, 1890.

Dates of first editions that were unavailable to us are given in parentheses. Dates or names in brackets indicate that they are not given in the book but have been otherwise verified.

English translations of many of the French books are available; we listed only those that are referred to in the text. Unless specifically stated otherwise, all citations are translated by the authors. We have thought it useful to list facsimile and other modern reprints of works.

—K.H.

Before the Nineteenth Century

Anonymous, *Le Cuisinier Gascon*. Amsterdam, 1740. (One of the loveliest of French eighteenth-century cookbooks.)

Marcus Gavius Apicius, *Les Dix Livres d'Apicius*. Translated from the Latin and commented on by Bertrand Guégan. René Bonnel, Paris, 1933. (The earliest extant cookbook in the Western World; Apicius died in 30 A.D. Guégan's scholarly and illuminating commentaries make this work invaluable.)

Robert Beverley, *The History and Present State of Vir-*

ginia. Richard Parker, London, 1705; modern edition, University of North Carolina, Chapel Hill, 1947. (Beverley was a historian and a perceptive observer. The chapters on the Indians, their way of life, and their cooking, are of special interest.)

Richard Briggs, *The New Art of Cookery, According to the Present Practice*. Spotswood, Campbell, and Johnson, Philadelphia, 1792. (First American edition of an English work.) (The first recipe including love apples [tomatoes] and the first for ice cream known by us to have been published in the United States are included in this book.)

William Byrd, *William Byrd's Natural History of Virginia or the Newly Discovered Eden*. Originally published in German, Bern, 1737; modern edition in German and English, translated by Richard Croom Beatty and William J. Malloy, Dietz Press, Richmond, 1940. (Byrd was a naturalist and a member of the Royal Society.)

Susannah Carter, *The Frugal Housewife, or Complete Woman Cook*. Edes and Gill, Boston, 1772; James Carey, Philadelphia, 1792, 1802; G. & R. Waite, New York, 1803. (One of the fine English cookbooks to come out in American editions. The plates are by Paul Revere. The 1803 edition has an interesting section of authentic American recipes.)

Mary Cole, *The Lady's Complete Guide: or Cookery in all its Branches*. London, (1788), 1791, third edition. (The lady listed her sources.)

[Frances Custis (?)], *A Booke of Cookery* and *A Booke of Sweetmeats*. Unpublished manuscript in the keeping of the Pennsylvania Historical Society. It was in the possession of Martha Washington and has long been attributed to the mother of her first husband, Daniel Custis (mistakenly, in our opinion. K.H.).

Lucy Emerson, *The New-England Cookery*. Josiah Parks, Montpelier, 1808. (Entire sections of this book are lifted verbatim, errors and all, from *American Cookery* by Amelia Simmons.)

John Evelyn, *Acetaria: A Discourse of Sallets.* B. Tooke, London, 1699; in facsimile, Women's Auxiliary, Brooklyn Botanic Garden, 1937. (One of the most delightful and erudite of cookbooks.)

Benjamin Franklin, *On the Art of Eating.* Commentaries by Gilbert Chinard. Princeton University Press for the American Philosophical Society, 1958.

John Gerard, *The Herball or General Historie of Plantes.* London, 1597. The same, "very much enlarged and amended by Thomas Johnson," London, 1636.

[Hannah Glasse], *The Art of Cookery, Made Plain and Easy; Which far exceeds any Thing of the Kind ever yet published....By a Lady.* Printed for the Author, London, 1747; same, by Mrs. Glasse, London, 1751, 1756, 1767, 1796; same, by Mrs. Glasse, Alexandria, Virginia, 1805. (This book is said to have been the most popular cookbook in the colonies. The American edition has a very interesting section on American cooking.)

Thomas Jefferson, *Thomas Jefferson's Garden Book* (1766–1824). Annotated by Edwin Morris Bette. American Philosophical Society, Philadelphia, 1944.

Louis Liger, *Dictionaire Pratique du Bon Ménager de Campagne et de Ville.* Ribou, Paris, 1715, first edition. (An invaluable work.)

Menon, *La Cuisinière Bourgeoise.* Foppens, Bruxelles, (1746), 1753. (One of the great cookbooks of all time. Vicaire cites forty-three editions, continuing into the nineteenth century.)

A. A. Parmentier, *Le Parfait Boulanger.* Paris, 1778. (The ageless classic on baking of bread.)

Samuel Pegge, *The Forme of Cury* (about 1390). J. Nichols, London, 1780. (One hundred and ninety-six recipes, compiled by the master cooks of Richard II, in what is generally regarded as the most ancient manuscript on cookery in English, are presented and edited by Mr. Pegge. He also includes a manuscript dated 1381 with some ninety recipes which is rarely cited although it is of great interest. Cury [pronounced as in curious] means cooking.)

Gulielma Penn, *Penn Family Recipes* (Transcribed 1702). Edited by Evelyn Abraham Benson. George Shumway, York, 1966. ("My Mothers Recaipts for Cookerys Presarving and Chyrurgery—William Penn." Only the cookery recipes are given. The manuscript is in the keeping of the Pennsylvania Historical Society.)

Elizabeth Raffald, *The Experienced English Housekeeper, for the use and ease of ladies, housekeepers, cooks, &c. Written purely from practice.* Millar, Law, and Cater, London (1769), 1789; Thomas Dobson, Philadelphia, 1801, 1818. (The American editions differ from the English only in minor details of style and spelling. The book was popular long before 1801. There are remarkable plates, one of which is a plan for "a curious new invented fire stove, wherein any common fuel may be burnt instead of charcoal.")

Amelia Simmons, *American Cookery, or the art of dressing viands, fish, poultry and vegetables, and the best modes of making pastes, puffs, pies, tarts, puddings, custards and preserves, and all kinds of cakes, from the imperial plumb to plain cake. Adapted to this country, and all grades of life. By Amelia Simmons, an American orphan.* Hudson & Goodwin, Hartford, 1796; facsimile, Oxford University Press, New York, 1958; Charles R. & George Webster, Albany, 1796, second edition. (This seems to be the earliest cookbook of American authorship to be published. The facsimile is of the copy in the keeping of the American Antiquarian Society and has the errata as corrected by the author; the copy at the Library of Congress does not.)

E. [Eliza?] Smith, *The Compleat Housewife; or, Accomplish'd Gentlewoman's Companion . . . fit either for private families, or such publick-spirited gentlewomen as would be beneficent to their poor neighbors.* William

Parks, Williamsburg, 1742. (This fine cookbook is the earliest known published in the United States. It is based on the fifth edition of the work, which first appeared in London in 1727.)

Guillaume Tirel *dit* Taillevent, *Le Viandier* (c. 1375). Techener, Paris, 1892; modern reprint, Morcrette, Paris, n.d. (Three manuscripts of different dates and a fifteenth-century edition of what is generally regarded as the earliest French cookbook are presented and discussed by Jerome Pichon and Georges Vicaire. *Viandier* means cook. The meaning of *viande* is parallel to that of meat; at one time they both meant simply food.)

The Towneley Manuscript. (A family manuscript of cookery from Towneley Hall in Lancashire, and still in family hands. The name Constantia Smith appears inside the book, and it is dated 1759.)

Hannah Woolley, *The Gentlewoman's Companion.* London, 1682. (A charming book from England's golden age of cookery.)

Nineteenth Century

Eliza Acton, *Modern Cookery for Private Families.* London, (1845), 1855; 1855 edition in facsimile, Elek, London, 1966. (One of the finest cookbooks in English literature.)

Louis Eustache Audot, *La Cuisinière de la Campagne et de la Ville.* Audot, Paris, (1818), fourth edition 1823, ninetieth edition 1912. (As the French home cookbook for a century, it exerted incalculable influence.)

Isabella Beeton, *The Book of Household Management.* S. O. Beeton, London, 1861; facsimile, Jonathan Cape, London, 1968. (A comparison of this work with the Audot tells much about why the French eat better than the English.)

Pierre Blot, *Hand-Book of Practical Cookery, for Ladies and Professional Cooks.* D. Appleton, New York

(1867), 1868, 1869; 1869 edition in facsimile, Arno, New York, 1973.

Jean Anthelme Brillat-Savarin, *La Physiologie du Goût.* Paris, (1826), 1834; modern edition, Pierre Waleffe, Paris, 1967.

Baron Brisse, *La Cuisine à l'Usage des Ménages Bourgeois.* Flammarion, Paris, n.d. [18—]. (A little-known work of considerable interest.)

Buckeye Cookery. Buckeye Publishing Co., Minneapolis, (1880), 1885. (The Minnesota classic.)

Antonin Carême, *L'Art de la Cuisine Française au Dix-neuvième Siècle.* Five volumes. Renouard et Cit, Paris, n.d. [1833–1835]. (The master cook and his masterpiece.)

Lydia Maria Child, *The American Frugal Housewife. Dedicated to Those Who Are Not Ashamed of Economy.* Carter, Hendee, Boston, (1832), 1833; 1833 in facsimile, Ohio State University Libraries, 1971. (Some of the earliest recipes for many homey dishes such as baked beans.)

Mary Hooker Cornelius, *The Young Housekeeper's Friend.* Charles Tappan, Boston, 1846, 1871. (And Mrs. Cornelius is a friend of ours.)

[Lafcadio Hearn] *La Cuisine Créole.* F.F. Hansell & Co., New Orleans, 1885; reprint, Favorite Recipes Press, Louisville, 1966. (We learn that even "during the long heated term [claret] is seldom absent from the table," and that "white wines of the lighter kinds" were favored for breakfast.)

Mrs. C. H. Cushing and Mrs. B. Gray, *The Kansas Home Cook-Book.* Crew & Co., Leavenworth, (1874), 1886; 1886 edition in facsimile, Arno, New York, 1973.

Fannie Merritt Farmer, *The Boston Cooking-School Cook Book.* Little, Brown, Boston, 1896, 1914, 1916, 1926, 194-, 1965; 1896 edition facsimile, Crown, New York, 1975. (The maiden aunt of home economists.)

Charles Gérard, *L'Ancienne Alsace à Table.* Levrault, Paris, (1862), 1877; reprint of 1877 edition, Alsatia,

Colmar, 1971. (A scholarly work on the food of Alsace through the centuries.)

Sylvester Graham, *A Treatise on Bread, and Bread-Making*. Light & Stearns, Boston, 1837. (He wrote on the evils of bolted flour; hence, graham flour.)

[Elizabeth Stansbury Kirkland], *Six Little Cooks; or Aunt Jane's Cooking Class*. Jansen, McClurg, Chicago, 1879; facsimile, Arno, New York, 1973. (A charming cookbook.)

Eliza Leslie, *Directions for Cookery, in Its Various Branches*. Carey & Hart, Philadelphia, (1837), 1843, 1848, 1870; 1848 edition in facsimile, Arno, New York, 1973. (Miss Leslie is one of our finest writers on cooking and this work is her classic.)

Eliza Leslie, *Domestic French Cookery*, chiefly translated from Sulpice Barué. Carey & Hart, Philadelphia, (1832), 1836. (This appears to be the first book on French cooking by an American. *The French Cook* by Louis Eustache Ude, a French chef, appeared in 1828. While no trace of Barué has been found, we find little support for speculation that Miss Leslie lifted from Ude.)

Eliza Leslie, *The Indian Meal Book: comprising the best receipts for the preparation of that article*. Carey & Hart, Philadelphia, 1847.

Eliza Leslie, *Miss Leslie's Lady's New Receipt-Book*. A. Hart, Philadelphia, 1850.

Eliza Leslie, *Miss Leslie's New Cookery Book*. Peterson, Philadelphia, 1857, 1859, 1874.

[Miss Eliza Leslie], *Seventy-Five Receipts, for pastry, cakes, and sweetmeats. By a lady of Philadelphia*. Munroe & Francis, (1828), 1832.

Mary J. Lincoln, *Mrs. Lincoln's Boston Cook Book. What to do and what not to do in Cooking*. Little, Brown, Boston, 1883, 1893, 1926. (The original textbook of the Boston Cooking School, antedating Fannie Farmer's book by thirteen years.)

Maria Parloa, *Miss Parloa's Kitchen Companion*. Estes and Lauriat, Boston, 1887.

M. E. Porter, *Mrs. Porter's New Southern Cookery Book.* John E. Potter, Philadelphia, 1871; facsimile, Arno, New York, 1973.

Martha Jefferson Randolph, Recipes. Unpublished manuscript in the keeping of the Alderman Library, University of Virginia. (It contains Jefferson family recipes, some going back to Monticello, some attributed to LeMaire [Jefferson's maître d'hôtel], some to Annie Trist [1851], and one to a E. W. Harrison [1876]. It thus spans nearly a century of the cooking of a prominent family; the decline in quality from the days of Thomas Jefferson is striking.)

Mary Randolph, *The Virginia Housewife: or Methodical Cook.* Davis and Force, Washington, 1824; Plaskitt, & Cugle, Baltimore, 1831, 1836 (Copyright 1828); E. H. Butler, Philadelphia, 1860; in facsimile, Avenel in cooperation with the Valentine Museum, Richmond, n.d. (Mrs. Randolph died in 1828, so it would appear that her son took the 1828 edition, changed the date of the author's preface [otherwise identical to that of the 1824 edition], and presented it as an 1831 edition. As compared to the 1824 edition, there are a few additional recipes. The only other significant differences involve spelling changes: "Gumbs" became "Gumbo" and "tomatas" became "tomatos." All subsequent editions were based on this 1831 edition. It remains one of our finest cookbooks.)

Lucien Tendret, *La Table au Pays de Brillat-Savarin.* Louis Bailly, Belley, 1892; modern edition, Rabelais, Paris, 1972. (One of the great classics on women's cooking.)

Marion Cabell Tyree, *Housekeeping in Old Virginia.* John P. Morton, Louisville, 1879. (The finest of the "contributed" cookbooks, and one of the earliest. The editor devotes 61 pages to bread making.)

[A. L. Webster], *The Improved Housewife, or Book of Receipts...By A Married Lady.* Hartford, (1844), 1845; 1845 edition in facsimile, Arno, New York, 1973.

S. C. Wightman, Manuscript cookbook in the authors' possession. Signed, and dated May 1826. It is from New England.

Twentieth Century—Cooking

Helen Lyon Adamson, *Grandmother in the Kitchen.* Crown, New York, 1965.

Ali-Bab [Henri Babinski], *Gastronomie Pratique.* Flammarion, Paris, (1906), ninth edition 1928.

Ali-Bab [Henri Babinski], *Encyclopedia of Practical Gastronomy.* McGraw-Hill, New York, 1974. (Half of the French original is excised.)

The American Heart Association Cookbook. Ruthe Eshelman and Mary Winston, editors. McKay, New York, 1973. (No cholesterol but chock full of sugar.)

American Heritage Cookbook. Helen Duprey Bullock, Helen McCully, and Eleanor Noderer, editors. American Heritage, New York, 1964; Penguin, Baltimore, 1967.

Esther B. Aresty, *The Delectable Past.* Simon & Schuster, New York, 1964.

Pearl Bailey, *Pearl's Kitchen.* Harcourt Brace Jovanovich, New York, 1973. ("I am not a gourmet chick." Warm and earthy.)

James Beard, *American Cookery.* Little, Brown, Boston, 1972. (The only major food writer to take a genuine interest in American cooking; affectionate but careless.)

James Beard, *Beard on Bread.* Knopf, New York, 1973. (Sugar in almost every recipe.)

Simone Beck, *Simca's Cuisine.* Knopf, New York, 1972.

Victor J. Bergeron, *Trader Vic's Book of Mexican Cooking.* Doubleday, New York, 1973. (Pure Tex-Mex. "Now, I know I'm going to make a lot of Mexicans sore as hell," he says.)

Paul Bocuse, *La Cuisine du Marché.* Flammarion, Paris, 1976.

Raymond Calvel, *La Boulangerie Moderne*. Eyrolles, Paris, 1952.

Poppy Cannon, *The Can-Opener Cook Book*. Thomas Y. Crowell, New York, (1951), 1953. (Not recommended.)

Jane Carson, *Colonial Virginia Cookery*. Colonial Williamsburg, 1968. (A remarkably well documented book; kitchens, utensils, cookbooks, and produce of colonial Virginia.)

Rebecca Caruba, *Cooking with Wine and High Spirits: A Lighthearted Approach to the Art of Gourmet Cooking*. Crown, New York, 1963; Cornerstone, New York, 1970. (A little too lighthearted.)

Samuel Chamberlain (Phineas Beck, pseudonym), *Clementine in the Kitchen*. Hastings House, New York, with *Gourmet* magazine, (1943), 1948.

Julia Child and Simone Beck, *Mastering the Art of French Cooking*, Volume II. Knopf, New York, 1970.

Julia Child, Louisette Bertholle, and Simone Beck, *Mastering the Art of French Cooking*, Volume I. Knopf, New York, 1961.

Julia Child, *From Julia Child's Kitchen*. Knopf, New York, 1975.

Ruth Ellen Church, *The American Guide to Wines*. Quadrangle, Chicago, 1963. (Not recommended.)

Craig Claiborne, *Craig Claiborne's Favorites* from *The New York Times*. Quadrangle, New York, 1975.

Craig Claiborne, *Craig Claiborne's Kitchen Primer*. Knopf, New York, 1969; Vintage, New York, 1972.

Craig Claiborne, *The New York Times Cook Book*. Harper & Row, New York, 1961.

Craig Claiborne, *The New York Times Menu Cook Book*. Harper & Row, New York, 1966.

Huguette Couffignal, *La Cuisine des Pauvres*. Robert Morel, Les Hautes Plaines de Mane, 1970. (A remarkable book on what the poor of this world find to eat.)

Robert J. Courtine, *Le Cahier de Recettes de Madame Maigret*. Laffont, Paris, 1974. (Maigret eats better than Nero Wolfe. See Rex Stout below.)

John Philips Cranwell, *The Hellfire Cookbook*. Quadrangle, New York, 1975. (Not recommended.)

Curnonsky, *Recettes des Provinces de France*. Productions de Paris, 1962. (A posthumous collection of articles and recipes on regional cooking.)

Curnonsky and Austin de Croze, *Le Trésor Gastronomique de France*. Delagrave, Paris, 1933. (A treasure.)

Elizabeth David, *The Baking of an English Loaf*. Printed for the author, London, 1969. (Flour, yeast, salt, and water; a perfect loaf.)

Elizabeth David, *French Provincial Cooking*. Harper & Row, New York, 1962; Penguin, Baltimore, 1964. (Along with her earlier *French Country Cooking*, the finest writing on the subject in the English language.)

Elizabeth David, *Spices, Salt and Aromatics in the English Kitchen: English Cooking, Ancient and Modern*, Volume I. Penguin, Harmondsworth, 1970.

Elizabeth David, *Syllabubs and Fruit Fools*. Printed for the author, London, 1969.

Roy Andries de Groot, *The Auberge of the Flowering Hearth*. Bobbs-Merrill, Indianapolis, 1973. (Recipes from a woman cook of a French country inn.)

Louis Diat, *French Cooking for Americans* or, *La Cuisine de Ma Mère*. Lippincott, New York, 1946.

Alexandre Dumaine, *Ma Cuisine*. Pensée Moderne, Paris, 1972. (The testament of the last of the great classic chefs.)

Auguste Escoffier, *The Escoffier Cook Book*. Crown, New York, 1941, 1961. (Purportedly a translation of his *Guide Culinaire*.)

Auguste Escoffier, *Le Guide Culinaire*. Flammarion, Paris, (1902), fourth edition 1921. (The bible of haute cuisine.)

Auguste Escoffier, *Ma Cuisine*. Flammarion, Paris, 1934. (A more personal cuisine, and a more interesting one, than that of *Le Guide Culinaire*.)

Jean-Noël Escudier, *La Véritable Cuisine Provençale et Niçoise*. Provencia, Toulon, 1964.

Célestine Eustis, *Cooking in Old Créole Days: La Cuisine Créole à l'Usage des Petits Ménages.* R. H. Russell, 1904; facsimile, Arno, New York, 1973.

M. F. K. Fisher, *Here Let Us Feast.* Viking, New York, 1946.

M. F. K. Fisher and editors, *La Cuisine des Provinces de France.* Time-Life, New York, 1969. (The fun book with blistering commentaries by Robert J. Courtine, now "out of print"; only a revised version is available.)

Marcella Hazan, *The Classic Italian Cook Book.* Harper's Magazine Press, New York, 1973; Knopf, New York, 1976. (The beautiful food of the Emilia-Romagna, *con amore.*)

Judith Herman and Marguerite Shalett Herman, *The Cornucopia: Good Reading and Good Cookery from more than 500 Years of Recipes, Food Lore, &c. (1390–1899).* Harper & Row, New York, 1973. (An excellent introduction to the pleasures of the past in cooking. The book is exemplary in that all sources are meticulously credited and it has a handsome bibliography.)

Annemarie Huste, *Annemarie's Cookingschool Cookbook.* Houghton Mifflin, Boston, 1974. (Not recommended.)

H. E. Jacob, *Six Thousand Years of Bread: Its Holy and Unholy History.* Doubleday, Doran, New York, 1944.

Evan Jones, *American Food: The Gastronomic Story.* Dutton, New York, 1975. (A handsome book with a great deal of interesting material, unfortunately poorly documented.)

Madeleine Kamman, *Dinner Against the Clock.* Atheneum, New York, 1973.

Madeleine Kamman, *The Making of a Cook.* Atheneum, New York, 1971. (A gifted French cook lets us in on kitchen technique.)

Diana Kennedy, *The Cuisines of Mexico.* Harper & Row, New York, 1972. (An extraordinarily handsome book that is considered by many to be the definitive book on Mexican cooking.)

Marie Kimball, *Thomas Jefferson's Cook Book.* Richmond-Garrett & Massie, Richmond, 1949. (You had better read the original; see Martha Jefferson Randolph.)

Marjorie Kreidberg, *Food on the Frontier: Minnesota Cooking from 1850 to 1900*. Minnesota Historical Society Press, St. Paul, 1975.

[Léo Larguier], *Clarisse ou la Vieille Cuisinière*. Abeille d'Or, Paris, 1922. (An impassioned, if sentimental, eulogy to women's cooking. Lots of old-fashioned recipes arranged by season.)

Dione Lucas and Marion Gorman, *The Dione Lucas Book of French Cooking*. Little, Brown, Boston, 1973. (The original Dione Lucas, 1947, should have been left alone.)

Albert Marinus, *Histoire du Pain* and *Notre Pain Quotidien*. Charles Peeters, Léau, for the author, n.d.

L. L. McLaren, *High Living*. Published for the benefit of the Telegraph Hill Neighborhood Association. Paul Elder, San Francisco, 1904; facsimile, Arno, New York, 1973. (An interesting and amusing book which illustrates the eclectic taste of San Franciscans.)

Helen Mendes, *The African Heritage Cookbook*. Macmillan, New York, 1971. (A serious discussion of black contributions to American cookery. The quality of the recipes does not come up to the text.)

Prosper Montagné, *Larousse Gastronomique: The Encyclopedia of Food, Wine & Cookery*. Crown, New York, 1961 (English translation of original *Larousse Gastronomique*, Larousse, Paris, 1938).

Prosper Montagné, *Nouveau Larousse Gastronomique*. Edited by Robert J. Courtine. Larousse, Paris, 1967.

National Republican Heritage Groups Council, *World Cookbook: Featuring Congressional & Culinary Achievements*. Atland, Washington, D.C., 1972. (Is this our heritage?)

Carolyn Niethammer, *American Indian Food and Lore*. Macmillan, New York, 1974. (The material on plants that the Indians use for food is interesting; the recipes show enormous cultural contamination.)

Edouard Nignon, *Les Plaisirs de la Table*. A Paris chez l'Auteur, [1926]. (A contemporary of Escoffier, Nignon was regarded by many as a finer cook [there is no flour in his soups, for instance] and certainly a more interesting writer.)

Hyla O'Connor, *The Early American Cookbook*. Prentice-Hall, Englewood Cliffs, N.J., 1974. (It is hardly possible for a book to be less documented.)

Richard Olney, *The French Menu Cookbook*. Simon & Schuster, New York, 1970.

Richard Olney, *Simple French Food*. Atheneum, New York, 1974. (Olney is a brilliant imaginative cook, yet he remains true to classic principles.)

Clementine Paddleford, *How America Eats*. Scribner's, New York, 1960. (Authentic Clementine.)

Clementine Paddleford, *The Best in American Cooking*. Scribner's, New York, 1970. (They cut every bit of Clementine out of this one.)

Fernand Point, *Ma Gastronomie*. Flammarion, Paris, 1969. (A posthumous book presenting the great chef's recipes from his notebook. Mme. Point, noted for her taste memory, and several of his most illustrious pupils assisted in the preparation of the book.)

Claudia Roden, *A Book of Middle Eastern Food*. Knopf, New York, 1972. (The beautiful fragrant food of ancient peoples presented by an intelligent and well-read cook.)

Irma S. Rombauer, *Joy of Cooking*. Bobbs-Merrill, Indianapolis, (1931), 1943, 1975; Signet, New York, 1973.

Waverley Root, *The Food of France*. Knopf, New York, 1958; Vintage, New York, 1966. (With love.)

Marcel Rouff, *La Vie et la Passion de Dodin-Bouffant*. Delamain, Paris, 1924; Stock, Paris, 1970. (In praise of the cooking of Adèle, *la cuisinière*, by the long-time collaborator of Curnonsky.)

Lorna Sass, *To the King's Taste*. Metropolitan Museum of Art, New York, 1975. (A sampling of recipes from

The Forme of Cury [c. 1390], unfortunately modernized beyond recognition.)

Ronald Sheppard and Edward Newton, *The Story of Bread*. Routledge & Kegan Paul, London, 1957.

Raymond Sokolov, *Great Recipes from The New York Times*. Quadrangle, New York, 1973.

Raymond Sokolov, *The Saucier's Apprentice*. Knopf, New York, 1976.

Rex Stout, *The Nero Wolfe Cook Book*. Viking, New York, 1973.

Louis Szathmáry, *The Chef's Secret Cook Book*. Quadrangle, New York, 1972. (Not recommended. [His substitution of store bread and liverwurst for Fernand Point's *foie gras en brioche* is recounted by us on page 143]).

Calvin Trillin, *American Fried: Adventures of a Happy Eater*. Doubleday, New York, 1974.

Oscar Tschirky, *Oscar of the Waldorf's Cook Book*. Dover, New York, 1973. (Originally *The Cook Book by "Oscar" of the Waldorf*. Werner, 1896).

Virginia Cookery—Past and Present: Including A Manuscript Cook Book of the Lee and Washington Families. The Woman's Auxiliary of Olivet Episcopal Church, Franconia, Virginia, 1957.

Joan Wiener and Diana Collier, *Bread: Making It the Natural Way*. Lippincott, New York, 1973. (Also the icky sweet way. "We're thoroughly hooked," they explain.)

Paula Wolfert, *Couscous and Other Good Food from Morocco*. Harper & Row, New York, 1973. (Already something of a classic.)

Twentieth Century—General

Michael Allaby and Floyd Allen, *Robots Behind the Plow: Modern Farming and the Need for an Organic Alternative*. Rodale Press, Emmaus, 1974.

Michael and Ariane Batterberry, *On the Town in New York: From 1776 to the Present.* Scribner's, New York, 1973.

Alan Berg, Nevin S. Scrimshaw, and David L. Call, *Nutrition, National Development, and Planning: Proceedings of an International Conference held at Cambridge, Massachusetts, October 19–21, 1971.* The MIT Press, 1973.

Daniel J. Boorstin, *The Americans: The Democratic Experience.* Random House, New York, 1973. (Assembly-line history.)

Rachel Carson, *Silent Spring.* ("The sedge is wither'd from the lake, / And no birds sing." Keats). Houghton Mifflin, Boston, 1962; Penguin, Baltimore, 1965). (She sounded the tocsin on man's befouling his environment.)

Vicki Cobb, *Arts and Crafts You Can Eat.* Lippincott, New York, 1974. (Feed the children synthetic dyes, she says.)

Susan Demarco and Susan Sechler, *The Fields Have Turned Brown: Four Essays on World Hunger.* Agribusiness Accountability Project, Washington, D.C., 1975.

Food Protection Committee, *An Evaluation of Public Health Hazards from Microbiological Contamination of Foods.* National Academy of Sciences–National Research Council, Washington, D.C., 1964.

Food Research and Action Center (Richard Pollack, Director) with Mark Irvings and Suzanne Vaupel, *If We Had Ham, We Could Have Ham and Eggs...If We Had Eggs.* Gazette Press, Yonkers, N.Y., 1972.

Food Research and Action Center (Richard Pollack, Director), *Out to Lunch: A Study of USDA's Day-Care and Summer Feeding Programs.* Gazette Press, Yonkers, N.Y., 1974.

Nikki and David Goldbeck, *The Supermarket Handbook: Access to Whole Foods.* Harper & Row, New York, 1973. (Well meant.)

Jerome Goldstein, editor, *The New Food Chain: An Organic Link Between Farm and City*. Rodale Press, Emmaus, 1973. (Readable essays on saving our farms and our cities.)

Mark J. Green, Editor, *The Monopoly Makers: Ralph Nader's Study Group Report on Regulation and Competition*. Grossman, New York, 1973.

Jim Hightower, *Eat Your Heart Out: Food Profiteering in America*. Crown, New York, 1975. (An exposé of agribusiness.)

Jim Hightower, *Hard Tomatoes, Hard Times: The Failure of the Land Grant College Complex*. Agribusiness Accountability Project, Washington, D.C., 1972. (A pioneering work on subsidized research toward a drearier society.)

Frances Moore Lappe, *Diet for a Small Planet*. Friends of the Earth / Ballantine, New York, 1971. (For vegetarians.)

Charles E. Little, *Challenge of the Land*. Preserved open space or costly urban sprawl? Pergamon Press, New York, 1968, 1969.

Thomas Robert Malthus, *On Population: An Essay on the Principle of Population, as It Affects the Future Improvement of Society*. (1798) Random House, New York, 1960. (Let them starve, the pastor said.)

Sidney Margolius, *Health Foods: Facts and Fakes*. Walker, New York, 1973. (An indiscriminate attack on charlatans and serious critics alike, by an author who prefers store bread.)

William Robbins, *The American Food Scandal: Why You Can't Eat Well on What You Earn*. William Morrow, New York, 1974.

Theodor Rosebury, *Life on Man*. Viking, New York, 1969; Berkley, New York, 1970. (A probiotic classic.)

E. F. Schumacher, *Small Is Beautiful: Economics As If People Mattered*. Harper Torchbooks, New York, 1973.

Adeline Garner Shell, *Supermarket Counter Power: The*

Intelligent Food Shopper's Guide to Eating Better for Less Money. Warner Paperback Library, New York, 1973.

Reay Tannahill, *Food in History*. Stein & Day, New York, 1973.

Jacqueline Verrett and Jean Carper, *Easting May Be Hazardous To Your Health*. How your government fails to protect you from the dangers in your food. Simon & Schuster, New York, 1974. (The findings, and the ordeal, of an F.D.A. researcher.)

Philip L. White and Diane Robbins, editors, *Environmental Quality and Food Supply*. Futura, Mount Kisco, 1974.

Philip L. White and Nancy Selvey, *Nutritional Qualities of Fresh Fruit and Vegetables*. Futura, Mount Kisco, 1974.

John Yudkin, M.D., *Sweet and Dangerous*. Peter H. Wyden, New York, 1972; Bantam, New York, 1973. (A British physiologist on the sugar sickness.)

Index